ISBN 978-1-334-07914-6
PIBN 10696864

This book is a reproduction of an important historical work. Forgotten Books uses state-of-the-art technology to digitally reconstruct the work, preserving the original format whilst repairing imperfections present in the aged copy. In rare cases, an imperfection in the original, such as a blemish or missing page, may be replicated in our edition. We do, however, repair the vast majority of imperfections successfully; any imperfections that remain are intentionally left to preserve the state of such historical works.

1 MONTH OF
FREE
READING

at

www.ForgottenBooks.com

By purchasing this book you are eligible for one month membership to ForgottenBooks.com, giving you unlimited access to our entire collection of over 700,000 titles via our web site and mobile apps.

To claim your free month visit:
www.forgottenbooks.com/free696864

English
Français
Deutsche
Italiano
Español
Português

www.forgottenbooks.com

Mythology Photography **Fiction**
Fishing Christianity **Art** Cooking
Essays Buddhism Freemasonry
Medicine **Biology** Music **Ancient**
Egypt Evolution Carpentry Physics
Dance Geology **Mathematics** Fitness
Shakespeare **Folklore** Yoga Marketing
Confidence Immortality Biographies
Poetry **Psychology** Witchcraft
Electronics Chemistry History **Law**
Accounting **Philosophy** Anthropology
Alchemy Drama Quantum Mechanics
Atheism Sexual Health **Ancient History**
Entrepreneurship Languages Sport
Paleontology Needlework Islam
Metaphysics Investment Archaeology
Parenting Statistics Criminology
Motivational

A Book called

OUR ANCESTORS
THE
STANTONS

By *WILLIAM HENRY STANTON*

THESE ARE DEEDS
Which Should not Pass Away
AND NAMES
That Must not Wither

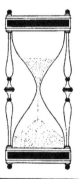

PHILADELPHIA
Privately Printed for WILLIAM HENRY STANTON
MCMXXII

TO
OUR PARENTS
THOSE BRAVE HEARTS WHO
GUIDED OUR TINY FEET · ·
CORRECTED OUR WAYWARD
STEPS AND LOVED US TILL
THE LAST · · THIS LITTLE
VOLUME IS AFFECTIONATELY
DEDICATED

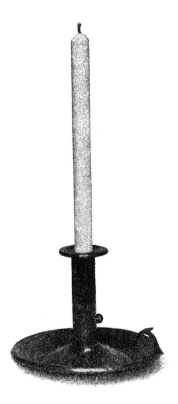

NOW FULL AND HIGH AND BRIGHTLY BURNING LIKE LIFE
IN YOUTH, BUT AS WE PASS ALONG LIFE'S HIGHWAY OR
PONDER O'ER THE PAGES OF THIS BOOK, IT SHORTER
GROWS UNTIL THE END.

INTRODUCTION

MY FIRST thought concerning this work was to record, perhaps in pamphlet form, some of the stories told by my parents and relatives of the early history of our ancestors, which, if not done, would largely be lost with the passing of the present generation. Accordingly I began collecting material, but soon found that there was much more available than I at first thought, and it seemed best to enlarge the scope of the work.

It was not intended to be of interest to the public, but rather that the personal history and intimate relationships told will be more valuable and more appreciated by the relatives, than a general history suitable for the public would have been.

In the prosecution of the work I have been impressed with the innate qualities, strong character, and loving service of our ancestors, and I feel sure I voice the sentiment of us all when I say that we, who are living, have failed to fully appreciate the true worth of our parents and relatives, who have toiled, achieved, and passed away. These people left their homes in the old

country

country and settled in a new and little-known land. That they were hardy and self-reliant is not questioned. The land they cleared, the homes they built, the businesses they conducted, and the impressions they made upon the sections where they lived, compel our admiration and respect.

Our present generation, instead of boasting of our ancestors, feel a deep sense of obligation to make of ourselves worthy followers of such a noble ancestry that worked under great difficulties and accomplished admirable results. If this little record, even to a slight degree, expresses our appreciation, I shall feel amply repaid. The work of collecting the items for the book has been one of pure pleasure. Every one has been so ready to help in any way possible, although each one has said that he knew nothing of value. However, the results prove otherwise.

It has been earnestly desired that the work should be authentic and it is hoped that no mistakes have crept in. On account of the nature of the early history, some of it so dim and little known, only fragments can be offered, but it was thought better to take the little rather than none at all. To give a fuller view, some contemporary pioneer experiences have been taken. It is believed that a record in detail of the home life of some early settlers would be valuable as giving an idea of the actual living conditions of the members of our family who were pioneers.

With thankfulness for such a noble ancestry and trusting that those living now will value it more as they know it better, this book is presented.

Ridley Park,
Pennsylvania,
1922.

IN APPRECIATION

EDNA MACY STANTON, of Lansdowne, Pennsylvania, who collected and prepared the genealogy of the Stanton family, aided in the editing of much of the text and contributed several articles, contracted, after a serious operation, the dread influenza and was called, on the Twenty-fourth of Second month, 1920, to leave the work she had so well carried along. Her loss was most keenly felt. Some appreciation of her character is expressed in a separate article by one of her friends.

It seemed most fitting that her twin sister, Ellen Stanton Pennell, should take up the unfinished work. Her services in the completion of the task begun by her sister have aided greatly in carrying, throughout the book, the original thought and spirit.

Their brother, William Macy Stanton, of Lansdowne, Pennsylvania, has arranged the engraving, the composition of the book, greatly assisted with the work during its progress, and attended to the printing and binding.

Many

Many other members of the family have offered valuable suggestions. Several of the recent pictures were taken by Alfred L. Bailey, of Tacoma, Ohio. The land-title data and maps have been prepared by Willis V. Webster, of Columbus, Ohio.

It is my desire to express my hearty appreciation of the kindness of all who have assisted in any way and especially to the above-mentioned persons who have given so much of their time.

Ridley Park,
Pennsylvania,
1922.

STILLWATER VALLEY

VIEW NORTH FROM THE HOME OF JOSEPH STANTON SHOWING RESIDENCE OF
BENJAMIN CLENDENON.

THE STANTON FAMILY

.utou.

HE primary object of this article is to review briefly the history of the Stanton family, to stress points of particular interest and to trace the line back to the earliest known ancestors. No claim is made that the statements herein presented are infallible, but they are as correct as the data now available permits. It is hoped that an exhaustive study of Stanton genealogy will sometime be made, both in this country and in Europe, as such would be of value, not alone to this family, but to the searcher for detailed history of the first two centuries of life in America.

Beginning with our branch in southeastern Ohio in 1922, we find that they came from southwestern Pennsylvania in 1800. They stopped there for only a few months while on their way from Beaufort, Carteret County, North Carolina, to Ohio. After a residence in North Carolina of about seventy-five years, they left that section of the country on account of slavery. They came to Beaufort from Newport, Rhode Island, after residing in that section of country for about eighty

11

eighty years. We find our earliest ancestor, Robert Stanton, was living in Newport in 1645. He was born in England in 1599 and was one of the settlers of Portsmouth, Rhode Island, in 1638. This much we may claim as fairly well established, but anything earlier than this is traditional and mostly conjectural.

THE STANTON (STAUNTON) ARMS.

Arms: Argent, two cheverons sable within a bordure engrailed the same.
Crest: Fox statant proper.
Mottoes: Below the arms, "En Dieu ma foy."
    Above the crest, "Moderata durant."

THE STANTON ARMS

The Stanton Coat of Arms was derived from Albini or Albencius who received the castle from Todeni.

The arms of Albini of Belvoir was a shield with a gold background upon which were two chevrons and a red border. He gave to the Lord of Stanton a shield with a silver background upon which were two black chevrons within a curved or indented black border. Later a helmet crest was adopted and was a fox standing and of the natural color.

There are two mottoes. The one below the arms is "En Dieu ma foy" (In God my faith); the other, above the crest, is "Moderata durant" (Moderate acquisitions are lasting).

The arms thus described is to be found in Burke's Heraldic Illustrations and is now borne by the Stauntons of Longbridge, who are a branch of the Stauntons of Staunton in Nottingham. This is undoubtedly the basis of all Stanton Arms and represents the original family.

Regarding the name Stanton, it is traced to Angl Saxon origin and is formed of two words—stan (ston and ton (town) or Stonetown. Now since the su name, sire-name or father name, originally came fro the place of residence, occupation, characteristic of t individu individual or some notable event in his life, we may conclude that some remote ancestor took the name of his town Stanton (Stonetown) for his surname.

In early times when writing was much less common and orthography not so well established, and when there was much less communication between neighborhoods and far more difference in pronunciation, we find writers spelling more by the sound of the name, and hence we have our name spelled Stanton, Staunton, Stainton, and Steynton. But we must remember that almost certainly all of the Stantons, however their names are spelled, came from one common ancestor.

It may be of interest, also, to note that the historic origin of the Stantons was in the eleventh century, in the southeast corner of Nottinghamshire, England, and in the northern end of Leicestershire. Here there lived a Sir Malgerus, or Mauger, Lord of Stanton. Little is known of him except that he appears to have been a Saxon.

Five miles southeast of this lordship we find Belvoir Castle, of much interest to the Stantons. It is believed to have been built by Robert de Todeni in the eleventh century. The "Lordship of Staunton" is five miles from Belvoir and seven from Newark. It is said to have been in the family of the name of Stanton or Staunton for more than thirteen hundred years, or about the date of the Saxon conquest, and we may infer that the family came with the Saxons.

The tower defended by Sir Malgerus against William the Conqueror at the time of his conquest in 1066 has ever since been known as "Staunton Tower."

Referring very briefly to the principal races that have

The MAKERS of the BOOK

have occupied England in historic times, we find that at the beginning of history the Britons were largely in possession of the island. Their possession continued up to the close of the first century when the Romans began their conquest. They occupied parts of the country until about the middle of the fourth century, and were followed by the great Germanic invasion of which the Jutes from Slesvig were probably the first. Later came the Saxons from the countries lying near the southwest shore of the Baltic Sea, and in turn were followed by the Angles from Slesvig, a corner of which is still known as Anglen.

Some of the original inhabitants were driven to the hill country and remote parts, such as Cumberland, Cornwall and the mountains of Wales, while many intermarried with the invaders and lost their nationality and distinctive character. The Angles gave their name to the country—Angles' Land, or England—and under Egbert (827) united many of the smaller countries into the Kingdom of England.

In the eighth century the Northmen or Norsemen, a race of vigorous self-reliant men, left the shores of Norway and Denmark, probably because of overcrowding and scarcity of food, and repeatedly robbed the southeast coast of England and the western coast of the continent of Europe, even going as far as the eastern end of the Mediterranean, but finally settling in large numbers in northern France, where for some two centuries they mixed with the Gauls, the ancestors of the modern French. Here they gave to the Gauls a vigor, hardihood and self-reliance which these people did not possess, and in turn received from them a culture and refinement which they did not have up to this time.

Such

Such was the ancestry of the Normans who, in 1066 under William the Conqueror, invaded and subdued England, bringing to the inhabitants many very desirable qualities, among which may be mentioned the executive and administrative ability which the English had not previously had in any marked degree.

Again, we find an amalgamation of the various races—Britons, Jutes, Saxons, Angles, Gauls and Norsemen—giving to the English many very desirable qualities not before possessed by any one of the races alone.

Such, then, was the blood of our ancestors who, in the seventeenth century, came to America for freedom, religious and otherwise, no doubt unconsciously urged on by a trace of the old Norse spirit of adventure and the quest for better homes for themselves and their children.

With regard to Robert Stanton of Newport—our earliest known ancestor—about all we know of him is that he was born in England in 1599, married Avis —————, had a son Robert, born in England, 1627. His two daughters—Sarah, born 1640, and Mary, born 1642, were most likely born in Portsmouth, Rhode Island, for we find he was one who settled Portsmouth in 1638; and later he lived in Newport and had a son John, born there Eighth month, 1645.

From the birth of his son Robert in England to the settlement of Portsmouth is eleven years, during which time he came to America, but the port from which he sailed and the date are unknown, and place of landing and his first place of residence are also unknown.

Many points in the lives of Robert Stanton of Newport, and Thomas Stanton of Connecticut, seem to indicate that they were connected, and, if not brothers, of quite different age and temperament, probably uncle and

and nephew. Then there is Paul Stanton of Maine, and Robert's brother John, who came with him, who should be studied, as also the much larger number in the next few generations.

We may note that Robert was born in 1599, Thomas born 1616 and came to America in 1635. From the age and character of Robert, he seems to have been a quiet and steady-going sort of person. He probably inclined toward Quaker belief even if not a member, and probably landed in Massachusetts, as it was the older and better known colony. Later, finding the religious intolerance out of harmony with his views, he would naturally move to more liberal Rhode Island; and as Quakers and Quaker sympathizers were ostracized, he would live a quiet and little-known life; this may account for our finding no record of visits between Robert and Thomas.

Thomas, being seventeen years younger and probably unmarried, came to America in any vessel that was convenient, and landed in Virginia. His religious views seem to have been different from those of Robert, even if not antagonistic. We see Thomas taking part in public affairs in Virginia, associating with the Indians and learning their language, which we would expect a young man to do, especially if he was inclined to deal with men, as he did very largely in the public life which he led afterward. But he left Virginia in a short time and went to Connecticut. If connected with Robert, he probably found the Puritan or Quaker type of mind more to his liking than that of the Cavaliers of Virginia, and so worked his way back to people of his own kind, not going to Massachusetts, where there was so much religious intolerance, but to a section where more liberal views could be comfortably held.

So

So far as we know, he was not a Quaker and few if any of his descendants seem to have been members of that religious society, while a very large part of the descendants of Robert have been Quakers.

William Alonzo Stanton, a descendant of Thomas Stanton of Stonington, Connecticut, did much research work and in 1891 published a large volume entitled "Thomas Stanton of Connecticut and His Descendants." His work is so good that the liberty is taken of reprinting from his book some information applying to both our families as now known.

The following traditions give interesting possible connections between the early branches of Stantons in this country and also the family's origin in England:

     *   *   *   *   *

"THE WELSH TRADITION.—The best documentary evidence for this is a record written in an old family Bible belonging to the Gere family of Syracuse, N. Y. This Bible was the property of Sophia Stanton, whose parents were both Stantons, and whose mother's parents were both Stantons. Sophia's Bible and her mother's Bible bear record that Thomas Stanton was born in Wales.

"The mother, Anna Stanton, was born in 1758, at Stonington. It is safe to say that Anna was informed as to this tradition by her father, Phineas, who was born in 1719, forty-two years after Thomas died.

"Half a century is not time enough for history to go very far astray, and I am inclined to think that either he or his wife, Ann Lord (alias Laward), was born in Wales. Even if this be true, however, he was not of Welsh ancestry, for 'Stanton' is a Saxon name. Wales is bounded on the east by Herefordshire and Shrop-shire. In Hereford are the following places: Staunton Park, Staunton-on-Arrow, and Staunton, all near the Welsh borders. In Shropshire are to be found the towns of Stanton, Stanton Lacy and Long Stanton.

"Would it be strange that a Thomas Stanton should be born
only

only a few miles at the farthest from some of these places, and if west of them his birthplace would easily be in Wales.

"Since writing the above I have had correspondence with William J. Stanton of North Danville, Vt., who was born in 1808. He says that his grandfather, Isaac Wheeler Stanton, often affirmed in a most positive manner that Thomas Stanton was born in Wales. His grandfather was born in 1743 at Stonington.

"Now what opportunity did Isaac W. have of knowing this? His grandfather was Joseph Stanton, who was born before Thomas died, and lived after Isaac W. was eight years old.

"Wm. J. Stanton then has his information from his grandfather, who was contemporaneous with those who in their youth had personal knowledge of Thomas, and whose parents were children of Thomas. This is even more direct testimony than in the case of Sophia Stanton's Bible. In addition to the above testimony is the following: Isaac Wheeler Stanton, when he moved from Connecticut to New Hampshire and Vermont, took an old desk with him in which was found a genealogical outline of Stantons, descendants of Thomas. It was written on coarse, dark-colored paper, in old-fashioned letters and style of writing, and testified that Thomas was born in Wales. Wm. J. Stanton says 'it looked to be a century old.' The desk was moved in 1784. I believe the Welsh tradition is true."

*   *   *   *

"THE LANCASHIRE TRADITION.—John Stanton of Hope Valley, R. I., has in his possession records received from his father, John Stanton, who was for some time town clerk of Charlestown, R. I., and who wrote quite a record of historical and genealogical information as to the Stanton family. These records assert that Thomas of Stonington, Ct., and Robert of Newport, R. I., were brothers, and came from Lancashire, Eng. This same tradition is found now among descendants of Robert of Newport. It does not necessarily conflict with the Welsh tradition, for Thomas may have been in Wales, then moved northward to Lancashire and come thence to America. Mr. Stanton can produce no authority for this record and does not know where his father got it. I have followed up this tradition far enough to learn that there are Stantons now living in Lancashire, and that the family is an old one there. Members of the family now in Preston,

Preston, the county seat of Lancashire, have testified to me that they can find no record of a Thomas who came to America. (Preston, Conn., is built on land that belonged to Thomas Stanton. Query: Was it named for Preston, Eng., by Thomas in memory of his boyhood home?)"

*   *   *   *

"THE LONGBRIDGE TRADITION.—The Hon. John D. Baldwin of Worcester, Mass., in 1883, printed his incomplete notes of Thomas Stanton and his descendants. Baldwin says of Thomas 'It is supposed, with strong probability, that he was the son of Thomas and Katherine (Washington) Stanton, of the Longbridge family.' This supposition was suggested to Mr. Baldwin by Mr. B. I. Stanton, then of Albany, N. Y., but now of St. Paul, Minn. Mr. B. I. Stanton for years has been preparing genealogies of the descendants of Robert Stanton of R. I. and of Paul Stanton of Maine. He is a descendant of Paul. In his search among English records he found a Thomas Stanton, born 1616, in Wolverton, Warwickshire, Eng., son of Thomas and Katherine (Washington) Stanton.

"Thomas, the father, was born 1595 and was in turn the son of Thomas Stanton, who was the son of John and Elizabeth (Townsend) Stanton of Longbridge, Warwick Co. No further record of Thomas, born 1616, has ever been found than the one made in the Visitation of the County of Warwick in 1619. He was then three years old.

"Mr. B. I. Stanton thought this might be Thomas Stanton of Connecticut. Mr. Baldwin adopted the suggestion and so printed it.

"It may be true, but it is not proven. If this was our Thomas he would have been 19 when he embarked at London in 1635, but he gave his age as 20. This could be explained, however, by the existence of a law forbidding emigration, without parent or guardian, under 20 years of age. It was not uncommon, therefore, for young men to 'borrow time,' as they termed it, and add a necessary year or two to their true age. Thomas may have 'borrowed time' to make himself 20 years old in 1635.

"This family of Stantons came to Wolverton from Longbridge, near the city of Warwick, in 1576, and became extinct in the first half of the 18th century."

The

THE STAUNTONS OF STAUNTON

"Malgerus' son and heir was Galfridus de Stanton who married Beatrice de Muschamp and had Sir William whose wife was Atheline de Musters. Their son was Sir Geoffery, his, Sir William who married Isabel Kirketon and died in 1326. These five were all Knights. The next one was Sir Geoffery de Staunton who was Sheriff of Nottingham. Soon after this the 'de' was dropped and when we come to later times we find the heir to be Colonel William Staunton who served in the army of Charles I. and who married Anne Waring. His son was Harvey Staunton, Esq., who was the last male heir of this ancient family after a continued male succession of five hundred years. Harvey's daughter and heiress was Anne Staunton who married Gilberto Charlton, Esq. Their son and heir was Job Staunton Charlton who married Mary Greenwood and whose daughter and heiress was Anne Staunton Charlton. In 1703 she married Rev. J. Aspinshaw, LL.D., rector of Elton Super-montem. In 1807 he, with wife and children, assumed by Royal License the surname and arms of Staunton. Their son and heir was Henry Charlton Staunton of Staunton Hall in 1858.'

"This is undoubtedly the original Stanton family. From them have sprung numerous branches. In the 15th century a Sir George Stanton went from this family to Ireland and became the progenitor of a numerous Irish posterity. The following, from the Boston (Mass.) Pilot of May 5, 1888, shows a still earlier departure into Ireland:

"'In England the name de Staunton dates from the Norman conquest, while in Ireland it appeared with the English Invasion. In 1220 Adam de Staunton granted lands to Christ Church, Dublin, and in 1373, in a summons to a great council to meet in Cork, Milo Staunton and Daniel Fitz-Thomas Roche were returned from County Cork. The attainders of 1691 include one Patrick Stanton, Great Island, County Cork.'

"Another branch of the Stauntons of Staunton settled in Warwick Co. prior to 1450 and bore the arms of the Nottingham family. Their hall is at Longbridge, a few miles from the city of Warwick, and they are known as

The

THE STAUNTONS OF LONGBRIDGE

"The Encyclopedia Britannica (9th edition) says, 'Of families holding knightly rank in Warwickshire before the commencement of the 16th century there now exist only ten, viz., Staunton of Longbridge,' etc.

"This family as a distinct branch runs thus: Thomas, John, Thomas, John, Thomas, Humphrey, John, John, John, John, William, John, William, the heir in 1858.

"Let us look a little into some interesting facts concerning John Staunton of Longbridge. He married Elizabeth, daughter of Townsend of Wales, they had three sons and two daughters. The eldest son was Thomas. Thomas had a daughter Judith Stanton who married Shakespere's friend and patron Hamnet Sadler. Shakespere's twin children, Judith and Hamnet, were named for Hamnet Sadler and his wife Judith Stanton. Sadler was a subscriber to Shakespere's will and was bequeathed a mourning ring.

"See also The Life of Wm. Shakespere (Duyckinck edition, P. xxvi) further reference to Mr. Staunton of Longbridge House and to Thomas Stanton, the English sculptor, as sculptor of Shakespere's bust in the church at Stratford-on-Avon, placed there between 1616 and 1623.

"An interesting description of this bust will also be found in Irving's Sketch Book.

"It was in 1576, at the time of the above John Stanton, that another son of his moved to Wolverton, between Warwick city and Stratford-on-Avon. He married Maria Pudsey and had five children. The eldest of these was Thomas Stanton who 30th July, 1616, married Katherine, daughter of Walter Washington of Radway, and had Thomas, born 1616 in Wolverton, who is thought by Baldwin to be the Thomas Stanton who came to America in 1635. This Wolverton branch became extinct in the male line during the first half of the 18th century and the estate reverted to John Staunton of Longbridge, who was born in 1704 and died in 1748.

"The last record of said Thomas Stanton, born 1616, in Wolverton, Warwick Co., Eng., is to be found on p. 277 of the Visitation of the County of Warwick in the year 1619. Taken by William

Camden,

Camden, Clarencieux King of Arms. (Harl. Mss. 1167.) Edited by John Fetherstone.

"The above book is Vol. 12 of the publications of the Harlian Society, established in 1869."

MISCELLANEOUS ENGLISH NOTES

"These notes are printed here as a possible clew to future research, and as facts of family and historic interest.

"1· In March, 1635, the pastor of The Church of St. Mary, Aldermanbury, London, was a Rev. Dr. Stanton (see N. E. Hist. and Gen. Reg., Jan. 1819).

"2. In Aug., 1635, Jo: Staunton, aged 27, sailed from London for Virginia, in ship George—Jo: Severne, master.

"3· Feb. 18, 1657, a Thomas Stanton of Mowlton, Suffolk Co., witnessed the will of Samuel Moody.

"4· In 1610, near Wolverton, Warwick Co., there was born a Thomas, son of Henry Stanton, who married ———— Rogers, Feb. 6, 1608.

"5. There was a Thomas Stanton at Little Eastcheap, London, in 1657. M. Middlebrooke, of Leeds, writes a letter to his nephew Rev. Michael Wigglesworth, at Malden, Mass., and orders it left at Mr. Thomas Stanton's in Little Eastcheap, to be conveyed to America. Said Wigglesworth was born in Hedron, East Riding, Yorkshire, Eng., in 1631, and in 1638 came to Quinnipiac, Conn.

"6· Dorothy Stanton, widow of Richard Wiseman, of Wigborough, Essex Co., about 1625 married John Rogers, of Dedham, Essex. Their grandson was Rev. John Rogers, D.D., who came to America with his father, Nathaniel, in 1636, and in 1682 became president of Harvard.

"7· In the northwest part of Leicestershire, some thirty miles from Belvoir Castle, is Staunton Harold. Its former owner was John DeStaunton, whose daughter and heiress, Margaret, married Ralph Shirley, and thus transferred the Staunton estate to the Shirley family. The present owner is Sir Sewallis Edward Shirley, 10th Earl of Ferrers and Viscount Tamworth. For further history of this family, see Timb's 'Abbeys, Castles and Ancient Halls of England and Wales,' Waren & Co., London.

"8· In

"8. In Oxfordshire, about five miles west of Oxford, is Stanton Harcourt. Here is the ancient manor of Stanton. It was among the vast estates that fell to the lot of the Bishop of Bayeux, a half-brother to William the Conqueror. Queen Adeliza, second wife to Henry, granted the manor of Stanton to her kinswoman, Milicent, wife of Richard de Camville, whose daughter married Robert de Harcourt. Since then the manor has been called Stanton Harcourt.

"9. An examination of Wills and Records at Bury St. Edmunds, Suffolk Co., shows in 1370 an Ada, widow of Henricus de Stanton, and their son Henry. In 1499 is mentioned a Robert, in 1504 a Roff, and in 1554 a Walter Stanton."

These extracts, then, give possible connections between the families of the early Stantons. Whatever the real connection, the truth remains that the family antidates our American colonies and had a worthy name and staunch tradition long before the Mayflower sailed.

Ridley Park,   W. H. S.
Pennsylvania,
1922.

THE WYATT WINDMILL

One of the few old windmills yet standing and operated by wind power. It is typical of the mills of the early American period which were familiar to the older Stantons.

This mill was built at Bristol, Rhode Island, about 1750. It was later moved several times, and now stands in Middletown, Rhode Island.

ENTERED ACCORDING TO ACT OF CONGRESS IN THE YEAR 1884 BY J. P. NEWELL, IN THE CLERK'S OFFICE OF THE DISTRICT COURT OF THE DISTRICT OF MASS.

HILL. HOLT.

COLLIN'S WHARF.   N. BAPTIST   STATE HOUSE.   FORT GEORGE.   PARSONAGE.   TRINITY CHURCH.   BILLING'S GATE WHARF.
CAR WHARF.   CHURCH.
                  COVE.   TOWN WHARF.   GOAT ISLAND.
CRAVELLY POINT.   TOWN WHARF.

FRIENDS' MEETING HOUSE.   CLARKE ST. CHURCH.   TRINITY   FRYE HOUSE.   PRESBYTERIAN CHURCH.   STONE MILL.   KING'S DOCK.
                                                                                                            DICKINSON'S WHARF.

NEWPORT, R. I., IN 1730.

ROBERT STANTON

ROBERT STANTON, the oldest member of our family in direct line of whom we have record,* was born in England in 1599. He married Avis, whose maiden name is unknown, and to them a son Robert was born in 1627.

Robert and Avis emigrated to America some time between 1627 and 1638. The family account states that their son Robert accompanied them.

Boylie's history of New Plymouth names John and Robert Stanton as among the earliest settlers there. John is believed to have been a brother of Robert. Arnold, the historian, says concerning Robert:† "In 1638 Portsmouth, then called Pocasset, was settled by William Coddington and others who left Massachusetts to avoid persecution on account of their religious opinions.

---

* In a clipping from an old Newport paper we read: "Copies of family record in my possession say that the Father of Robert of Newport was Thomas—and that he died at his son's house, very aged—Thomas Stanton of Stonington probably brother of Robert. (Signed) A. A. W."
† Arnold's history of Rhode Island, Page 133.

opinions. . . . Robert Stanton was one of the
names signed to the compact for forming the colony."
Robert was living in Newport in 1645 and either
accompanied

AN OLD HOUSE IN NEWPORT

IT IS THOUGHT THAT THIS HOUSE WAS IN EXISTENCE AT THE TIME ROBERT STANTON
LIVED IN NEWPORT. IF IT WAS NOT, IT IS TYPICAL OF THE DOMESTIC ARCHITECTURE
OF HIS TIME.

accompanied or soon followed Governor Coddington when he went to Portsmouth.

George Fox began to preach about 1643. In 1655 the first Friends arrived from England, and persecution began. Mary Stanton, a young woman from Rhode Island, quite young at the time, was whipped in Massachusetts in 1658 for being a Friend. Mary, the daughter of Robert and Avis, was sixteen years old and doubtless the one who suffered for her religious belief. Whether Robert Stanton joined the Society or not is unknown, but he appears to have sought freedom of religious belief in coming from Massachusetts to more liberal Rhode Island. If Robert was

not

OLD STONE MILL, NEWPORT, RHODE ISLAND

THIS TOWER IS THOUGHT TO BE THE RUINS OF A WINDMILL BUILT FOR ARNOLD, GOVERNOR OF RHODE ISLAND, 1615-1678. THE TOWER WAS UNDOUBTEDLY A FAMILIAR SIGHT TO THE OLDER STANTONS.

not a Friend, some members of his family were,* and
a large number of his descendants are members at the
present time.   Robert Stanton died at Newport, aged
seventy-three, and was buried Eighth month Twenty-
ninth, 1672.

Children of Robert and Avis Stanton:

Robert	b. 1627	In England
Sarah	b. 1640	m. 12–1661 Henry Tibbits d. 1708
Mary	b. 1642	
John	b. 8–1645	In Newport, Rhode Island d. 10–3–1713
Daniel	b. 1648	In Newport, Rhode Island m. Elizabeth ——
		Lived in Barbados, West Indies, d. 1690.
Prudence	b. 1649	

The Daniel Stanton (born 1708, died 6–29–1770),
who was a prominent minister of the Society of Friends
in Philadelphia, and was very active in urging Friends
to liberate their slaves and take a stand against slavery,
is said to have been a grandson of Daniel, the son of
Robert.

* A record of Friends' Meeting at Newport mentions John, son of Robert and
Avis, as the first Stanton to join Friends.

Sarah or Mary or both may have joined before the family moved to Newport,
and so Newport Friends had no record of Mary's persecution.

A LIGHTHOUSE ON LOWER NARRAGAN-
SETT BAY, SOUTHEAST OF NEWPORT,
RHODE ISLAND.

JOHN STANTON

OHN STANTON, son of Robert and Avis, was born at Newport, Rhode Island, Eighth month, 1645. He married Mary Horndale, his first wife, in 1667, in Friends' Meeting. His second wife, Mary Clarke (b. 1641, d. 4–7–1711), was the widow of Governor John Cranston and daughter of Jeremiah and Frances (Latham) Clarke. John Stanton was a prominent man in Newport, Rhode Island, where he died Tenth month Third, 1713.

The children of John and Mary Horndale Stanton:

Mary	b. 1668	d. 1747	m. John Coggeshall.
Hannah	b. 1670	d. 1712	m. Edward Carr.
Patience	b. 1672		
John, Jr.	b. 1674		m. Eliz. Clarke. Died in Richmond, Rhode Island.
Content	b. 1675		
Robert	b. 1677	d. 1712	m. Penelope ————.
Benjamin	b. 1684	d. 1760	m. Martha Tibbits.

By his second wife, Mary (Clarke) Cranston, John Stanton had a son Henry born in Newport, Rhode Island, Fifth month Twenty-second, 1688.

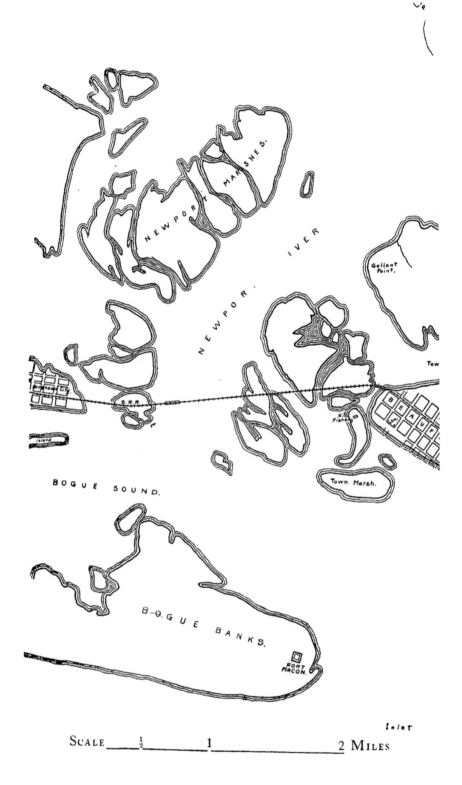

NEWPORT MARSHES.

NEWPORT RIVER

Gallant
Point.

Tow

Morehead City

Gallant
Point.

S.R.R.

B E A U F

U.S.
Fishery

Island

BOGUE SOUND.

Town Marsh.

BOGUE BANKS.

FORT
MACON.

Inlet

SCALE ½ 1 2 MILES

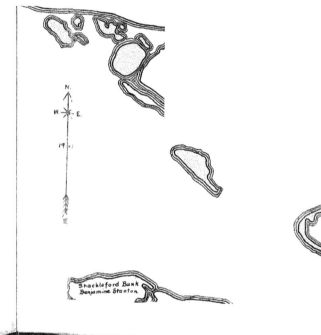

N.

W. — E.

19 41

Inlet

Miles

Shackleford Bank
Benjamine Stanton

Middle
Marshes

HENRY STANTON

HENRY STANTON, son of John Stanton and Mary (Clarke) Cranston, was born at Newport, Rhode Island, Fifth month Twenty-second, 1688. He was married to his first wife, Mary Hull, in Rhode Island, Fifth month Twenty-second, 1707, by Edward Thurston, Justice. He removed to Carteret County, North Carolina, between 1721 and 1724 and there he later married his second wife, Lydia Albertson.

He took with him from Rhode Island to North Carolina the old Stanton clock, which is now (1919) in the possession of one of his descendants, Dr. Byron Stanton, of Cincinnati, Ohio.

The children of Henry and Mary Hull Stanton:

Mary	b. 1708	died in infancy
Alice	b. 1709	
Mary	b. 1712	
Catherine	b. 1713	married Isaac White
Hannah	b. 1716	
Henry, Jr.	b. 1719	
Joseph	b. 1724	

His

His children by his second wife, Lydia Albertson, were:

Benjamin ⎫
Sarah ⎪
Avis ⎬ b. at Beaufort, North Carolina
John ⎭

Henry Stanton, Sr., Henry Jr., and Benjamin, his sons, and three of the sons of Henry Jr., Benjamin, Joseph and John Howard, were ministers of the Society of Friends.

A SCHOONER OFF NEWPORT,
RHODE ISLAND, 1921

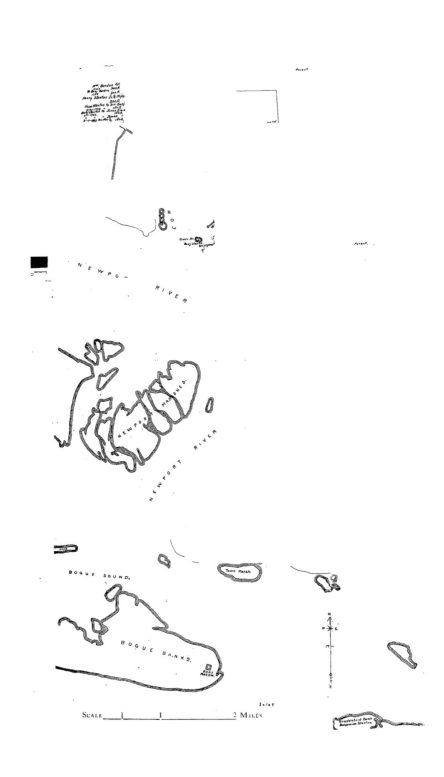

Forest

COR

Newport River

NEWPORT MARSHES.

NEWPORT

NEWPORT RIVER

Forest.

BOGUE SOUND.

Town Marsh.

BOGUE BANKS.

FORT MACON.

Inlet

N.
W   E
S

SCALE   1   1   2 MILES

His children by his second wife, Lydia Albertson, were:

Benjamin ⎫
Sarah   ⎪
Avis   ⎬ b. at Beaufort, North Carolina
John   ⎭

Henry Stanton, Sr., Henry Jr., and Benjamin, his sons, and three of the sons of Henry Jr., Benjamin, Joseph and John Howard, were ministers of the Society of Friends.

A SCHOONER OFF NEWPORT,
RHODE ISLAND, 1921

THE STANTON · CLOCK

THIS CLOCK CAME BY A LONG LINE OF DESCENT FROM THE ORIGINAL STANTON
OWNER TO BYRON STANTON OF CINCINNATI, BY WHOM IT IS NOW POSSESSED.

THE OLD STANTON CLOCK

HE old Stanton clock is ticking away in the room in which I am now writing, as faithfully and as correctly as it has for the last two hundred years or more.

I am not able to give the full early history, but according to tradition the clock was brought to this country from London by a seafaring descendant of Robert Stanton, the first one of our family to come to America. The only descendants of Robert Stanton who were mariners were Robert's son Robert and his grandson Henry. As Robert never married, it is not probable that he brought the clock to America, but Henry was a man of family and possessed of a large estate. It seems, therefore, probable that he was the original purchaser. As Robert, Jr., died in 1712 and Henry abandoned his seafaring life before the year 1736, the clock was, no doubt, brought to this country before or early in the eighteenth century, so there can be no question as to its early Americanization.

Henry was born in Newport, Rhode Island, May twenty-second, 1688, and removed to Carteret County,
North

35

North Carolina, before 1736, for the records of the Monthly Meeting of Friends of Newport River, North Carolina, for that year, show that the meetings were "to be held at the house of Henry Stanton until otherwise ordered." He, no doubt, took the clock with him on his removal to North Carolina, where it descended to my grandfather, Benjamin Stanton, after whose death it was the property of his widow, Abigail (Macy) Stanton, by whom it was brought to Harrisville, Jefferson County, Ohio, in 1800. On her death, June fifth, 1825, the clock was left to my father, Benjamin Stanton, of Salem, Ohio, who died in 1861, and by him was left to me.

It was made by Joshua Wilson, who, I have learned from a book on horology in the Boston Public Library, was a clockmaker in London before the year 1700. From the fact that Joshua Wilson was of sufficient prominence to be mentioned in works on horology as a clockmaker, in London, in 1700, it would seem probable that he had been there a number of years before that time, so there is little doubt that my clock antedates the year 1700, and as the pendulum was not used for the regulation of timepieces until the year 1662, it is evident that no pendulum clock in the world is forty years older than the one in my possession.

The works, which are of brass, the weights, and the pendulum are the same as in the original. The pinions are of brass and the verge of steel. As Abigail Stanton and her family came north in ox-carts, the clock case, owing to its size and weight, was left in North Carolina, and from 1800 to 1825 the clock "hung on the old cabin wall."

After the death of Abigail Stanton, the clock was taken to Salem, Ohio, where Dr. Benjamin Stanton
caused

EDITH COOPER, A GREAT-GRANDCHILD OF DR.
BENJAMIN STANTON. THE PHOTOGRAPH WAS
TAKEN IN 1889, JUST BEFORE THE CLOCK WAS
REMOVED TO THE HOME OF DR. BYRON STANTON,
CINCINNATI, OHIO.

THROUGH GENERATIONS THE CLOCK HAS STOOD,
"THROUGH DAYS OF SORROW AND OF MIRTH,
THROUGH DAYS OF DEATH AND DAYS OF BIRTH."

IF ITS SWINGING PENDULUM COULD BUT TALK, WHAT TALES IT COULD
TELL OF THOSE FOR WHOM IT LONG AGO TICKED OUT THE LAST HOUR.
THE LITTLE MAID GAZES EARNESTLY AT THE CLOCK OF HER ANCESTORS
AND HER HEART BEATS FASTER AS THE UNREAL PAST IS MADE REAL AND
LINKED WITH THE PRESENT.

caused a new case to be made as nearly like the original
as he was able to draw it. It is of poplar, painted black,
and is seven and one half feet high; the hood lifts off;
the face is of brass, twelve inches by twelve inches.
Within the polished brass hour circle are black figures
to indicate the hours, and between these are black
arrow heads to show the half-hours, and the days of
the

the month are shown in a small square opening below the hands. In the corners outside the hour circle were brass fretwork ornaments, which were lost many years ago, so that the entire face is of polished brass except within the hour circle, where it is of unpolished brass of dark color.

The pendulum is thirty-nine inches long, of apple wood, which is but little affected by atmospheric conditions. Unfortunately it has been broken more than once, but as it would be difficult to replace with so good material, it has been fastened together and still does duty as well as ever. It hangs by a steel spring, which allows it to swing without friction, and carries a heavy iron bob.

The long pendulum and the brass wheels, which have borne the wear of two centuries, have made the clock an unexcelled timekeeper.

Cincinnati,
Ohio,
1919.

Byron Stanton.

BENJAMIN STANTON

BENJAMIN STANTON, son of Henry Stanton and Lydia Albertson, was born in Carteret County, North Carolina, Seventh month, 1746, and died Twelfth month Twelfth, 1798. He lived and died in the house in which he was born. The house was on Ware Creek, which flows into Newport River, about four miles north of the town of Beaufort, the terminus of a railway. He was a minister of the Society of Friends.

The first wife of Benjamin Stanton, Elizabeth Carver, died young. Their one child, James, born Tenth month Ninth, 1770, married Rebecca Chaddock; they had no children. On Ninth month Twenty-ninth, 1773, Benjamin married Abigail Macy in Friends' Meeting, at New Garden, North Carolina, and they lived the remainder of his life at his home in Carteret County, where all their children were born.

Children of Benjamin and Abigail (Macy) Stanton:
David   b. 11–3–1774   died in infancy
Elizabeth b. 12–24–1775   m. Joshua Scott
Sarah   b. 1–12–1778   m. Richard Williams

Avis

THE LOCATION OF BENJAMIN STANTON'S SHIPYARD

SMALL SEAGOING VESSELS WERE BUILT HERE. JUST BACK OF THIS SHIPYARD STOOD HIS WINDMILL ON THE WESTERN EDGE OF THE HUMMOCK FIELD.

VIEW NORTH FROM BENJAMIN STANTON'S SHIPYARD

LOOKING ACROSS THE MOUTH OF WARE CREEK UP CORE CREEK, THE INLAND WATERWAY.

Avis	b. 12-1-1779	m. Jesse Thomas
Anna	b. 6-12-1782	m. Aaron Brown
Henry	b. 2-25-1784	m. Clara Patterson
Abigail	b. 3-23-1786	m. Benjamin Mitchner
David	b. 5-1-1788	m. Lucy Norman
Lydia	b. 10-11-1790	m. William Lewis
Benjamin	b. 7-28-1793	m. Martha Townsend
Joseph	b. 1-2-1797	m. Mary Townsend

Benjamin acquired a large landed estate in Carteret and Craven counties. The large ordnance used during the Rebellion for taking Fort Macon on Bogue Banks and commanding Beaufort harbor was planted on Shackleford's Banks, which had been owned by him.

OLD FORT MACON

LOCATED ON SOUTH END OF BOGUE BANKS, BEAUFORT, NORTH CAROLINA. BUILT TO DEFEND THE CITY.

He owned a shipyard and was engaged for a while in ship-building. He had inherited slaves from his father, but these he had emancipated about the year 1787 when members of the Society of Friends in North Carolina followed the example of Friends in the more northern states and manumitted

HUMMOCK FIELD

OWNED BY BENJAMIN STANTON, SR., AND WILLED TO HIS SONS, BENJAMIN AND
JOSEPH. THE SOIL IS BLACK WITH A LARGE PER CENT OF SHELLS.

CORE SOUND GRAVE YARD

THIS IS PROBABLY THE BURIAL PLACE OF MANY OF THE OLDER STANTONS. THERE
IS NOT A MARKER OF ANY DESCRIPTION TO INDICATE THE IDENTITY OF THE GRAVES.
MUCH OF THE GROUND IS COVERED WITH HEAVY TIMBER AND A DENSE UNDERGROWTH.

n one thousand se

ounced and Decla

Said Benjamin He

his last Will and te

esence of us then O

John Mar

Joseph Dew

unty {
799 }   The above

by the oa to

ᴑRTH CAROLINA.   DATED 11-5

the courts, where, though at first unsuccessful, they finally obtained a decision of the highest court in favor of the freedom of the manumitted people. Thereupon, an act was passed by the legislature of North Carolina, authorizing any persons to seize any colored person so manumitted

LOCATION OF CORE SOUND MEETING HOUSE

THE ORIGINAL HOUSE STOOD ABOUT WHERE THE WHITE MONUMENT IS LOCATED. THERE WAS NO MARKER ERECTED TO INDICATE THE EXACT LOCATION. THE BUILDING SHOWN IS A METHODIST CHURCH AND FACES EAST. WHILE THE MEETING HOUSE FACED THE SOUTH.

manumitted and cast him or her into prison, and providing that on proof being made that such person of color had been manumitted, he or she should be sold at auction. Notwithstanding this barbarous enactment, Benjamin Stanton, and after him his widow and children, succeeded in protecting the slaves set free by him and some of them emigrated to Ohio with the family in 1800.

One of the slave women set free by Benjamin Stanton once saved the life of his son Benjamin, then a very small child. A boat had been pulled upon the beach and into it the child had clambered. At high tide the boat had floated and when the tide began to recede the boat started out to sea, but fortunately not so far but that the colored woman, who discovered the child's danger, was able by wading almost

her

OLDEST HOUSE IN BEAUFORT, NORTH CAROLINA
THIS HOUSE IS NO DOUBT TYPICAL OF THOSE STANDING DURING THE LIFETIME OF BENJAMIN STANTON, SR.

... the Estate of Benj[r] Stanton

... in April 1799

& Beds	one loom and Warping Beams
	one Riding Chaires
	one and a half hogshead
...table	of Molasses
	carried over

two Cots
one Desk
one Mahogany table
and Candle Stand
two Black Walnut table
two Chests
fifteen Chires
two Dozen phino t Bottles
one Case with Bottles
Breafast and furniture
Consisting of Glass
Chaney & Delph
one Looking Glass
four pewter Dishes
two ditto Basons
one Doz White Metal
Spoons
Eight Coarse Earthen
Dishes
two Dutch ovens
four Iron potts
two Skillets
three Iron Kettles
one Bell metal Kittle

one and a half hogoh
of Molases
two hundred Weight of
Siin twine
one old Siin
one Dutch fann
one Cask Rice
one bbl penn
two hand mill
three Whip Saws
part of a sett of Coopers tods
Nine Barrels fish
two ditto Rosin
ten Deer Skins
part of an old porpoise
Siin
Eight Row hides
four Calf Skins
forty one fish Barrels
two Sailing Boates
one Large Skow
fourteen Stocks Junipe
one Gun Barrel
two Mens Riding Saddle
Caried over

true Inventory of what
Abigail Stanton

Inventory of the estate
of Benj. Stanton

teen White Mugs
tea pots
Shugar Dishes
n Earthan Juggs
urteen fire hats
wool ditto
and half Dozn White
tal Spoons
Ink Stands
Earthan pot
Chappone d fire
te Baskets
Large Box Wafers
tennant Saws
papers Shoemakers
paper awl Blades
paper Small fish hooks
papers Nee Buckles
Shoe Buckles
pr plated ditto
black one ditto
and half Dozen
Buttons
Coopers Whittles
of Knitting needles
Buckle Brushes
pr Sizars

four papers Ink
powder
one paper pins
Silk twist
Sixty
half pound fine thred
part of five pieces
Ribbons
Eight Stock locks
three p" chest hin
- ges
one Gunn Lock
one Keg White Lead
part of a box pipes
five yards Check
Muslin
Six yards and quarter
pair Muslin
Seven yard a half
rig ditto
five Cravats
two Large Muslin
Shawls
two and three quar
ters yard flowerd
muslin
one yard and a qt
Check
one and three quart
yard Jeans

one yard half quarter of
Casimire
four yards thick sett
four Red Cloacks
Seven yard worsted
Corduroy
two yards Red Broad Cloth
one and a half yard plu
eight yard blue Broad
Cloth
Eighty Eight yard Calico
Seventeen ditto Ravens
Duck
one Whole piece Raven
Duck
twenty yard Buckram
Seventeen and three yd
yard ozynaburgo
two Skeines Marlin
two Drum lines
four ditto Serin augers
two old ditto
two Stone Juggs
Sixty four pounds Coffee
fifteen yards of Red Dura
- nt
one Iron Square
one water pot
two pr Worsted Stocking
thirty nine and three quart
yard Velvet
one old Chest Drours
Caried over

her full depth into the water to catch the boat and pull it ashore.

Some of the colored people set free by Benjamin Stanton took the family name and their descendants still bear the name of Stanton.

*   *   *   *   ~

When Benjamin Stanton was twenty-one years old, and living in North Carolina, about forty-five years after his father left the old home town of Newport, Rhode Island, and when his future wife, Abigail Macy, was fourteen years old, living in Nantucket, there was a little social held in Newport that gives an insight into the life of that day. The description is taken from "Newport Illustrated," published in 1854.

> "From the Newport Mercury, of 1767, we extract the following, as giving a lively picture of the manner in which a clergyman's salary was paid when money was scarce and only to be obtained by the few:
>
> "'Last Wednesday thirty-seven young ladies of this town made the Rev. Dr. Stiles' lady a visit. They sent their wheels and carried flax enough for a moderate day's spinning, having agreed to have no trial who should spin most, but to spin good, fine yarn, and as much as they could without fatiguing themselves, and, accordingly, they spent the day in a very agreeable, industrious manner, and at sunset made Mr. Stiles a present of about one hundred fifteen-knotted skeins of yarn fine enough for shirts for the best gentleman in America.'"

NEW GARDEN MEETING HOUSE, NORTH CAROLINA

REPRODUCED FROM A CRAYON DRAWING.

RECORDS OF THE STANTONS IN NORTH CAROLINA

SHOWING A LIST
OF PURCHASES AND
SALES OF LAND.

VIEW FROM BOGUE BANKS

CARROT ISLANDS, BENJAMIN STANTON'S FISHERY AT LEFT.
SHACKELFORD BANK, ON RIGHT, OWNED BY HIM.

LIST OF PURCHASES AND SALES OF LAND BY THE STANTONS IN CARTERET CO., NORTH CAROLINA

As found by Willis V. & Thomas
Webster, 6-   -1921.

Joshua Porter & wife to Henry Stanton, 1992A. near Bogue Inlet, 4-28-1721.

George Cogdell to Henry Stanton Shipweight, 150A. on the north side of Newport river, 3-6-1732.

Geo. Cogdell to Henry Stanton Shipweight, 440A. between Eastman's & Bell's Creeks, and known as the "Swimming Poynt," 3-6-1732.

Carey Godby & wife to Henry Stanton, 437A. on Core Sound, on the east side of Broad creek on Newport river, 1-13-1732.

George 2nd to Cap. Henry Stanton, 380A. east side of Newport river, south of Powell's creek, 3-8-1736.

George 2nd to Cap. Henry Stanton, 480A. on the headline of Captain Henry Stanton, between Ware & Russells creeks, 9-25-1741.

George 2nd to Henry Stanton, 640A. on north west side of Black creek, on north side of Newport river, 8-4-1740.

Henry Stanton Sr. to Son Henry Stanton Jr. 300A. on N. E. side of Newport river, between Powell & Ware creeks, 9-27-1745.

John Small to Joseph Stanton, 122A. on W. side of Harlows creek, 7-15-1759.

John Bell to Henry Stanton, 80A. on head of Harlows creek, 5-14-1754.

Joseph Borden to Joseph Stanton, 500A. E. side of Core creek, 3-   -1764.

John Russell to Benj. Stanton, 80A. uppermost tract on North river, 11-18-1767.

Robert Williams to Henry Stanton, 1A. on W. side of Black creek, Saw & Grist mill, 2-6-1771.

George P. Lovick to Henry Stanton, 400A. on N. side of Newport river, on Black creek, 6-17-1771.

David Shepard to Henry Stanton, 1A. on Black creek, including Stanton's mill, 5-7-1773.

David Shepard to Henry Stanton, an island below the mill, on Black creek, 6-24-1774.

Hope Stanton to Benj. Stanton, one half of 300A. on W. side of Core creek, part of my father, Benj. Borden's land, 3-20-1779.

Thos. Bratchard to Benj. Stanton Jr. 100A. on N. side of Newport river, between Powell and Ware creeks, on Core creek, 2-21-1785.

David Hall to Benj. Stanton Jr. 100A. on N. side of Newport river, on Core creek, 4-1-1785.

James Peartree to Benj. Stanton Jr. 100A. on N. E. side of Newport river, on E. side of mouth of Core creek, between Powell & Ware creeks, 9-7-1785.

Diedrich Gibble to Benj. Stanton, 100A. on N. side of Newport river, 3-22-1786.

James Bell to Benj. Stanton Sr. & Jr. one fourth part of 300A. near head of Harlows creek, 11-30-1785.

James Bell to Benj. Sr. & Jr., 50A. on head of Harlows creek, 11-30-1785.

Nehemiah Harris to Benj. Stanton, 50A. Carrot island, 3-25-1790.

John Stanton to Benj. Stanton, 200A. on W. side of North river, 11-14-1791. Part of 300A. patent to Richard Russell.

State to Benj. Stanton Jr. 50A. east of Core creek & north of Eastman creek, 1789. State

State to Benj. Stanton Jr. 50A. joining Core creek, & N. of Eastman creek, Patent issued 11-17-1789.

Joseph W. Davis to Benj. Stanton 50A. of Banks land, between Old Topsail inlet & Drum inlet, 10-7-1792.

Francis Mace to James Stanton, 50A. on Bogue Banks, between Old Topsail inlet & Bogue inlet, 10-31-1796.

Joseph King to James Stanton, ½ Lot & House in Beaufort 8-23-1800.

Joshua & Elizabeth Scott and Richard & Sarah Williams to James Stanton their interest in land on North river, willed to unborn child by Benj. Stanton, 11-10-1801.

Benj. Stanton Jr. to Benj. Stanton Sr. & Dedrich Grebble, 480 A. on east side of Newport river, between Ware & Russell creeks, the land pat. by Capt. Henry Stanton, 9-25-1741, but never taken out and costs paid until Benj. Stanton Sen. finished the work and obtained it by heirship & purchase and now owns the most of it, 6-1-1785.

State to Owen Stanton, 200A. on North river, west side, 3-8-1817.

Owen Stanton to Otway Burns, land on Core creek whereon I now live & 200A. on North river, joining the land of Otway Burns, 12-15-1820.

Adm. of Abram Pigott to James Stanton, one negro boy named Isaac, 1- -1813. Consideration 275.00 dollars.

State to Benj. Stanton Sr. & Lemrick Harris, on W. side of Parrots bay, 1788.

State to Benj. Stanton Sr. 50A. on W. side of North river, by his own entry, 3-13-1788.

State to Owen Stanton 120A. within the reputed bounds of the lands he now lives on, patented by Thos. Austin, including vacant land at N. end, 4-7-1788.

State to Benj. Stanton Jr. 80A. on E. side of Core creek, joining his own land, 3-29-1788.

State to Benj. Stanton, 10A. on Ware creek just above my shipyard, 5-22-1792.

James Stanton to Stephen Fulford, house & ½ lot, Beaufort, 12-1-1804.

Henry Stanton to Silas Carpenter, 300A. on which I now live, between Powell & Ware creeks on Core creek, N. of Newport river, 3-13-1745.

Henry Stanton to James Easton, 437A. on Core sound, on the E. side of Broad creek, on Newport river, 1-13-1732.

Henry Stanton to Son Richard Russell, 100A. near Core creek, 3-11-1737.

Henry Stanton to Isaac White, 150A. on N. side of Newport river, 11-7-1751. (Isaac White married Catherine Stanton.)

Henry Stanton Jr. executor of Henry Stanton Sr. to Henry Chew Sr. 640A. on N. side of Newport river, on Black creek, 3-7-1753.

Benj. Stanton to John Russell, 50A., 11-18-1767.

Benj. Stanton to John Shepard, 80A. near head of North river, 6-17-1772.

Benj. John & Sarah Stanton to Peter Starkey, 266A. part of 800A. on Bear bank, 1-25-1769.

Henry Stanton to Isaac Scriven, 80A. near head of Harlows creek, 11-4-1768.

Henry Stanton to Wm. Borden, 200A. on Bogue banks, 6-17-1776.

Henry Stanton to Son John Stanton, by will, 5-1-1751, 190A. on N. side Newport river.

John Stanton to Henry Dickson, 190A. on N. side of Newport river, 1-23-1773.

Henry Dickson to Henry Stanton, 190A. N. side of Newport river, 11-6-1775.

Benj. & Hope Stanton to James Scrivens, 80A. E. side of Harlow creek, 12-17-1779.

Hope Stanton, widow & sole Executrix of Henry Stanton, deceased, and Benj. Stanton eldest son of Henry Stanton to Robert Williams, 1A. & all the Saw mill & M of the Grist mill purchased of David Shepard, also a piece of marsh land below the mill, between the tail race and main creek, also 400A. above the mill on both sides of Black creek, 9-24-1777.

Benj. Stanton to Elizabeth Tomlinson, 75A. adjoining Beaufort, 6-17-1783.

Benj. Stanton Sr. to Nehemiah Harris, a part of old patent whereon Benj. Stanton now lives, 3-17-1790.

Owen Stanton to Peter Piser, 120A. on west side of Harlow creek, 3-29-1793.

Benj. Stanton to Joseph W. Davis, 200A. between Powell & Ware cks., 1-22-1794.

Benj.

Benj. Stanton to Jonas Small, 150A. W. side of Core creek, 6–1–1793.

Benj. Stanton to Wm. Gardner, 24A. N. side Newport river, near Deep creek, 11–22–1796.

Benj. Stanton to Edward Kenneday, 300A. on N. side of Newport river W. of Little Deep creek, 2–20–1798.

Benj. Stanton to Jonas Small, 150A. on N. side of Core creek (pt. of Wm. Borden patent of 1747), 2–17–1796.

Abigail Stanton, by Atty. lease to Ludwig Roberts, 300A. her homestead, 10–27–1800. Yearly rental of $50.10 for seven years beginning 1–1–1801.

Abigail Stanton to Benj. Cheney, Power of Atty., 5–7–1800.

Benj. Cheney appoints George Read Atty. in his stead, 12–1–1804.

Abigail Stanton to J. W. Davis, her right in land willed her by her father, Benj. Stanton.

Henry Stanton to J. W. Davis, his right in land willed him by his father, Benj. Stanton, including the Hummock field and Shipyard, 9–2–1805.

Benj. Stanton, son of John, to Jacob Davis, 100A. (part of 300A.) on west side of North river, 12–12–1807.

David Stanton to J. W. Davis, 50A. willed me by father Benj. on E. side of Core creek & S. side of Ware creek, 1–8–1810.

David Stanton to Benj. Thomas, Power of Atty., 11–1–1809.

Benj. Stanton, by Bryant Hellen Atty. to J. W. Davis, on east side of Newport river, ½ the plantation on which father last lived, & my interest in North river farm willed to the unborn child, 2–5–1816.

John Stanton to Wm. Davis, 100A. (part of 300A.) on west side of North river, 3–10–1814.

Henry Stanton to Quakers, 3A. for a pasture south of Quaker meeting house, 9–23–1737. (At Powell creek & the public road.)

Nicholas Briant to Quakers, the land upon which stood Core Sound meeting house. (Just north of the 3A. for pasture.)

State to Benj. Stanton et. al. 10A. being a cockle shole on the east side of Newport Channel on the west point, running down the said channel including a small island marsh, 8–27–1793.

State to Jonathan Stanton, 90A. Bounded on west by Mallard Dickerson's land & on south by Wm. H. Dickerson's land, 12–31–1847.

State to Horton Howard, 75A. Lying near or joining Benj. Stanton's land and in or opposite the mouth of Core creek and joining the east side of the channel of said creek including the Green Bank, 9–7–1789.

State to Benj. Stanton, 50A. of marsh land, being an island on the west side of Newport channel & on the east point of the Great shole opposite to his own landing near David Coopers & Enoch Wards entry, 4–1–1784.

State to Benj. Stanton, 7A. on the east side of Newport river, at the south side of the mouth of Core creek, joining his own land including his shipyard, 4–1–1784.

State to Benj. Stanton & Didrich Gibble, —A. on west side of North river joining their own land, 5–17–1785.

State to Benj. Stanton Jr. 30A. marsh land, being part of sundry small islands adjoining each other on the west side of Newport channel & on the north east point of the Great shoal opposite Benj. Stanton Sr. landing joining his entry, 12–8–1786.

State to Benj. Stanton Jr. 10A. marsh land, on the east side of the main channel in Newport river, being two small islands joining each other lying opposite the mouth of Island creek, 12–8–1786.

State to Benj. Stanton Jr. 10A. on the east side of Core creek, joining the lands of John Easton & his own, 12–8–1786.

RECORDS OF THE STANTONS IN NORTH CAROLINA

SHOWING AN ABSTRACT
FROM THE MINUTES OF
CORE SOUND MONTHLY
MEETING.

**TREES OPPOSITE SITE OF CORE SOUND
MONTHLY MEETING HOUSE**

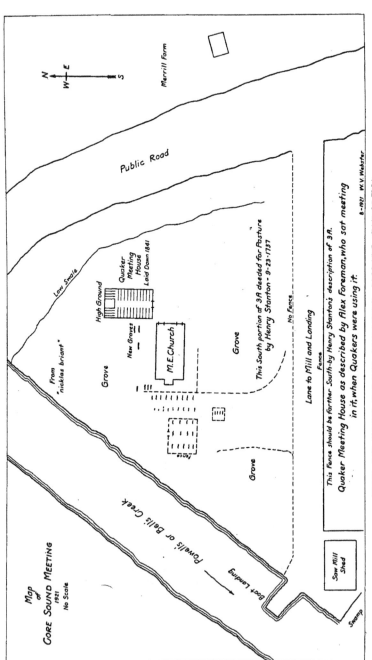

Map
of
CORE SOUND MEETING
1921
No Scale

Powell's or Bell's Creek

Boat Landing

Swamp

N
W — E
S

Merrill Farm

Public Road

Low Swale

From
"nicklas briant"

Grove

High Ground

Quaker Meeting House
Laid Down 1841

New Graves

M.E.Church

Grove

No Fence

Grove

Fence

Grove

Lane to Mill and Landing

This South portion of 3A deeded for Pasture by Henry Stanton - 9-23-1737

This Fence should be further South-by Henry Stanton's description of 3A. Quaker Meeting House as described by Alex Foreman, who sat meeting in it, when Quakers were using it.

8-1921 W.V. Webster

Saw Mill Shed

MAP OF CORE SOUND MEETING, NORTH CAROLINA

ABSTRACT OF MINUTES OF CORE SOUND MONTHLY MEETING

Taken from the original minute book
by Willis V. Webster, 8-3-1921.

8-1-1733. Core Sound Meeting organized. Monthly meeting every first third day in the month successively for time to come, and that the first day before the monthly meeting shall be a representative meeting and to be kept at the house of Henry Stanton till the meeting orders it other ways. Nickolas Briant for men, and Mary Stanton for women, to inquire into the order of Friends in respect to the minute of our yearly meeting held at Perquimans, North Carolina.

1739. Record book ordered made.

1742. 50 shillings per year for care of the meeting house and yard.

1742. Henry Stanton and wife given certificate to visit their friends in the other county.

1742. Henry Stanton, Senior appointed clerk of the monthly meeting.

11- -1742. Certificate to Henry Stanton Junior.

1743. Received a certificate for Henry Stanton, Senior.

7-3-1745. Henry Stanton Senior and Lydia Albertson laid their intentions of marriage before the meeting.

1746. Henry Stanton and Henry Stanton Junior sign the wedding certificate of John Small and Elizabeth Small.

4-12-1750. Henry Stanton son of Henry and Mary his former wife, and Hope Borden daughter of Benjamin Borden and Ruth his wife, late of, and from Boston in New England, now of Carteret County, North Carolina, married. Witnesses—Lydia, Mary, Catherine, Benjamin, Henry and Joseph Stanton and 21 others.

3-7-1751. Henry Stanton Senior, lays a plan to visit Rhode Island before the meeting.

9-10-1752. Henry Stanton gives up his plan to visit Rhode Island.

1754. Henry and Hope Stanton sign a wedding certificate.

1755. Joseph Stanton and Meriam Small declare their intentions of marriage.

1758. Henry and Joseph Stanton to help find shingles to repair the meeting house roof.

6- -1759. John Tomlenson and Henry Stanton desire a certificate to visit Rhode Island.

1760. Hope, Joseph and Henry Stanton and others appear on a marriage certificate.

1-28-1761. Henry Stanton appointed clerk.

1761. Henry and Joseph Stanton with others sign marriage certificate.

11-24-1761. Henry Stanton returns from a visit to Nantucket and Rhode Island.

1762. Henry and Joseph Stanton mentioned in meeting records.

1762. A meeting is proposed for Clubfoot's creek by Bishops bridge.

3-17-1762. Joseph, Henry, Miriam and Hope Stanton sign papers.

1-19-1763. Henry and Joseph Stanton and John Tomlinson appointed Trustees of meeting house, burying ground and yard.

1764. Henry Stanton requests a certificate to visit Rhode Island.

1765. Miriam, Hope and Joseph Stanton sign papers.

2-29-1766.

53

2-29-1766. William Britton and Alice Stanton publish intentions of marriage.

7-9-1766. Henry Stanton's name appears.

1767. Sarah, Avis, Hannah, Henry, Hope, Joseph and Benjamin Stanton appear on Bartholomew Howard and Ruth (Stanton) Howard's marriage certificate as witnesses.

10-18-1767. Two certificates were produced for Benjamin and Sarah Stanton.

1768. Henry and Joseph Stanton mentioned.

2-12-1769. James Newby and Sarah Stanton announce their intention of marriage.

7-11-1769. James Newby and Sarah Stanton married. Witnesses, Miriam, Hannah, Benjamin, John, Henry and Joseph Stanton et. al.

1771. Henry Stanton and Parmenas Horton should wait upon the Governor in regard to church matters.

6-12-1771. Joseph and John Stanton and John Mace representatives to Quarterly meeting.

4-7-1771. John Tomlinson and Elizabeth Albertson (widow) married. Witnesses, Owen, Benjamin Junior, Hannah, Henry Junior, Joseph, Henry and Benjamin Stanton et. al.

3-11-1772. John Stanton applies for a certificate. Joseph and Benjamin appointed to make inquiry.

6-10-1772. Henry Stanton requires a certificate.

1-13-1773. Benjamin Stanton having requested a few lines by way of a certificate to New Garden monthly meeting, the same is ordered to be got ready ag. next first meeting.

7-14-1773. Robert Williams and Benjamin Stanton son of Henry appointed representative to Quarterly meeting.

7-14-1773. Benjamin Stanton requests a certificate to New Garden Monthly meeting. Ordered that Joseph Stanton and William Britton make inquiry.

8-11-1773. Certificate ordered signed. (Benjamin Stanton and Abigail Macy married at New Garden 9-27-1773.)

1774. Henry, Benjamin and Joseph Stanton et. al. sign the denial papers of Robert Williams.

1-10-1776. James Bishop and Hannah Stanton declare intentions of marriage and were married. Witnesses, Abigail, Abigail, Joseph, Henry, Benjamin, Benjamin Junior and Owen Stanton.

8-14-1776. Benjamin Stanton son of Henry and John Tomlinson appointed rep. to Quarterly meeting.

10-8-1776. Henry Stanton Junior requests a certificate to Pasquotank Monthly meeting. John Tomlinson appointed to prepare it with Henry Stanton.

1-8-1777. It was ordered that John Tomlinson prepare a certificate for Henry Stanton signifying his parents and friends approbation of his intentions of marriage to Hannah Nixon of Little River.

11-12-1777. At a Monthly meeting, Owen and Benjamin Stanton Junior, appointed to represent the state of the meeting to Quarterly meeting. Benjamin Stanton Senior is appointed to prepare certificate for William Bishop. Benjamin Stanton Junior appointed clerk. Also Joseph and Benjamin Stanton Senior to visit those who want membership with us.

1-14-1778. Henry Stanton is requested to record births and deaths as collected by our members. (Only a few pages of this record remains.)

2-11-1778. Joseph Bishop and Abigail Stanton declare their intentions of marriage. Married 3-22-1778. Witnesses, Joseph, Benjamin, Benjamin Junior, William, Henry, Borden, Henry, and Hope Stanton and Ruth Howard, Abigail Stanton and Lydia Bishop.

5-13-1778. Benjamin Senior and Junior Stanton appointed to attend Quarterly meeting.

6-10-1778. Owen Stanton and Elizabeth Bishop declare intentions of marriage. Benjamin Stanton clerk, 8-7-1778, they did not know the meeting approved on account of sickness.

6-12-1778.

6-12-1778. Joseph Bishop and William Stanton to attend Quarterly meeting. Owen Stanton and Elizabeth Bishop married. Witnesses, Joseph, Henry, Benjamin, Benjamin Junior, William, Borden, Mary, Hope, Abigail Stanton et. al.

6-9-1779. Benjamin Stanton Junior returns his certificate given him Third month.

7-14-1779. Benjamin Stanton Senior and Joseph Bishop appointed representatives to Quarterly meeting. John Tomlinson and Benjamin Stanton Junior are appointed to draw papers recommending Benjamin Stanton Senior as minister to the select meeting. Representatives ask for Quarterly meeting to be settled at Contentney.

8-11-1779. Recommendation for Benjamin Stanton signed.

8-22-1779. William Stanton and Lydia Bishop married. Witnesses, Benjamin, Joseph, Borden, Henry, Owen, Hope, Abigail Stanton and Ruth Howard et. al.

12-8-1779. Benjamin Stanton Senior, to visit Adams creek meeting. Benjamin Stanton Junior and Jesse Thomas to go with him. 3-8-1780. They give an account of visit.

4-12-1780. Benjamin Stanton Junior, and Alice Macy (or Mace) declare intentions of marriage.

9-13-1780. Benjamin Stanton Junior, recommended minister. Is accepted.

5-9-1781. Henry Stanton son of Henry being about to move to Contentney, requests a certificate.

3-13-1782. Jesse Thomas marries Huld Bell. Witnesses, Owen, Benjamin, Benjamin, Junior, William and Abigail Stanton et. al.

8-14-1782. Henry Stanton produced a certificate from Contentney Monthly meeting which was read and accepted and he and Nelly Melton declare their intentions of marriage. Benjamin Stanton Junior et. al. are appointed to inquire, etc. Susannah Stanton also produced a certificate and was accepted.

10-9-1782. Friends appointed to attend report the marriage accomplished. As the last named Henry Stanton died some one or more years before this transcript was made out we think this notice of marriage sufficient.

11-13-1782. Boundary line between Contentney and this as follows: Begin at head of Dawson Swamp; along said swamp to Trent River, and down Trent River to the mouth of Resolution branch, and up the said branch to the head and said boundaries are agreed to by Contentney monthly meeting.

1-8-1783. Benjamin Stanton the younger wants to take a trip to some northern Counties.

2-12-1783. Benjamin Stanton Senior and Owen Stanton are appointed to labor with such as have slaves.

5-14-1783. Benjamin Stanton wants to visit meetings. 6-11. Returned from visit. Monthly meeting sometimes at Core Creek and sometimes at meeting house on the Neuse River.

3-11-1784. Benjamin Stanton, Junior, son of Henry Stanton late of Carteret County and Hope Stanton his wife, married to Mary Moore, daughter of John and Mary Moore of Mattamuskeet, of Hyde County. Witnesses, Benjamin Senior, Owen and Elizabeth Stanton et. al.

1-1-1785. Owen and Benjamin Stanton appointed to visit families.

6-4-1785. William Stanton appointed overseer. Appoint a committee to see about building a shed to accommodate the women for preparative and monthly meeting.

8-7-1785. Joseph Bishop and Elizabeth Bundy marry. Witnesses, Joshua Bundy, Borden, Owen, Benjamin, William, Hope, Susannah and Abigail Stanton and Ruth Howard et. al.

9-3-1785. Owen Stanton and Jesse Harris to procure a workman and material and construct a partition in the meeting house.

1-7-1786. Benjamin Stanton Junior wishes to visit Trent and other meetings.

1786. Benjamin Junior, Borden, Owen, Benjamin, William, Mary and Susannah Stanton are mentioned.

4-1-1786. Monthly Meeting held at Clubfoot Creek upon Neuse River.

3-4-1787.

3-4-1787. Josiah Bundy son of Moses Bundy and wife, Jane, marries Methia Owen. Witnesses, Owen, Benjamin Junior, Benjamin, Hope, Abigail, Lydia and Nellie Stanton.

8-4-1787. Benjamin, Owen, and Borden Stanton appointed to attend Quarterly Meeting and Benjamin Stanton Junior, if he is able to go desires to visit Friends meetings generally.

10-6-1787. At a Monthly Meeting held for Core Sound upon Neuse, Benjamin Stanton, Junior, informs this meeting that he visited and had meetings at all the meeting houses in Pasquotank and Perquimans Counties. Also Contentney Monthly meeting. Also Tar River and Jack Swamp meetings and Northampton Monthly meeting, and that it was considerable to his own mind.

11-14-1787. Benajah Steele marries Sarah Bundy, daughter of Joshua Bundy of Craven County. Witnesses, Borden and Susannah Stanton, Abner Hall and Hannah Bundy et. al.

5-3-1788. Our last yearly meeting held at Guilford.

7-5-1788. Owen Stanton appointed to collect subscriptions instead of Benjamin Stanton who desires to give up.

10-12-1788. Daniel Frazier Junior, marries Nellie Stanton widow of young Henry Stanton deceased. Witnesses, Benjamin Junior, Owen, William, Benjamin Senior and Joseph Stanton.

1-3-1789. Appoint Benjamin Senior, Borden and Owen Stanton and William Mace representatives to First Quarterly Meeting, to be held on Contentney the Third Seventh day of this month.

3-7-1789. Owen Stanton requests to be released as overseer.

11-8-1789. Jesse Thomas of Jones County upon Trent marries Martha Briant.

3-6-1790. Last Yearly Meeting held at Center, Guilford County. James Stanton accused of fornication which he doth not deny.

2-5-1791. Friends of the lower First day meeting on Trent conclude on a place to build a meeting house on north side of Trent River near the mouth of Buck Horn branch.

3-5-1791. Yearly Meeting alternately at Symons creek and New Garden meeting houses.

2-6-1791. Aaron Brown marries Mary Howard. Witnesses, Owen, Benjamin, Senior and Junior, Borden, William, Elizabeth, and Sarah Stanton et. al.

1-1-1791. Meeting adjourned to 1-5 on account of a severe snow storm. Very few Friends met.

1-5-1791. Friends meeting house built on Buck Horn branch.

4-7-1792. William Stanton has removed to Trent. Abigail Stanton recommended as an elder.

1-5-1793. Josiah Bundy goes to Trent (Certificate 4-6-1793).

3-2-1793. Hepsibah Stanton assists with the meeting.

6-1-1793. Benjamin and Owen Stanton et. al. to select a site for a meeting house at Mattamuskeet, agreed it should be located at the lower end of James Hall's plantation near a grave yard, by a large mulberry tree. This meeting concurs.

1-5-1794. Joshua Scott, son of Adam and Hannah Scott, and Elizabeth Stanton daughter of Benjamin and Abigail Stanton marry. Witnesses, Benjamin, Owen, Sarah, Avis, Anna Stanton et. al.

6-7-1794. Benjamin and Owen Stanton et. al. appointed to devise some means so women friends can have more conveniences for holding business meetings.

10-4-1794. Benjamin Stanton et. al. appointed representative to Quarterly meeting.

3-7-1795. Benjamin Stanton informs this meeting that he expects to go to Philadelphia on account of his outward business and requests a few lines to friends, he being a minister. The clerk is directed to furnish the same. Jesse Thomas was disowned for marrying a woman not of our society in less than two weeks after the death of his wife.

5-2-1795. Benjamin Stanton returns from his voyage.

1-2-1796.

1-12-1796. Benjamin and Owen Stanton et. al. appointed to attend Quarterly meeting.

2-6-1796. Horton Howard appointed clerk.

3-5-1796. Benjamin Stanton expects to go to Philadelphia on outward business and requests a few lines. He got them. Quarterly meeting at Contentney, Wayne County, and Yearly Meeting at New Garden.

4-2-1796. Owen Stanton and Horton Howard representatives to Quarterly meeting.

11-6-1796. Richard Williams, son of Robert Williams and his wife, deceased and Sarah Stanton daughter of Benjamin and Abigail Stanton married. Witnesses, Benjamin, James, Owen, Owen Junior, Abigail, Avis, Anna Stanton, Horton Howard, Joshua Scott, Jesse Thomas and Elizabeth Scott.

9-3-1797. Jesse Thomas Junior, son of Jesse Thomas of Jones County, marries Avis Stanton daughter of Benjamin and Abigail Stanton. Witnesses, Benjamin, Abigail, Owen, Anna, Miriam, Elizabeth Stanton et. al.

1798. Yearly meeting at Little River and Piney Woods.

2-25-1798. Horton Howard marries Mary Dew. Witnesses, Elizabeth Scott and Avis Thomas, etc.

3-31-1798. Benjamin Stanton and Horton Howard representatives to Quarterly Meeting.

5-3-1798. Enoch Harris marries Lany Dew. Witnesses, Benjamin, Owen, Elizabeth Stanton, Horton Howard, Sarah Williams, Elizabeth Thomas et. al.

3-30-1799. Horton Howard given a certificate as he expects to travel into the back parts of Virginia, Pennsylvania and Northwest Territory. 7-27. Back from trip.

8-31-1799. Certificate to Horton Howard and two sons Henry and Joseph to Westland Monthly Meeting, Pennsylvania. Josiah Bundy and three sons, Benjamin, Moses and Stanton, same place.

9-29-1799. Aaron Brown, son of Edward Brown and Sarah, of Jones County, North Carolina, marries Anna Stanton daughter of Benjamin and Abigail Stanton, Carteret County. Witnesses, Borden, Owen, Henry, Owen Junior, Abigail, Miriam, Abigail Junior, Hannah, Elizabeth Stanton, Elizabeth Scott, Avis Thomas, Sarah Williams et. al.

3-29-1800. The sons of Abigail Stanton request certificates to western Pennsylvania and Northwest Territory.

2-8-1801. Owen Stanton Junior, son of Owen Stanton Senior, and wife Elizabeth marries Abigail Davis, daughter of Joseph W. Davis and wife Susuhenna.

3-30-1804. Owen Stanton and Jesse Harris representatives to Quarterly Meeting.

1805. Great Contentney became Contentney.

6-28-1807. Abigail and Owen Stanton appear on a marriage certificate.

5-1-1808. Jacob Davis, son of Joseph Wicker Davis, marries Mary Stanton, daughter of Owen and Elizabeth Stanton. Witnesses, Rebecca, Owen, Elizabeth, Junior, and Anna Stanton et. al.

3-26-1809. Aaron Lancaster, son of William marries Miriam Stanton, daughter of Owen Stanton. Witnesses, Ruth, Elizabeth, Owen, Elizabeth, David, Owen Stanton Junior et. al.

1810. Owen Stanton representative to Quarterly meeting.

1810. Owen Stanton and James Stanton are witnesses to a marriage.

7-31-1814. Elijah Harris marries Ruth Stanton, daughter of Owen and Elizabeth Stanton. Witnesses, Owen, Elizabeth, Anna Stanton et. al.

1818. Elizabeth and Anna Stanton et. al. witnesses to marriage.

1819. Same.

1820. Contentney Quarterly Meeting to be held once a year at Core Sound.

9-27-1828. Jonathan Mace marries Susannah Stanton, daughter of Owen Stanton. Witnesses, Jonathan and Abigail Stanton et. al.

3-28-1829. Jonathan Stanton disowned for selling slaves and liquor.

7-8-1829. Abigail Stanton's name appears on a marriage certificate.

10-30-1841. Core Sound Monthly Meeting laid down.

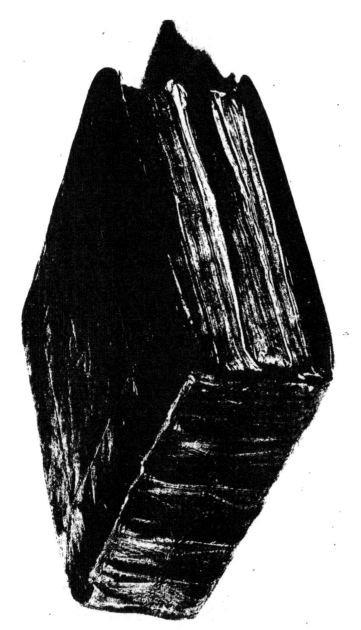

THE STANTON BIBLE

Printed in 1712, in England. The first recorder was Benjamin Stanton. Now in the possession of William Macy Stanton.

THE STANTON BIBLE

THE original Stanton Bible was given to me in 1893 by my aunt Mary P. Dawson, who had had possession of it from her father's death in 1863.

The Bible was handed on to me because of the "Macy" in my name. It seemed proper to my aunt that I should have this family treasure, since I was named for the Macys and was the youngest Stanton in her family who was a descendant of Abigail (Macy) Stanton, to whom the Bible at one time belonged and who brought it in a cart when she moved from North Carolina to Ohio in 1800.

The Bible is a heavy volume and somewhat out of true book proportion on account of trimming the pages when the book was rebound. It is, of course, impossible at this time to determine its original size or the kind of material in which it was originally bound. It is conclusively known that Henry Stanton had the Bible rebound in St. Clairsville, Ohio, and its present size and appearance would indicate that previous rebindings had been necessary. The present cover is of natural colored leather that is still in good condition.

dition. The leather is stamped on one side with an
"H" and on the other with an "S"—Henry Stanton's
initials.   The

SPECIMEN OF TYPE PAGE

A REPRODUCTION OF A PAGE FROM THE STANTON BIBLE SHOWING THE KIND OF TYPE
USED, THE WOOD-CUT INITIAL LETTER, AND THE WORN CONDITION OF THE PAGE'S EDGE.

The paper on which the text is printed is a hand-made
paper similar to the book paper so often used in the
early part of the eighteenth century. Many of the

pages

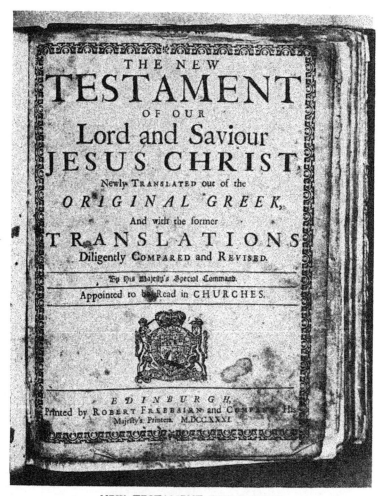

NEW TESTAMENT TITLE PAGE

A REPRODUCTION OF THE TITLE PAGE FOR THE NEW TESTAMENT PORTION OF THE
STANTON BIBLE. THIS PAGE SHOWS THE OLD WOOD-CUT LETTERS OF VARYING SIZES
THAT WERE USED IN THE SAME LINE OF TYPE, ALSO THE TIME AND PLACE OF PRINTING.

pages are badly worn, and· a few completely gone
from the book. The book's edges are brown from age
and ragged from continuous use. It is easy to discern
                                                    from

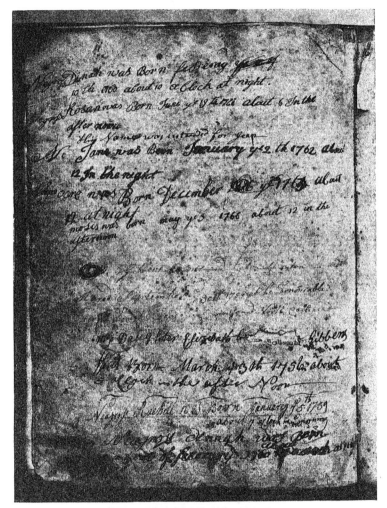

PAGE FROM FAMILY RECORD

A REPRODUCTION OF ONE OF THE MANY FLY-LEAVES THAT HAVE BEEN USED TO RECORD
THE FAMILY HISTORY. THIS PARTICULAR PAGE SHOWS THE RECORD OF THE BIRTHS OF
SEVERAL OF THE SLAVES OF THE FAMILY.

from the pages' worn edges the favorite selections of our sires. Some portions of the text have unstained and unwrinkled pages, while in other parts of the Holy Writ the fingers of the devout have worn the paper thin and sear.

An attempt was once made to reinforce the tattered paper by pasting a transparent paper over the entire page. The idea was excellent, and the intent beautiful, but the materials, although the best at the time, were unsuited for a perfect result. The paper used was heavy and stiff and somewhat obscures the printing underneath.

The Bible, although now in one volume, was originally composed of two. The Old Testament was printed in London in 1712, and the New Testament in Edinburgh in 1731. In addition to the Old and New Testaments, the Bible contains the Apocrypha. The text is bold and plain and all the large type and the illuminated initial letters are from wood cuts.

Some of the family records have been written in the Bible from time to time, and a very interesting part of the information recorded is the birth-date and names of the slaves.

There is no record that establishes the identity of the original purchaser, or of the names of any possible owners before Benjamin Stanton. As there is a record of Benjamin Stanton's first marriage, and of the death of his first wife, it is reasonable to conclude that the Bible belonged to the Stanton and not the Macy family.

Notwithstanding the uncertainty that obscures the early history of this Bible, suffice it to say that it is a precious and venerable treasure whose identity is established

established with Benjamin and Abigail Stanton, and whose hereditary existence in our family is due to the devout thought and reverent love for the better things in life, which held Abigail (Macy) Stanton to the Bible's possession through her long, widowed life and to bequeath the Bible to her son Henry for his use when she was past the vale of its teachings.

Lansdowne,
Pennsylvania,
1921.

THE OPEN BIBLE

The Sea Captain

STORY told me when a small boy by my father, Eli Stanton, was of "an Old Uncle" who was captain of a vessel. He did not say this "uncle" was a Stanton, but gave me that impression. Nor did he say whether the vessel was a fishing vessel or a merchantman, but the story seems to fit the practice on board a fishing vessel. It was customary to keep a man on watch for schools of fish or for whales and when one was sighted to endeavor to secure the catch.

One day when this old uncle, the captain, was high up on the mast in the "lookout," there was a cry of "Man overboard!" As soon as the captain learned who it was, he knew the man could not swim, so watched for him to come up and then dived from the lookout, cleared the side of the vessel, caught the drowning man, brought him aboard, and thus saved his life. Such action must have required a brave heart as well as a "strong arm." I have often wondered how many of us now living would attempt a deed so heroic.

W. H. S.

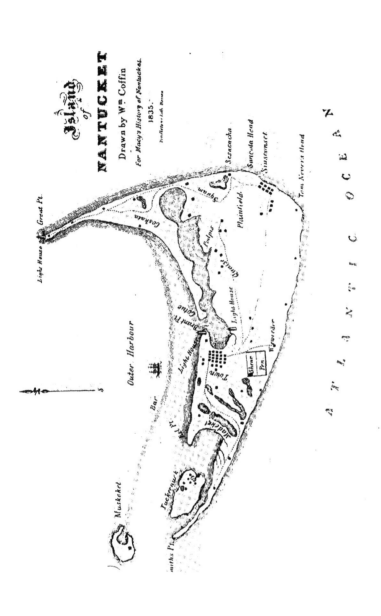

MAP OF NANTUCKET ISLAND

THOMAS MACY

BEFORE his embarkation for America Thomas Macy lived in the parish of Chilmark, near Salisbury, England. The date of his arrival in this country is not known, but it was probably in 1635. He is known to be the ancestor of all the Macys in America, for no other had a male descendant. The first record of Thomas Macy in this country is dated September sixth, 1639, when he took the freeman's oath at Newbury, Massachusetts. In this same year a number of the citizens of Newbury decided to move a short distance to a more open space which they named Salisbury, after Salisbury in England. Thomas Macy's name appears sixty-sixth on the list of first settlers of this little town.

The laws made in Massachusetts in regard to Friends in 1656–7 and those in regard to all who did not attend the Puritan Church, in 1658, explain why a determined and energetic man like Thomas Macy concluded to find a place, if possible, where there was unlimited religious liberty. He had been fined for not attending the Puritan Church and for giving shelter to some

Quakers

SOUTHEASTERN VIEW OF NANTUCKET, MASS.

THE ABOVE VIEW SHOWS THE APPEARANCE OF NANTUCKET AS IT IS SEEN FROM THE SHORE OF THE INNER HARBOR SOUTHEAST FROM THE TOWN. THE LIGHT-HOUSE ON BRANT POINT IS SEEN IN THE DISTANCE ON THE RIGHT; BEYOND IN THE EXTREME DISTANCE ARE SEEN VESSELS NEAR THE SAND-BAR, SOUTH FROM THE OUTER HARBOR, AND NEARLY TWO MILES FROM THE NORTHERN SHORE,

FROM BARBER'S HISTORICAL COLLECTIONS, 1839.

Quakers during a storm. The latter incident, however, occurred after he had decided to move. Thus, he was driven from Massachusetts by the same persecuting spirit that drove the Pilgrims from the shores of England.

On July second, 1659, he and nine others concluded the purchase of the Island of Nantucket from Thomas Mayhew. Later that same year Thomas Macy with his family and two or three others embarked in a small sailboat and started for Nantucket. They found there about three thousand Indians, who received them kindly, but no white settlers were there. After occupying temporary quarters for the winter, at the west end of the island, he selected for a permanent home, land near Reed Pond, called Wattacomet, a mile and a half northwest of the present town of Nantucket.

He died April nineteenth, 1682, aged seventy-four, and was buried on his place. His wife, Sarah (Hopcott) Macy, was also a native of Chilmark, England. She died in 1706, aged ninety-four years.

JOHN MACY

JOHN MACY, son of Thomas and Sarah Macy, was born July fourteenth, 1655. He married Deborah Gardner, daughter of Richard Gardner and Sarah Shattuck. He was but four years old when his father moved to Nantucket. He was the only son who married, and all the Macys in America are descended from him, as well as from his father, Thomas Macy. He died October fourteenth, 1691.

OLDEST HOUSE IN NANTUCKET

BUILT 1686.

No doubt Abigail Macy (Stanton) visited this house when living in Nantucket. It was the bridal home of Jethro and Mary (Gardner) Coffin. The ground was given them by her father; and the lumber furnished by his father, who had timber land at Exeter, New Hampshire. It is said Jethro did much of the construction work. They were married in this new home.

JOHN MACY

JOHN MACY, second of the name, 1675–1751, married Judith Worth, daughter of John Worth and Miriam Gardner. He and his wife were the first of the family to join the religious Society of Friends. The first Friends Meeting established on the Island of Nantucket dated from 1708, and they joined in 1711. Many other members of the family joined soon afterwards.

DAVID MACY

DAVID MACY, born September Twelfth, 1714, son of John Macy and Judith Worth, married Dinah Gardner, daughter of Solomon Gardner and Anna Coffin. Among those who went to North Carolina, in 1771, on account of the decline in whale fishing at Nantucket, were David Macy and many of his family. He left Nantucket April Twenty-eighth, 1771, for New Garden, Guilford County, North Carolina. Died October Thirteenth, 1778.

SETH MACY

This story of Seth Macy was contributed by **Dr. Byron** Stanton. Seth Macy was a brother of David Macy and an uncle of Abigail (Macy) Stanton.

ETH was among those who never married. He was a sea captain. I remember hearing my father relate as a tradition which came down to him in the Macy family, a story of Seth Macy, which I have recently seen in print. In the summer of 1754 the ship Grampus, Seth Macy, Captain, left Nantucket for London with a cargo of oil. Her owner, Jethro Coffin, was on board. Both owner and Captain were Quakers, as also were most of the crew. Nevertheless, as England and France were then at war, Seth urged Jethro to arm the vessel. But Jethro, true to his non-resistance principles, refused. The voyage was about two-thirds accomplished when, as Seth had feared, they fell in with a French privateer which gave chase. Jethro directed Seth to yield without resistance, but Seth was not that kind of Quaker. "Go thou below, Jethro, I am commander of this vessel."

Macy so managed his vessel as to give the Frenchmen the impression that he was about to "bring her to" in order to surrender, when, suddenly changing the course of the ship, she bore down on the privateer, whose officers discovered Macy's design too late to prevent its execution.

"If thou dost intend to run her down," said Jethro, "ease thy helm a little and give them a chance for their lives."

"Stand by to lower the boats," thundered Macy. A groan of horror escaped his own crew, for not until this moment had they really seen the design of their Captain, and the swarthiest cheek grew pale. . . . The schooner lay in the trough of the sea, her decks covered with confusion, and the huge bulk of the Grampus poising on the last high wave above her. . . . "Down with the boats from the quarter deck; launch the long boats!" The command could not have been uttered or executed sooner with safety, but it came too late. The aim of Seth had been too fatally sure. His own boat narrowly escaped being sucked into the whirlpool made by the sinking schooner. Not one of the Frenchmen's crew rose or again saw the light of day.

WILL OF DINAH MACY

Whereas I Dinah Macy widow, of the county of Gilford and State of North Carolina well knowing the uncertainty of life and certainty of Death and being aged but of sound mind and memory do leave the following lines as my last will and Testament relating to such Temporals as I am posysed of—First it is my will that all my Just debts and funeral expenses be paid up and discharged by my Executors here after named in due time.

2 ly. I give unto my Daughter Anna Macy my large looking glass and my large puter platter with my small tin Comister and small leather trunk with my large stone pitcher and stone jug and large walnut chair.

3 ly. I give unto my Daughter Abigail Stanton my woosted gound and my dark coulored huey coat, two new hankerchiefs checked also one coperas coulord and three checked also cloth of a checked apron.

4 ly. I give unto my Grand Daughter Dinah Macy my handirons, fire shovel and tongs with my Surred History and Ellwoods history and my two chairs.

5 ly. I give unto my Daughter in law Hannah Macy my Duffed blanket one toe sheet my Round table my pillows.

6 ly. I give unto my Grand Daughter Anna Ozment one garlick sheet also I give her one checked apron and my warming pan.

7 th. I give unto my Grand Son Thadeus Macy one black heifer four years old.

8 th. I give unto my Grand Daughter Hyrybuck Russell one half of the feathers out of my bed with one bolster and one pillow also one sheet apron.

9 th. I give unto my Grand Daughter Miriam Swaine one sheet apron.

10th

73

10 th. I give unto my two Grand Sons Isaac Macy and David Macy all my carpenter tools and farming tools with all the remainder of my letters to be equally divided between them, also I give my large chest and David my small one with my coverlid.

11 th. I give unto my two Grand Daughters Abigail Macy and Anna Macy each one large silver spoon with one feather bed and the remaining part of the other feather bed, my iron stand, my bucket and large tea pot to be equaly divided between them with my two bed steads and cord.

12 th. I give unto my Grand Daughter Sarah Macy my point puter cup.

13 th. I give unto Daughter Anna Macy and my Daughter in law Hanna Macy all the remaining part of my wearing apperal and house hold furniture to be equally divided between them, and lastly I constitute and appoint my son in law Enoch Macy and Daughter in law Hanna Macy my whole and sole executor and executrix of this my last will and testament Ratifying and allowing what so ever they may lawfully do or cause to be done in witness where of I have here unto set my hand and affixed my seal this 18th day
(1796)
of the 5th mo. and year of One thousand seven hundred and Ninty Six.

Signed, sealed and acknowledged to be Dinah Macy's last will and testament in the presence of us

Thadeus Macy   Dianah Macy (Seal)
Dianna Joy
State of North Carolina}   February Court 1797
Gulford County

Thadeus Macy proved the execution of the with in will in open court and on motion let it be recorded. Then came in Enoch Macy and Hannah Macy and qualified as Executors agreeable to law.—Test.

                John Hamilton clk.

MAP OF NANTUCKET TOWN AND VICINITY, NANTUCKET ISLAND.

ABIGAIL (MACY) STANTON

ABIGAIL STANTON (1753–1825), wife of Benjamin Stanton, was a native of Nantucket. When nineteen years of age, in 1772, she emigrated with her parents, David and Dinah Macy, to New Garden, North Carolina.

After a residence of nearly two years, she was married to Benjamin Stanton, of Carteret County, that state, where she resided during the twenty-five years of her married life, and occupied as a dwelling the house where her husband was born and lived through life, and which was therefore the birthplace of all their children.

Abigail

75

NEW GARDEN MEETING HOUSE, NORTH CAROLINA
PHOTOGRAPH TAKEN 1875.

THE HOUSE OF ALBERT PEEL

THE LUMBER OF THE OLD NEW GARDEN MEETING HOUSE WAS PURCHASED AND PORTIONS
OF IT USED IN BUILDING THIS HOUSE. THE CEILING BOARDS AND DOORS ARE OF YELLOW POPLAR
AND ARE SAID TO BE FROM THE MEETING HOUSE WHOSE WEATHERBOARDING WAS RE-USED
ON THE CENTRAL PORTION OF THE DWELLING.

THE SITE OF NEW GARDEN MEETING HOUSE

THE LOCATION OF NEW GARDEN MEETING HOUSE

THE FOUR SQUARE STONES WITH INCLINED TOPS MARK WHERE THE FOUR CORNERS OF
THE HOUSE STOOD. BENJAMIN STANTON AND ABIGAIL MACY WERE MARRIED HERE
9-29-1773.

THE LETTERED STONE
TABLET WHICH STANDS
ON THE SITE OF THE
NEW GARDEN MEETING
HOUSE AND MARKS FOR

ALL TIME THE SPOT
WHERE OUR ANCESTORS
WORSHIPED AND WERE
MARRIED

THE HOMESITE OF DAVID MACY
NORTH OF GUILFORD COLLEGE, NORTH CAROLINA.

Abigail Stanton, after the death of her husband, which occurred in December of 1798, soon determined to emigrate to Jefferson County, Ohio, with her six minor children. Accordingly, in the Spring of·1800, accompanied by her son-in-law and his wife, Aaron and Anna Brown, she left her old home with all its endearing ties, in order to escape the great evil, with its blighting effects, that overshadowed all—taking a part of her husband's former slaves with her, and leaving behind her three oldest married daughters, Elizabeth Scott, Sarah Williams, and Avis Thomas, with their husbands and children. After crossing the Allegheny Mountains, she remained some three or four months near Brownsville, Pennsylvania, awaiting the coming into market of the land where she designed settling, and in the fall of that year, she purchased land from the Government, one mile west of where Mount

Pleasant

Pleasant was subsequently located, paying for all squatter improvements thereon, including two log cabins, one of which she occupied a short time. In 1802 she erected a more commodious cabin and occupied it. She was one of the first pioneers in that vicinity. Though her family consisted of six minor children—the eldest being her son Henry, who was but sixteen years old—she kept pace with her neighbors in the

THE HOME OF DAVID MACY

THE SMALLER PORTION OF THE BUILDING SHOWN WAS PROBABLY STANDING DURING HIS LIFETIME, AND IF SO, ABIGAIL MACY LIVED HERE AT THE TIME OF HER MARRIAGE TO BENJAMIN STANTON.

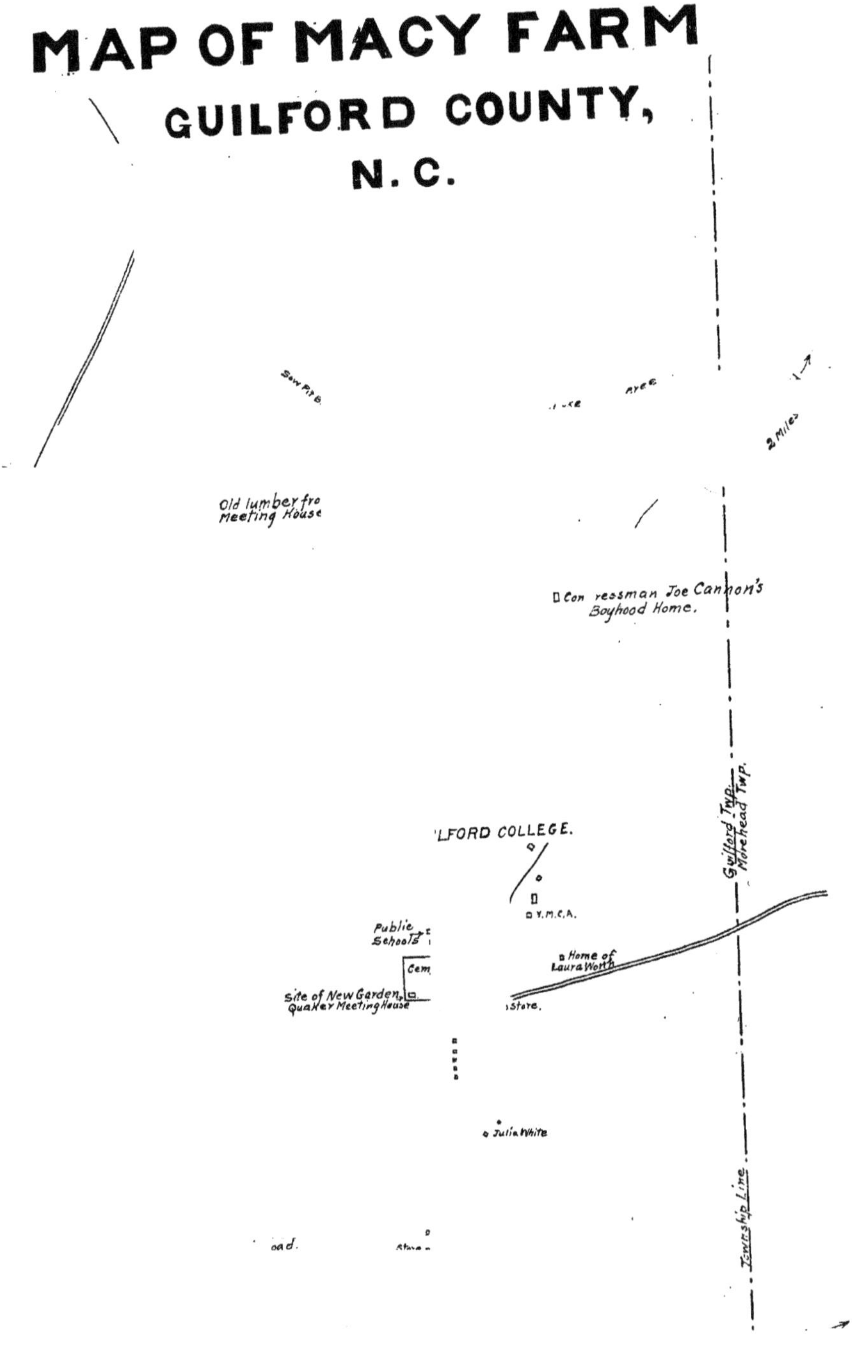

MAP OF MACY FARM
GUILFORD COUNTY,
N. C.

Saw Pipe

.1 ..«e   Ave e

2 Miles

Old lumber fro
Meeting House

☐ Con ressman Joe Cannon's
Boyhood Home.

Guilford Twp.
Morehead Twp.

'LFORD COLLEGE.

☐ Y.M.C.A.

Public
Schools

Cem.

☐ Home of
Laura Worth

Site of New Garden
Quaker Meeting House

Store.

Township Line

☐ Julia White

oad.   Stine .

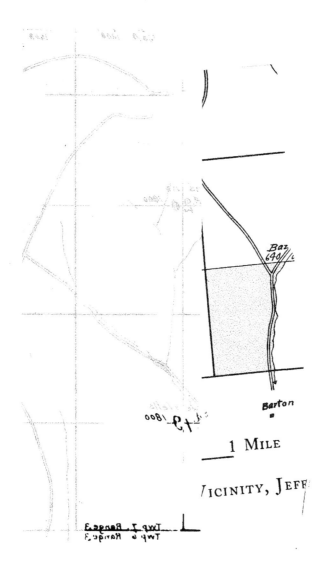

Ba_c
640

Barton

1 MILE

VICINITY, JEFF

SCALE $\frac{1}{4}$ $\frac{1}{8}$ 1 MI

MAP OF MOUNT PLEASANT AND VICINITY

Range 4.
Range 3.

OUR ANCESTORS—THE STANTONS

MAP OF MACY FARM

GUILFORD COUNTY,
N. C.

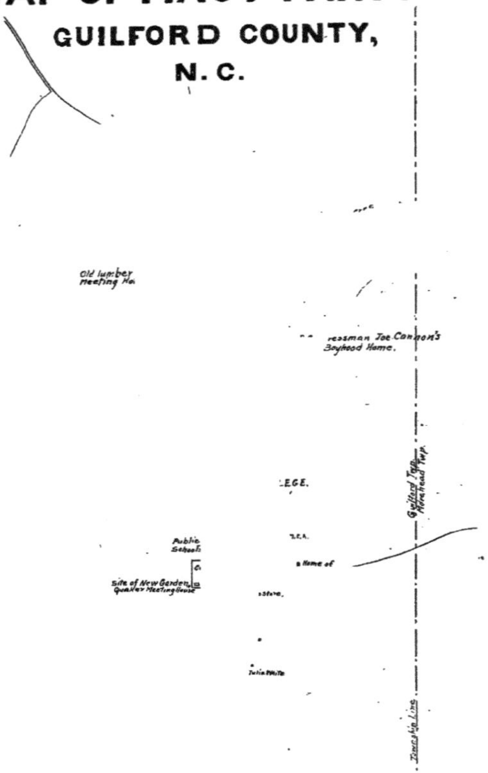

Old lumber
Meeting Ho.

Residence Joe Comfort's
Birplace? Home.

.E.G.E.

Guilford Twp.
Morehead Twp.

Y.C.A.

a Home of

L.F.M.

Public
School

Site of New Garden
Quaker Meetinghouse

Twin Wells

Township Line

the improvement of her farm, and hers was among the first bearing orchards. Within two years, her three eldest daughters left the South and came and settled in her vicinity.

If the property in the South belonging to the heirs of Benjamin Stanton had been in a land of freedom, it would have been of great value; but surrounded by slavery and abandoned by all the kindred, only a small sum was realized for it.

For the first ten or twelve years following 1802, Abigail Stanton's children were all located within two miles of her residence, and her house was the great resort of her children and grandchildren. She sold her farm after occupying it for seventeen years, and during the last years of her life, though her home was with her youngest daughter, Lydia Lewis, in Harrisville, she spent much of her time with her daughters Avis Thomas, at Mount Pleasant, and Abigail Mitchner, near Cadiz.

Her three younger sons, David, Benjamin, and Joseph, studied medicine and became successful practitioners. Sixty grandchildren were numbered among her descendants. All her children, ten in number, arrived at maturity and were married, making twenty in all, and not a death had crossed her threshold.

Her grandson, the son of Dr. David Stanton, the late Edwin M. Stanton, the great war secretary, in performing such conspicuous part in putting down the Rebellion and sweeping slavery from the land, showed conclusively that the old blood of the exiles was not extinct in her posterity.

She was a member of the Society of Friends by birthright, had strong faith in the doctrines of that sect, and for many years was an Elder in the Society. She

She died at Harrisville, in the month of June, 1825, in the seventy-third year of her age. Her funeral was attended by a large number of relatives and friends. She was buried in Friends' burying ground, at Harrisville, Harrison County, Ohio.

The above article was compiled from one written by N. M. Thomas in June, 1881.

THE KETTLE AND CRANE IN THE DOOR-YARD

THE MATRON

ABIGAIL STANTON

A Tale of the Days That are Gone

There was a time when all men lived in huts
And cabins made of logs amongst the woods,
And chopped down trees and split them up with gluts,
And did almost without cash, or goods;
Then women cared little for caps or hoods;
But they were ever full of mirth and glee,
And children sported round in mirthful broods
As happy as such urchins well can be,
Or sporting o'er the lawn, or couched on parent's knee.

And there was one I knew among the train,
A widowed matron with a little flock,
Who sought with ardent efforts to maintain
A steady course beneath misfortune's shock,
Watching with steady eye, each dangerous rock
On which the incautious bark is often driven,
Stemming like mariner the waves that broke
Along the channel, craggy and uneven,
Till some safe port be gained on earth—perhaps in heaven.

For she was cradled on yon rugged isle
Where men catch vigor from the foaming wave,
And freedom from the wind, and strength from toil,
And patience from misfortune, and grow brave
In combating the wrong—still wont to lave
The limbs of freemen in the briny flood;
For in that rugged spot I ween no slave,
E'er crouched beneath a haughty tyrant's rod,
Nor man superior owned, save when he bowed to God.

83

But there with frantic tumult to the shore
The waves came sweeping o'er the driven sand
When swelled with wind to full majestic roar,
And booming onward, wild, sublime, and grand,
As urged by some unseen all potent hand,
Spurning resistance and defying bound,
Till checked their fury by the opposing strand,
They shrink, retiring with a sullen sound
Back to their coral caves and ocean depths profound.

Such was her birthplace, and her pedigree
Was of that hardy stock by Whittier sung,
Who ever scorned to bow the supple knee,
Or bend the neck to priest who urged the wrong,
But sought a residence the wilds among
That crowned this little isle in former day,
Where free in thought, in deeds of virtue strong,
Scorning each bigot power's tyrannic sway,
He whiled a long, long life in virtuous deeds away.

And from his hardy line there sprung a race
Of sturdy seamen, daring, bold and brave,
Whose chief delight has ever been to chase
The huge sea monster in the icy wave,
Mounting the foaming surges still that lave
From frozen Greenland to the southern pole,
Braving the fury of the storms that rave,
And toss old ocean with tumultuous roll,
With heart unawed by fear, with an undaunted soul.

Nantucket! such thy sons have ever been,
And such heaven grant that they may still remain;
And such thy daughters, too—and such I ween
Was she, the heroine of this simple strain,
Dauntless in peril, ardent to maintain
A life of virtue in this world of wrong,
With prayerful efforts seeking to retain
Patience in suffering and temptation strong,
Fostering all virtuous traits to women that belong.

There was she nurtured on that little spot,
Nor was she anxious for a wider sphere.
But who so wise to scan man's future lot,
Or say on earth where ends life's strange career?
For some short space perhaps we linger here,
Veering and changing, tossing to and fro;
Child of mutation—bard, nor sage, nor seer,
Can tell what change his lot may undergo,
Careering through this world of mingled joy and woe.

Her lot was cast upon a sunny strand,
Where southern zephyrs breathe through myrtle groves,
And flowery bowers, by fragrant breezes fanned,
Seemed formed for fit retreats of joy and love,
Where clustering vines on gay magnolias move
Their graceful tendrils to each passing wind,
And fawns and lambs in sportive circles rove
'Mid verdant groves with flowery woodbine twined,
All like some fairy scene for perfect bliss designed.

And there the gentle wave with graceful swell
Came rippling shoreward o'er its pearl-clad bed,
And many a coral wreath and sparkling shell,
Their beauteous tints and burnished luster shed,
And sportive schools of finny tenants sped
In playful gambols through the briny flood,
And flocks of swans along the margin fed,
Or on the swelling wave majestic rode,
Where playful sea fowls sport in many a noisy brood.

And there she lived in that enchanting land,
By nature's bounty decked for blessed abode,
But, ah! it was not blessed, for despot hand
Its rosy walks with poison thorns had strewed,
And Tyranny there sat enthroned in blood,
The cruel master and the crouching slave,
And crushed humanity poured out a flood
Of bitter tears, such as are wont to lave
The oppressor's cruel path, while none bedew his grave.

There vice and ignorance triumphant reign,
And pomp and poverty stalk side by side,
And lust and vanity and all the train
Dragged by the car where powers despotic ride,
And whips and implements of torture dyed
In human blood, and altars, too, and throne
Were built of skeletons of those who died,
As millions trodden down and crushed have done,
Victims on slavery's shrine, unpitied and unknown.

Alas, my native land! Is this thy state?
And thus forever, ever, must it be?
Ah! would to Providence that cruel fate
Had ne'er discovered, or had kept thee free!
Oh, that in the long future I could see
Some hope that thou wouldst break the galling chain
That binds alike thy shackled slave and thee
In degradation, where you must remain
While men their fellow-men in bondage base retain.

Land of the sunny south,—land of my birth,
Land of my childhood and my father's tomb—
Of all the spots on this delightful earth,
There's none on which I would so blithely roam
As on thy flowery plains, could I but come
And find thee free from that o'ershadowing cloud,
That hovers o'er thee, like impending doom,
Where murmuring thunders mutter long and loud—
Oppression covering all with one impervious shroud.

Oh, strike that bloody banner, crimson red!
Undo the fetter and unbind the chain!
Nor let the voice of mercy ever plead,
Plead for the bondman still, and plead in vain,
From thy broad scutcheon wipe that gory stain.
So shall thy groves once more with peace abound,
And in thy courts the full harmonious strain
Of hope, and joy, and gladness shall resound,
And plenty pour her horn and comfort flow around.

How widely have I wandered from my theme!
I fain would sing of one as yet unsung—
But all before me, like some fleeting dream,
The visions of the past career along,—
Could I but catch and pour them forth in song,
With what strange transport would my sonnet glow
From pictures of the past, drawn bright and strong,
The sympathizing soul should quickly know
To smile for others' joy—to weep for others' woe.

The matron, with the partner of her lot,
There lived and loved and was beloved in turn,
For in the stately hall or in the cot,
.'Mid those who banquet, or 'mid those who mourn,
She held her court—and ever prompt to earn
The bliss, the consciousness of doing good,
She caused the sinking lamp of hope to burn,
Misfortune's thorny track with comfort strewed,
And votaries, of vice to paths of virtue, wooed.

Beneath the shelter of their friendly dome
No unpaid bondman spread the costly board,
But there the needy ever found a home—
A shelter for the vassal and the lord.
The hardy sailor with misfortune scarred,
And ministers of peace together joined,
Nor Jew, nor Turk, nor husbandman, nor bard,
E'er asked protection which he did not find,
For all were brethren there, who represent mankind.

And there the matron watched the little flock
That clustered round her, with maternal care,
And strove to teach their youthful feet to walk
In paths of virtue, and to shun the snare
That vice still spreads for footsteps unaware
Of her insidious charms; and of their store
To want and misery to yield a share—
For "He," she taught, "who giveth to the poor
But lendeth to the Lord, and shall receive the more"—

In the strict paths of justice still to tread,
To shun vile falsehood as the gate to death,
The woe-worn wanderer on his way to lead,
To strive to copy "Him of Nazareth,"
In prayer and praise to spend their earliest breath,
Nor censure erring man with word severe,
To trust in Providence with constant faith,
To mercy's voice to lend an open ear,
And strive from every eye to wipe off every tear.

As some strong archer, conscious of his power,
With deadly arrow seeks the brightest shield,
As strongest bulwark and the loftiest tower,
Are, by the invader, first compelled to yield,
Even so the heights of human bliss have reeled
Beneath thy shafts, oh, Death! Thus, by one stroke,
Low smitten to the dust, and scathed and peeled,
Were the rich comforts of that little flock—
Their safeguard—snatched away, their arm of safety broke.

In yon lone churchyard now with pines o'ergrown,
Fast by that house whose courts he loved to tread,
To bend the knee to sue the Eternal Throne,
Or lift in humble thanks his reverend head,
'Mid those who erst his friendly counsel led,
He lies in calm repose—his labor done.
No restless spirit haunts his peaceful bed,
And by no monument the spot is known,
Save a green, grassy mound, and an unlettered stone.

Now, all forsaken is that lonely spot,
And silent as the mansions of the tomb,
Save where the owlet pours its solemn note,
From midst the lofty fir tree's shady gloom;
Save that some pensive wanderer here may roam,
'Mid the cool grove, or by the gentle rill,
To listen to the drowsy beetle's hum,
Or catch with startled ear the piercing thrill,
That issues from the throat of the lone whippoorwill.

As some tall ship before a lively gale,
Dashed by misfortune on a desert coast,
'Mid cheering speed beneath her swelling sail,
Scarce sees the danger till by breakers tossed,
Her hull all shattered and her pilot lost,
So seemed the matron now, tossed to and fro.
Sorrow and care at once her mind engrossed.
Ah! who hath ever known a widow's woe,
Or felt an orphan's loss, save they who shared the blow?

She stood astonished on the barren shore,
Amid the remnant of her helpless crew,
And heard the sea with angry tempests roar,
Whose snares and dangers, oh! too well she knew.
O'er it the winds of disappointment blew,
And vice and ruin haunted every coast,
The wrecks of ruined hopes its shores bestrew,
And honor forfeited and virtue lost,
And many a righteous aim amid temptation tossed.

And on the other side there lay the land,
And such a land! Oh, Heaven! where hast thou seen?
For there oppression ruled with iron hand,
And spread out darkness where the light had been;
For chattled slavery blighted all the scene.
Where once the garden grew there sprang a thorn,
And o'er the cultured fields erst clothed in green,
There fell a mildew; and the rosy morn
By superstitious reign was turned to night forlorn.

"Oh, Thou, the father of the fatherless,"
'Twas thus e'en now methinks I hear her pray,
"Support in want, and succor in distress,
The orphan's shelter, and the widow's stay,
Be Thou in mercy pleased to send a ray
Of light to guide through this terrene abode;
Permit not Thou the unskilled feet to stray,
But guide them safely in the peaceful road,
That leads through Nature's temple, up to Nature's God.'

The matron spake and sunk to soft repose,
When, in the airy vision of the night,
On wild imagination's wing she rose,
And stood upon the mountain's lofty height
That skirts the Atlantic plain, bounding the sight
Of civilized abode.   Beyond there lay
A vast extended region, where the light
Of science scarce had sent a wandering ray
To announce the rising morn, the approach of social day.

Beside her feet there sprang a little rill
That running westward o'er its rocky bed,
Grew wide and deep, until it seemed to fill
A long extended valley where it sped
Onward with gentle current, till it led
A thousand streamlets from their mountain source,
Which, with their cool and crystal waters, fed
And added to its majesty and force,
As far, and farther still, it swept its boundless course.

Far to the north as visioned eye could reach,
A silvery lake extends its bright expanse,
Cool sylvan groves along its borders stretch
And playful wavelets on its margin dance;
The quivering lightbeams from its surface glance,
Reflecting sky, and bank, and bush, and tree,
Which, all invert, in sportive eddies pranced,
So broad, so bright, so clear, it seemed to be,
As 'twere the mirror of some sylvan deity.

And from its eastern margin poured a flood
Of waters, terrible, sublime and dread—
It seemed as if the forming hand of God
Had reared the mountains, and scooped out the bed
To hold the mighty deep, and then had sped
To fill old ocean to his farthest shore,
And opening wide the floodgates, all that led
From Heaven's great reservoir, had thence let pour
A foaming cataract, in all its wild uproar.

On the steep slopes and vales beyond the stream
An unpierced forest reared its tangled head;
So thick and dark its wild recesses seem,
As though a sunbeam scarce could pierce its shade.
The wolf and wild deer in its shelter strayed,
And through its haunts the untaught Indian trod,
The wild flower here the craggy cliff arrayed,
And there the panther held his dread abode,
All wild as fire created by the hand of God.

So still, so wild, so wide, the scene appeared,
That solitude might here erect her throne.
To cottage in this widespread forest reared,
The world of vice and crime might ne'er be known.
In that new soil the seeds of virtue sown
Might grow unstifled by the thorns of wrong,
The seeds of slavery's mildew were not sown,
Nor chains, nor fetters in these wilds belong,
But Freedom there might pour her sweetest, wildest song.

The dream departed, and the matron woke—
Fresh rays of hope, like morn, illumed her soul,
As though a joyful day again had broke,
And from her heart did clouds of sorrow roll.
Reason and fortitude assumed control
Once more in her uncrushed, heroic mind,
And, constant as the needle to the pole,
Her powers and energy were all combined,
In that wild wilderness a resting place to find.

Like bird of passage that collects her brood
When burning sun or wintry storms arise,
And seeks amid some distant solitude,
For milder chme and more congenial skies,
So seeks the matron now, with purpose wise,
To fly the impending storms that gather round,
She combats danger, want and toil, and flies
To seek a home amidst the wilds profound.
And here, amid the wilds, a home at length she found.

—Dr. Benjamin Stanton.

Written about 1845
at Salem, Ohio

THE GINGER JAR OF
ABIGAIL STANTON,
WHO BROUGHT IT
FROM NORTH CARO-
LINA TO OHIO IN
1800.

THE JAR WAS FILLED
WITH GINGER TO BE
USED AS A MEDICINE.
NOW IN THE HOME OF
ROBERT SMITH

ANECDOTES
CONCERNING ABIGAIL (MACY) STANTON

SOON after her husband's death, Abigail (Macy) Stanton turned her face towards the remote and almost unexplored wilderness west of the Ohio River. She made the journey with a considerable body, all members of the Society of Friends, who, like herself, felt the gall of slavery's presence too keenly to remain under its shadow. They crossed the river at Portland, now known as Rayland. The trees had to be felled before the teams could proceed. Abigail Stanton's wagon is said to have been the first to enter this section of the country. They got to Concord, now called Colerain, by First-day. Here they stopped, rolled some logs together, sat down, and felt they had a very good meeting.

The Stantons located one mile west of Mount Pleasant, Ohio, on a tract of land containing four hundred and eighty acres. Surrounded by the difficulties of pioneer life, Abigail established a home under an administration so wise that as her children grew
and

and passed out into the world, it was to positions of honor and usefulness.

She was a member of the Society of Friends by birthright, had strong faith in the doctrines of that sect, and for many years was an Elder in the Society.

Her son Henry was the first person to do his harvesting in Mount Pleasant Township, Jefferson County, Ohio, without furnishing his men with liquor. He told them one morning that he felt that he could not do it. They all left, but two of them came back the next morning and with some other help he got his harvesting done more easily than usual.

Barnesville,
Ohio,
1919.
        Robert. Smith
        Maria H Smith.

ROBERT SMITH

*   *   *   *   *

Of the children of Benjamin and Abigail Stanton all except David married members of the Society of Friends.

At the time of the division in that Society, Sarah Williams and Henry Stanton and their families sided with the branch called Orthodox and the others with the branch known as Hicksites.

Of the eighty-two grandchildren of Benjamin and Abigail Stanton, sixty-eight arrived at the age of majority, fourteen died between the age of a few months and seventeen years.

Cincinnati,   BYRON STANTON
Ohio,
1919.

THE RAYLAND FERRY SITE

OHIO RIVER JUST ABOVE THE MOUTH OF SHORT CREEK WHERE ABIGAIL (MACY)
STANTON CROSSED WITH HER WAGON WHEN SHE CAME TO OHIO IN 1800.

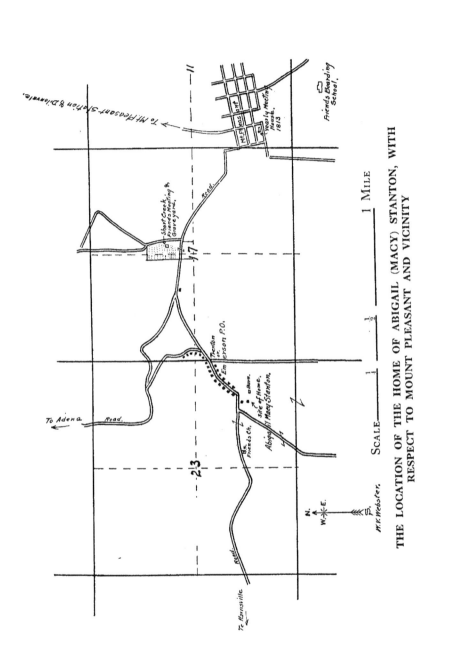

W. K. Webster.

THE LOCATION OF THE HOME OF ABIGAIL (MACY) STANTON, WITH
RESPECT TO MOUNT PLEASANT AND VICINITY

Scale

1   ½   ¼   1 Mile

THE SITE OF THE FIRST FRIENDS' MEETING

THE FIGURE IN THE CENTER OF THE PHOTOGRAPH MARKS THE PLACE WHERE THE
FIRST MEETING IN OHIO WAS HELD. THE WORSHIPERS SAT ON LOGS.

Abigail (Macy) Stanton was a widow twenty-seven years. She had in her time five broken bones, the first when thirty years old. She, with her husband and other Friends, were going on horseback to New Garden to attend their Yearly Meeting, a distance of two hundred miles. When they were about half-way there, her creature stumbled and threw her off and broke her wrist. They splintered it with oak leaves and she put it in a sling and went on, rather than be left alone or have her husband stay from meeting. About the year 1794 she fell at the doorstep and broke her ankle very badly. Then, soon after she came to Ohio, she was going to a neighbor's and went to get over the fence and the top rail rolled off and threw her back and she fell on her wrist and broke it. Some time between that and 1810 she got on horseback and the horse reared and threw her off, breaking both bones of one leg below the knee, which always remained crooked, so she used a crutch or crutches as long as she lived. The summer of 1810 she was walking in the yard and fell and broke her thigh,
but

but with all her cripplements she rode on horseback. I well remember seeing her and father start off to ride eight miles to Harrisville about three weeks before her death. She rode on one creature and he on another, he carried her crutch and in a pair of leather saddle bags on the saddle under him was her wardrobe, a very common way of transportation in those days.   AUTHOR UNKNOWN.

"THE STOLEN BONNET"

Great-great-great-grandmother Abigail (Macy) Stanton, when she and her children were moving from North Carolina to Ohio, camped at night. Grandmother, to make her Quaker bonnet safe for the night, pulled down a limb of a nearby tree and tied her bonnet

THE BURIAL PLACE OF ABIGAIL (MACY) STANTON
HARRISVILLE, OHIO. THE IDENTIFICATION OF THE GRAVE IS NOT KNOWN.

A PEAR TREE PLANTED BY ABI-
GAIL (MACY) STANTON AT HER
HOME NEAR MT. PLEASANT,
OHIO. THIS TREE WAS TOP-
GRAFTED IN THE 1850'S BY
RICHARD ROBERTS.

AN APPLE TREE PLANTED BY
ABIGAIL (MACY) STANTON AT
HER HOME NEAR MT. PLEASANT,
OHIO. THE VARIETY OF THE
TREE IS KNOWN AS "GRAND-
MOTHER APPLE."

THE LOCATION OF THE SPRING AT THE HOME OF ABIGAIL (MACY) STANTON

THE SPRING HAS BEEN COVERED UP, AND THE WATER PIPED TO A NEARBY SPRING HOUSE. THE SPRING WAS PERHAPS TWENTY-FIVE FEET INSIDE THE CORNER OF THIS YARD.

FOUNDATION STONES OF THE HOUSE OF · ABIGAIL (MACY) STANTON

THE HOUSE WAS BURNED IN 1877 AND A NEW ONE WAS ERECTED, A PART OF THE OLD FOUNDATION BEING USED.

bonnet to it. During the night the bonnet was stolen and she had to continue her journey without one.

DEBORA H. WEBSTER.

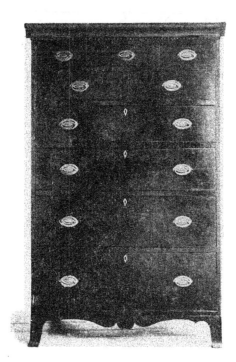

A HAND-MADE CHEST OF DRAWERS

FORMERLY OWNED BY ABIGAIL (MACY) STANTON WHO GAVE IT TO HER DAUGHTER AVIS. IN 1848, PROBABLY AT THE SALE OF HOUSEHOLD GOODS OF JESSE AND AVIS THOMAS, IT WAS PURCHASED BY EZEKIEL ROBERTS, AND REMAINED IN THIS HOME UNTIL 1903 WHEN IT CAME INTO THE HOME OF RICHARD E. AND MIRA G. S ROBERTS, OF EMERSON, OHIO. IN 1921 IT CAME INTO THE POSSESSION OF WILLIAM H. STANTON.

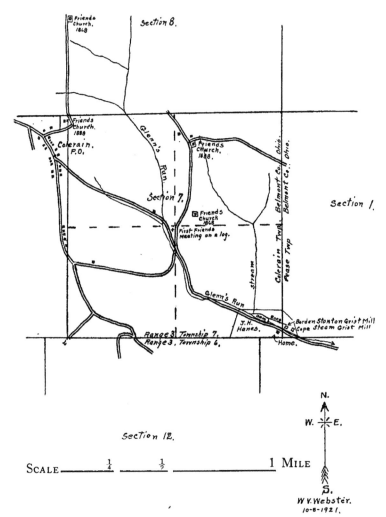

THE LOCATION OF BORDEN STANTON'S MILL
NEAR COLERAIN, OHIO

BORDEN STANTON'S MILL

BUILT IN 1801 AND OPERATED AS A WATER-POWER MILL FOR SEVENTY-FIVE YEARS
NOW USED AS A STABLE. THE MODERN STEAM-POWER MILL CAN BE SEEN AT THE
RIGHT.

BORDEN STANTON

BORDEN STANTON, a half-nephew, came out with Abigail (Macy) Stanton in the fall of 1800, and the following year built a water-power grist mill on Glenn's Run about four and one-half miles southeast of the home of Abigail (Macy) Stanton. And thus undertook as early as possible to furnish the pioneers with power to grind their wheat and corn and other grains for food.

The

**DOWN-STREAM VIEW OF BORDEN STANTON'S
MILL DAM**

THUS DIMMED BY NATURE'S GROWTH SINCE THE WHEEL WAS STILLED-BY TIME.

THE WHEEL-END OF BORDEN STANTON'S MILL

WHERE THE PRIMITIVE POWER PLANT STOOD.

The fall of water secured was sixteen feet, and an overshot water wheel of this diameter was used. The dam breast was built of stone and earth; and the race followed the northeasterly bank of the stream down a few hundred feet to the mill. This was a large and substantially built hewn log structure, and is in quite good condition today, although used only as a stable. The business is now being conducted in a steam-driven mill a short distance below. There are in existence several pieces of machinery belonging to the original water-power mill, such as conveyors, wooden gear wheels and similar parts. The heavy timbers used to support the machinery indicate very good workman-ship, and are sound after more than one hundred years.

Borden

THE ENTRANCE TO THE RACE
BORDEN STANTON'S MILL DAM.

THE SITE OF BORDEN STANTON'S RESIDENCE
LOCATED ACROSS THE STREAM AND ROAD FROM THE MILL.

BORDEN STANTON'S MILL AND MILLER'S HOME
VIEW FROM DOWN STREAM "BY THE WATERS THAT ARE PASSED."

Borden Stanton lived just across the stream and roadway from the grist mill. There we find one of the old mill-stones used now as a well-curb. There were formerly two sets of burrs in the mill. He sold this mill to Joseph Cope in 1813. It was run as a water mill for many years, but on account of the growing scarcity of water was abandoned and the steam mill erected. It is now known as the Hanes mill.

A MILL-STONE FROM BORDEN STANTON'S MILL
NOW USED AS A WELL-CURB AT THE SITE OF HIS FORMER HOME.

**WOOD COGWHEELS AND CONVEYOR FROM BORDEN
STANTON'S MILL**

THE LARGE WHEEL IS OF BLACK WALNUT WOOD.

**HANES—THE MILLER
OF TODAY**

ANECDOTE
CONCERNING BORDEN STANTON

EGARDING Borden Stanton, the valued minister among Friends, who built the water-power grist mill on Glenn's Run, William Stanton, of Pasadena, relates a story told him by his father, Dr. Benjamin Stanton, of Salem:—

When Borden Stanton emigrated from North Carolina he went to what is now, and perhaps was then, Belmont County, Ohio, just across the Ohio River from what is now West Virginia, but was then a part of "Ole Virginny."

Soon slaves began to disappear from that part of Virginia, and it became known that if a "Virginny nigger" fell under the guidance of Borden Stanton's sons it was difficult for his pursuer to get further trace of him. So the Virginians "put up a job" on the Stanton boys. They caused word to be given to the Stantons, privately, that on a certain night a skiff would cross the river with one or more runaway slaves, but there were no runaways. Instead there were some rough Virginians who sought to abduct the young Quakers and carry them across to Virginia. My father did not give the particulars for which I was so eagerly listening, but he did say that the Virginians were glad to go home without the young Stantons.

William Stanton

The Move From Carolina
and the New Settlement in Ohio

(Taken from Friends' Miscellany.)

A brief account of the regular movements of the Carolina
Friends who went to settle over the Ohio River in the year
1800: to which is prefixed a copy of Borden Stanton's letter
to Friends of Wrightsborough Monthly Meeting in Georgia,
on the proposal of their also removing to settle in what was
then called The North Western Territory; dated the Twenty-
fifth of the Fifth month, 1802, being as follows:

EAR friends: Having understood by William Patten and
William Hodgin from your parts, that a number among
you have had some thoughts and turnings of mind re-
specting a removal to this Country; and, as I make
no doubt, you have had much struggling and many reasonings
about the propriety of it; and also, considering the undertaking as a very arduous one, that you have been almost ready
at times to be discouraged and faint in your minds; under
a sense of which I have felt a near sympathy with you.   As
it has been the lot of a number of us to undertake the work
a little before you, I thought a true statement (for your information) of some of our strugglings and reasonings concerning
the propriety of our moving: also of our progress on the way, and
the

the extension of Heavenly regard to us-ward; together with the progress of Friends, both temporally and spiritually, since we have got here, might afford strength and encouragement to you in the arduous task you have in prospect.

"I may begin thus, and say that for several years Friends had some distant view of moving out of that oppressive part of the land, but did not know where until the year 1799; when we had an acceptable visit from some travelling Friends of the Western part of Pennsylvania. They thought proper to propose to Friends for consideration, whether it would not be agreeable to best wisdom for us unitedly to remove north-west of the Ohio river—to a place where there were no slaves held, being a free Country. This proposal made a deep impression on our minds; and it seemed as if they were messengers sent to call us out, as it were from Egyptian darkness (for indeed it seemed as if the land groaned under oppression) into the marvellous light of the glory of God.

"Nevertheless, although we had had a prospect of something of the kind, it was at first very crossing to my natural inclination: being well settled as to the outward. So I strove against the thoughts of moving for a considerable time; yet the view would often arise that it was in accordance with pure wisdom for Friends to leave that part of the land, but I had often to turn the fleece, as Gideon did, and to ask Counsel of the Lord, being desirous to be rightly directed by Him: more especially as it seemed likely to break up our Monthly Meeting which I had reason to believe was set up in the wisdom of Truth.

"Thus I was concerned many times to weigh the matter as in the balance of the sanctuary; till, at length, I considered that there was no prospect of our number being increased—by convincement, on account of the oppression that abounded in that land.

"I also thought I saw in the light, that the minds of the people generally were too much outward, so that 'there was no room in the inn' of the heart for much religious impression; being filled with other guests: and notwithstanding they have been visited with line upon line and precept upon precept, yet they remain in too much hardness of heart.

"Under a view of these things, I was made sensible, beyond doubting, that it was in the ordering of wisdom for us to remove; and that the Lord was opening a way for our enlargement, if
found

found worthy. Friends generally feeling something of the same, there were three of them who went to view the country, and one worthy public Friend. They traveled on till they came to this part of the Western Country where they were stopped in their minds, believing it was the place for Friends to settle. So they returned back, and informed us of the same in a solemn Meeting; in which dear Joseph Dew, the public Friend, intimated that he saw the seed of God sown in abundance, which extended far north-westward. This information, in the way it was delivered to us, much tendered our spirits, and strengthened us in the belief that it was right. So we undertook the work, and found the Lord to be a present helper in every needful time, as He was sought unto; Yea, to be as 'The pillar of Cloud by day and the pillar of fire by Night:' and thus we were led safely along until we arrived here.

"The first of us moved west of the Ohio in the Ninth month, 1800; and none of us had a house at our command to meet in to worship the Almighty Being.

"So we met in the woods, until houses were built, which was but a short time.

"In less than one year, Friends so increased that two preparative Meetings were settled; and in the last Twelfth month a Monthly Meeting, called Concord, also was opened, which is now large. Another preparative Meeting is requested and also another first and week-day Meeting. Four are already granted in the territory, and three Meeting-houses are built. Way appears to be opening for another Monthly Meeting; and I think, a Quarterly Meeting.

"Having intimated a little of the progress of Friends in a religious line, I may say that as to the outward we have been sufficiently provided for, though in a new Country, Friends are settling fast and seem, I hope, likely to do well. Under a sense of these things, and of the many favours the Lord has conferred on us, I have been ready, and do at times cry out, 'Marvelous are Thy works, Oh Lord God Almighty! just and true are all Thy ways.' And Oh! that we may ever be sufficiently thankful, and ascribe the praise to Him alone to whom it is due.

"Now I may inform you a little of the nature of this Country. It is in the main, very hilly; though most of the land may be
profitably

profitably cultivated, and produces abundantly. Corn, from thirty to forty bushels per acre, ploughed twice. Sometimes more when well worked. Some places have produced from fifty to sixty bushels per acre. Wheat, from twenty to twenty-five bushels. The soil appears to be very natural to grass of the best quality: and we make plenty of good sugar. Salt Works are being erected, and in some places considerable quantities are made so that I think people may live here as independent of European Trade as in any country.

"Feeling my mind clear of apprehended duty towards you, and not desiring to enlarge, I bid you farewell. Commending you to God and to the word of his grace, that is able to make a way for you where there may seem to be no way, and to direct you aright in all things, yea, to make you wise unto salvation, and to build you up in that most holy faith, without which I believe you will not journey safely along. I conclude with unfeigned love.

Your friend,

BORDEN STANTON.

*   *   *   *   *   *

"It appears by a copy of the minutes of a Monthly Meeting on Trent river, in Jones' County, North Carolina held in the Ninth and Tenth months, 1799, that the weighty subject of the members thereof being about to remove unitedly to the territory north-westward of the Ohio river, was and had been before that time, deliberately under their consideration and the same proposal was solemnly laid before their Quarterly Meeting held at Contentney the Ninth of the Tenth month; which on weighing the matter and its circumstances, concluded to leave said Friends at their liberty to proceed therein, as way might be opened for them, yet the subject was continued till their next Quarter. And they having (before the said Monthly Meeting ceased) agreed what certificates be signed therein for the members, to convey their rights respectively to the Monthly Meeting nearest to the place of their intended Settlement, showing them to be members whilst they resided there;—such Certificates for each other mutually were signed in their last Monthly Meeting held at Trent aforesaid, in the First month, 1800; which was then solemnly

and

and finally adjourned or concluded; and their privilege of holding it together with the records of it, were delivered up to their Quarterly Meeting held the Eighteenth of the same month, 1800.

"They removed accordingly; first to the Settlement of Friends on each Side of the Monongahela river, in Fayette and Washington Counties, in Pennsylvania, to reside a little while, in order to prepare for beginning their intended new settlement over the Ohio. Having brought their Certificates with them, they laid their circumstances, with extracts from the minutes of their former Monthly and Quarterly Meetings in Carolina, before Redstone Quarterly Meeting held the Second of the Sixth month, 1800, and received the advice and assistance of Friends there.

"Thus they proceeded and made their Settlement in the year 1800; and were remarkably favoured with an opportunity to be accommodated with a quantity of valuable land, even at the place which was chosen for their settlement by the Friends who went to view the Country, before the office was opened for granting lands in that Territory. And thus they were allowed to enter for, and secure divers sections (so called) or tracts of land, containing square parcels of about six hundred and forty acres each even as some of the first purchasers, before many others came in to interfere with them; which appeared as a marvellous affair to themselves and others."

*   *   *   *   *   *

"The following notes are taken from the memorandums of a Friend who visited those new Settlements in the Tenth month, 1802.

"Crossing the Ohio river, we rode about twelve miles to Plymouth. The next day being first of the week, we attended Friends' Meeting there, at which about fifty persons were assembled under a degree of Solemnity.

"At this meeting we met with our valued friend Borden Stanton, one of those lately removed to this new country, under an apprehension of duty, from North Carolina. His residence is at a place called Concord, a few miles distant; where we attended the preparative Meeting on the Thirteenth, at which were about thirty grown persons. A number of sensible valuable Friends belong here, towards whom near sympathy and unity were left.

"Hence

"Hence we went home with our Friend Joseph Dew to Short Creek, and next day were at preparative Meeting there.

"About sixty Friends attended, besides some children: and it was a satisfactory season.

"Sixteenth—We attended Concord Monthly Meeting, which had been established by Redstone Quarterly Meeting about ten months before; being the first Monthly Meeting held on the west side of Ohio river. About forty-five of each sex attended; and it was a uniting and satisfactory opportunity. Our friend Joseph Dew was favoured in a brief, lively testimony on the baneful effects of covetousness, as destructive to the prevalence of pure religion.

"On first-day we were again at Concord, where they have a comfortable Meeting-house, newly erected. It was nearly filled with Friends and neighbours, and Truth was measurably in dominion.

"After visiting a number of families, we turned homewards, riding along a crooked path much of the way towards the river, about seven miles, and crossed the Ohio at Zane's Island to Wheeling, in Virginia.

"In a letter from Borden Stanton, dated on the Fifth of the Eleventh month, 1803, he says, 'I am now on my way to pay a religious visit to Friends and others in some of the Southern States. As to the situation of Friends in this land (Ohio) they are still increasing very fast. There is a monthly meeting established at Bull Creek, by the name of Middleton, and another at the Miami's, by the name of Miami Monthly Meeting; also several meetings indulged within the limits of Concord Monthly Meeting, some of which are about to be established.

"Our numbers have so much increased, that we have unitedly agreed to divide Concord Monthly Meeting, and referred the subject to Redstone Quarterly Meeting; and I have no doubt the division will take place in its season.' "

THE SITE OF WESTLAND MEETING HOUSE NEAR BROWNSVILLE, PENNSYLVANIA

Abigail (Macy) Stanton and family attended this Meeting for a few months while stopping at Redlands on their way from Carolina to Ohio in 1800. The arrow indicates the location of the old meeting house.

WESTLAND MEETING HOUSE GROUND

JOSEPH TOWNSEND & SARAH, HIS WIFE

To

James Crawford,
Nathan Heald
Abraham Smith
John Townsend
John Heald &
Isaac Jinkinson.

Recorded in Book 1, Vol. 1, Page 355.
Dated 12th day of 4th Month, 1792.
Recorded 4th day May, 1792.

Consideration, twenty (20) pounds.

"Whereas the said Joseph Townsend obtained a patent for a tract of land situate on the drains of Monongahela River and Two Mile Run, in said County of Washington, called 'Fecund Valley' containing 186 Acres of land, and the allowance of six per cent, dated the 8th day of the sixth month (called June), 1790 and inrolled in the Roll's Office of said Commonwealth in Patent Book No. 15, Page 291.

"And whereas the Society of the people called Quakers of Westland Meeting did nominate and appoint the said James Crawford, Nathan Heald, Abraham Smith, John Townsend, John Heald and Isaac Jinkinson as Trustees for the purpose of securing a certain lot of ground, included in said survey, for the purpose of a meeting house, burying ground and other necessary proposed for the only particular use and behoof of said Society, Now this indenture witnesseth, & etc.

"For the only particular use and behoof of the said Society, of the people called Quakers of Westland Meeting aforesaid and their successors forever; the following described and bounded part of the aforesaid tract of land, beginning at a stone corner in James Powell's line and running thence by said Joseph Townsend's land N 86, W 33 p to a stone, S 30 W, 31½ p to a stone, S 48 E 47½ p to a stone and hickory bush, thence by the same and land of James Powell and N 13 E 57 p to the place of beginning, containing *Ten Acres* (10), be the same more or less.

"To have and to hold unto the said Trustees for the only proper use and behoof of the Society of the people called Quakers of Westland Meeting aforesaid and their successors forever."

A CABIN IN THE WOODS

"OUR CABIN, OR LIFE IN THE WOODS"

The following description of the life of the early settlers is taken from Howe's "History of Ohio." The article was written by John S. Williams, editor of the American Pioneer, and published in that journal in October, 1843.

John S. Williams was a half-brother of Richard Williams, who married Sarah Stanton, the third child of Benjamin and Abigail (Macy) Stanton, in North Carolina. They moved to Belmont County, Ohio, in 1802. Richard was a half-brother of Elizabeth (Williams) Garretson, the grandmother of Joseph W. Doudna, of Barnesville, Ohio.

This John S. Williams left North Carolina with his mother, a widow and her family, in 1800 and settled on Glenn's Run, about six miles northeast of Saint Clairsville and about four and a half miles from Abigail (Macy) Stanton.

The experiences of the Williams family seems to have been typical of those of the pioneers of that time and place, and this account is given here to show the conditions under which Abigail (Macy) Stanton started her home, at the same time and only a short distance from the location of the Williams' cabin.

"Emigrants poured in from different parts, cabins were put up in every direction, and women, children and goods tumbled into them. The tide of emigration flowed like water through a breach in a mill-dam. Everything was bustle and confusion, and

116

and all at work that could work. In the midst of all this, the mumps, and perhaps one or two other diseases, prevailed and gave us a seasoning. Our cabin had been raised, covered, part of the cracks chinked, and part of the floor laid when we moved in on Christmas day. There had not been a stick cut except in building the cabin. We had intended an inside chimney, for we thought the chimney ought to be in the house. We had a log put across the whole width of the cabin for a mantel, but when the floor was in we found it so low as not to answer, and removed it. Here was a great change for my mother and sister, as well as the rest, but particularly my mother. She was raised in the most delicate manner in and near London, and lived most of her time in affluence, and always comfortable. She was now in the wilderness, surrounded by wild beasts; in a cabin with about half a floor, no door, no ceiling overhead, not even a tolerable sign for a fireplace, the light of day and the chilling winds of night passing between every two logs in the building, the cabin so high from the ground that a bear, wolf, panther, or any other animal less in size than a cow, could enter without even a squeeze. Such was our situation on Thursday and Thursday night, December 25th, 1800, and which was bettered, but by very slow degrees. We got the rest of the floor laid in a very few days, the chinking of the cracks went on slowly, but the daubing could not proceed till weather more suitable, which happened in a few days; doorways were sawed out and steps made of the logs, and the back of the chimney was raised up to the mantel, but the funnel of sticks and clay was delayed until spring. . . .

"Our family consisted of my mother, a sister of twenty-two, my brother, near twenty-one and very weakly, and myself, in my eleventh year. Two years afterwards Black Jenny followed us in company with my half-brother, Richard, and his family. She lived two years with us in Ohio, and died in the winter of 1803–04.

"In building our cabin it was set to front the north and south, my brother using my father's pocket compass on the occasion. We had no idea of living in a house that did not stand square with the earth itself. This argued our ignorance of the comforts and conveniences of a pioneer life. The position of the house, end to the hill, necessarily elevated the lower end, and the determination

mination of having both a north and south door added much
to the airiness of the domicil, particularly after the green ash
puncheons had shrunk so as to have cracks in the floor and doors
from one to two inches wide. At both the doors we had high,
unsteady, and sometimes icy steps, made by piling up the logs
cut out of the wall. We had, as the reader will see, a window,
if it could be called a window, when, perhaps it was the largest
spot in the top, bottom or sides of the cabin at which the wind
could not enter. It was made by sawing out a log, placing sticks
across, and then, by pasting an old newspaper over the hole,
and applying some hog's lard, we had a kind of glazing which
shed a most beautiful and mellow light across the cabin when the
sun shone on it. All other light entered at the doors, cracks and
chimney.

"Our cabin was twenty-four by eighteen. The west end was
occupied by two beds, the center of each side by the door, and
here our symmetry had to stop, for on the opposite side of the
window, made of clapboards, supported on pins driven into the
logs, were our shelves. Upon these shelves my sister displayed,
in ample order, a host of pewter plates, basins, and dishes, and
spoons, scoured and bright. It was none of your new-fangled
pewter made of lead, but the best London pewter, which our
father himself bought of Townsend, the manufacturer. These
were the plates upon which you could hold your meat so as to
cut it without slipping and without dulling your knife. But,
alas, the days of pewter plates and sharp dinner knives have
passed away never to return. To return to our internal arrange-
ments. A ladder of five rounds occupied the corner near the
window. By this, when we got a floor above, we could ascend.
Our chimney occupied most of the east end; pots and kettles
opposite the window under the shelves, a gun on hooks over the
north door, four split-bottom chairs, three three-legged stools,
and a small eight by ten looking-glass sloped from the wall over
a large towel and combcase. These, with a clumsy shovel and a
pair of tongs, made in Frederick, with one shank straight, as the
best manufacture of pinches and blood-blisters, completed our
furniture, except a spinning-wheel and such things as were necessary to work with. It was absolutely necessary to have three-
legged

legged stools, as four legs of anything could not all touch the floor at the same time.

"The completion of our cabin went on slowly. The season was inclement, we were weak-handed and weak-pocketed; in fact, laborers were not to be had. We got our chimney up breast high as soon as we could, and got our cabin daubed as high as the joists outside. It never was daubed on the inside, for my sister, who was very nice, could not consent to 'live right next to the mud.' My impression now is that the window was not constructed till spring, for until the sticks and clay were put on the chimney we could possibly have no need of a window; for the flood of light which always poured into the cabin from the fireplace would have extinguished our paper window, and rendered it as useless as the moon at noonday. We got a floor laid overhead as soon as possible, perhaps in a month, but when it was laid, the reader will readily conceive of its imperviousness to wind or weather, when we mention that it was laid of loose clapboards split from a red oak, the stump of which may be seen beyond the cabin. That tree grew in the night, and so twisting that each board laid on two diagonally opposite corners, and a cat might have shook every board on our ceiling.

"It may be well to inform the unlearned reader that clapboards are such lumber as pioneers split with a frow, and resemble barrel staves before they are shaved, but are split longer, wider and thinner; of such our roof and ceiling were composed. Puncheons were planks made by splitting logs to about two and a half or three inches in thickness, and hewing them on one or both sides with the broadaxe. Of such our floor, doors, tables and stools were manufactured. The eave-bearers are those end logs which project over to receive the butting poles, against which the lower tier of clapboards rest in forming the roof. The trapping is the roof timbers, composing the gable end and the ribs, the ends of which appear in the drawing, being those logs upon which the clapboards lie. The trap logs are those of unequal length above the bearers which form the gable ends, and upon which the ribs rest. The weight poles are those small logs laid on the roof, which weigh down the course of clapboards on which they lie, and against which the next course above is placed. The knees are pieces of heart timber placed above the butting poles, successively, to prevent the weight poles from rolling off.

"The

"The evenings of the first winter did not pass off as pleasantly as evenings afterwards. We had raised no tobacco to stem and twist, no corn to shell, no turnips to scrape; we had no tow to spin into rope-yarn, nor straw to plait for hats, and we had come so late we could get but few walnuts to crack. We had, however, the Bible, George Fox's Journal, Barclay's Apology, and a number of books, all better than much of the fashionable reading of the present day—from which, after reading, the reader finds he has gained nothing, while his understanding has been made the dupe of the writer's fancy—that while reading he had given himself up to be led in mazes of fictitious imagination, and losing his taste for solid reading, as frothy luxuries destroy the appetite for wholesome food. To our stock of books was soon after added a borrowed copy of the Pilgrim's Progress, which we read twice through without stopping. The first winter our living was scanty and hard; but even this winter had its felicities. We had part of a barrel of flour which we had brought from Fredericktown. Besides this, we had a part of a jar of hog's lard brought from old Carolina; not the tasteless stuff which now goes by that name, but pure leaf lard, taken from hogs raised on pine roots and fattened on sweet potatoes, and into which, while rendering, were immersed the boughs of the fragrant bay tree, that imparted to the lard a rich flavor. Of that flour, shortened with this lard, my sister every Sunday morning, and at no other time, made short biscuit for breakfast—not these greasy gum-elastic biscuit, we mostly meet with now, rolled out with a pin, or cut out with a cutter; or those that are, perhaps, speckled by or puffed up with refined lye, called saleratus, but made out, one by one, in her fair hands, placed in neat juxtaposition in a skillet or spider, pricked with a fork to prevent blistering, and baked before an open fire—not half-baked and half-stewed in a cooking stove.

"In the ordering of a good Providence the winter was open but windy. While the wind was of great use in driving the smoke and ashes out of our cabin, it shook terribly the timber standing almost over us. We were sometimes much and needlessly alarmed. We had never seen a dangerous looking tree near a dwelling, but here we were surrounded by the tall giants of the forest, waving their boughs and uniting their boughs over us, as if in defiance of our disturbing their repose, and usurping their long

and

and uncontested rights. The beech on the left often shook his bushy head over us as if in absolute disapprobation of our settling there, threatening to crush us if we did not pack up and start. The walnut over the spring branch stood high and straight; no one could tell which way it inclined, but all concluded that if it had a preference, it was in favor of quartering on our cabin. We got assistance and cut it down. The axeman doubted his ability to control its direction, by reason that he must necessarily cut it almost off before it would fall. He thought by felling the tree in the direction of the reader, along the chimney, and thus favor the little lean it seemed to have, would be the means of saving the cabin. He was successful. Part of the stump still stands. These, and all other dangerous trees, were got down without other damage than many frights and frequent desertions of the premises by the family while the trees were being cut. The ash beyond the house crossed the scarf and fell on the cabin, but without damage.

"The monotony of the time for several of the first years was broken and enlivened by the howl of the wild beasts. The wolves howling around us seemed to moan their inability to drive us from their long and undisputed domain. The bears, panthers, and deers seemingly got miffed at our approach or the partiality of the hunters, and but seldom troubled us. One bag of meal would make a whole family rejoicingly happy and thankful then, when a loaded East Indiaman will fail to do it now, and is passed off as a common business transaction without ever once thinking of the Giver, so independent have we become in the short space of forty years! Having got out of the wilderness in less time than the children of Israel, we seem to be even more forgetful and unthankful than they. When spring was fully come and our little patch of corn, three acres, put in among the beech roots, which at every step contended with the shovel-plough for the right of soil, and held it too, we enlarged our stock of conveniences. As soon as bark would run (peel off), we could make ropes and bark boxes. These we stood in great need of, as such things as bureaus, stands, wardrobes or even barrels, were not to be had. The manner of making ropes of linn bark was to cut the bark in strips of convenient length and water-rot it in the same manner as rotting flax or hemp. When this

was done, the inside bark would peel off and split up so fine as
to make a pretty considerably rough and good-for-but-little kind
of a rope. Of this, however, we were very glad, and let no ship
owner with his grass ropes laugh at us. We made two kinds of
boxes for furniture. One kind was of hickory bark with the outside shaved off. This we would take off all around the tree, the
size of which would determine the calibre of our box. Into one
end we would place a flat piece of bark or puncheon cut round
to fit in the bark which stood on end the same as when on the
tree. There was little need of hooping as the strength of the bark
would keep that all right enough. Its shrinkage would make the
top unsightly in a parlor now-a-days, but then they were considered quite an addition to the furniture. A much finer article
was made of slippery-elm bark, shaved smooth, and with the
inside out, bent round and sewed together where the ends of the
hoop or main bark lapped over. The length of the bark was
around the box and inside out. A bottom was made of a piece
of the same bark dried flat and a lid like that of a common band-
box made in the same way. This was the finest furniture in a
lady's dressing room, and then, as now, with the finest furniture,
the lapped or sewed side was turned to the wall and the prettiest
part to the spectator. They were usually made oval, and while
the bark was green were easily ornamented with drawings of birds,
trees, etc., agreeably to the taste and skill of the fair manufacturer.
As we belonged to the Society of Friends, it may be fairly pre-
sumed that our bandboxes were not thus ornamented. . . .

"We settled on beech land which took much labor to clear.
We could do no better than clear out the smaller stuff and burn
the brush, etc., around the beeches which, in spite of the girdling
and burning we could do to them, would leaf out the first year
and often a little the second. The land, however, was very rich
and would bring better corn than might be expected. We had
to tend it principally with the hoe, that is, to chop down the
nettles, the water-weed, and the touch-me-not. Grass, careless,
lambs-quarter, and Spanish needles were reserved to pester the
better prepared farmer. We cleared a small turnip patch, which
we got in about the tenth of August. We sowed timothy seed,
which took well, and the next year we had a little hay besides.
The tops and blades of the corn were also carefully saved for our
horse,

horse, cow, and the two sheep. The turnips were sweet and good, and in the fall we took care to gather walnuts and hickory-nuts, which were very abundant. These, with the turnips which we scraped, supplied the place of fruit. I have always been partial to scraped turnips, and could beat any three dandies at scraping them. Johnny-cake, also, when we had meal to make it of, helped to make up our evening's repast. The Sunday morning biscuit had all evaporated, but the loss was partially supplied by the nuts and turnips. Our regular supper was mush and milk, and by the time we had shelled our corn, stemmed tobacco, and plaited straw to make hats, etc., the mush and milk had seemingly decamped from the neighborhood of our ribs. To relieve this difficulty, my brother and I would bake a thin Johnny-cake, part of which we would eat and leave the rest till morning. At daylight we would eat the balance as we walked from the house to work.

"The methods of eating mush and milk were various. Some would sit around the pot, and every one take therefrom for himself. Some would set a table and each have his tin cup of milk, and with a pewter spoon take just as much from the dish or the pot, if it was on the table, as he thought would fill his mouth or throat, then lowering it into the milk, would take some to wash it down. This method kept the milk cool, and by frequent repetitions the pioneer would contract a faculty of correctly estimating the proper amount of each. Others would mix mush and milk together.

"To get grinding done was often a great difficulty by reason of the scarcity of mills, the freezes in winter and the droughts in summer. We had often to manufacture meal (when we had corn) in any way we could get the corn to pieces. We soaked and pounded it, we shaved it, we planed it, and, at the proper season, grated it. When one of our neighbors got a hand-mill, it was thought quite an acquisition to the neighborhood. In after years, when in time of freezing or drought, we could get grinding by waiting for our turn no more than one day and a night at a horse mill, we thought ourselves happy. To save meal we often made pumpkin bread, in which, when meal was scarce, the pumpkin would so predominate as to render it next to impossible to tell our bread from that article, either by taste, looks, or the amount of nutriment it contained. Salt was five dollars per bushel, and we used none in our corn bread, which we soon liked as well without it. Often has sweat ran into my mouth, which tasted as fresh and flat as distilled water. What meat we had at first was fresh, and but little of that, for had we been hunters we had no time to practice it.

"We had no candles and cared but little about them except for summer use. In Carolina we had the real fat light-wood, not merely pine knots, but the fat straight pine. This, from the brilliancy of our parlor, of winter evenings, might be supposed to put not only candles, lamps, camphine, Greenough's chemical oil, but even gas itself to the blush. In the West we had not this, but my business was to ramble the woods every evening for seasoned sticks, or the bark of the shelly hickory, for light. 'Tis true our light was not as good as even candles, but we got along without fretting, for we depended more upon the goodness of our eyes than we did upon the brilliancy of the light."

A HIGH CHAIR

BOUGHT IN 1851 BY JOEL DAWSON FOR HIS DAUGHTER
ANNA, FIRST WIFE OF NATHAN W. BUNDY.

BENJAMIN STANTON, M. D.

Benjamin Stanton, M. D.

BENJAMIN STANTON, son of Benjamin Stanton and Abigail Macy, was born in Carteret County, North Carolina, Second month Twenty-eighth, 1793. His father died when Benjamin was five years old. His mother moved to the Territory of Ohio in the year 1800, taking all her minor children with her. He spent his boyhood on his mother's farm near Mount Pleasant, Ohio. He studied medicine at Mount Pleasant and removed to Salem, Columbiana County, Ohio, in the year 1815, where he married Martha Townsend on Eighth month Twenty-first, 1816.

Some

125

Some months after their marriage Benjamin and Martha Stanton moved into a frame house, still standing (1885), near the corner of Main and Chestnut Streets, Salem, Ohio, and there all their children were born. They lived there until 1854, when they moved to a brick house he had just built at the corner of Green and Chestnut Streets, where he died Second month Twenty-seventh, 1861, in his sixty-eighth year.

He was a skilful physician; a student not only in his profession but also in other branches of learning. He was a member of the Society of Friends (Hicksite). He was a public-spirited and highly-esteemed citizen, prominent in all good works. He was quiet and reserved, retiring and domestic in his habits, but hospitable and fond of his family and friends.

He was one of the earliest Abolitionists at a time when Abolitionists were but a handful of people, hated and despised, and when to be an Abolitionist required a degree of moral as well as physical courage. His home was a place of rest and refuge for many a fugitive slave on the way to Canada. He died just at the beginning of the struggle which was to result in the overthrow of slavery—a struggle he had often predicted. He often said he had no hope that the slavery question would ever be settled in America, except through war between the North and South; he did not expect to live to see it, but sooner or later it must come.

Of

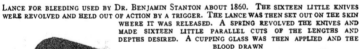

LANCE FOR BLEEDING USED BY DR. BENJAMIN STANTON ABOUT 1860. THE SIXTEEN LITTLE KNIVES WERE REVOLVED AND HELD OUT OF ACTION BY A TRIGGER. THE LANCE WAS THEN SET OUT ON THE SKIN WHERE IT WAS RELEASED. A SPRING REVOLVED THE KNIVES AND MADE SIXTEEN LITTLE PARALLEL CUTS OF THE LENGTHS AND DEPTHS DESIRED. A CUPPING GLASS WAS THEN APPLIED AND THE BLOOD DRAWN

Of his father's family, some were tall and slender and others short and stout. They were familiarly spoken of as "the long Stantons" and "the short Stantons." His sisters Avis and Lydia and his brother Henry were of "the long Stantons," as was also Benjamin himself, his height being six feet and two inches, as also was that of his son Joseph. Three other sons were five feet eleven and one-half inches to six feet in height.

The foregoing accounts were mostly furnished by William Stanton, of Pasadena, California, which were in turn furnished to him some years ago by the late Benjamin I. Stanton, Esq., then of Albany, New York.

DAUGHTERS OF DR. BENJAMIN STANTON

LAURA BARNABY

REBECCA WEAVER

AN ANECDOTE

William Stanton, of Pasadena, relates a story about his niece, Loretta Barnaby. She often had at her house some school friends who were the daughters of an old Quaker farmer who lived about two miles from Salem, Ohio. On one occasion she accepted an invitation to go home with the young ladies. They introduced her to their father and added that she was a granddaughter of Martha Stanton: "Oh!" said the old man, "I have known Martha Stanton for a great many years. Martha is an *old* woman, and so am I." "No, Father," said one of his daughters, "thee is not an old woman, thee is an old man." "Yes," said the old Friend, "I am an old man, and so is Martha."

MEDICINE MORTAR

THIS BELONGED TO JAMES BAILEY, A GREAT-UNCLE
OF LINDLEY P. BAILEY. THE DOCTORS IN THAT DAY
POUNDED AND GROUND HERBS AND ROOTS FOR
MEDICINE.

SPRING LANCE

Used by Peter Sears, Sr., now in the family of his granddaughter Mary B. (Sears) Niblock.

OLD TOOTH PULLER

Used in Barnesville, Ohio, about 1850. They were called "Pullicans."

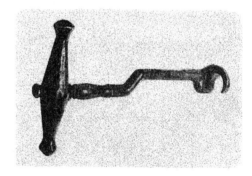

OLD TOOTH TWISTER

One of the instruments of early days used to remove a "double tooth." The hinged hook was placed over the tooth, then by a strong twist the tooth was pulled over and out.

WILLIAM STANTON

William Stanton, of Pasadena, California

WILLIAM STANTON, fourth son of Benjamin and Martha (Townsend) Stanton, began his professional life as a civil engineer in 1851, a profession he pursued for about three years. On account of financial disturbances, railroad building ceased for a time and he turned his attention to the study of medicine, entering the Cleveland Medical College in 1854 and pursuing his studies at his home in Salem, Ohio, until October, 1855, when he entered the Miami Medical College, at Cincinnati, and graduated therefrom in the spring of 1856. After graduation he went to New Brighton, Pennsylvania, where he engaged in practice with his brother David while

while the latter went to Philadelphia to attend a post-graduate course in the Medical Department of the University of Pennsylvania. In October, 1857, William returned to Cincinnati and accepted an appointment as Intern in the St. John's Hospital, where he remained until the spring of 1858.

Thinking the practice of law preferable to the practice of medicine, he took up that study, matriculated at the Cincinnati Law School in October, 1858, graduated from that school in 1859 and began the practice of law in Cincinnati, where he succeeded in doing a good business. He represented Hamilton County in the Ohio legislature from 1862 to 1868.

In 1875 he retired from the practice of law and removed to New Brighton, Pennsylvania, and in 1878 to Sewickley, Pennsylvania, where he remained until 1888.

In 1870 he married Ellen K. Irish and they had one daughter, who is now the wife of Oliver S. Picher, of Winnetka, Illinois. Ellen Stanton died in 1897, and in 1903 he married Sophronia H. Nevin, daughter of the late William Harbaugh, of Sewickley, Pennsylvania.

In 1888 he removed to Pasadena, California, which has been his home ever since.

Cincinnati,   BYRON STANTON.
Ohio,
1920.

BYRON STANTON

BYRON STANTON

BYRON STANTON, M.D., son of the late Dr. Benjamin and Martha Stanton, of Salem, Ohio, was born at that place August 14, 1834. He received his education in the public schools and Friends' Academy of Salem, and for a short time followed the profession of civil engineering. He then studied medicine for eighteen months with his father and entered Miami Medical College, Cincinnati, Ohio, graduating from that college in 1857. He served as interne at the St. John's Hospital for one year and then began the practice of medicine with his father at Salem, Ohio.

In October, 1861, he entered the army as Assistant Surgeon of the First Regiment, Ohio Light Artillery. In December, 1862, he was promoted to the rank of Surgeon and assigned to the 120th Ohio Volunteer Infantry, with which regiment he served

(except

132

(except for two months when he was a prisoner in a Confederate prison, and for four months when Acting Surgeon of the 11th New York Cavalry) until May, 1865, when he was appointed by the President Assistant Surgeon U. S. Volunteers and assigned to duty at the U. S. General Hospital at Cleveland, Ohio, and after the closing of that hospital in July, 1865, to the charge of the U. S. General Hospital (Harper Hospital) in Detroit, Michigan.

After the close of the war and while still in the service of the United States, he was appointed Superintendent of the Northern Ohio Lunatic Asylum, at Cleveland, where he remained for nearly four years and then resigned the position to resume the practice of his profession in Cincinnati (1869), since which time he has been in continuous practice in that city.

In 1877 he was appointed Professor of Diseases of Women and Children in the Miami Medical College, a position he resigned in 1900. Since that time he has held an emeritus professorship in that college and in the Medical Department of the University of Cincinnati. He served one year as President of the Cincinnati Medical Society, one year as President of the Cincinnati Obstetrical Society and one year as President of the Academy of Medicine of Cincinnati. He has been Consulting Obstetrician to Christ Hospital since 1889, was one of the founders of the American Association of Obstetricians and Gynecologists, and now holds an honorary life membership in that society.

He served the city for two years as a member of the City Council, two years as a member of the Board of Aldermen, and four years (1886–1890) as Health Officer. For six years he was a member of the Board of Medical Advisers of the Cincinnati Hospital and from April, 1893, to January, 1911, was a member of the Ohio State Board of Health, and for three years its President. He was a member of the Board of Trustees of the Associated Charities of Cincinnati from 1887 to 1911.

At the annual meeting, May, 1921, of the Ohio Commandery of the Loyal Legion Byron Stanton was elected Commander. This is the only time that this great honor has been conferred by the Ohio Commandery upon a medical officer and comes as a fitting tribute to the respect and esteem in which he is held. He realizes the responsibility and appreciates the high honor.

A short time before entering the army, he was married to
Edith M. Weaver, of Salem, Ohio, whose demise occurred while
he was still in the service; and in October, 1866, he married Harriet
A. Brown, of Cleveland, Ohio, with whom he lives on Savannah
Avenue, Cincinnati, Ohio.

EDNA MACY STANTON.

Lansdowne,   ELLEN STANTON PENNELL.
Pennsylvania,
1921.

OHIO'S JEWELS

A GROUP OF BRONZE FIGURES DESIGNED FOR AND FIRST ERECTED AT THE
WORLD COLUMBIAN EXPOSITION, CHICAGO, 1893. NOW STANDING NEAR THE
CAPITAL BUILDING, COLUMBUS. THE FIGURE IN FRONT AND FACING THE
SOUTH IS EDWIN M. STANTON. THE OTHERS ARE: GARFIELD, HAYES,
CHASE, SHERMAN, GRANT AND SHERIDAN.

Edwin McMasters Stanton

IT is not possible here to do justice to such a character, but it is earnestly hoped that some one will collect and record the facts concerning this great man. However, we cannot pass without noting some selections from "Edwin McMasters Stanton," by F. A. Flower, giving some glimpses of his character.

"William H. Whiton, who was chief clerk in the office of Military Railways during the Rebellion, and knew the inner workings of the War Department intimately, relates this incident:

"I went to the War Office after 10 o'clock, one night, to consult Mr. Stanton. I found the mother, wife, and children of a soldier who had been condemned to be shot as a deserter, on their knees before him pleading for the life of their loved one. He listened standing, in cold and austere silence, and at the end of their heart-breaking sobs and prayers answered briefly that the man must die. The crushed and despairing little family left and Mr. Stanton turned, apparently unmoved, and walked into his private room. My own heart was wrung with anguish. It seemed to me that Mr. Stanton must be a demon—the very incarnation of cruelty and tyranny.

"I was so dazed that, forgetting myself, I followed him into his office without rapping. I found him leaning over a desk, his face buried in his hands and his heavy frame shaking with sobs. 'God help me to do my duty; God help me to do my duty!' he was repeating in a low wail of anguish that I shall never forget. I quickly withdrew, but not until I had seen a great light. I have loved, almost reverenced Edwin M. Stanton ever since. His own heart

EDWIN McMASTERS STANTON

The great Civil War Secretary. Born 12-19-1814. Died 12-24-1869.

heart perhaps was suffering more intense agony than the hearts of his humble petitioners, but he was compelled to steel his outward face for the bloody duties of war, while within, his soul was warm with sympathy and sorrow for its victims.

"Whenever Lincoln moved away from the White House he knew of it and provided one or more trustworthy officers to watch and protect him; he sent warnings to him by telegraph to keep away from the missiles of battle at the front; he frequently advised, almost commanded, Grant to avoid exposure to death; while watching Lincoln's life-blood ebb away at midnight he lifted himself out of the confusion of the hour to telegraph precautions for the safety of Grant, when en route from Philadelphia to Washington; he created time to visit or write to every sick or wounded officer and, when battles were in progress, stood at the telegraph instruments night and day urging extra energy in bringing away and caring for the wounded.

"Adjutant-General Townsend remembers that soon after hostilities ceased he laid before Stanton the findings of a court-martial which condemned a soldier to be shot. 'Usually,' says the General, 'which fact gave commanders such great strength in the field, the Secretary never reversed the findings of his officers; but this time he drew back in horror. 'Blood enough, blood enough,' was all he said, and the man was not shot.' In armed conflict he was the ideal embodiment of aggressive ferocity, of the spirit of war, but 'in peace shuddered at the sight or thought of blood and his heart was wrung by the pains and sorrows even of strangers.'"

An attractive picture of the real Stanton is drawn by Mrs. General Rufus Saxton, of Washington, as follows:

"Secretary Stanton was our guest at Beaufort, North Carolina, in January, 1865. On arriving he said that fatigue would compel him to retire early; but after dinner, entering our bare, uncarpeted sitting-room, with its few dim candles but a large wood fire on the broad hearth, he sat down in front of the blaze and chatted brightly. Examining the books on the table, his face grew animated and he exclaimed: 'Ah, here are old friends,' and taking up a volume of Macaulay's poems, he turned to me saying: 'I know you love poetry. Pray read us something—anything. Poetry and this fire belong together.' I read 'Horatius at the Bridge,'

Bridge,' and returning the book to him said: 'I know you love poetry, Mr. Stanton; please read to us.' He at once complied, reading finely 'The Battle of Ivry' and other poems.

"He was in his most genial mood. Every nerve seemed relaxed, and as one after another of the numerous guests departed, he still sat in front of the dying embers till long after midnight, repeating snatches of poetry or indulging in that 'leisurely speech or the higher power of silence—the quiet evening shared by ruminating friends.'

"The next morning we drove him out on the 'Shell Road,' where the live-oaks were draped with graceful gray moss, the birds singing and the air was soft and bland. His capacity for enjoyment seemed intense. He leaned back silent in the carriage, gazing at the blue sky, seeming in spirit to 'soar with the bird and flutter with the leaf.' The Titan War Secretary was replaced by the genial companion, the man of letters, the lover of nature—the real Stanton, who expressed again and again his rapturous enjoyment of the surroundings.

"He was racked by asthma from childhood; denounced and assailed incessantly during his entire career as Secretary of War; crowded out of office after a stormy but patriotic struggle in which he prevented President Johnson from seizing the army, shackling Congress, and renewing the war; and, then, worn out, poor, and broken-hearted, laid down to die—only 55 years old."

A Near Stanton Connection

MARY (Sears) Niblock relates: "In the earlier days often the suitor would visit with all the family and would some_times propose in their presence to the one he loved. It happened one day as David Stanton (father of Edwin M. Stanton, the Great War Secretary) was visiting Grand_mother Sears (Anna Doudna) that he saw her trying to cut some goods with the scissors, which were very dull, and he said to her: 'Anna, if thee will be my wife I'll promise always to keep thy scissors sharp'; but she could not accept him, and answered, 'I am engaged to Peter Sears.'"

STATUE OF EDWIN M. STANTON
By the Court-house in Steubenville, Ohio.
Unveiled in 1911.

THE RESIDENCE OF HENRY STANTON

THE LOWER PART OF WEATHERBOARD DORE, IT IS THOUGHT, WAS BUILT BY HIS SHORTLY AFTER 1812. THE OTHER PORTION WAS ADDED BY HIS

Henry Stanton

Clary Stanton

HENRY AND CLARY (PATTERSON) STANTON

AS grandfather and grandmother, Henry and Clary Stanton, grew older, grandfather was much troubled with shaking palsy and needed more care than grandmother could give him, so after the death of their son Edmund, who then owned the home place a mile south of Speidel, Belmont County, Ohio, they had their home with their son Joseph until his death, when they moved to our home near the Sandy Ridge Road, two miles east of Barnesville, Ohio. Here they spent their declining years kindly cared for by my father, Joel Dawson, and my mother, Mary Patterson Dawson, who was their daughter.

I was a young boy when they came, but I remember them very distinctly. Grandfather Henry was tall and slender, looked very much like Benjamin Stanton (whose picture is shown on page 125). He had blue eyes, rather thin sandy hair and a very heavy sandy beard.

141

beard. In his later years he walked with a cane, and was much stooped. On account of his palsy, he could not shave himself and after my father's death it was my duty to do it for him. After I learned to keep the razor sharp it seemed to please him, for he said that I was the best barber he had found. I became quite expert and at a test shaved him in just one minute. At another time when some one was paying him some money, he handed me a five-dollar bill and said, "Take this, Henry. Thee has been very good in shaving me." I mostly did it twice a week, First- and Fourth-day mornings.

He often wore a knit jersey coat, which was warm and soft and much praised by him. It had the usual small rolling collar. A Friend, commenting on this, remarked that he was surprised to see him wearing a rolling collared coat. Grandfather replied, "It must be worrying thee more than me, for I did not know that it had a collar." And he continued to wear it.

At

HENRY STANTON'S SHAVING
BRUSH AND WOODEN "MUG"
USED UNTIL 1863.

WHEREAS Henry Stanton of Jefferson county & State of O[hio]
[Ben]jamin Stanton (now Deceased) & Abijail his wife and Clary Patterson
[coun]ty and State Daughter of Joseph Patterson & Mary his wife having
[declared their inten]tions of Marriage with each other before a Monthly Meeting of the religious Soci[ety]
[of Friends at] Short Creek according to the good order used among them and having con[sent]
[of pa]said proposal of Marriage was allowed of by said Meeting Now these
[are to certify whom] it may concern that for the full accomplishment of their said inten[tions]
[this ___ d]ay of the third Month in the year of our LORD one thousand eight hu[ndred]
[___] the said Henry Stanton & Clary Patterson appeared in a public [meeting]
[___] [m]e held at Short Creek aforesaid and the said Henry Stanton taking the
[said Clary Pat]terson by the hand did openly declare that he took her the said Cla[ry]
[___] his wife promising with Divine assistance to be unto her a loving and fait[hful]
[husband until] Death should separate them and then in the same assembly the [said Clary]
[Pat]terson did in like manner declare that she took him the said He[nry Stanton]
[t]o her husband promising with Divine assistance to be unto him a lo[ving]
[wife] until Death should separate them (or words of like import) An[d]
[the] said Henry Stanton and Clary Patterson (she according to the c[ustom]
assuming the name of her husband) did as a further confirma[tion]
[then] and there to these presents set their hands

AND we whose names are also hereunto subscribed being
[pres]ent at the Solemnization of said Marriage and subscription
[ha]ve as witnesses thereto set our hands the day & year above written

George Carson		Abigail Stanton	Henr[y]
[Li]dia Carson	Anna Foulke	Jordan Patterson	Clary
	Rebecca Taylor	David Stanton	Josep[h]
	Rebekah James	Anseling Patterson	Mar[y]
	Esther Briggs	John Hall	Abiga[il]
	Anne Michener	Joshua Scott	Achso[n]
	Ann Loyd	Rich. Williams	Lydia
	Jonathan Taylor	Christopher Taylor	Elisab[eth]
	Reuben P. Taylor	Joseph Stanton	Av[a]
	Mary Kinsey	Jesse Thomas	Anne
	George Kinsey	Aaron Brown	Abiga[il]
	Ann Taylor	Benjamin Michener	Sara[h]

At the beginning of the Civil War, people were generally asked to contribute clothing, bedding and such articles as were needed for wounded soldiers. In due time two men called and, knowing that grandfather was a plain and consistent Friend, opposed to war, acquainted him with the object of their visit, fearing lest they offend him. He heard them through and without comment said, "There is a basket under the bed. Take what you want." They selected what they wanted, thanked him, and left.

ONE OF CLARY STANTON'S WEDDING GLOVES

On account of his nervousness he could not drink from an open cup, so father had a tin cup made for him with a tight cover and a small tin tube fastened in it at an angle. His drink was placed in this pint cup from which he could take it without spilling it or shaking it out. He always took his cup with him when he went visiting.

As his palsy grew worse he could not lie down, but sat in an armchair which he had made soon after he was married, and leaned his head forward on a small support or stand made for the purpose, and thus secured his rest and sleep.

Grandmother was a very small person with blue eyes, skin as white as a lily, in later years her hair as white as snow and lots of it, and sharp nose and chin. She was a very pretty little old woman, always ready to meet you with a smile. When she and grandfather walked together they looked more like father and daughter. She was very strong and wiry and a great worker. For many years she had

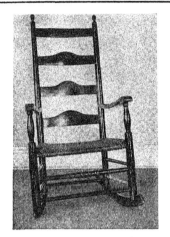

**THE ROCKING CHAIRS OF HENRY AND CLARY
(PATTERSON) STANTON**

THESE CHAIRS HE HAD MADE BY A "CHAIR MAKER" ABOUT TWO MILES EAST
OF HIS HOME SOON AFTER MOVING TO GOSHEN TOWNSHIP, BELMONT COUNTY,
PROBABLY IN 1810.

had no teeth, but her gums were remarkably hard and she took pride in showing how she could bite a crust of bread.

Grandfather always kept his own horse and carriage to carry them to meeting and any place they wished to go. I generally harnessed the horse and had her ready for them to get into the carriage and go, but many, many times I went with them to drive and take care of the horse. Poll was her name. She was a very faithful animal and seemed to know when she was hitched to their carriage. When they got in she would just pace off with them a mile to the meeting house, always turning at the proper place and stopping at the porch to let them out without a word or touch of the line. She raised a colt almost every year, so that there was usually one trotting beside her when she was on the road. She died on our place several years after they had passed away. The carriage, I think, was sold at a sale.

Grandfather

A REPRODUCTION OF THE *Last Writing* OF HENRY STANTON

TRANSCRIPT OF THE LAST WRITTEN WORD OF
HENRY STANTON

2nd, Mo. 25th 1853.

I have this day accomplished the 69th year of my voyage over a sea of glass mingled with fire and I would often have been shipwrecked had I not through unmerited mercy been favored to run into port and set under the beautiful low and wide spreading power of resignation and regale on the delicious and soul sustaining fruit that fall from its branches. Love (I trust confined) to God and man.

H. STANTON.

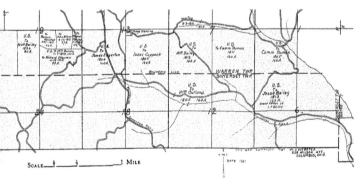

MAP—SHOWING THE EARLY *Land Transfers* IN WHICH THE STANTONS AND BUNDYS WERE INTERESTED

Grandfather and grandmother occupied the large down-stairs sitting-room, which was furnished with their own furniture and bedding. They ate at our table, but always contributed financially for their care. They both passed away in this room, grandmother a few years first.

Columbus,
Ohio,
1919.

Henry S Dawson

ANECDOTE
RELATED BY CHALKLEY DAWSON
RECORDED BY EMMA C. WEBSTER

Once in grandfather Henry Stanton's boyhood days, he and Rebecca Updegraff were walking from Wheeling Creek up the hill to Mount Pleasant with a small company of young people. The overflow of mischief, which at times comes to all young people, prompted them to exchange head-gear. As they walked along, they met one of the older men of the meeting. He observed this exchange, thought it unbecoming to Friends, and reported it to the overseers.

FIREPLACE AND MANTEL IN THE HOME OF HENRY STANTON
THE CRATE WAS ADDED LATER.

SPECTACLES AND CASE USED BY HENRY STANTON

HIS GRANDDAUGHTER, SARAH I. (DAWSON) FRENCH HAD THEM IN HER POS-
SESSION UNTIL A FEW YEARS BEFORE HER DEATH, WHEN SHE PRESENTED
THEM TO WILLIAM HENRY STANTON.

BLACK WALNUT "PEGS"

FROM THE PORCH OF THE HENRY STANTON HOUSE. THE "PEGS" WERE
USED FOR CLOTHES "HOOKS."

WASH BOWL AND PITCHER OF HENRY AND CLARY (PATTERSON) STANTON

REPUTED TO HAVE BEEN BROUGHT FROM NORTH CAROLINA. NOW IN THE POSSESSION OF
ELIZABETH (SMITH) LIVEZEY.

POCKET BOOK USED BY
HENRY STANTON ABOUT
1860

It was later used by Eli Stanton and is
now in the possession of William Henry
Stanton.

ANECDOTE

RELATED BY CHALKLEY DAWSON
RECORDED BY DEBORAH WEBSTER

RANDFATHER at-
tended the funeral of a
colored man at the
Stillwater Meeting
House. As was customary,
the bodies were laid in rows in
the cemetery. This colored
man was laid outside in the
unused ground. After the
burial, grandfather went to
one of the overseers and said,
"If I live until the rows are
filled, I wish to be laid beside
this colored man."

A CORNER OF THE HENRY
STANTON HOUSE

It is of interest to note the nicely dressed
sand-stone foundation, the logs at the
left edge, the nailing strips on the logs
and the wide lap weatherboarding.

ANECDOTE

Grandfather Henry Stanton once made the remark, "The time will come when a bushel of salt can be bought for a bushel of wheat." This shows the scarcity of common articles and the difficulty in obtaining them at that time.   —*Related by Chalkley Dawson.*

**A SYRUP CRUET OF HENRY AND CLARY
(PATTERSON) STANTON**
USED BETWEEN 1810 AND 1860.

HENRY STANTON ONE TIME GAVE A SILVER-SMITH SIX SILVER DOLLARS FROM WHICH TO MAKE SIX TEA-SPOONS. THE SILVER LEFT OVER WAS TO PAY THE SILVERSMITH FOR HIS LABOR. THREE OF THE SPOONS ARE NOW IN THE HOME OF MARIA H. SMITH.

An account of the property that my Daughter Mary P Dawson has had 10th mo 1843.

	$.	C.
to 6 chairs — — —	6	
to 1 bureau — —	9	
to 1 bed and bedding	30	
to 1 table — — —	5	
to 1 cow — — —	8	
to sundrys for cupboard	10	25
to 20 dollars cash — —	20	

A REPRODUCTION OF A NOTE-BOOK RECORD MADE BY HENRY STANTON

SAMPLER
MADE BY ANNA STANTON

REBECCA (STANTON) SMITH'S BUREAU
NOW IN THE HOME OF HER DAUGHTER ELIZABETH (SMITH) LIVEZEY.

A Visit to Henry and Clary Stanton in 1846

 I REMEMBER going with my father and mother once when they visited Uncle Henry Stanton. As nearly as I can remember, I was fourteen years old, in which case it must have been over seventy years ago.

The first night we stopped at Dearman Williams'. His mother was a Stanton and he was a nephew of my father. He had a son about my own age. This son was deter-mined that I was to see all there was to be seen in Salineville. So, after supper when it was quite dark, he took me a short distance from the house, rolled a sand bag off the top of an iron pipe, applied a lighted match and the flames shot up twenty feet or more. The well was bored for salt, but they struck gas. The value of natural gas was then unknown and the gas well was useful only as a curiosity.

My young cousin then took me into a coal mine that belonged to his grandfather, James Farmer. Being youngsters, and the vein of coal being thick, we were able to walk without stooping. We came at last to the floor where the miners had been at work. There he put down his candle, the only one we had, to show me how the coal was mined. He had taken but two or three strokes with the pick when the candle turned over and went out. He groped about until he found it, only to discover that he had no matches. He reassured me by telling me that the water in the mine had no outlet but the mouth of the mine and that if we would follow this stream, which was flowing at our feet, it would take us out of the mine. So, taking me by the hand and occasionally stooping to feel which way the water flowed, we stumbled along until at last we saw starlight.

We were two days and a half going from Salem to Uncle Henry's farm in Belmont County. Part of the road was fearful—I cannot understand how we traveled over it without breaking the springs. So far as comfort goes, and about as far as time goes, it is not so hard to travel from Chicago to California now as it was from Salem to Belmont County then. It seems absurd in these days of railroads and automobiles—to say nothing of flying machines—that that distance, ninety miles, should keep those two brothers apart. I am afraid to trust my memory, but it seems to me they had not met for thirty years. The meeting between these two old brothers was very affecting to see. Uncle Henry was con-siderably older than father, who must have been somewhere near fifty-five at that time. There was, nevertheless, a strong likeness between the two men.

Cincinnati,
Ohio,
1919.

Byron Stanton.

**THE RESIDENCE OF JOEL AND MARY P.
(STANTON) DAWSON**

MARY DAWSON'S PARENTS, HENRY AND CLARY (PATTERSON) STANTON, SPENT THEIR LAST
DAYS IN THIS HOUSE IN THE FIRST-FLOOR FRONT ROOM AT THE LEFT OF THE ENTRANCE.

A VISIT TO HENRY STANTON

IN this house in the late winter of 1862 and 1863 I saw Great-grandfather Henry Stanton. This is the only time that I remember seeing him, but that visit made a vivid impression on me. He was sitting in his favorite armchair, with his long cane with a round knob on top resting between his knees. I was sitting on a small table or stand close to the left-hand side of the fireplace. Some young man, probably Henry S. Dawson, leaned against the table with his arm back of me, and as I leaned against it, I remember how strong and solid it seemed. There were a number of friends and relatives in the semi-circle about the soft-coal fire in the grate. A bed stood in the corner of the room to the left and near it was an open door to the kitchen. There was the light from a candle or lamp there and some of the family were busy with the after-supper work. The sitting

sitting-room was dark except for the light from the open fire. I noted Great-grandfather's smooth-shaven, rather thin, oval face, sandy complexion, light thin hair, his stooped back and his round shoulders. He wore a dark-brown knit blouse or "jersey." His attitude was very kindly but quiet. His conversation was in subdued tones.

Recently I had the pleasure of visiting this room for the first time since I saw Great-grandfather there. Having endeavored on my way to the house to recall just what I would see, and standing upon my arrival where I formally sat, I was astonished to see how accurate my memory had been. The length, width and height of the room; the number, position and size of windows and doors; the place for the bed; the kitchen—all were exactly as I had remembered. The chimney was built in the room instead of flush with the wall as I had thought.

The first visit was made when I was about two and a half years old, the second, fifty-seven and one-half years later.

Ridley Park,
Pennsylvania,
1921.

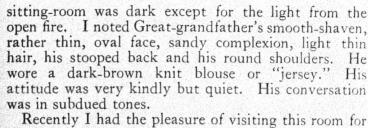

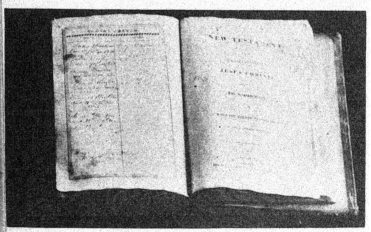

HENRY STANTON'S BIBLE
In possession of Myra Dawson Bundy in 1922

ANECDOTES
ABOUT HENRY STANTON
RELATED BY HENRY DAWSON.

GRANDFATHER told me that he attended the first Friends' Meeting for worship held in the Concord neighborhood, near Mount Pleasant, Ohio. Logs were rolled to a suitable position for seats, and here under the open sky they worshipped God.

* * * *

Early in the Nineteenth Century Friends' Quarterly Meeting held at Stillwater met once during each year at Pennsville, Morgan County, Ohio. On one of these occasions when several friends were spending the night at a home in Pennsville, the conversation drifted to the propriety of Friends wearing buttons on the back of their coats. Grandfather Henry Stanton listened to the discussion in silence, then said, "I do not know whether there are buttons on my coat or not, I'll go see."

* * * *

When Edwin M. Stanton finished his law course and had been admitted to the Bar, he asked his Uncle Henry Stanton to patronize him. Grandfather replied in words to this effect: "Thee may rest assured I will do all I can to keep from needing thy help."

* * * *

Grandfather Henry Stanton collected a number of articles advocating the principles of Friends concerning war. He intended to send them to his nephew, Edwin M. Stanton, Secretary of War, but before they were mailed Secretary Stanton sent out his great declaration, "If any soldier is found deserting or showing cowardice, shoot him on the spot." The articles were not sent.

* * * *

When the time came to take leave of Grandmother Clary at the funeral, Grandfather said, "Come, look upon her, as others shall soon look upon us."

154

MARY P. (STANTON) DAWSON
FOR EIGHTEEN YEARS SHE WAS CONFINED TO A WHEEL-CHAIR.

MARY P. (STANTON) DAWSON

ONE of the earliest recollections of my child-hood is of Grandmother Dawson, as we called her, whom my mother cared for during the last years of her life. Many valuable lessons I then learned at her knee. She sat in a wheel-chair all day, for she could not walk a step during

155

during the last eighteen years of her life. When night came, my mother put straps under her arms and about her back and then hooked them to a swinging crane that my father rigged up and by means of a windlass he hoisted her up in the air and swung her around and down on the bed where she lay with a pillow under her knees, for she was unable even to straighten them. This was, of course, a very interesting process to me as a child.

Her chair had a foot-board on it and she would get me to stand up on this board at her knee and spend a part of her time teaching me and telling me Bible stories. By the time I was old enough to start school she had taught me so that I could read through the First Reader and could write some, too. This all came in very handy in after life. She was without doubt the most patient and peaceful person to be so badly afflicted whom I have ever known. The lessons she taught me from books, however, were no more important than the ones she taught me from her every-day life by her example of meekness and gentleness and by not complaining of her hard lot in life.

The

**MARY P. (STANTON) DAW-
SON'S PITCHER**
NOW IN THE HOME OF MYRA DAWSON
BUNDY'S FAMILY.

When night
arms and about
crane
cut of a windlass
came around and
them under her
straighten them.
the process to me

and she would get
come and spend a
reading me Bible
go to start school
went through the
This all came
without doubt the
be so badly
The lessons she
were more impor
in her every-day
gentleness and b

Th

The rheumatism had stiffened her joints and knotted her hands so that about all she could do was to feed herself and write a little once in a while. During her stay with us she wrote a good bit of poetry. I remember one piece in particular that she wrote about my first pair of trousers that my mother had made for me and of which I was so proud. She wrote it in a humorous strain and I wish I could have kept it, but in our moving from one place to another it was lost. However, I discovered among some old pictures a fairly good one of the house in which she spent the last few years of her life and in which she died.

Her two daughters, Aunt Myra Bundy, of Kansas, and Aunt Sarah French or Aunt "Sis," as we called her, from Columbus, Ohio, used to come to visit her and I would look forward to their coming with great anticipation, for I was just a little country boy and did not travel much from home. Aunt "Sis" could tell such wonderful stories of life in a big city which were very interesting to me, but now that I have grown up and live in the midst of the hurry and bustle of one, the glamor has passed away and I wish that I could be a boy again at Grandmother's knee in the peaceful quietness of that old country home. I visited that spot just last summer and it did not seem that over twenty years have passed since I lived there. Nothing was left of the old home but the foundation, and I had only the memories of the happy days spent there. One scene in particular stands out most vividly on the canvas of the past, and that was at Grandmother's deathbed. It was the first death that I had ever witnessed and it made a great impression on my boyish mind. She had been failing for some time and gradually the end came, and while we were all gathered around her bedside

bedside she passed quietly into that great Beyond wher
there is no more suffering and pain, there to dwe
forever with her Master whom she always loved s
well. She was a lifelong member of the Society c
Friends and always kept strictly to the teachings an
beliefs of that faith.

Steubenville,
Ohio,   WARREN C. BUNDY.
1920.

Mary P. Dawson was confined to her wheel-chair eighteen
years. For seven years she was with her daughter, Myra
Bundy, two years with Ruanna Bundy, and the last nine
years of her life she lived in the home of Nathan W. and
Agnes H. Bundy, at Tacoma, Ohio.

Warren C. Bundy is a son of Nathan Bundy and his
second wife, Agnes Hanson. Nathan W. Bundy's first wife
was Anna Dawson, daughter of Joel and Mary P. (Stanton)
Dawson.

JOEL DAWSON
PHOTOGRAPHED ABOUT 1850.

JEPTHA BUNDY

MYRA (DAWSON) BUNDY

THE POEM REFERRED TO IN THE ARTICLE ON MARY P. DAWSON, BY WARREN C. BUNDY, HAS BEEN FOUND SINCE THE RECEIPT OF HIS CONTRIBUTION AND IS REPRODUCED BELOW.

IT IS IN THE HANDWRITING OF MARY P. (STANTON) DAWSON.

Dear Aunt Fanny

There came of late to our little town
A modern dude of some renown
A modern dude! Yes, now don't you guess it;

And he's come to stay; not just to visit.
He said "five long years have rolled around
Since on this planet I - was found.
So looking around, one day in solemn mood,
I said, I am going now to be a dude,"
He has rosy cheeks and dark brown hair
With keen black eyes and forehead square.
He wears a hat with a turned up rim
And a black ribband band, which looks right prim.
His pleated waist is of gingham brown
With a sailor collar, which lays flat down.
His pants are nice, and quite neatly made,
Of the latest style of cottonade.
But Alas! the tailor didn't make any pocket!
But then he is such a busy little poppet.

That a little pocket he never misses
Because it is such fun to leave off dresses.
His feet are encased in new button shoes,
And his little round legs, in long ebon hose.
Now I have described him so very minute
That don't you   think he looks real cute?
Oh but he is funny romping and rude.
And goes about whistling "I am a dude"

         Yours truly,

             Warren Bundy

AN EARLY AND UNFINISHED SAMPLER
BY MARY P. STANTON. THE INITIALS
J. P. M. P. ARE PROBABLY FOR HER
GRANDPARENTS, JOSEPH PATTERSON
AND MARY PATTERSON.

A SAMPLER PROBABLY MADE BY MARY
P. STANTON. POSSIBLY IT WAS MADE
BY HER OLDER SISTER, ANNA. THE
INITIALS H. S., C. S., J. S., ETC., DOUBT-
LESS ARE FOR HER PARENTS, HENRY
AND CLARY STANTON AND THEIR CHIL-
DREN, JAMES, JOSEPH, ANNA, EDMUND,
JORDEN, MARY PATTERSON, HENRY
AND DANIEL. IT IS NOT SO EVIDENT
FOR WHOM THE INITIALS R. S AND
D. S. WERE MADE.

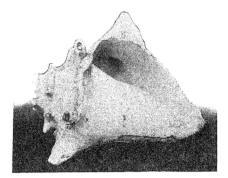

CONCH SHELL USED AS A HORN BY MARY P. DAWSON TO CALL THE MEN ON THE FARM TO DINNER.

THE CHAIR ON WHICH MARY P (STANTON) DAWSON SAT DURING A TRIP TO KANSAS. SHE WAS UNABLE TO WALK AND WAS CARRIED BY TWO MEN WHEN IT WAS NECESSARY TO CHANGE CARS.

HAND-MADE SLAW CUTTER USED BY MARY P (STANTON) DAWSON.

KNITTING MACHINE

MARY P. (STANTON) DAWSON MADE MANY PAIRS OF SOCKS AND STOCKINGS ON THIS MACHINE YEARS AGO AND SOLD THEM TO THE STORES.

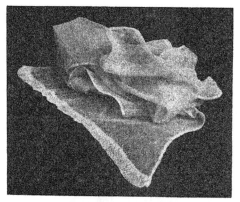

MARY P. (STANTON)
DAWSON'S NECKTIE

NOW IN THE POSSESSION OF
EVA T. STANTON.

MEMORIES

By Mary P. Dawson

Written after her seventieth birthday.   Tacoma, Ohio, 1891

As by my window I lonely sit,
   Pondering o'er the bygone years,
Crowded scenes o'er memory flit
   Of joys and sorrows, hopes and fears.

And the place I loved so well,
   Where my thoughts oft unbidden roam,
Is the scene of my early childhood,
   My old familiar, happy home,

Where we children, young and old,
   Altogether numbered eight,
With father and mother at the head,
   All sat beside our cup and plate.

We all enjoyed the greatest wealth—
   That which nature gives to busy hands—
The rosy cheek and blooming health,
   Acquired in new and forest lands.

Daily as we grew to mature age,
   Guarded around with loving care,
Our parents read aloud the Sacred Page
   And breathed for us a silent prayer.

They arrived at manhood one by one,
   And assumed life's burden and care;
One by one they passed away,
   Leaving now and then a vacant chair.

They all are gone! gone long before me
    To the happy, bright beyond.
Oft methinks they are watching o'er me,
    And their spirits hovering around.

Oft in my dreams I see their faces,
    While I am slumbering on my bed,
In their old familiar places,
    But awaken, alas! they all have fled.

There are only four of my parents' connections,
    And only two near, to speak a word,
That ever met at our collections
    Around that ample family board.

May I through mercy all unmerited
    Some time enter the happy throng,
And meet the loved ones gone before
    And sing with them the mystic song.

When here below my journey ends
    And leaves the place by loved ones trod,
May I be permitted to lie beside them
    And our dust mingle beneath the sod.

HENRY STANTON DAWSON

HENRY STANTON DAWSON, son of Joel and Mary Patterson (Stanton) Dawson, was born Third month Nineteenth, 1847, in the old house, which stood on their farm two miles east of Barnesville, Ohio. He was married Third month Third, 1870, to Ellen Castello, from Guernsey County, Ohio. They lived most of their married life in Columbus, Ohio, where he was engaged in the nursery and fruit-tree business for over twenty years. There two sons were born to them—Stanley French and Clarence.

Clarence is now clerking in Columbus, Ohio, and French is in the theatrical business. His work has taken him from home most of the time for several years, but no difference where he is, he always remembers his parents and has written them a letter or a card every day. Surely he is keeping the commandment, "Honor thy father and thy mother."

W. H. S.

ELLEN CASTELLO DAWSON

WHEN mother was not very strong, Ellen Castello came to help in our house and soon won our hearts. She was bright and cheery. It seemed that she knew just what little folks liked. When we did not wash quite clean—a way little folks have of doing—she would say she guessed we left that for a starter, or else maybe we would never get dirty any more.

She had travelled in Europe and lived in Philadelphia, and entertained us with stories and songs. There was one song about "Old Mr. Grumble" that we liked especially and wanted her to sing it every day, but she said that she could only sing that one on ironing day. It ran like this:

"Old Mr. Grumble he did say and said it to be true, true,
That he could do more work in one day then his wife could
    do in two, two."

His wife traded places with him and ploughed, while he attempted to milk, feed the pig, wind the yarn and churn. Difficulties met him at every turn and his face was long when she came in to help him. Then the last stanza:

"And when he saw where she had ploughed the furrows so
    straight, straight,
He said a woman could do more work in one day than a man
    could do in eight, eight."

While working on one of the buildings, father fell from the roof and was badly hurt. He crawled to the kitchen door, but

could

168

could get no farther. Ellen, who was rather below average height and slender, heard him call and found him lying on the ground. She picked him up and carried him into the house. How she did it she could not tell, as father was about five feet ten inches tall, of medium weight. A doctor was called, who said that two ribs were broken. In those days there were no trained nurses in the neighborhood but, as was customary, the relatives and friends arranged to take turns "sitting up" with him to relieve the family who cared for him during the day. Our cousin, Henry Dawson, then a young man, volunteered to help and came several nights. Of course he met Ellen and seemed to enjoy her as much as we children did.

One night she prepared a midnight lunch for him, placed it on the table, and covered it with a table cloth. Henry did not find it, but ate some cold buckwheat cakes he found in the cupboard. In the morning Ellen complained to father that he had eaten all her chicken feed, but Henry replied, "Well, a 'hen' got it anyway."

Henry was a good nurse, and seemed to enjoy coming so much that father told Ellen that at first he came to sit up with him, but now to see her. Ellen was delightful, every one liked her—especially Henry. Their acquaintance changed to friendship, then to love, and later they were married.

W. H. S.

IN REMEMBRANCE

WHEN I was a girl and dependent on my own resources I spent several years in the homes of Eli and William Stanton, helping in the rearing and caring for the children. While thus occupied I had many very happy experiences and remember distinctly the deep impression the character of the men and women of those immediate families made upon me, and I now look back with gratitude for their association during the time I strived to lighten their burdens and cares.

Ellen Dawson

CHALKLEY DAWSON

CHALKLEY DAWSON was a son of Joel and Sarah (Bundy) Dawson. His father, Joel Dawson, later married Mary Patterson Stanton. The history of his life appears in the following extract from an article written by him on his eighty-second birthday:

"I was born near Barnesville, Ohio, on the first day of Second month, 1836, and have now completed my eighty-second year. My father and mother were both born and raised near Barnesville, Ohio. My grandparents came to this state from North Carolina in the early days of its settlement. They were Quakers and left New England in the time of the religious persecution there and went to the South, where they could worship God and not be molested on account of religious views. Quakers and slavery never did go together, hence they were compelled to move again.

"I was raised on a farm and went to school in the winter months and worked on the farm during the summer season, except for two years, one of which I attended Friends' Boarding School at Mount Pleasant, Ohio, and one at Westtown Boarding School, Westtown, Pennsylvania. My earlier education was from the common schools, but I was reared strictly under the Quaker rule.

"I was

170

"I was married to Martha Garretson, of Barnesville, on the 28th of Ninth month, 1859, and settled on a small farm. As I could not raise much and as there was but little market for what I did raise, I concluded to go West and grow up with the country. Consequently I sold my farm and moved to Keokuk, Iowa. There I found I was up against another hard proposition—the land had to be broken up and lay over one year before it could be farmed. I went to work and in five years had a pretty good farm of eighty acres and was making some money, when my greatest loss came. I lost my wife. She was called away in 1867, leaving me four small children, in a new country amongst strangers. In the spring of 1868 I was compelled to return east to my kindred to get my children so placed among them that they could be properly cared for, and I succeeded in getting them settled to my entire satisfaction.

"With my children all cared for, I applied myself to my profession, that of an engineer and surveyor. For seven years I worked at laying out the pikes in Belmont County and had the care of the construction of the same. I laid out and constructed over fifty miles of pikes in Belmont County.

"On completing the pikes in 1873, on the tenth of Eighth month I married my second wife, Rebecca Ann Branson, of Flushing, Ohio. With a new wife and a new home, I also started a new business, forming a partnership with my cousin, Nathan Bundy, to go into the coal business. We sank a shaft one hundred and seventy-five feet deep at Barnesville, but on account of the limited market for coal, it was not a success. My second wife died fourth month 18th, 1877. It seemed as if the whole world was frowning on me. I was left with five children, and a large debt hanging over my head.

"On January 16th, 1883, I married my third wife, Margaret T. Tapper, of Barnesville, Ohio. We came to Bellaire and started housekeeping, I bringing my family with me. Once more I began to get ahead in the world and have fairly well succeeded. Now in old age I have the assurance of a competence and some to spare to worthy causes, when I am done with things here.

"During my life I have buried all my children, six in number, and three wives. My third wife was stricken with paralysis, and died October 19th, 1914, and was buried at Bellaire, Ohio.

"One

"One of the most important steps of my life was when I was made a Mason, and I have been one for over fifty-nine years. I have made many a friend through its influence, and through its social and festival occasions I have spent many an enjoyable time.

"In a business way, I have been connected with the electric-light plant and helped to manage its affairs for five years. I helped to organize the Farmers' National Bank and have been a director and vice-president ever since its organization. For three terms I served Belmont County as surveyor.

"As to my church life, I will say that I was born a Quaker and attended that church until some time after 1883, when I began to attend the Presbyterian church and later became one of its members.

"A few days before my wife was stricken and died, I was stricken with paralysis and have not been well since. I was forced to give up the active duties of life, and now my work is finished and I await His coming. Many loved ones are waiting to greet me on the other shore, for which my eyes are now watching. Second month, First, 1918."

Chalkley Dawson

Chalkley Dawson was married for the fourth time on August 13, 1919, aged 83½ years, to Mrs. Lohr, of Columbus, Ohio.

ANECDOTES
RELATED BY CHALKLEY DAWSON.   RECORDED BY EMMA C. WEBSTER

John Sullivan, the first president of the Central Ohio Division of the Baltimore and Ohio Railroad, told me of an epidemic of cholera in Wheeling, West Virginia, about 1832. It was fatal. "There was no sound of tools in the town except those used in making coffins, and no business except hauling out the dead."

*   *   *   *

Some years ago I attended a reunion at Westtown Boarding School, but found no one there I knew. A friend very kindly offered to try to find some of my old schoolmates. Finally I was introduced to a man as Chalkley Dawson, but he did not seem to remember me and repeated the name several times, "*Chalkley* Dawson." Then his face lighted up—"Oh, *Chalk* Dawson; certainly I remember thee," and we had a pleasant time talking over old school days.

Anecdotes

ANECDOTES

PIONEER LIFE IN IOWA

RELATED BY CHALKLEY DAWSON
RECORDED BY EMMA C., MARY L., and DEBORAH H. WEBSTER

Many privations and hardships were experienced in pioneer life in Iowa in the early sixties. We bought eighty acres of prairie land, of which only ten acres were broken. I continued to break ten acres at a time, thus having new land each year. The first year I plowed with a double ox team and planted corn by lifting the dirt at the edge of each furrow and dropping a few grains every few feet. This produced a very poor grade of corn, but it was good enough for cattle food.

*   *   *   *

One day when I was plowing, the oxen shied and I saw a rattlesnake. A fifteen-foot whip, which I carried in order to touch up the front oxen, proved to be very useful in killing the snake. A second rattler was encountered one evening on my way to Ann Gibon's house. I pulled off my boot, took it by the strap and killed the snake.

*   *   *   *

We attended a marriage one evening. There was a little snow on the ground, but not enough to cover the trail, which consisted of wagon tracks across the prairie. We spent a pleasant evening, ignorant of the fact that more snow had fallen, entirely obliterating our trail. As far as eye could see, the ground laid as one white sheet. I knew that the tendency of man is to move in a circle, so I decided to trust to the oxen I was driving. They brought us safely to our door. As we looked back, we could see our track a long straight line.

*   *   *   *

We were not always able to keep the cold out of our houses. I remember one morning, on waking, we found the baby's hair frozen to the pillow, her mother's breath having caused the moisture.

*   *   *   *

The house was guarded by a fire-break, which was made by plowing three furrows a little way from the house, then leaving about two rods and plowing three more furrows and burning the grass between. This was usually a safe protection, but sometimes, when there was a high wind, the fire would come across the break.

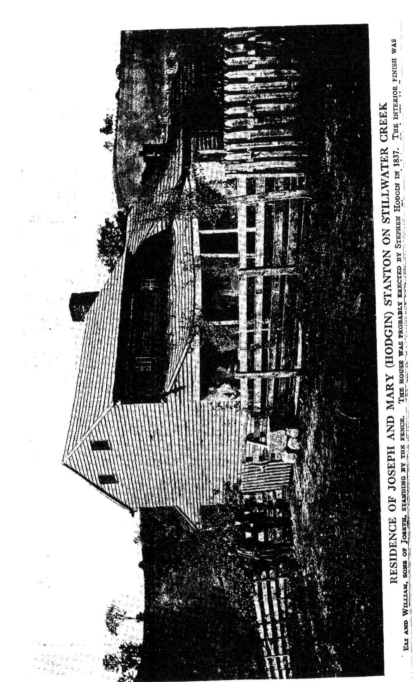

RESIDENCE OF JOSEPH AND MARY (HODGIN) STANTON ON STILLWATER CREEK

Eli and William, sons of Joseph, standing by the fence. The house was probably erected by Stephen Hodgin in 1837. The interior finish was

Joseph Stanton

Mary Stanton

JOSEPH AND MARY (HODGIN) STANTON

OSEPH STANTON, son of Henry and Clary Stanton, and Mary Hodgin, daughter of Stephen and Elizabeth Hodgin, were married Ninth month Twenty-seventh, 1832, at Stillwater Meeting House. They lived for a short time in Goshen Township, a half mile east of the Henry Stanton home four miles east of Barnesville, and later bought a farm on Stillwater Creek, about two miles north of Stillwater Meeting House, where they lived the remainder of their lives.

They

COMBINATION PEN AND PENCIL
Used by Joseph Stanton about 1855 when clerk of Stillwater Monthly Meeting.

175

THE OLD JOSEPH STANTON HOUSE

LOCATED ABOUT HALF A MILE EAST OF THE HENRY STANTON HOME. IN THIS HOUSE JOSEPH AND MARY
(HODGIN) STANTON STARTED HOUSEKEEPING AND HERE THEIR SON ELI WAS BORN. THEIR OTHER
CHILDREN WERE BORN IN THEIR LATER HOME ON STILLWATER CREEK.

SPRING AT THE OLD JOSEPH STANTON HOUSE

THE SPRING WAS NEAR THE HOUSE AND FURNISHED ALL THE WATER USED. WE WOULD THINK IT A
HARDSHIP TO HAVE TO CARRY WATER AS FAR AS IT WAS NECESSARY HERE, BUT THERE WAS MORE TIME
AND MUCH LESS WATER USED. IT IS OVERGROWN WITH FLOWERS AND IVY NOW IN 1920, BUT THE ROUGH
STONE WALL IS STILL GOOD AND THERE IS AN EXCELLENT FLOW OF WATER.

... Joseph Stanton of Belmont County, Ohio, son of Henry Stanton of the County
... and Clara his wife; and Mary Hodgin, daughter of Stephen Hodgin of the
... and State aforesaid, and Elizabeth his wife, having declared their intentions of mar...
with each other, before a monthly meeting of the religious society of Friends,
Stillwater; and having consent of Parents, their said proposals of marriage were allow...
said meeting. These are to certify whom it may concern, that for the full a...
ment of their said intentions, this 26th day of the ninth month in the year of our ...
32, they, the said Joseph Stanton, and Mary Hodgin appeared in a public meet...
... said people held at Stillwater aforesaid; and the said Joseph Stanton, taking the
... Hodgin by the hand, declared that he took her the said Mary Hodgin to be his
... ising, with divine assistance, to be unto her a loving and faithful husband until ...
... ould separate them; and then the said Mary Hodgin did in like manner declare that
... him the said Joseph Stanton to be her husband, promising, with divine assistance to be
... a loving and faithful wife until death should separate them.

... they the said ... Stanton ... Mary Hodgin did as ... further con...
... thereof, then and there to these ... to set their hands.   Joseph Stanton
... we whose names are also hereunto subscribed, being   Mary Stanton
at the solemnization of said marriage, have as witnesses ...
... our hands the day and year above written   Relations Names

	Edith Scholfield	Benj. Hoyle	Henry Stanton
... Mary Jones	James Dawson	Mary Hoyle	Stephen Hodgin
son Rachel Schofield	Henry Dowina	Sarah Bailey	Elizabeth Hodgin
... Sarah William	Sarah Middleton	Robert Milhouse	Clara Stanton
... Cidney Schofield	Rachel Engle	Benjamin Clendenon	Jesse Bailey
Patten Anna Williams		Amy Clendenon	Eli Hodgin
Mary V Dowina		Robert Fox	Mary Hodgin
Anna Garretson		Eliza Starbuck	Stephen Hodgin, Jr.
Sarah Engle		Sarah Clendenon	Richard Fawcett
David Smith		Mary Fawcett	Deborah Fawcett
		Sarah Dawson	Anna Stanton
		Sarah Patton	Edmund Stanton
			James Stanton

**JOSEPH STANTON'S
BIBLE**
NOW IN THE POSSESSION OF
JOSEPH ELI STANTON.

They were prominent members of the Society of Friends. Both were Elders in the Meeting for a number of years. Joseph was appointed Clerk in 1852 and served the Meeting in that capacity for seven years, until his death in 1859. Mary Stanton was granted a minute as companion to Rebecca Mitchner, a minister, to Philadelphia Yearly Meeting in 1853. Joseph Stanton was appointed to accompany Benjamin Hoyle, a minister, to Baltimore Yearly Meeting in 1849. The minutes of the Monthly Meeting show that both Joseph and Mary Stanton were frequently appointed on committees from soon after their marriage until their deaths.

They were good neighbors, always trying to help the needy and deserving.

ROBERT PLUMMER, JR.
1813–1894
SON OF ROBERT, WHO DONATED THE
ACRE OF GROUND FOR THE GRAVE-
YARD AND FRIENDS' MEETING HOUSE,
A HALF MILE NORTH OF STILLWATER
MEETING HOUSE.

serving. At butchering time they saw that those in need had a good meal of spareribs and sausage, and when they butchered a beef, many of the neighbors would get a small portion of it, a custom that was common in those days.

One time Joseph and Mary Stanton were calling on their near neighbors, Robert and Jane Plummer, when Robert called Joseph's attention to the large stock of cook-stove wood he had prepared. Joseph remarked, "One hickory log will do my wife a year." Jane commented, "Well, Mary Stanton does not have to cook as much as I do." All enjoyed the inference that Robert had a good appetite.

In those days people were mostly ahead of their work; for example, they would have their year's supply of wood cut. They did not let their work push them as it does so many of us nowadays.

Mary Stanton's father, Stephen Hodgin, was very much annoyed by a neighbor's turkeys. One day when they got into his garden, he threw a stick to drive them away and accidentally struck one and knocked it over. He immediately picked it up, cut off its head, and prepared it for roasting. Then he invited the owners down to help eat it and the matter was settled without further trouble.

Joseph and Mary Stanton had five children: Eli, Anna, William, Eunice and Elizabeth. All lived to be married and to have families except Eunice, who died when about six years old.

About the year 1856 Mary began to notice a weakness in her ankles and knees, which gradually grew worse, until she could not walk or turn herself in bed. She spent the days in an armchair on castors, so she could

could be pushed around. She was in that condition several months, when she took a heavy cold which affected her lungs. She lived about a week after that and passed quietly away just twenty-five years, to the day and hour, after they were married. The family was very lonely after that. Eli was married to Mary P. Bundy before his mother's death. Joseph and his three remaining children kept house the following winter. In the spring, Third month Thirtieth, 1859, Anna was married to Nathan Bundy. As carriages were scarce then, Joseph and his twelve-year-old daughter Elizabeth went to the wedding on horseback. William was in the wedding company. It was a double wedding; Nathan Bundy's brother, Caleb Bundy, and Deborah Hanson were married at the same time. Contrary to custom, the marriage reception was at the home

ANNA STANTON BUNDY, WILLIAM STANTON, ELIZABETH STANTON BAILEY
Photograph About 1912

home of the man's father, Ezekiel Bundy.   The next day they were at Elijah Hanson's and the next at Joseph Stanton's.   From the second reception the Stantons had to go home early to make sponge for bread, and prepare for the "infair" dinner.   The neighbors were very good to come in and help and when the day came, everything was in readiness.

Joseph had a housekeeper, who stayed with him, doing good service until his death, Seventh month Twenty-sixth, 1859, two years, lacking two months, after his wife's death.

After her father's death Elizabeth lived with her brothers and sisters, doing what she could to help them. She very much felt her loneliness, but every one was very kind to her and made her feel less the loss of a father and mother who had been so inspiring and so exemplary not only to her but to her brothers and sisters and who had stood as staunch pillars in the Meeting which they loved and as beacon lights for good in a community which they strived to serve.

Tacoma,
Ohio,
1919.

Elizabeth Stanton Bailey

JOSEPH STANTON'S WATCH
NOW IN THE POSSESSION OF
JOSEPH ELI STANTON.

HAT WORN BY JOSEPH STANTON ABOUT 1858
TYPICAL OF THE HATS WORN BY OLDER FRIENDS OF THAT PERIOD.

THE KIND OF BONNET WORN BY MARY (HODGIN) STANTON
THIS ONE BELONGED TO ASENATH BAILEY, THE MOTHER OF LINDLEY P. BAILEY, AND WAS WORN BY HER ABOUT 1900.

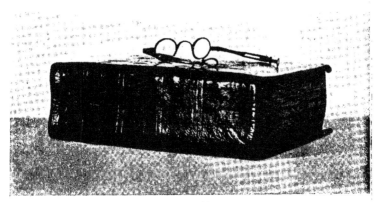

JOSEPH STANTON'S SPECTACLES
NOW IN POSSESSION OF ELIZABETH STANTON BAILEY

**BUREAU FROM THE HOME OF JOSEPH
AND MARY (HODGIN) STANTON**
THE ONE WITH WHICH SHE BEGAN HOUSEKEEPING
IN 1832. NOW IN THE HOME OF ELIZABETH
STANTON BAILEY.

STONEWARE JAR

THIS JAR FILLED WITH LARD WAS GIVEN BY HENRY STANTON
TO HIS SON JOSEPH AT THE TIME OF HIS MARRIAGE IN 1832.

THE INVALID CHAIR OF MARY (HODGIN) STANTON

THIS CHAIR WAS MADE FOR HER WHEN, ON ACCOUNT OF SPINE
TROUBLE, SHE COULD NOT WALK. IT WAS ORIGINALLY PROVIDED
WITH A FOOT-REST AND CASTORS. IT WAS USED IN THE HOME OF
ELI STANTON ABOUT THIRTY YEARS AND NOW IS IN THE POSSESSION
OF ELIZABETH STANTON BAILEY.

VINEGAR CRUET
USED BY JOSEPH AND MARY (HODGIN)
STANTON BETWEEN 1832 AND 1857.

**A SPLINT-BOTTOM
CHAIR**
A GENUINE SPECIMEN IN THE HOME OF
ALBERT AND MARY B. NIBLOCK.

A FEW OF THE APPLE TREES THAT ARE STILL STANDING OF THE ORCHARD PLANTED BY JOSEPH STANTON IN FRONT OF HIS HOME ON STILLWATER CREEK IN 1857.

PRESERVING FRUIT BEFORE THE DAYS OF CANNING

I REMEMBER in 1853 or 1854 mother doing our first canning. Until that time we had always dried our fruit, only making a small amount of apple butter and sometimes a little peach butter. These we cooked long enough to make them so rich they would keep without sealing.

Mother boiled sweet apples until they were tender, put them in a press until all the juice was out, then boiled down the juice until it was molasses. This we ate with cream and, as I remember, it was most delicious.

ELIZABETH STANTON BAILEY.

Tacoma,
Ohio,
1921.

SUGAR BOWL AND MUG

LEFT: THIS SUGAR BOWL WAS BOUGHT BY JOSEPH STANTON AT HIS UNCLE JAMES
STANTON'S SALE AND WAS USED IN HIS FAMILY UNTIL HIS DEATH IN 1859.
RIGHT: THIS MUG WAS KEPT IN THE CORNER OF MARY (HODGIN) STANTON'S CUP-
BOARD AS A "CATCH-ALL" FOR SMALL THINGS OF IMPORTANCE.

TIN PLATE AND JELLY JAR

LEFT: TIN PLATE PRESENTED BY HENRY STANTON TO HIS GRANDDAUGHTER
ELIZABETH STANTON (BAILEY) AND USED BY HER WHEN A LITTLE GIRL.
RIGHT: JAR USED FOR JELLY BY MARY (HODGIN) STANTON. MARY M. COLPITTS
HAS IT NOW (1921) FILLED WITH THE JELLY WHICH HER GRANDMOTHER
MADE AND PUT IN IT IN 1855 OR 1856.

TEAPOT AND PITCHER

LEFT: TEAPOT USED BY MARY (HODGIN) STANTON.
RIGHT: PITCHER OWNED BY MARY (HODGIN) STANTON WHEN SHE WAS MARRIED IN
1832 AND USED IN HER HOME FOR THIRTY YEARS. IT WAS LEFT WITH TEA IN IT ONE
WINTER EVENING AND DURING THE NIGHT THE TEA FROZE AND CRACKED THE BOTTOM
OF THE PITCHER. SINCE THAT TIME IT HAS BEEN VALUED AS A "KEEPSAKE."

SOFT SOAP

SOAP-MAKING was one of the various duties of the housewife, when I was a little girl. The ash hopper in which the lye was made was located in the door yard. It consisted of four posts about five feet high set in the ground; inside of these and supported by them was a conical wood box or hopper about three feet square at the top and a foot square at the bottom. It rested on an inclined board with grooves cut near the outside to conduct the lye to one end and into a vessel set to receive it. Four or five bushels of wood ashes were thrown on top of the straw and a bucket of water was poured into a hollow formed in the ashes. As the water soaked into the ashes more water was added at intervals for three or four days. When the liquid commenced to seep through, a kettle was placed to receive the lye and when there was a big iron kettle full, it was put over the fire and the lye boiled until it was strong enough to "eat" a feather. Then the grease and meat rinds were put in and when they were acted upon by the lye the solution was boiled again until it roped from the stick with which it was stirred. The process was now finished and when the liquid cooled it was pronounced to be good soft soap and was kept in a barrel. Mother made enough soap in the spring to last for a year.

ELIZABETH STANTON BAILEY.

Tacoma,
Ohio,
1921.

ASENATH (HODGIN) EDGERTON

BORN 7-21-1823. DIED 1-30-1905. MARRIED JOHN EDGERTON
3-31-1857. AN OLDER SISTER OF JOHN E. HODGIN.

FOUR GENERATIONS

TAMER D. HODGIN, RACHEL H. COPPOCK, ADA J. BOWLES,
ELSIE R. BOWLES. AGES 85 TO 3 YEARS.

JOHN E. AND TAMER D. HODGIN

BORN 11-12-1830 AND 8-6-1836. HE IS A NEPHEW OF MARY
(HODGIN) STANTON.

ANY of the Friends living in Georgia wanted to leave that state on account of trouble from the Indians, and also that they might live in a country free from slavery.

William Hodgin and William Patten investigated conditions n Belmont County, Ohio, in 1802. In 1803 they brought out heir families, and with them came Stephen Hodgin, a brother of Villiam; also the Williams, Todd, Vernon, Sidwell, Millhouse, Childrey, Hayes, Stubbs and other families.

William Hodgin died in North Carolina in 1820 when on a trip o Georgia on a visit.

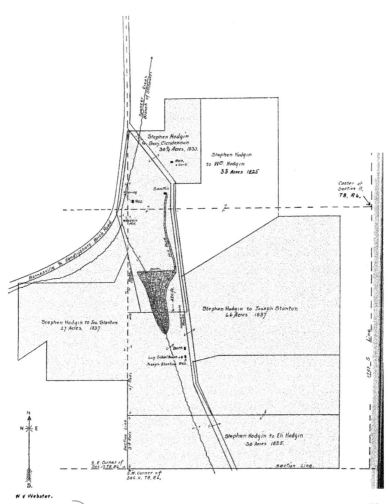

MAP OF THE JOSEPH STANTON, STEPHEN HODGIN,
BENJAMIN CLENDENON FARMS AND THE
CLENDENON AND HODGIN MILLS

RED ROOSTER WEATHER VANE
FOUND IN THE OLD HOSEA DOUDNA HOUSE.

THE BEAR STORY

An account of the narrow escape that Alphonsus and Abigail Kirk's family had from a hungry bear, as recorded by their granddaughter, Rachel Price, who was a cousin of Mary (Hodgin) Stanton.

LPHONSUS and Abigail Kirk were married in 1695 and settled on a farm near Wilmington, Delaware. One morning a beef had been killed, and soon after Abigail Kirk was left alone with two younger sons. A large bear, attracted by the smell of fresh meat, came near the door of the cabin before he was noticed. Upon seeing him the mother ran to close the door. It was a double door, the kind used before windows with glass were in general use. When the bear reared and placed his paws on it, thus making it impossible to close the upper half, she held it against his paws while she called to her son to hand her the rolling pin, and with it she beat the bear's paws until it jumped down and she could fasten the door. The bear then climbed on to a shed roof and tried to enter a second-story window. The mother sent her two little boys to the cellar and told them to climb into a chest there and shut down the lid all but a small crack for air, while she went upstairs to prevent his entering through the window. The shed roof gave way and he fell to the ground. She then threw him some pieces of the fresh meat which he ate eagerly and started off.

The next morning the men tracked the bear through the snow, by bloodstains from injuries received from his fall, and killed him.

EDNA MACY STANTON.

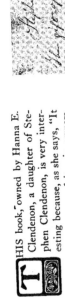

"THIS book," owned by Hanna E. Clendenon, a daughter of Stephen Clendenon, is very interesting because, as she says, "It has in it the names of its six owners. First is a printed library slip bearing the name of Philip Price. Under that is written, 'Transferred to his mother, Ruth Price, 1817.' On the next fly-leaf, 'Presented to Stephen Hodgin by his Aunt, Ruth Price.' Under that, 'Presented to Benjamin Clendenon by his father-in-law.' That, I am sure, is in Grandfather's handwriting. Then the handwriting of Stephen Clendenon, also his son, and lastly my own, with the date 1910, when Father gave the book to me."

*

* *

AMY (HODGIN) CLENDENON

BORN IN SAVANNAH, GEORGIA, IN 1800. DIED
AT COAL CREEK, IOWA, IN 1868. SHE WAS A
SISTER OF MARY (HODGIN) STANTON.

"AUNT AMY!"—father's aunt—I have heard him speak of her as long ago as I can remember; she seems to have held a very warm place in his heart, and indeed in the hearts of his brother and sisters. As she lived on the next farm below, we may be sure there were many visits to "Aunt Amy's"; and doubtless the name was often associated in mind with sweet cakes, "turn-over pies", cherries—eaten in the trees,—peaches, apples and nuts. And too, such good meals, which seemed much better than the ones at home—just because they were at "Aunt Amy's".

What a pleasure it was to him to remember her, and to live over again those happy days!

W. H. S.

STEPHEN CLENDENON
BORN 5–28–1833. DIED 5–4–1913. MARRIED
ELIZABETH BRANSON 3–25–1859. PHOTOGRAPH
ABOUT 1871.

ELIZABETH BRANSON
CLENDENON
BORN 3–29–1834. DIED 8–4–1913. MARRIED
STEPHEN CLENDENON 3–25–1859. PHOTOGRAPH
ABOUT 1871.

LYDIA CLENDENON
SMITH
DAUGHTER OF BENJAMIN AND AMY CLENDENON.
PHOTOGRAPHED ABOUT 1862.

HANNAH CLENDENON
STANLEY
BORN ABOUT 1835. DIED 12–00–1867. MARRIED
ISAAC STANLEY 12–00–1866. DAUGHTER OF
BENJAMIN AND AMY CLENDENON.

AN OLD IRON TEA-KETTLE

HANNA ELIZABETH CLENDENON, OF OSKALOOSA, IOWA, GIVES ITS HISTORY AS
FOLLOWS: "WHEN I WAS A LITTLE GIRL I WAS PRESENTED WITH A LITTLE IRON
TEA-KETTLE AND THIS STORY WAS TOLD TO ME:

"'IN 1813 STEPHEN AND ELIZABETH HODGIN WENT FROM OHIO TO PENNSYLVANIA
ON HORSEBACK.   WHILE THERE GREAT-GRANDMOTHER WAS PRESENTED WITH THIS
TEA-KETTLE FILLED WITH SEED POTATOES, AND SHE WAS TOLD THAT THE TEA-KETTLE
BELONGED TO HER GREAT-GRANDMOTHER.' I STILL HAVE THIS RELIC OF EARLY TIMES
IN A PERFECT STATE OF PRESERVATION."

THE RESIDENCE OF BENJAMIN CLENDENON

LOCATED ON STILLWATER CREEK ABOUT TWO MILES NORTHEAST OF BARNESVILLE,
OHIO, AND A LITTLE ABOVE AND ON OPPOSITE SIDE OF VALLEY FROM HIS WATER-POWER
SAW MILL. THE HOUSE WAS BUILT ABOUT 1840. THE WEATHERBOARDING IS
MODERN. THE CHIMNEY IS OF DRESSED STONE. AT ONE TIME A COLONY OF BEES
MADE ITS HOME IN THE GARRET AND ENTERED THROUGH THE LOWER PART OF THE
LEFT-HAND GABLE WINDOW. "UNCLE" BENJAMIN FREQUENTLY TOOK A SUPPLY OF
HONEY FROM ITS STORES.

**STEPHEN CLENDENON'S HOUSE ON STILLWATER
CREEK**

LOCATED ACROSS THE ROAD FROM THE SAW MILL. STEPHEN MOVED TO IOWA IN 1864.

SPLINT BOTTOM CHAIR

USED BY AMY (HODGIN) CLENDENON ABOUT 1850. NOW IN THE
HOME OF SARAH B. HALL.

THE LOCATION OF BENJAMIN CLENDENON'S SAW MILL

BENJAMIN CLENDENON'S SAW MILL

THIS was a water mill located on Spencer branch of Stillwater Creek about two and one-quarter miles northeast of Barnesville and a half mile below Joseph Stanton's residence. It stood in a depression in the bank across the road from his son Stephen Clendenon's house. The dam was about eight hundred feet up the stream, as shown in the map. The race followed the bank near the roadway to the mill, which was located about where the person is standing in the picture. There was a fall of about eight feet, giving power to an over-shot water wheel. The saw was of the vertical reciprocating type.

Father told me years ago that one very cold day when Uncle Benjamin Clendenon was running the mill, his wife, Aunt Amy, kept the tea-kettle boiling all day so he could have hot water to melt the ice on the wheel—one of the bearings probably.

Henry S. Dawson recently told me that once when Stephen was sawing in severe weather his hands were numb from the cold, and as he rode on the carriage with his hand on the log he failed to notice that the saw was approaching his fingers until the end of one had been taken off. He stopped the saw, went into the house where his wife wrapped up the finger—then back to sawing.

W. H. S.

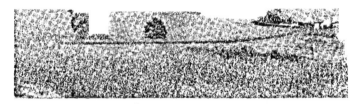

THE LOCATION OF BENJAMIN CLENDENON'S MILL DAM

THE ARROW INDICATES WHERE THE MILL STOOD. THE RACE RAN ALONG THE EDGE OF THE VALLEY BELOW THE ROAD.

"HIGH MILL"

TYPICAL OF THE LARGER OLD-TIME GRIST MILLS. LOCATED NEAR M₄ OHIO.

AN OVER-SHOT WHEEL

A SPECIMEN OF THE LATER TYPE SHOWING CONSTRUCTION OF THE BUCKETS. LOCATED NEAR BARBERTON, OHIO.

WOODEN WHEEL SHA

THE REMAINS OF THE WOODEN SHAFT "HIGH MILL." THE SHAFT IS ALMO FEET IN DIAMETER.

Eli Stanton

Married Twelfth Month Ninth 1857

Mary P. Brandy

ELI AND MARY P. (BUNDY) STANTON

HE NEVER allowed his horses to be driven with a whip" is an index to the character of Eli Stanton. A gentle, loving, sympathetic man, he worked ardently for a pleasant home, and for advancement and improvement in his surroundings. He was ever ready with a word of encouragement and with a helping hand to the needy.

This eldest son of Joseph and Mary (Hodgin) Stanton was by nature of good mechanical ability, and early in life contemplated taking up some line of cabinet making for a profession. He made several pieces of furniture for his home. A bookcase of black walnut made by him is still in the possession of his daughter Sarah. However, having been raised on a farm and educated

in

A BLACK-WALNUT BOOKCASE MADE BY ELI STANTON WHEN
A YOUNG MAN, AND A BUREAU USED IN HIS FAMILY FOR MANY
YEARS.   BOTH IN POSSESSION OF SARAH B. HALL.

in agriculture, when his father, a successful farmer,
offered him opportunities in that line, he accepted and
enjoyed the preparation of the soil, the planting of the
seeds, the raising and the harvesting of the crops on
his father's farm on Sandy Ridge two miles east of
Barnesville,

William B
bitha

NTON. *Marri*

ELI AND MARY P. STANTON
Taken about 1868.

Barnesville, Ohio. He became a progressive agricul-turist, and stock raising was added to his interests. Cattle were a specialty, he being among the first to introduce thoroughbred Shorthorns into his vicinity. He was an active member of the Grange.

On a farm not far from the Stanton home lived John and Ruth (Patten) Bundy. On the Ninth of Twelfth month, 1857, Eli Stanton married their daugh-ter, Mary P. The waiters at their marriage were: 1st, Caleb Bundy, Hannah Clendenon; 2d, Nathan Bundy, Anna Stanton; 3d, William P. Bundy, Tabitha Doudna. This little woman, for she could walk under her husband's outstretched arm, was always a good example to others. Her method of disciplining her children was to ever set them the right example and then

RESIDENCE OF ELI STANTON

A VIEW SOUTHEAST FROM THE RESIDENCE OF ELI STANTON, LOOKING TOWARDS THE
OLD GOSHEN FRIENDS' MEETING HOUSE. PART OF THE FARM FORMERLY OWNED
BY HENRY DOUDNA IS SHOWN AT THE RIGHT AND THE FARM OF JAMES STANTON AT THE
LEFT.
Photographed in 1884 by W. H. S.

then gently and patiently see that they followed it.
Kindness to every one was characteristic of her. She
was careful never to wrong any one in thought or deed,
believing that whoever robs others with evil suspicions
robs himself of his own peace of mind. She was industrious and happy, doing what she could for the up-
lifting of humanity. The motto by which she lived
was, "Life is given for noble deeds that we may pro-
mote our own happiness in proportion as we contribute
to the comfort of others."

Eli and Mary Stanton went to housekeeping in an
old log house on Sandy Ridge, erected by Jesse Bailey.
No photograph remains of the house, but a sketch has
been made, which faces page 215. The present road
passes directly over its foundation. In this old house
with its whitewashed walls, rag carpets and green
paper window shades, three children were born to this
happy couple.

William

William Henry (8–2–1860). Will was an energetic little boy, who dearly loved his family and his home. With the mechanical turn inherited from his father, he enjoyed everything mechanical and the study of science. After a year at Friends' Boarding School, Barnesville, and three years as apprentice to the machinist trade and four years as instrument maker and four years at DePauw University, while studying at Rose Polytechnic Institute, he was offered a position with the Philadelphia Quartz Company, to have charge of the building and development of new factories. While with that company he lived for twenty years at Anderson, Indiana, where he met and married, on Sixth month Fifteenth, 1898, Miss Louise Smith. Since then he has lived in Buffalo, New York, Robinson, Maryland, and for the last seven years in Ridley Park, Pennsylvania. Now, in his sixtieth year, he has retired from active work.

Sarah B. (11–23–1861). This eldest daughter, with black curly hair and blue eyes, brought much happiness into her parents' home. She was educated at Friends' Boarding School, Westtown, Pennsylvania. For a number of years she taught in her home neighborhood and there met and married, on the Twenty-eighth of Tenth month, 1890, Wilfred T. Hall, son of Thomas P. and Rebecca Hall. They went to housekeeping on his mother's farm, near the house where Nathan and Anna (Stanton) Bundy first lived after their marriage. Dairying and farming have claimed Wilfred's attention. In 1898 they bought a part of the Robert Plummer farm near Tacoma, Ohio, and in 1907 moved there, living in the house built by William Bundy.

Bundy. This, with additional land, is their present farm.

To them three daughters were born, all of whom attended Friends' Primary School and Friends' Boarding School near Barnesville, Ohio. Eva (9–26–1891). On the Twenty-fifth of Sixth month, 1914, Eva married Guy Woodward, of Plainfield, Indiana. They located in Anderson, Indiana, where he was manager of the plant of the Philadelphia Quartz Company. While there, Eva gained the love and esteem of all who knew her and again when Guy was transferred to the plant at Buffalo, New York, her influence was felt. To be a helpmate to her husband, to set an example of "the things worth while" in their daily lives was her ambition. Hers was an energetic, buoyant life with a deep interest in relatives and friends, yet above all was her great love for her husband and home. Into their short married life they crowded more of joy and happiness than many do in long years. On the Twenty-sixth of Second month, 1919, she died of influenza. Thus early called "Home," she left a void hard to fill. Bertha Rebecca (12–16–1892). Bertha married Albert W. Guindon of Bristol, Vermont, on the Twenty-sixth of Ninth month, 1918. They went to the beautiful Green Mountain state to live. There they follow the business of farming for which Albert prepared himself at Cornell University, New York. Helen E. (6–13–1899). On the Fifteenth of Second month, 1919, Helen married Harold L. Holloway of Barnesville, Ohio. He is a mechanic of unusual ability and has been trained under expert instructors. On the Twenty-first of Twelfth month, 1919, a son, Paul W., was born.

Emma

Emma C. (10-5-1864). This second daughter, in looks resembling her father, came to add, in her quiet manner, joy to the happy household. She was educated at Friends' Boarding School, Barnesville, Ohio, and at Westtown Boarding School, Westtown, Pennsylvania. In 1888, on the Twenty-third of Eighth month, she married Willis Vail Webster, son of Thomas and Lydia P. (Richardson) Webster, of Quaker City, Ohio. They built a small house near Quaker City and there established their home. Willis taught school for a number of years, then led a busy life as a surveyor. In 1914 his health was poor and he retired from business. The family then and since that time has lived at 838 Wilson Avenue, Columbus, Ohio. Five children came to bless their home. Harlan Stanton (9-6-1889). Harlan received his education in the Quaker City, Cambridge and Columbus Public Schools, with two years at Friends' Boarding School near Barnesville, Ohio. Like many other boys, he found electricity and wireless very attractive and after patient perseverance installed a station that gave wonderful results for that early day of wireless. He says: "The best results I have had with my wireless outfit were in the years 1910 and 1911. My station was located at the rear of our home, 838 Wilson Avenue, Columbus, Ohio, and at this time was well equipped. My antenna was two hundred and fifty feet long, comprised of four aluminum wires suspended from one end on a pole about seventy-five feet high, and at the other end from a pole about ninety-five feet high. With this station I could pick up messages from the English Government Station at Nova Scotia, stations at Cape Cod, Key West, Florida, and the naval station at Norfolk.

Norfolk. I often heard the United Fruit Company station at New Orleans giving orders to their boats and to their office at Colon, Panama. At one time I heard the Government Station at Seattle, Washington, talking to a station at Katalla, Alaska. They were inquiring about a boat that had been wrecked. In a day or so the papers contained an account of a shipwreck near Katalla." He married Mary Avis Smith, then of Estherville, Iowa, on the Third of Ninth month, 1912. They have one son, Willis William, born Seventh month eighth, 1914. Their home is in East Canton, Ohio, where Harlan has a position as chemist.

Raymond Nathan (7–27–1893). Raymond, like his brother, received his education in the public schools of Quaker City, Cambridge, and Columbus, Ohio, and at the Friends' Boarding School near Barnesville, Ohio. During vacation he secured employment as engineer in a plant in Columbus, where art glass for automobiles was prepared. While on duty, his clothing was caught in the machinery, throwing him backwards. His head struck the floor, causing instant death on the Fifth of Ninth month, 1912. Interment was made in the family lot in Green Lawn Cemetery, Quaker City. Raymond was of a cheerful, studious disposition. Wherever he went, he made friends. Our great loss we trust was his eternal gain. Thomas (6–25–1897), at Quaker City, Ohio. Thomas was educated in the public schools of Cambridge and Columbus, Ohio, and at the Friends' Boarding School near Barnesville. Since leaving school he has been employed as a draftsman. Mary Lydia (6–11–1904), at Cambridge, Ohio. Debora Harriet (7–6–1906), at Columbus, Ohio. Both girls are attending the public school in Columbus.

The

The winter of 1871 brought sadness to the home of Eli Stanton. The devoted wife and mother, after an illness of about six weeks, was called to her Heavenly Home, leaving a heart-broken husband and three children under twelve years of age. What a void, what an utter loneliness was felt in that home only those of us who have lost the mainstay of our lives can know. Not only in the home, but among the relatives and neighbors was this loss keenly felt, for she had taken an active interest in the affairs of the neighborhood and her quiet, gentle life had touched and inspired the lives of many. A cousin, Sarah Clendenon, came and made her home with the stricken family. The aunts did all in their power to make happy those motherless children. William has happy recollections of his joy and pride in a suit made by Aunt Jennie in which she stitched the name William H. Stanton in the lining of the coat, and the frequent visits of Aunt Annie and Aunt Lizzie to their home were red-letter days.

On the thirtieth of Seventh month, 1873, Eli Stanton married Deborah H. Bundy, daughter of Elijah and Eliza Hanson, of Stillwater, Ohio. She brought to his home her little daughter, Mary C. Bundy, and her step-daughter, Mary E. Bundy.

This was an unusual home, where five children lived happily together representing three different families and all treated like own children by each of the step-parents. On the Twenty-sixth of First month, 1875, a son was born, Nathan Eli. Together they all worked and played harmoniously for twelve years, when the home was again visited by the unseen messenger, who called the father, Eli Stanton, to the mansions above the sky. His going left his wife a widow for the third time

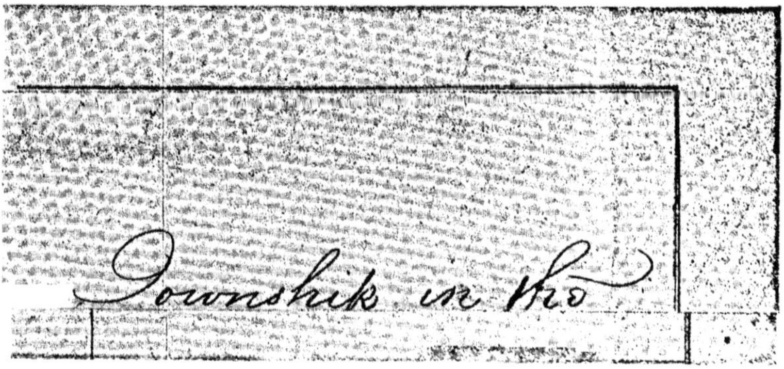

Township in the

ried 7-30-1873

Whereas; Eli Stanton of Warren County of Belmont and State of Ohio, son of Joseph Stanton State aforesaid, and Mary his wife (both deceased), and Deb daughter of Elijah Hanson of the County of Belmont and State Eliza his wife, having declared their intentions of Marriage before a Monthly Meeting of the Religious Society of Friends h and having consent of surviving parents, their said proposa allowed by said meeting. These are to certify whom it may for the full accomplishment of their said intentions, this th month, in the year of our Lord, eighteen hundred and seventy Eli Stanton and Deborah Bundy appeared in a public meeti people held at Stillwater; and the said Eli Stanton taking Deborah Bundy by the hand, declared that he took her, the said to be his wife, promising with Divine assistance, to be unto her faithful husband until death should separate them: and Deborah Bundy did in like manner, declare, that she took Eli Stanton to be her husband, promising with Divine assistance, a loving and faithful wife, until death should separate them. they the Eli Stanton and Deborah Bundy (she according to marriage, adopting the name of her husband) did as a further thereof, then, and there to these presents set their hands,

And we whose names are also hereunto subs at the solemnization of said marriage, have, as witnesses thereto, day and year above written.

Robert Plummer	Dempsy Bundy	Benjamin Hoyle
Rachel Green	Rebecca M. Bundy	Edmund Hays
Eli Kennard	A. Sedgfield	
Mary Kennard	Hiram Sedgfield	Nathan Bundy
Sarkuel Walton	Ann Eliza Wilson	Anna P. Bundy
Barclay Smith	Anna Edgerton	William Stanton
Sinclair Smith	Esther Wilson	Jane D. Stanton
Aaron Frame	Deborah A. Smith	Leighton Bailey
Abijah Frame	Rebecca D. Bundy	Lizzie S. Bailey
Elizabeth Patterson	Mary J. Starbuck	
Jesse Bailey	Tacy H. Starbuck	
Asenath Bailey	Hannah Smith	
George Tatum	Ruth B. Doudna	
Hannah Tatum	Eliza Bundy	
Asenath Crew	A. J. Blower	
	Wm. Bundy	
	Asenath Bundy	
	Sidney Bailey	

ELI STANTON   **DEBORAH H. B. STANTON**
PHOTOGRAPHS TAKEN IN 1874 IN CLARKSBURG, WEST VIRGINIA.

me and his three oldest children, now between the
es of twenty and twenty-five years, without parents,
it with the love of a step-mother which has enriched
eir lives.

Nathan Eli, the only other child, now a boy of ten
ars, was educated in the district school and later
nt to Westtown Boarding School for a short time.
the summer of 1893, when he was eighteen years
l, he, accompanied by his mother, went to Iowa,
here he engaged in farming. From that time, except-
one year spent in Houston County, Minnesota,
til Third month, 1920, he lived in Iowa. For sev-
l years he devoted himself to grain farming and hog
sing, then turned to dairy work, retailing bottled
lk and supplying hotels, dining cars and restaurants.

n 1914 a silver medal was awarded him by the Dairy
ttle Congress held in Waterloo, Iowa, and both a
er and a gold medal by the Agricultural College
Ames for market milk tested from samples taken at
four different seasons of the year.

On

On the Twentieth of Sixth month, 1907, he married at Barnesville, Ohio, Sarah E. Stanton, daughter of Daniel and Rebecca Bundy Stanton. To them three children were born: Edith Rebecca (4-15-1908), Mervin Daniel (2-13-1910), William Hanson (1-8-1914).

They have all three attended the city schools in Estherville, Iowa. On Third month first, 1920, they moved to a large farm near Rush City, Minnesota, where they now reside. His mother, Deborah H. B. Stanton, makes her home with them.

In closing, the words of Thomas Carlyle seem most fitting to apply to such a man as Eli Stanton:

> "The work an unknown good man has done is
> like a vein of water flowing hidden under ground,
> secretly making the ground green."

Lansdowne,
Pennsylvania,   *Edna Macy Stanton*
1919.

Rocking-chair used by Eli Stanton until 1885.

A great comfort to him during year of his declining health.

ELI STANTON'S SILK
WEDDING HAT WORN
1873 AT THE TIME
OF HIS MARRIAGE TO
DEBORAH H. BUNDY.

WATCH BOUGHT AND USED BY ELI STANTON. LATER GIVEN BY HIM TO HIS SON,
WILLIAM H., WHEN THE LATTER WENT TO PHILADELPHIA IN 1880.

THE ORIGINAL KNOB TO OPEN THE CASE WAS LOST. THE ONE NOW ON THE WATCH
WAS MADE BY WILLIAM H. STANTON WHILE WORKING FOR JAMES W. QUEEN & CO.

BULLET MOLD FOR SQUIRREL RIFLE
TWO HUNDRED BULLETS TO THE POUND.

SMALL SQUIRREL RIFLE BOUGHT IN 1865 AND USED BY ELI STANTON. MADE BY
THE LOCAL "GUNSMITH," WILLIAM FOLGER, BARNESVILLE, OHIO.

"I FIRST SAW IT LYING ACROSS FATHER'S KNEES AS HE SAT IN THE KITCHEN OF THE
OLD LOG HOUSE."

                                                        W. H. S.

READER USED BY RUTH PATTEN, AND DATED BY HER 8TH OF 2ND MONTH, 1826.

FLY-LEAF OF RUTH PATTEN'S READER SHOWING HER SIGNATURE AND THAT OF HER
DAUGHTER, MARY PATTEN (BUNDY) STANTON.

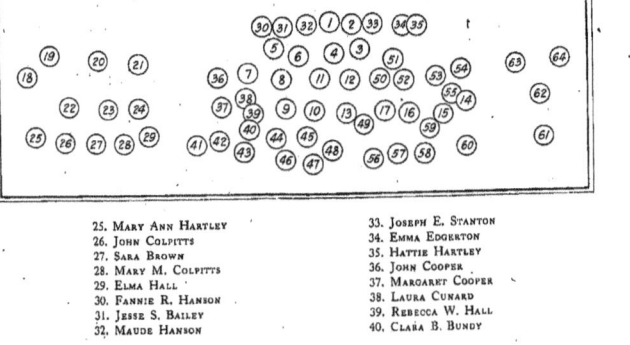

STANTON
NTON
TANTON
STANTON
TON
ON
STANTON
TON
HALL
ALL
STANTON
ANTON
NDY
ANTON
ANTON
8. BAILEY
BAILEY
RRTON
OGERTON
NDY
CETT
BUNDY
BUNDY
AWCETT

25. MARY ANN HARTLEY	33. JOSEPH E. STANTON	41. STEWART WATT
26. JOHN COLPITTS	34. EMMA EDGERTON	42. ANNA W. WATT
27. SARA BROWN	35. HATTIE HARTLEY	43. WILLARD BUNDY
28. MARY M. COLPITTS	36. JOHN COOPER	44. FREDERICK R. BUNDY
29. ELMA HALL	37. MARGARET COOPER	45. MARY ANNA BAILEY
30. FANNIE R. HANSON	38. LAURA CUNARD	46. HELEN HALL
31. JESSE S. BAILEY	39. REBECCA W. HALL	47. MARY HOLLOWAY
32. MAUDE HANSON	40. CLARA B. BUNDY	48. CLARA VON HOFSTEN
		49. OSCAR J. BAILEY
		50. MELISSA BUNDY
		51. CALEB HANSON
		52. MARY D. BUNDY
		53. CLINTON T. BUNDY
		54. FLORENCE HOOE
		55. SARA C. HOLLOWAY
		56. ANNA MARY BUNDY
		57. BERTHA HALL
		58. EVA HALL
		59. ANNA C. STANTON
		60. CHARLES HOLLOWAY
		61. WILSON TAYLOR
		62. MYRTLE TAYLOR
		63. EVALYN P. BUNDY
		64. T. CARVER BUNDY

GUESTS AT THE *Wedding Reception* OF NATHAN E. AND SARAH E. STANTON. *Married 6-20-1907.*

Whereas,

These are to Certify,

And We,

Witnesses.

A specimen of my Epistolary and Writing

Mary P. Bundy

MADE AT MOUNT PLEASANT BOARDING SCHOOL.

A WORK BOX GIVEN TO MARY P. BUNDY BY ELI STANTON ABOUT 1856, BEFORE THEIR MARRIAGE.

NOW OWNED BY THEIR DAUGHTER, SARAH B. HALL.

EARLY QUEENSWARE FRUIT JAR USED BY Y P. STANTON ABOUT 1860. A TIN CAP PLACED OVER THE OPENING AND THE SEALED AIR-TIGHT BY MELTED ROSIN.

CELLAR USED BY ELI AND MARY P. TON FOR MANY YEARS. NOW OWNED BY EMMA C. WEBSTER.

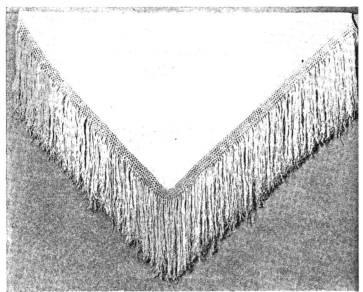

MARY P. STANTON'S WHITE SILK WEDDING SHAWL

WOODEN WORK-BOX USED FOR MANY YEARS
MARY P. STANTON. NOW OWNED BY H
DAUGHTER, EMMA C. WEBSTER.

QUILT PIECED BY MOTHER, MARY P.
STANTON, IN 1867, FROM AUNT SARAH
(BUNDY) MOTT'S DRESSES (THE AUNT
FOR WHOM I WAS NAMED). THE PINK
SQUARE IN EACH BLOCK WAS MADE
FROM A LITTLE SACK OF MINE. THE
QUILT HAS BEEN GREATLY PRIZED BY
ME FOR OVER FIFTY-FIVE YEARS.
SARAH B. HALL.

ELI STANTON'S OLD LOG HOUSE

A MEMORY RECONSTRUCTION BY WILLIAM HENRY STANTON. WATER COLOR BY WILLIAM MACY STANTON

HOME! How shall one describe it? Home and
Mother! Seems to me that a word describes
it better than sentences and paragraphs.
Childhood's home! When details and efficiency did not intrude—cares and responsibilities were unknown. The sun was always shining,
the fire burned brightly. The cold was not noticed,
but rather the cheer of the open fire. Meals were very
simple, but how good and satisfying. Father knew
everything and could do anything; Mother cured everything, mental and physical. Father was tall, strong and
manly; Mother petite, cheery and helpful. And
when I wanted to go with Father to town or to the
field his answer was, "Go ask Mother." After dinner was over and Mother was dressed for the
afternoon, if I asked where she was going—"To
Stanton's," or, at another time, "To a meeting," but
never would be "Father."

True, the house was old—log house—nearly
forty years. There was moss on the north side of the
roof, the big chimney was cracked and ragged, a great

THE OLD LOG HOUSE

HOME! How shall one describe it? Home and Mother! Seems to me that a word describes it better than sentences and paragraphs. Childhood's home! When details and efficiency did not intrude—cares and responsibilities were unknown. The sun was always shining or the fire burned brightly. The cold was not noticed, but rather the cheer of the open fire. Meals were very simple, but how good and satisfying. Father knew everything and could do anything; Mother cured every ill, mental and physical. Father was tall, strong and manly; Mother "petite," cheery and lovable. And when I wanted to go with Father to town or on an errand his answer was, "Go ask Mother." After the dinner was over and Mother was dressing for the afternoon, if I asked where she was going—"To Eli Stanton's"; or, at another time, "Who's coming?" her answer would be "Father."

True, the house was old for a log house—nearly sixty years. There was moss on the north side of the roof, the big chimney was cracked and ragged, a part

of

of the cellar wall had fallen down, and a new house wa
being talked about.   How well I remember the weath
ered gray logs, the white lime mortar that filled th
cracks between; the small windows with the littl
lights of glass; the low, but wide, front door; the white
washed walls; the beams of the ceiling with the board
of the floor above; the very wide, open fireplace which
Father had divided, using one end for cook stove an
the other for a coal grate; and the partition separatin
the two bedrooms from the living room.   The board
of the partition were wide, yellow poplar with th
edges beaded and placed vertically, and not painted
but kept scoured and clean.   At the left end of the roon
was the narrow three winding-step stair to the secon
story and again to the garret.   In the bedroom were th
bi

TRUNDLE BED

THE FOUR-POST AND TRUNDLE BEDS WERE USED BY MOST OF THE PIONEERS.   THIS
ONE IS IN THE HOME OF WILLIAM F. GIBBONS.

ELI STANTON'S CLOCK
USED IN HIS HOME ALL OF HIS MARRIED LIFE. NOW IN THE POS-
SESSION OF HARLAN S. WEBSTER.

big red four-post beds and under one our "trundle bed," to be pulled out for use; the rag carpet; looking glass and comb case on the wall over the little square stand; green paper window blinds rolled up and tied with brown braid; a corner cupboard; and on the narrow mantelpiece the clock and a brass candlestick.

Through the big door at the left of the fireplace we entered the kitchen—a big, square room with such a big fireplace for wood. There was a plain built-in cupboard

cupboard and a little shelf for the water bucket and "tin," and a stair in the corner to the loft. At the left hand of the fireplace the "Triumph" cook stove stood in summer, but in winter it was moved to the living room because the kitchen was too cold for cooking.

Here in the living room, in the cold days of winter, the sausage, with sage in it, was fried for breakfast and the big buckwheat cakes were baked and turned with the big maple paddle Father made "before they were married." These cakes were often served with apple butter and real cream.

And what a delightful odor when Mother opened the oven door and took out the mince pies with the rope formed

BRASS CANDLE STICK
USED IN THE HOME OF ELI AND MARY P. (BUNDY) STANTON IN THEIR EARLY MARRIED LIFE.

formed on the edge and a couple of fern leaves drawn on the brown-tinted crust.

As the days grew shorter and the sun set gray, we gathered the last of the peaches and apples and made cider, and then sorghum molasses down by the spring. There they ground the cane. Can't you hear the feeder "hollerin'" "Git up, git up!" and hear the crunching of the cane and the rushing out of the light-green juice, and see the smoke from the low stone chimneys of the furnace curl over the roof, and the shed filled with sweet-scented steam?

Then the call of the wild came, and on a warm afternoon following a frost we laid in a supply of nuts—walnut, chestnut, hickory, beech and butternut—always so much in demand in winter.

At evening time who has not watched the flicker of the firelight on the windowpane and the men coming in with lanterns from work or from feeding at the barn? Heavy wraps were laid off and the news of the afternoon was discussed.

For supper we often had cornbread, shortened with "lard cracklings" finely ground, and well cooked. This, with rich milk, made a full meal and satisfied every desire.

Sometimes on a cold First-day evening Father would rattle the ashes from the grate, leaving hot coals above and below, then set one of the mince pies under the grate to warm. That was our supper, and how good it was—never a bad dream.

How we enjoyed the visitors when they came! No announcement; they just drove up to the horse block and unloaded and put the horses in the stable. There was lots to talk about—news about the families and the neighborhood

neighborhood; the 'phone had not told everybody every-thing. Then there was always plenty of fresh meat on hand—just a call, "Chickee, chickee!" a handful of feed, and some rooster would slip out of his feathers into the pot and on to the table before a particle of flavor had been lost. Then came the gravy and mashed pota-toes—we never got enough, just stopped for lack of space.

Back of the house and not far from the corner was the well, with a "sweep" weighted with a chunk of wood and a couple of plow points to help balance the bucket and water. At the other end a long black walnut lath was attached to the sweep with a small rope and to the old oaken bucket by a few feet of chain. The water

was

A WELL SWEEP

USED IN THE EARLY DAYS TO DRAW WATER FROM SHALLOW WELLS. IT WAS EASY
TO MAKE AND WHEN A POLE WAS USED INSTEAD OF A CHAIN IT REQUIRED VERY
LITTLE MATERIAL THAT COULD NOT BE FOUND ANYWHERE IN THE WOODS.

was always cool and, maybe, sanitary. Beyond was the cave which answered for cellar and refrigerator. When we heard the inclined cave door slam we knew that it was time to come for dinner or supper—and obeyed promptly.

The garden lay between the house and road. It was large and fenced with black-walnut palings about six feet high. Inside, everything good and beautiful grew. At the side of the yard next to the garden were lilacs, snowballs, old-hundred roses and maiden blush; at the right-hand end of the yard was the split chestnut log woodhouse and the big cedar tree that could be seen from long distances in many directions.

But now all are gone—not a stick nor stone remains —only happy memories and a grateful heart to those who made that home.

Ridley Park,
Pennsylvania,
1921.

Wm H. Stanton.

A CAVE DOOR

LOCATED NEAR FOX CHASE, PENN-
SYLVANIA.

THE HOME OF PETER AND ANNA (DOUDNA) SEARS

BUILT BY THOMAS WILLIAMS IN 1807 OR 1808. IT WAS THE FIRST HEWN LOG HOUSE IN THAT
SECTION AND WAS LATER PURCHASED BY MATTHEW BAILEY. HE WAS THE GREAT-GRAND-
FATHER OF EDWIN W. SEARS AND MARY B. NIBLOCK, WHO HAVE FURNISHED SO MANY
RELICS WITH THEIR HISTORY.

SPRING-HOUSE AT PETER SEARS' HOME

THE HOUSE WAS COVERED BY A SHAVED CLAPBOARD ROOF. THE "BOARDS" WERE SPLIT,
SHAVED AND PUT ON BY MATTHEW BUNDY OVER FIFTY YEARS AGO. IT IS OF INTEREST TO
NOTE THE WELL-PRESERVED LOGS AND THE EXCELLENT WORKMANSHIP. PHOTOGRAPH, 1920.

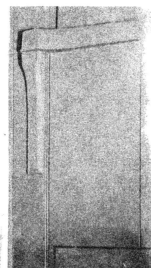

A WOODEN HINGE

FROM THE SOUTH DOOR IN THE PETER SEARS HOUSE. IT HAS BEEN IN USE ABOUT ONE HUNDRED AND TWELVE YEARS.

OUTSIDE CHIMNEY BREAST

FROM THE PETER SEARS HOUSE. THE BRICK CHIMNEY IS MODERN.

THE SPRING AT THE PETER SEARS HOUSE

THIS SPRING WAS USED IN ITS PRESENT FORM FOR OVER ONE HUNDRED YEARS. THE SANDSTONE WALL APPEARS GOOD FOR ANOTHER CENTURY.

LOGS FROM THE ELI STANTON LOG HOUSE

THE HOUSE WAS BOUGHT BY ANDREW BLOWERS, TORN DOWN IN 1869 AND RE-ERECTED BY HIM ON HIS FARM ABOUT TWO MILES BELOW ON "SANDY RIDGE." HERE IT SERVED AS A DWELLING FOR ABOUT THIRTY YEARS AND WAS REPLACED BY A NEW BUILDING. "I WENT TO THE OLD HOUSE IN 1907, BUT FOUND ONLY A PILE OF LOGS. IN 1919 I WENT AGAIN TO SEE THE LOGS AND IF POSSIBLE TO GET A SOUVENIR, BUT COULD NEITHER SEE NOR LEARN OF ANY PIECE OF THE LOGS ABOUT THE PRESENT HOME. JUST AS I WAS LEAVING I DECIDED TO VISIT A NEARBY TOBACCO HOUSE WHERE TOBACCO WAS BEING STRUNG AND PLACED IN THE HOUSE. THIS WAS INTERESTING, AS I HAD NOT SEEN GREEN TOBACCO FOR FORTY-FIVE YEARS, SINCE I WORKED IN IT ON THE HOME FARM. AS I LOOKED ABOUT THE HOUSE AND NOTICED THE ROUND LOGS, THE NOTCHING AT THE CORNERS AND THE 'CHINKING' AND 'DAUBING' BETWEEN THE LOGS, I GLANCED UP AT THE EAVES AND INSTANTLY RECOGNIZED THE OBJECT OF ALL MY SEARCH. THERE WERE SEVERAL LARGE, BEAUTIFULLY HEWN AND WELL-PRESERVED LOGS IN THE TOP COURSES. A LITTLE INQUIRY OF MRS. E. L. PHILLIPS CONFIRMED MY BELIEF THAT THEY WERE PART OF THE LOG HOUSE IN WHICH I WAS BORN. MR. PHILLIPS KINDLY CONSENTED TO CUT OUT A SECTION OF ONE OF THE LOGS AND SHIP IT TO ME." THE ORIGINAL OLD LOGS ARE MARKED WITH AN "X."

W. H. S.

THE LOG FROM THE ELI STANTON HOUSE

THE SECTION OF A LOG CUT FROM THE TOBACCO HOUSE REFERRED TO ABOVE AND FROM WHICH THE SPECIMEN ON THE SAMPLE PAGE WAS MADE.

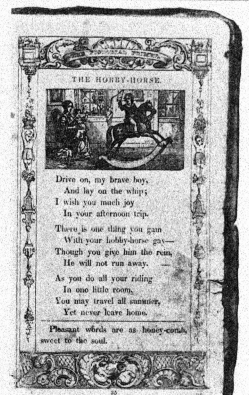

THE HOBBY-HORSE.

Drive on, my brave boy,
  And lay on the whip;
I wish you much joy
  In your afternoon trip.

There is one thing you gain
  With your hobby-horse gay—
Though you give him the rein,
  He will not run away.

As you do all your riding
  In one little room,
You may travel all summer,
  Yet never leave home.

Pleasant words are as honey-comb,
sweet to the soul.

THE AUTHOR

REPRODUCTIONS OF SOME
OF THE PAGES FROM THE
PRIMER USED BY WILLIAM
H., SARAH B., AND EMMA
C. STANTON. BOUGHT
ABOUT 1866.

HOSEA AND MARY DOUDNA

A TYPICAL EARLY STAIRWAY

CHIMNEY, CLOSET AND STAIRWAY IN THE HOUSE OWNED BY HORACE SMITH, EMERSON, OHIO.

A TOBACCO HOUSE

OBACCO HOUSES WERE VERY COMMON IN THE EARLY DAYS IN SOUTH-EASTERN OHIO. THE TOBACCO WAS STRIPPED FROM THE STALK JUST BEFORE THE FROST IN THE FALL, WAS THEN STRUNG ON STICKS ABOUT FOUR FEET LONG, PLACING A COUPLE OF LEAVES ALTERNATELY ON EACH SIDE OF THE STICK. IT WAS THEN HUNG BETWEEN POLES IN THE YARD UNTIL IT HAD WILTED, THEN WAS HUNG BETWEEN SIMILAR POLES IN THE HOUSE AS CLOSE TOGETHER AS POSSIBLE AND FROM THE TOP TO WITHIN A FEW FEET FROM THE GROUND. A STONE FLUE WAS BUILT THE LENGTH OF THE HOUSE, WITH OPENINGS IN THE COVERING STONE. A WOOD FIRE IN THIS FLUE FILLED THE HOUSE WITH SMOKE AND HEAT AND SO CURED THE TOBACCO. THE FURNACES ARE NOW ARRANGED SO THAT THE HEAT ONLY ENTERS THE HOUSE, THE SMOKE BEING DELIVERED OUTSIDE, WHICH RESULTS IN PRODUCING A MUCH MILDER TOBACCO.

THE SUGAR TREE

ONE THAT STOOD BESIDE THE SPRING. FOR MANY
YEARS IT FURNISHED SAP FOR TWO TO THREE GALLONS
OF MAPLE SYRUP.

THE SUGAR TREE BY THE SPRING

FOR nearly sixty years I knew the sugar tree by the spring. And what a wonderful tree it was, with its great roots sunk deep in the rich, moist soil, its shapely gray trunk and graceful branches! What a pleasure it was to see its first tender-tinted shoots of early spring, the unfolding leaves, the winged seed pods fluttering down or blown to leeward in every wind, the luxuriant foliage of summer with its dense cool shade, the gorgeous mass of autumn color—tints so rich that no artist's brush could have done them justice and which faded so gradually that none could mark a time to sigh for the loss of their beauty. And as the ground grew cold and frosty, with what royal prodigality did the old tree fling down a finer carpet than the rarest tapestry! Surely the kindness of nature is exemplified in

228

ELI STANTON'S SPRING

LOCATED NEAR THE OLD LOG HOUSE. THE SUGAR TREE STOOD
A LITTLE TO THE LEFT.

n the old sugar tree which in the coming and going
)f the seasons yielded such wealth of beauty and
.weetness.

Doubtless this tree was of goodly size when the
:lder Jesse Bailey lived nearby. Throughout the whole
)f Father's life it stood, and doubtless it saw more than
our generations come and go ere the coming of that
pring when the rays of the kindly sun failed to stir
t from the long winter's sleep.

THE SUGAR TREE

THE NOBLE TRUNK THAT LIFTED THE TREE AND
GIVES IT FOOD AND LIFE

A GOURD DIPPER

THE KIND USED BY THE EARLY SETTLERS.
PHOTOGRAPHED AT THE HOME OF JAMES AND
EUNICE (SMITH) HENDERSON.

 N THE EARLY DAYS CANE SUGAR WAS VERY EXPENSIVE AND OFTEN COULD NOT BE BOUGHT, SO THE PIONEERS MADE MAPLE SUGAR AND SYRUP BY BOILING DOWN THE SAP OF THE SUGAR OR HARD MAPLE. AS SOON AS THE GROUND THAWED IN EARLY SPRING THEY BORED USUALLY TWO THREE-QUARTER-INCH HOLES IN THE TRUNK OF THE TREES NEAR THE GROUND AND DROVE A SPILE OR TUBE ABOUT A FOOT LONG TO CARRY THE SAP INTO THE WOODEN TROUGH OR BUCKET PLACED TO RECEIVE IT. MONEY WAS SCARCE AND TRANSPORTATION DIFFICULT, SO OUR FIRST SETTLERS MADE EVERYTHING THEY COULD WITH THEIR SIMPLE TOOLS. THE SPILES WERE SPLIT FROM SOFT WOOD, SUCH AS WHITE WALNUT, SHAVED DOWN WITH A "DRAWING-KNIFE," A HOLE BORED IN THE END WITH A HAND "GIMLET" AND A GROOVE CUT BY POCKET KNIFE TO THE OTHER END TO CONDUCT THE SAP. THE TROUGHS WERE CHOPPED OUT ENTIRELY BY A COMMON CHOPPING AX. THE SAP WAS COLLECTED AT FREQUENT INTERVALS AND HAULED IN BARRELS OR TUBS ON A SLED TO THE SIMPLE SHED NEAR THE CENTER OF THE "SUGAR CAMP" AND BOILED DOWN IN BIG IRON KETTLES OVER OPEN FIRE. THEN THE SYRUP WAS TAKEN TO THE HOUSE TO BE FINISHED OFF, OR REDUCED TO SUGAR.

HAND-MADE MAPLE SUGAR TUB

WITH DOUBLE-LOCKED HOOPS. MADE BY HENRY DOUDNA PROBABLY MORE THAN ONE HUNDRED YEARS AGO. NOW OWNED BY EDWIN W. SEARS.

SAP TROUGH

MADE BY NATHAN W. BUNDY.

THE BUILDING OF ELI STANTON'S BARN
AND HOUSE

WE WERE living in the old log house in the winter of 1866-67, which was a busy one in our home. The kitchen in the east end was too cold to be occupied in winter, so father built a dividing wall in the fireplace in the living-room. He set a coal grate in the left end and placed a cook stove in the other half. Coal was used for fuel in the grate as well as in the stove, but wood was burned in the large kitchen fireplace. The house was in need of extensive repairs to make it comfortable; even when repaired, as a log house it would always have its disadvantages. The house was too small and neither house nor barn was properly located, so it was decided to erect new buildings. The barn must necessarily be built first, as the old one would have to be moved before completing the new house.

During the winter, timber was cut in the various woods on the farm and hauled to a portable saw mill on the farm of William Bundy about a mile northeast of our house. The logs were sawed into posts, stringers, nail-ties,

231

A VIEW OF THE RESIDENCE OF ELI STANTON

nail-ties, joists, and rafters. Oak was used for flooring boards and weatherboarding. The shingles were made of white oak rived with froe and hand-maul; then with "shaving horse" and "draw knife" were shaved and jointed by hand. On one section of the roof, ten feet square, black walnut shingles were used. When the roof was removed by Anderson and Dough-lass in 1906, they found the black walnut shingles in a better state of preservation than the oak.

When the warm days of spring came, great piles of lumber and timbers were located near the site for the new barn. One bright morning we children were greatly excited by hearing some one remark, "The car-penters are coming." We rushed out to see and hear Aaron Frame and some of his helpers driving down the stony hill of the lane. They drove to the old barn and there a large chest of tools was unloaded and placed inside. They also brought several axes, a cross-cut saw, boring machine, trussels and other tools. They then went away in the direction of the north woods. Soon we heard chopping and occasionally a tree fall. Of course, I, a small boy, was anxious to know what they were doing and at the first opportunity went over to where the men were at work.

The barn was to measure forty-five by fifty feet, and eighteen feet six inches from the main floor to the eaves, with the stable story eight feet six inches high. The largest posts in the stable story were twelve by fifteen inches, the main floor sills ten by twelve inches; the girder over the main floor nine by thirteen inches, and forty-five feet long. Some of the timbers were so long, they could not be sawed by the portable mill. In order to make these long timbers, the carpenters had to select a sound tree of sufficient height, and large

large enough and yet not too large to make a timber of
the proper size. When the tree was down it was
trimmed to the required length and cut off. The log
was rolled, or pried up, and placed on blocks a few
inches from the ground. It was then "laid off" in
order to get the finished timber to the best advantage.
A strong cord was immersed in Venetian Red water-
paint and the surplus paint raked off on the edge of
the can as the line was carefully withdrawn. At one
end of the log the line was held down to the point
where the side of the timber was to be formed, while
at the other end the line was held tight, then raised
up about a foot and snapped down, spattering a line
of red paint from end to end of the log. The workman, with a common chopping-ax, stood on the log
and beginning some two feet from the end chopped a
series of V-shaped vertical notches about two feet
apart, just into the line, then split off the long "jug-
gles" between the cuts. This left the surface more o
less rough, according to the grain of the timber. Agai
he chopped notches a few inches apart, until the whol
surface had been carefully cut down to the line. Nex
came the man with the broadax. He stood on th
ground at the side of the log and started at one en
chipping off the high spots and leaving a fairly fla
smooth surface. With only the line to start by, h
must use his eyes and plumb-bob to guide him in kee
ing the surface vertical. When two sides of the l
had been finished, it was turned on to one finished si
and two more lines made; then these sides were dress
in the same way as the first one. The weight of t
log was now reduced to perhaps half. This reducti
in weight was quite an item in hauling the timber
the location for the barn.

Aar

BROADAX

Aaron Frame, the head carpenter, probably had a drawing of the proposed building, but I am sure he had no such detailed drawings as would be used to-day. He seemed to have a mental picture of the plans and to remember everything that had to be done.

The barn was to be of the style known as a "bank barn." It was built against a bank, so that teams could be driven up the bank and over a short bridge on to the second or main floor of the building.

When the real construction work was started on the barn, the posts and other timber were cut to length, "boxed" to size, morticed, tennoned and drawbored for wooden pins. Such a number of mortices and tennons! What a quantity of braces! I think four bushels of pins were required. The pins were one inch in diameter by eight inches in length, shaved to an octagonal shape and pointed at one end. They were made from the toughest seasoned white oak fence rails.

The

The site had been graded by the farm plow and the surplus earth removed by a big wooden "scoop" made and loaned to us by grandfather John Bundy. This scoop was made of white oak boards with a steel cutting edge and iron straps over the bottom and sides to take the wear. Indeed, it was a "man's sized" tool, and with the oxen, Buck and Berry, a good-sized boy to drive and a strong man at each handle of the scoop, one had the nearest approach to the modern steam shovel which I have ever seen.

Stone for the piers was quarried on the farm. The piers were set and leveled off. Stone was so near the surface

OX YOKE

A GOOD SPECIMEN OF THE EARLY TYPE OF YOKE. THE "HUSKY" BOYS OF OUR ANCESTORS KNEW HOW TO CARRY THE YOKE WITH ONE BOW OUT AND PUT IT ON BERRY—IF HE COULD. THEN REMOVE THE OTHER BOW, HOLD UP THE OTHER END OF THE YOKE AND, SWINGING THE BOW, CALL OUT, "COME UNDER, BUCK, COME UNDER, BUCK," AND OLD BUCK—THE FAITHFUL OLD ANIMAL THAT HE WAS—WOULD OBEY. IN THE POSSESSION OF CLARENCE FAWCETT, CONCORDVILLE, PENNSYLVANIA.

surface of the ground that every pier rested firmly on solid bed-rock. After the frame was completed, the site graded and foundations in, we were ready for the "raising." Pike poles had been borrowed and prepared for use in raising the barn. There were no hoisting engines or windlass, nor do I remember a rope being used. The pike poles were small saplings about three inches in diameter with the small end encircled by an iron band and a sharp, thick iron spike set in the centre. The lower end was provided with a couple of stout cross-pins to serve as handles. The poles were of various lengths from about six to twenty-four feet long.

Now came the test of all the carpenters' plans and work. If a mistake had been made, it certainly would show when the frame was put together.

The stable frame was first assembled by "bents" or a series of posts; stringers, main floor sill, and braces running across the building. These were assembled and pinned together as they lay on the ground, with the base of the bent at its future place on the stone piers. When this bent was finished, the top was raised by hand and set on trussels; then raised again and set on short pike poles. These poles were raised higher and as the side of the bent rose, longer poles were used until the bent was lifted into a vertical position.

The most perfect individual work, as well as team work, was required. Each piece had to be carried from the yard to the building and put in place, then the complete bent raised by hand and held in place until it was secured. The timbers were so heavy that the united efforts of all were required to raise the frame. The other bents were assembled and raised in a similar

way

way, but as they neared the vertical, the ties, connecting them with the ones standing, were put in place and the pins "driven home," making all rigid and secure.

When the frame of the first story was finished, the main floor joists were put in place and covered by loose planks on which men could walk while assembling and raising the remaining bents.

The second story was higher than the first, but the timbers were not so large. The centre bent had a girder nine by thirteen inches spanning the width of the building so that the floor would be free from posts. This girder was supported in the centre by a king bolt and braces, which transferred the weight to the ends of the girder and to the side posts.

When all the bents were in place, the building was "up to the square," then the plates to support the lower ends of the rafters had to be erected. Last came the purlines with their posts and braces to support the centre of the long rafters. These two bents running across the top of the other bents were particularly hard to handle on account of their height and the absence of a floor underneath. By afternoon all the frame was in place and thoroughly rigid and secure.

Among Aaron Frame's helpers I remember his son Amasa, and William Hoyle. Joel Bailey, the neighborhood blacksmith, made, by hand, in his shop nearly a mile south on Sandy Ridge Road, the big king bolt, the long strap hinges and the lightning rods.

It is with pleasure I remember the willingness of th helpers and the neighborhood men to obey and carr out the instructions of the head carpenter. To th genuine workman, there was so great a pleasure i
carin

caring for and using his simple tools, that the work was easily and economically done and each piece finished exactly as desired.

Relatives and friends for miles around had been invited to the "raising." About one hundred were present. At such neighborhood affairs as raisings and huskings each one gave his services free. In fact, it was as much a social as a business affair. The spirit of kindness and friendliness was marked. With no daily paper, no telephone and little communication with the outside world there developed a neighborhood sociability that was delightful. Many of the wives and daughters came and helped to prepare and serve the excellent dinner. There were no tropical fruits nor after-dinner mints, but a substantial meal well cooked, which satisfied every want.

The barn was finished by fall and proved to be in every way satisfactory.

* * * * *

The following winter I remember father and mother sitting before the open fire, one First-day afternoon, laying out the floor plans of the house.

Building a country home in 1868 was quite a different matter from building a house today. So many parts of the house were made or prepared on the farm and comparatively few things bought. Father had been collecting from time to time yellow poplar for the door and window frames and inside trim and selecting white oak for the floors.

Stone was quarried from large sandstone rocks on the farm. The mason with his heavy stone pick dug a series of small holes a few inches apart and a couple of inches deep along the line where he wanted to split

the

the large stone. In each hole he placed a small iron wedge, then lightly hit each wedge in rapid succession until the stones split in two. When the stones were broken into the size required for the foundation wall, he knocked off the rough edges with a "stone hammer." They were then hauled to the location for the house. Here the stone placed on a trussel was laid off to the proper size. The surplus material was knocked off by chisel and mallet or picked away by a heavy stone pick. This rough surface was then finished by a "bush pick," which resembled an ax; the edge was made up

WEDGES FOR SPLITTING STONE

of a series of small square steel bars pointed as a pick. Soon the surface was quite smooth and the stone ready to be laid in the wall.

Samuel Williams, the head carpenter, first erected a shop where they made the door and window frames and most of the doors. The window sash, shingles, weatherboarding, newel post, stair rail and balusters were bought ready to be put in place.

When the cellar and foundation were done the sills were morticed and tennoned and put in place, the joists put on and the frame morticed, tennoned, braced, erected

erected and pinned in the regular way. The carpenters used a hand-boring machine, but often used the old-style auger for medium and large-sized holes. They ripped the mouldings out of poplar boards and planed them by hand. The flooring boards were made in the barn where a rip saw driven by horsepower had been set up. The white oak boards were ripped to about four or five inches in width. The saw was then removed and a head put on in its place to "tongue" and "groove" the edges of the boards. This saved much time and work, but the boards were not straight or of uniform width. However, most of the floors were laid of such boards and "straight nailed." When the boards varied too much in thickness, the projecting edges were "adzed off" and thus made less noticeable.

Lime for the plaster had been made in a little ravine on the north end of the farm. The limestone dug from the edge of the ravine was piled in a round heap in alternate layers with fire-wood and the whole pile covered with sod. Small holes were left for the entrance of air and the exit of smoke. The fires were started and sufficient heat produced to drive off the carbon dioxide and change the limestone to quick lime. Due to the slow and imperfect combustion, great quantities of smoke poured out, so I well understood the origin of the old saying, "smoking like a lime-kiln." After the wood had burned out and the pile cooled, the sod was cleared away and the pile of lime was ready to haul to the house. Sand for the mortar and plaster came from the lane where it had washed from the soft sandstone of the hills.

The linseed oil for the paint was bought "raw," then boiled in a large iron kettle back of the house. This made a "boiled" or quicker drying oil.

Each

Each room downstairs had an open coal grate. Upstairs there was no provision for heating the rooms, except an opening made in a chimney, so a stove could be used in case of sickness.

The raising of the house was a simple matter compared with the raising of the barn. So before the first cool winds of autumn came we were snugly settled in our new house.

Credit and respect were richly deserved by the men and women of that time for their kindness and for their willingness to help others, with no thought of recompense other than the joy of service.

One cannot but compare these carpenters and their helpers with the structural steel men as reported in the papers of today—the character of the men, the quality of the work, the great pleasure they took in whatever they did, to say nothing of the wages and hours. The buildings still speak for the good design and careful work. They are today plumb, level and square. The roofs do not "sag" nor do the doors "drag" after fifty-three years of service.

While some repairs and replacements have bee necessary to the outside, these buildings still stan monuments to honest materials and the conscientiou workmanship of those who built them.

Ridley Park,   WILLIAM HENRY STANTON.
Pennsylvania,
1921.

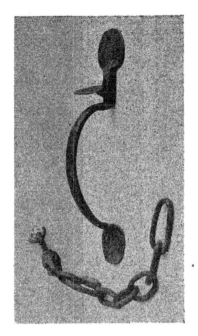

DOOR LATCH FROM THE HOUSE IN WHICH
JOSEPH AND MARY STANTON BEGAN HOUSE-
KEEPING.

BEHIND THIS LATCH ARE SOME BITS

OF WHAT THEY USED—OUR ANCESTORS—THE STANTONS

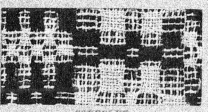

COVERLET
Woven by Charity Bundy

SAMPLES OF DRESSES WORN BY MARY P. STANTON
The center one is from her wedding dress of changeable silk,
later dyed black.

BOLTING CLOTH
Full size reproduction of the
cloth from the grist mill built
by Isaac Patten, or Captina Creek
and later known as Cole's Mill.

HOMESPUN LINEN
TOWEL
MADE BY MARIA (ENGLE)
BUNDY ABOUT 1848.

HOMESPUN LINEN
THREAD
MADE FROM HOME GROWN
FLAX BY ANNA (EDGER-
TON) BUNDY WHEN SHE
WAS A GIRL.

HOME WOVEN
FLANNEL
MADE BY DEBORAH H. B.
STANTON IN 1874. IN USE
FORTY-FIVE YEARS.

"HOMESPUN STUFF"
THIS PIECE OF CLOTH CAME FROM THE
FLANNER FAMILY OF STILLWATER
NEIGHBORHOOD ABOUT 1860. THE DATE
IT WAS WOVEN AND THE WEAVER'S NAME
ARE NOT KNOWN.

WHITE OAK VENEER
CUT FROM ONE OF THE LOGS OF ELI STANTON'S
"OLD LOG HOUSE."

N the oldest buildings hand-made nails or spikes were used. These were often made by the local blacksmith. The one shown is from the Ezekiel Bundy Barn, built about 1840, burned down 1880.

The small nail is from the first Joseph Stanton house. It appears to have been cut from sheet metal like our common cut nail, but the head is formed by "pinching" or contracting the wide part of the "blank" and making a tapered portion immediately under the head at right angles to the lower portion. Possibly the larger part was heated to form the head. Since the nail tapers two ways there is a tendency to split the timber any way the nail is "set" in reference to the grain of the wood.

The screw is from a door hinge in the same house. Note that it has no "point." It was necessary to have a hole the full depth of the screw. It is said a boy invented or suggested the "gimlet-pointed" screw now universally used.

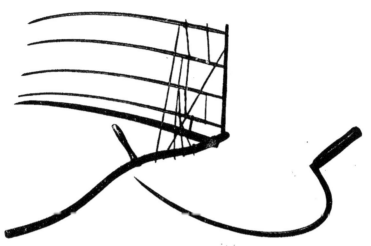

THE GRAIN CRADLE AND SICKLE

This sickle belonged to Chalkley Bundy and was used as early as 1840.

THE SICKLE

THE SICKLE HAS A FINE BEARDED EDGE TO BETTER CUT THE SMOOTH HARD STRAW OF WHEAT, OATS AND OTHER GRAIN. THE SICKLE WAS BEST ADAPTED TO THE ROUGH STUMPY GROUND OF THE PIONEER, WHERE THE GRAIN GREW VERY RANK ON NEW RICH GROUND AND OFTEN FELL DOWN AND TANGLED BADLY. THE REAPER GATHERED A SMALL QUANTITY OF GRAIN BY THRUSTING IN THE POINT AND SEPARATING A PORTION, THEN GRASPING IT BETWEEN THE THUMB AND MIDDLE FINGER SLIPPED THE SICKLE DOWN AND TOWARDS THE HEEL. THEN WITH A RAKING STROKE FROM HEEL TO POINT, CUT OFF THE HANDFUL, WHICH WAS LAID DOWN TO BE BOUND INTO SHEAVES. IT WAS AN OLD SAYING THAT "A BOY WOULD NOT LEARN TO REAP UNTIL HE HAD CUT HIS LITTLE FINGER."

WHERE THE GRAIN STOOD WELL AND WITH FAIRLY SMOOTH GROUND THE GRAIN "CRADLE" DID MUCH FASTER AND EASIER WORK. IT IS USED MUCH AS THE MOWING SCYTHE, EXCEPT AT THE END OF THE STROKE THE UPPER END OF THE "SNATH" OR HANDLE IS ELEVATED, BRINGING THE FINGERS HORIZONTAL ON THE STUBBLE; THEN A BACKWARD MOTION WITHDRAWS THEM, LEAVING THE CUT STALKS OF GRAIN THAT WERE GATHERED ON THE "FINGERS" LYING IN A ROW, READY TO BE RAKED TOGETHER AND BOUND INTO A SHEAF. THE FIRST HORSEPOWER "REAPERS" CARRIED A MAN TO RAKE THE SHEAF OFF, AS SOON AS ENOUGH GRAIN HAD BEEN CUT TO MAKE ONE. THEN CAME THE "DROPPERS," WHERE THE BUNCH OF GRAIN WAS DROPPED OFF BY THE FOOT, AND THEN THE SELF-BINDERS AND THE "HEADERS," WHICH CUT, THRASHED AND SACKED THE GRAIN AT ONE OPERATION. EACH TOOL FIT THE CONDITION. THE "HEADER" WOULD HAVE BEEN JUST AS USELESS TO THE PIONEER AS THE SICKLE IS NOW TO THE GREAT "WHEAT KINGS" OF THE NORTHWEST.

THE FLAIL

BEFORE THE DAYS OF POWER THRASHING MACHINES GRAIN, SUCH AS WHEAT, OATS, RYE, BARLEY, GRASS AND VEGETABLE SEEDS, WERE THRASHED FROM THE STRAW BY SPREADING IT IN A CIRCULAR ROW AND DRIVING HORSES OR OXEN OVER IT TO "TRAMP OUT" THE GRAIN. THE STRAW WAS FREQUENTLY TURNED SO AS TO BRING ALL PARTS UNDERNEATH THE ACTION OF THE FEET OF THE ANIMALS. SMALL AMOUNTS WERE ARRANGED IN A PILE AND THE GRAIN BEATEN OUT BY A "FLAIL" OR HINGED CLUB. THIS CONSISTED OF A CONVENIENT HANDLE ABOUT SIX FEET LONG; ATTACHED TO THE END BY A LEATHER STRAP OR STOUT CORD WAS THE FLAIL OR WOODEN CLUB ABOUT THREE FEET LONG AND O LARGER DIAMETER.

IN USE THE HANDLE WAS RAISED WITH A SWINGING MOTION AND DIRECTED DOWNWARD WITH A QUIC BLOW, SO THAT THE CLUB STRUCK THE STRAW HORIZONTALLY AND WITH SUCH FORCE THAT THE GRAI WAS QUICKLY BEATEN FROM THE STRAW. THE GRAIN WAS THEN SHAKEN FROM THE STRAW, SWEP UP AND SIFTED WITH A HAND-SIEVE TO REMOVE THE CHAFF.

THE GRAIN FLAIL IN USE

HAND-MADE HORSESHOE
NAILS
PROBABLY MADE BY JOEL BAILEY.

JOEL BAILEY'S BLACKSMITH SHOP

FROM ABOUT 1858 TO 1876 JOEL BAILEY CONDUCTED A BLACKSMITH AND WAGON SHOP ON, THE SANDY RIDGE ROAD NEARLY THREE MILES EAST FROM BARNESVILLE AND SERVED THAT SECTION OF THE COUNTRY.

HE WAS A SKILLED MECHANIC AND MADE MUCH OF THE HARDWARE AND MADE OR REPAIRED MANY OF THE TOOLS AND IMPLEMENTS USED IN THAT NEIGHBORHOOD BESIDE SHOEING THE HORSES.

HIS FARM ADJOINED THAT OF PETER SEARS' AND IS NOW OWNED BY EDWIN W. SEARS AND SISTER. MANY OF THESE ILLUSTRATIONS WERE MADE FROM ARTICLES IN THEIR HOME.

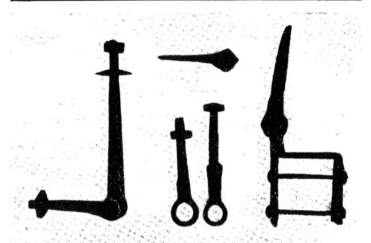

THESE SPECIMENS OF HAND-MADE HINGES WERE FOUND IN THE BLACKSMITH SHOP
OF JOEL BAILEY AND WERE PROBABLY MADE BY HIM. THEY REPRESENT THE TYPE
OF HARDWARE GENERALLY USED BY THE EARLY SETTLERS.

HAND-MADE NAILS

FROM THE JOEL BAILEY BLACKSMITH SHOP. THE
BUILDING WAS ERECTED ABOUT 1855 AND TORN
DOWN IN 1921.

HAND-MADE WOODEN RAKE AND FORK

Used in binding and thrashing grain.

GRAIN FLAIL

Hanging on the road door of Joel Bailey's shop. The door appears to be the original one and is more than fifty years old.

FORKING THE STRAW

In thrashing.

A PAIR OF HAND-MADE HAMES

PASTERN LOCK

In the days of horse thieves such a lock was put on a horse's foot and was not uncomfortable to the horse while in the stable, but the horse soon became lame if it walked any distance.

JOSEPH AND MARY (HODGIN) STANTON'S QUILTING FRAME

**QUILT PIECED BY
MARY P. BUNDY**

Now owned by William H. Stanton.

THE QUILTING

Elizabeth Stanton Bailey says that Joseph and Mary (Hodgin) Stanton's Quilting Frame, shown opposite, was made probably by Edwin Wilson, and that she remembers it in 1856 or '57. After the death of Joseph Stanton it became the property of Nathan and Anna Stanton Bundy. It was often loaned to Eli and Mary P. Stanton, and later given to Lindley P. and Elizabeth Stanton Bailey, who now have it in their home. The quilt shown was pieced recently by Elizabeth Stanton Bailey.

IN mid-summer, '68, Father said to Mother that in a few days the carpenters would be ready to raise the frame of the new house and that some extra help would be needed; so it was arranged that they should invite a few relatives and friends—the men would help with the raising and their wives and daughters would help prepare and serve the dinner—a nice combination of business and pleasure. But as our good neighbor "Betty" Hall on the next farm south says; "It was not idle pleasure, to sit with empty hands was a disgrace; every one worked, and while we talked and laughed we had a quilt in the quilting frame. The floor

249

BEDSPREAD

WHITE MUSLIN KNOTTED WITH COTTON IN AN
ALL-OVER DESIGN. USED IN THE HOME OF
ELI STANTON IN THE SIXTIES. MADE BY
RUTH (PATTEN) BUNDY.
NOW IN THE POSSESSION OF SARAH B.
(STANTON) HALL.

floor in the sitting-room was covered with a rag carpet
and there were chairs, painted to represent rosewood
and striped in yellow and stenciled with gold. The
soft wind from the south and the songs of the birds
came in through the open door. There we sat, some
on one side of the frame, some on the other, and
with the left hand under the quilt and the right on
top we stitched in the rope and shell pattern which
had been laid out and which was carried along from
one strip to the next. How the needles clicked on
the thimble! and Mary Doudna talked just as short
and fast and laughed just as cheery as she has done
for the fifty odd years since that day. Such a good
time we had! Every one knew every one else and
meetings were not so frequent but that there was
much to be talked about that was new and of interest.
There were the children, a subject never old; dress-
making, new dishes and new butters and jellies for
the almost endless cooking and preserving and maybe
just a dash of kindly gossip to provide a little spice
for

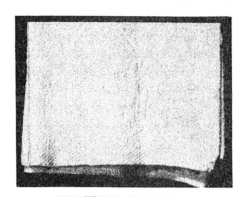

OLD-STYLE BEDSPREAD

MADE WARM BY A LAYER OF COTTON BETWEEN THE TWO
COVERS, WHICH WERE QUILTED IN MANY AND VARIED DE-
SIGNS. A STYLE QUITE COMMON IN PIONEER DAYS.

for an occasion so pleasant that it was dinner time almost before we knew it." Mother was not well— had not been for some years, so the help was even more generous than was usual and was greatly appreciated. Aunt Lizzie was busy in the big log kitchen helping "Lib" Duvall, our "girl," thus taking the burden from Mother, and with her helpers she set the dinner tables together and arranged to seat all the men at once. It was a wholesome, jolly company that sat down that day, and if "a good appetite is the best of sauce" the dinner must have tasted very good to all.

After this hearty meal the men went back to work and the women reset the table and had dinner themselves. Then more quilting, and by late afternoon the house was raised, the quilt finished and all with the most delightful and stimulating social intercourse.

Such kindly neighbors and such sincere friends were a real blessing to us, and we valued them very highly.

So

So far as we know not one of the men who helped us that day is living now, and only three of the women —Aunt Lizzie (Stanton) Bailey, "Aunt" Betty Hall and "Aunt" Mary Doudna.

Ridley Park,   WILLIAM HENRY STANTON.
Pennsylvania,
1921.

EIGHT-POINT STAR QUILT

PIECED BY ELIZABETH STANTON BAILEY.
DARK PART MADE OF HER MOTHER'S LAST
DRESS, LIGHT PART MADE OF THE LAST DRESS
HER FATHER BOUGHT FOR HER.

OLD LOG PUMP
LOCATED IN LOYDSVILLE, OHIO.

PUMP MAKING IN THE EARLY DAYS

A HOUSE, in the early days, was always located near a spring, because this spring was the sole source of water for the house and from this supply the water must be carried. Somewhat later wells were dug close to the houses and were considered great conveniences. The

water

water was at first drawn from these wells by means of a sweep and bucket. Later this method was replaced by a wooden pump. I remember such a pump being made at the home of my father, Eli Stanton.

Alpheus Blowers came in a one-horse wagon to build our pump, bringing with him a big chest of tools, high trestles and long iron boring rods. The upper part of the pump was made from a mulberry log cut in our own woods, hewn to size and to an octagonal shape. This was placed on trestles four feet high and secured in place by angle-iron hooks driven in the trestle and the log. Small iron pins were driven in the top of the log at each end to sight by while boring. A third trestle with an adjustable bearing was used to support the outer end of the boring rod. A hole two inches in diameter was bored through the center of the log. This hole was reamed out to about three and a half inches from the top to where the bucket, or the lower valve, was to be set. The lower end was reamed to about five inches, then the end of the next lower section was shaved down to fit this hole. A heavy iron band encircled the upper section to prevent splitting, when put into the well, and the sections were driven tightly together.

The augers were of shell type, the smaller one had a pointed thread or screw to pull it in, as with the common auger. The other end of the boring rod had an auger handle about four feet long. All the boring was done by hand.

The pumpmaker brought with him the ironwork for the handle of the pump and made and fitted it to the pump. He also made the piston or sucker, with its valve, and the lower valve. The bucket had an iron

bale

bale with which to pull it up when necessary. It was served with a few layers of small twine and covered with a soft wax to make the joint water tight.

Quite a little artistic taste was displayed in the design of the pump, with its top cover, handle, spout and necessary ironwork. It was large and rather heavy, but was a very reliable pump which gave good service for many years.

W. H. S.

BROOM-CORN COMB

Used to scrape the seed from broom-corn when preparing it for use.

THE REEL

THE YARN AFTER BEING SPUN WAS WOUND INTO SKEINS ON
THIS REEL. FORMERLY IN THE HOME OF
ROBERT H. SMITH, SR.

RECOLLECTIONS OF SPINNING AND WEAVING

PINNING Wool. "White as wool" is a comparison that surely could not have been meant for wool that had not been subjected to a cleansing process. In the days when we prepared the wool for spinning we used to think the quantity of oil in it was almost limitless. It was necessary to wash it in two sudsey waters and rinse it through as many clear waters before spreading it on boards or short grass in the sunshine to dry. After it was dry we picked it apart by hand in order to dislodge any bits of litter or burs that might be lodged in the fibers.

The

WOOL CARDS
USED BY PETER SEARS' FAMILY ABOUT 1850.

The next step in the preparation of the wool was the carding. This was done by hand with two wool cards. These cards had rows of steel wires set in a wooden or leather back and somewhat resembled the currycomb of the present day. They were held by means of handles at the sides; one of them was taken in the left hand, a piece of wool placed on it, and with the right hand the other card was drawn down over it repeatedly until the strands of the wool were straightened out. The wool was then lightly rolled into rolls an inch or slightly more in diameter. Later on the carding mills took the labor of carding out of the homes, the wool being sent to the mills and there made into rolls. These rolls were longer and smaller in diameter than the home-carded rolls.

After the carding came the spinning. The spinning wheel was constructed with a long, low standard supporting at one end the great wheel; at the other end the head, with a spindle. Spinning was very interesting; it required close attention to learn to pull just enough on to the roll with the left hand and at the same time turn the great wheel with the right hand just enough to make an evenly twisted thread of wool.
The

THE LARGE—OR WOOL—SPINNING WHEEL

MARY (HODGIN) STANTON HAD A WHEEL SIMILAR TO THIS ONE ON WHICH SHE SPUN THE
YARN FOR THE FAMILY STOCKINGS. THE "FINGER" SHOWN BELOW WAS USED BY HER TO
"SPIN" THE WHEEL AND SAVE HER HAND.
WHEEL FROM THE DANIEL STANTON HOME.
FINGER OWNED BY ELIZABETH STANTON BAILEY.

The spinner took hold of the roll about five or six
inches from the spindle and stepped backward, pulling out the roll and turning the wheel at the same time.
As the great wheel turned it made the spindle revolve
very rapidly and the wool, being held out at an angle
from the end of the spindle, slipped off and was twisted
tightly.

tightly. After a length had been twisted the spinner held the roll at right angles to the center of the spindle, turned the wheel, and the woolen thread was wound on to the spindle. Then another length was spun, until there remained only two or three inches on the roll attached to the thread spun, then the spinner placed an end of another roll on it and the fibers of the wool readily twisted together. Thus were the rolls added and a continuous thread produced until the spindle was filled with thread. The yarn was then reeled from the spindle on to a clock reel. This reel had a six-spoke wheel, not with a rim, but with six pegs on which to wind the yarn, and was so constructed that at every fortieth revolution it clicked for the purpose of measuring one tie or knot. After a thread was looped around these forty threads another knot was begun. The practice was to reel four of these knots on to the reel and make a loop with a strand of yarn to avoid the tangling of the threads. This was then called a skein of yarn and was slipped off the reel and another skein begun; and so on until the spinning was done. If the yarn was intended for blankets or for cloth for clothing, it was now ready to be prepared for the loom; if for knitting or crocheting, something more was necessary.

The coloring was done either in the wool or when the yarn was in the skein.

Spinning Flax. The spinning of flax was an important branch of domestic industry. The flax or lint was procured from the fibers of the inner bark of the flax plant and was spun on a small wheel. This wheel had an attachment for holding the distaff, upon which a bundle a bundle of flax was loosely wound, and was operated by foot in order that the spinner might have both hands free to manage the flax fiber as it came from the distaff.

After spinning a fine thread we reeled it from the spindle; then, placing two skeins of single thread on the swifts and taking the ends of the skeins, we wound them two-double into balls which were then twisted together on the spindle of the wheel. This was our linen sewing thread used to make garments from home-woven woolen and linen material, and all these garments were made by hand, since we had no sewing machines. The ability to spin the fine flax fiber into sewing thread and thread to be used in fine linen web was considered an accomplishment.

DISTAFF

Weaving. Since cloth-ing is one of the first ne-cessities of civilized man the loom for weaving must have been one of his earl-iest inventions. The loom we used consisted of a square wooden frame, supported on four posts, to which the working parts of the loom were attached. The center beam at the back was the warp or chain beam and beneath this was the wooden cylinder on which the warp or chain was wound.

SMALL SPINNING WHEEL

THIS TYPE OF WHEEL WAS USED TO SPIN FLAX FOR SEWING THREAD AND FOR LINEN CLOTH. A WOMAN WAS CONSIDERED EXPERT WHEN SHE COULD SPIN FINE, EVEN SEWING THREAD. FROM THE DANIEL STANTON HOME.

DETAIL OF HAND-LOOM
SHOWING BATTEN, REED, AND THE SHUTTLE READY TO BE THROWN.

HAND-LOOM
SHUTTLES.
THE ONE WITH
SMALL OPEN-

ING FOR CLOTH,
THE LARGE FOR
CARPET.

HAND-LOOM
USED FOR WEAVING RAG CARPET. LOCATED IN CHESTER, PENNSYLVANIA.

REED FOR HAND-LOOM

The reed carried the warp or chain and was used to beat up the woof or filling.
This reed was very fine and carried 640 threads. The coarsest reed carries 300.
In use about 1865.
Owned by Pharaby Bundy Sears.

wound. The beam extending across this a little below the center was the breast beam which supported the weaver. Beneath this was the cylinder upon which the web was wound as it was woven. The top of the frame supported the batten, which was attached to a movable horizontal bar by two vertical pieces, one at each end. Another bar across the top of the frame supported a set of pulleys and the heddles. The heddles consisted of two frames from which cords were attached to the loop or eye of each thread in the warp; usually each alternate thread was attached to one heddle and the other thread to the other heddle. The heddles were connected by cords, which passed over the pulley in the top of the frame, with treadles operated by the weaver. The batten contained a reed through which the threads of the warp passed. The weaver pressed on the treadle and raised the alternate threads of the warp while depressing the others, thus forming an angle for the thread of the weft or filling, which was placed in position by throwing the shuttle; the other treadle was then pressed by the foot and the thread "beaten up" as the batten struck it.

Weaving consisted of three operations: (1) setting the warp threads for the web; (2) working the weft threads into the warp, to and fro, by means of a shuttle; and

and (3) beating up weft threads by means of the batten.

Cloth was woven for household needs and for clothing for the family: blankets and both single and double coverlets for bedding; cassinette and jeans for the men and boys, flannel and linsey for the women and girls.

The one-strand flax thread spun on the small foot-operated wheel was woven on the hand-loom into linen material for clothing, sheets, table linen, towels, pocket handkerchiefs, etc. The coarse part of the flax, called tow, was used in making material for bagging, matting, etc.

Truly, a few score years ago the term "busy housewife" was not a mere name given by custom, but a title faithfully earned by long hours of painstaking toil.

Rush City,
Minnesota,
1921.

Debrah H. B. Stanton

SPINNING JENNY
In the home of Lydia P. Webster, Quarer City, Ohio.

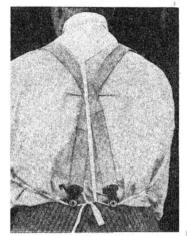

DICKY—A CAMOUFLAGE

IN THE EARLY DAYS, WHEN LINEN WAS SCARCE
AND EXPENSIVE, SOME OF OUR ANCESTORS USED
THIS FALSE WHITE SHIRT-FRONT.
IN THE POSSESSION OF MARY B. NIBLOCK.

LINEN TOWEL
HAND-WOVEN BY PHARABY BUNDY SEARS.

LINEN SOCK
HOMESPUN AND HAND-KNIT.
MADE IN THE FAMILY OF PETER SEARS.

MAKING COLORED STOCKINGS

I N THE days of homespun stuffs the dyeing of the fabrics was also done at home. The process became the periodic forerunner of the knitting season. After the wool had been picked over carefully and the boys had brought some walnut bark to the house, mother would put a layer of bark, then a layer of wool into a half-barrel. When the barrel was almost full, she would cover the wool and bark with water, weight down the cover, and allow the barrel to stand for several days. The wool was then wrung out and aired, and, if it was not dark enough in color, it was put back in the dye and the operation repeated. When the wool was dyed to the desired shade, it was washed and dried and then sent to be carded and made into rolls. When this wool came home mother would spin it into yarn ready to be knitted into stockings for us. I remember many times lying on the floor listening to the hum of mother's spinning wheel.

Tacoma,
Ohio,
1921.

ELIZABETH STANTON BAILEY.

FIVE-INCH TELESCOPE AND
EQUATORIAL MOUNTING
Made by William H. Stanton in 1901.

WILLIAM HENRY STANTON

WILLIAM HENRY STANTON, son of Eli and Mary P. (Bundy) Stanton, spent his boyhood years on a farm two miles east of Barnesville, Ohio. His father was a good farmer and desired that his son should follow the same occupation. But William at a very early age showed a decided inclination for mechanical work and was never so happy as when using tools or constructing machinery. His father's toolshed was his workshop, in which much of his time was spent, often to the detriment of the farm work. With a few crude tools and material that he was able to pick up about the place he constructed a small steam engine and boiler that developed sufficient power to run small machines.

I, an interested uncle, felt discouraged about the boy's future, thinking all farm boys should show an inclination for farm work or if they did not, there was little chance for success in any line. But his father, a wise, foreseeing man, felt he should be allowed to do the work for which he had a natural liking and talent.

When

When William was through the Friends' Primary School and had had three terms at Friends' Boarding School, he worked a few months in the blacksmith shop of Joseph Kennard, then was bound apprentice for two years at the machinist's trade with Charles Kugler, of Barnesville, Ohio. Here he was very happy, for

TURNING LATHE

THE IRON TURNING LATHE WHICH WAS IN THE SHOP OF CHARLES KUGLER IN BARNESVILLE AND HIS SUCCESSORS FOR SO MANY YEARS WAS PURCHASED BY WILLIAM F. GIBBONS A FEW YEARS AGO, AND HAS BEEN CHANGED TO A WOOD LATHE. IT HAD THE USUAL SIMPLE HEAD AND TAIL STOCK AND WAS BACK-GEARED. THIS WAS THE ONE ON WHICH WILLIAM H. STANTON SERVED HIS APPRENTICESHIP IN 1878 AND 1879. THE IRONWORK WAS MADE PROBABLY BEFORE 1870 BY THE BLANDY MACHINE COMPANY, ZANESVILLE, OHIO. "THE SHEARS" WERE MADE IN BARNESVILLE AND ARE ABOUT 6 X 16 INCHES IN SECTION AND 16 FEET LONG AND ARE OF SOLID BLACK WALNUT. A PORTABLE SIDE-REST WAS USED, HELD IN PLACE BY A STIRRUP EXTENDING OVER THE BASE AND BELOW THE SHEARS AND FASTENED BY A SUITABLE BLOCK AND LARGE WOODEN WEDGE. THE REST WAS SET PARALLEL BY GUESS AND AFTER A TRIAL WAS KNOCKED A LITTLE RIGHT OR LEFT UNTIL THE TOOL TURNED PARALLEL WITH THE CENTERS. A HANDY TOOL IN ITS DAY, BUT NO MATCH FOR THE MODERN HIGH-SPEED LATHE.

TURNING LATHE FOR WOOD

"I WORKED ON THIS LATHE WHILE BOUND APPRENTICE TO CHARLES KUGLER TO LEARN THE MACHINIST'S TRADE IN 1878 AND 1879. IT STILL RUNS AND LOOKS AS GOOD AS IT DID FORTY YEARS AGO. I HAVE SELDOM ENJOYED ANY WORK MORE THAN OPERATING THIS LATHE. IT WAS A RARE PLEASURE TO CUT AWAY THE MATERIAL AND SHAPE THE GRACEFUL CURVES, TO MAKE THE SURFACE SMOOTH, TO POLISH AND BRING OUT THE BEAUTY OF THE GRAIN AND COLOR OF THE WOOD. I TURNED EVERYTHING—CHESSMEN, BASEBALL BATS, NEWEL POSTS, STONE CUTTERS' MALLETS, OR WHATEVER WAS WANTED. IT WAS REAL FUN TO LEARN A TRADE."—W. H. S.

for he had a splendid opportunity to learn about the various metals, woods and other materials used and about the different kinds of machines made and repaired in the shop.

When the two years had passed he felt he wanted greater opportunities to develop his talent, so applied for a position in the shop of James W. Queen and Company, of Philadelphia, manufacturers of optical, mathematical and philosophical instruments. When he started there, in 1880, he found the work lighter than the work in the machine shop but much more accurate and intricate, so he had a chance to exercise all the skill he possessed. He made it a rule to try to understand the principle and use of every instrument he made or repaired. He realized that future efficiency depended on close application and intelligent work, so naturally he made rapid progress and won the esteem of the heads of departments and of the members of the firm. While there he made for Professor George F. Barker, of the University of Pennsylvania,

Pennsylvania, the first secondary electric battery made in the United States and the first Toepler-Holtz induction electric machine made in the country.

William attended the Franklin Institute night school but realized he needed a better education and, as an opportunity was presented, he entered De Pauw University, Greencastle, Indiana. He started in the preparatory school and earned money to pay his way by teaching Physics and by making apparatus for the University. At various times he traveled with Professor John B. De Motte and operated the instruments and apparatus used in his scientific lectures. After spending about four years at De Pauw he felt it would be an advantage to add some studies at a technical school. Dr. W. V. Brown, of the University, kindly offered to help him prepare to enter Rose Polytechnic Institute at Terre Haute in the fall of 1889. He greatly enjoyed the work at this school as well as the care of the scientific instruments of which he was in charge. He made rapid progress but was soon offered a position as manager of a plant for the manufacture of silicate of soda established by the Philadelphia Quartz Company in Anderson, Indiana. This was probably as good an offer as he could expect to receive after completing the course at the technical school, so he left his school work and took the position.

When saying good-bye to some of his professors, C. A. Waldo, Professor of Mathematics, said to him, "Now, Stanton, when you get out, don't just read a little here and there, have a hobby, take up one line of reading or study and follow the subject until you feel you are through with it; then take up another." This advice William remembered and followed. He

now

now admits he has been interested in sixteen different subjects:

Landscape Gardening	Electric Power
Bees	Wage Systems
Weather	Geology
Natural Gas	Earth and Rock Ex-
Coal Mining	cavation
Smokeless Combustion	South American Trip
Astronomy	and Spanish
Corporation Law	Finance
American Law	Family History

As manager of the Anderson Plant of the Quartz Company he keenly felt the responsibility he had assumed, but with his determination to win he placed the plant on a profitable basis from the first. The success of this plant induced the Company to build other plants in different parts of the United States, for most of which he had the planning and oversight in building. In 1904 he was put on the executive board of the Company and in 1913 made General Manager of all their plants, which are now located at Anderson, Indiana; Buffalo, New York; Chester, Pennsylvania; Kansas City, Kansas; and Rahway, New Jersey.

His duties as General Manager required him to live near the executive office in Philadelphia, so in 1913 he moved to Ridley Park and built the home where he now lives. In 1919 he was made Vice-President of the Company. After thirty years of service devoted to their interests he gave up active duties and now holds a position as Consultant to the Company. All through this period of years it seemed he had no thought of pecuniary compensation, but rather a nobler incentive—"What can I do to advance the interest

WILLIAM H. STANTON'S HOME
ANDERSON, INDIANA
BUILT 1892.

interest of the Quartz Company?" This certainly
would be a profitable attitude for all ambitious young
men to assume.

William has ever been interested in movements for
the uplift of the community in which he lived. While
in Anderson he was made President of the Maplewood
Cemetery Association. He was interested in laying
out the driveways, locating the trees and shrubbery
with pleasing results. He was also made president
of the Union Coal Company, which opened a shaft
mine

WILLIAM H. STANTON'S HOME
RIDLEY PARK, PENNSYLVANIA
BUILT 1913.

LITTLE STEAM ENGINE
MADE BY WILLIAM H. STANTON WHEN FIFTEEN YEARS OLD.

FOOT-POWER TURNING LATHE FOR WOOD
IT WAS ON THIS LATHE THAT WILLIAM H. STANTON FIRST PRACTISED TURNING AND
MADE MOST OF THE PARTS OF THE LITTLE STEAM ENGINE.
THE LATHE WAS MADE BY ISAAC PATTEN, THE BUILDER OF COLE'S MILL. IT HAS
BEEN OWNED BY JOHN BUNDY, ELI STANTON, DANIEL STANTON, WILLIS AND LEWIS
BUNDY AND IS NOW OWNED BY FRED R. BUNDY.

THE FALL BUTCHERING

LONG in the early winter when the ground froze 'most every night and we had had some snow, when the pigs began to walk slow and waddle from eating too much corn, then it was time to "kill hogs" and lay in the year's supply of pork. So the men hauled a couple of loads of big firewood to the barn lot and made a "log heap"; big logs were placed on two sides and smaller stuff between; scattered through the center was a small load of soft sandstones and heavy scraps of iron; kindling was prepared, but kept in the dry. The big hogshead was brought from the cellar and the hoops tightened. A sled was placed convenient to the fire and the hogshead set in a hole in the ground and leaned against the sled. The hogshead was now filled nearly full of water. Tomorrow was to be a great day.

Long before daylight there was an unusual stir about the house—small boys felt that they were needed, then if ever, to see what was going on. Kindling was brought out and placed in the windward end of the pile; then a match—and the smoke began to curl up

up and soon the blaze, then the whole pile caught fire—
how it lighted up the yard! Such popping and snap
ping! Great sparks were shot out—sometimes in our
direction, and smaller ones went up with the smoke
and drifted off across the fields. There were weird and
flickering shadows all around and so much heat that
we had to back off. Daylight was coming and the
fire seemed to lose itself in the day.

Then father came with his rifle—with the bullet
pouch and powder horn slung across his shoulder. He
scattered a little shelled corn in the lot where the hogs
were, and as a pig faced him there was a
sharp crack of the rifle and the pig dropped
with a little depression between his eyes.
No disturbance, no pain—only arrested
development. Then father measured out
a little powder, poured it into the gun,
then a patch and bullet, and he set the
rifle by his side and under the left arm
so he could hold the hickory ramrod with
both hands and push the bullet down;
then a "cap" from the little, round, green
paper box, a little more corn and—the
same result. When enough pigs for the
year's supply had been selected they
were brought up to the fire, which had
burned down, leaving the stones and iron
red hot. Now the big two-hand tongs
from the wash-house fireplace—and the
hot stones were soon transferred to the
hogshead and the water heated to near
boiling. A neighbor or two had come in—
and now the real business began.

Two

Two of the men grabbed a pig by the hind feet—the only convenient handles which nature put on a hog—and soused him in the bath, head foremost, up and down, rolled him around and then out, turned him end for end—and launched him stern foremost and rolled him over, then out on the sled, and such a scraping, scouring, scrubbing, washing and rinsing he got, that his mother would not have known him. Now they slipped a stout pointed club between his legs and hung him on a strong pole so he swung free from the ground. Here he "lost heart" and liver, too; his stomach was "all upset" and he changed from pig to pork.

The surplus fat was collected, cut in small pieces and heated in a big iron kettle over a wood fire, then ladled into a sack and squeezed between great wooden pincers or clamps, and the lard caught in big stoneware jars and set away to cool. The best of the cracklings were saved and ground in the sausage grinder to make "crackling corn bread." The other cracklings, some of the livers and the various scraps were boiled up later with small potatoes and corn meal and made "scrapple" for the chickens which, they confided to me, tasted mighty good on a cold morning.

There were spareribs and back bones cut out and our good neighbors and friends were remembered with a "mess" of them or a heart, some sausage, etc., which was very real proof of friendship.

Next day the hams, shoulders and sides were trimmed up and the scraps worked into sausage; only the best of the side meat was saved, the rest worked into lard and sausage. Then came the serious discussion as to how much salt and pepper and sage should be mixed
with

with the sausage before grinding; it ended by guessing that about so much would be right, and it was.

The meat was now rubbed over with salt and stacked up to be smoked in the early spring, unless some unreliable citizen with more appetite than moral character reduced our supply. Some of the sausage was fried, packed in crocks and covered with melted lard to preserve it for later use.

In the spring when the sun shone warm and the snow melted rapidly on the roofs it was time to smoke the meat. You remember the little house, the little old stove in the center, no pipe to it, the hickory wood-fire that burned slowly and smoked, how it made the eyes smart, how you held your breath? And don't you remember the sweet aroma of the smoke-house, or is it the thought of smoked country ham and gravy, light-cakes and the delightful visits when our friends came to see us and stayed to supper, that we remember?

WILLIAM HENRY STANTON.

Ridley Park,
Pennsylvania,
1921.

SAUSAGE GRINDER
ONE OF THE EARLY-DAY TYPE. USED BY DANIEL STANTON.

UP TO TOWN WITH A LOAD OF GRIST

NE day Mother said the flour in the bin was getting low and Father said he guessed he would have to take a grist to mill, but added, "I would rather go to mill than go for the doctor." They said I could go along if I would be a good boy.

A little later, in the barn, we picked out five two-bushel grain sacks that were strong and had not been snagged nor eaten by the mice. Then we went to the middle bin in the granary on the south side of the barn—the wheat bin where I had caught many a mouse by setting a little "figure-4" trap under a brick —and there, with the old black half-bushel measure, we put ten bushels of real Red Mediterranean wheat into the sacks. My job was to hold the sack so Father could hold the half-bushel on his knee, catch a side with each hand and pour the wheat in while I held out the front of the bag. When the sacks were filled some straw was spread on the bottom of the bed of the wagon which stood on the same floor. The sacks, two bushels of wheat in each, were shouldered and carried to the wagon. That was a "man's job."

Two

Two of our horses, Trim and Nellie, were harnessed and then we went to the house to "wash up and dress." After this was done, I did not feel so comfortable, but it had to be. We now backed the wagon out, hitched up and were off. Mother had some butter and several dozen eggs to "take to the store." These had to be watched and the egg basket held in hand when the road was very rough, for there were no springs to the wagon.

Our progress was not rapid, for Father said, "Don't trot the team down hill, it is too hard on the horses' front feet." On the level there was frequently deep sand and the hills were so stony and steep that a slow walk was "high speed."

Out of our lane and on to the Sandy Ridge Road there was always plenty to see. We did not travel this road very often, so everything was new and interesting. The rail fences seemed so high, the cuts so deep. The birds, the trees and an occasional ground squirrel were all of interest and suggested plenty of questions. Yes, some of Hosea Doudna's apples were getting ripe—Aaron Frame was plowing that hill field for wheat. We could see away across country —Grandfather Bundy was plowing, too; the woods were beginning to color a little, soon frost and cool nights would come. They were threshing at Robert H. Smith's. We met and spoke to Dr. J. W. Judkins and wondered who was sick out our way. Barclay Smith was plowing, too, and the ground seemed dry and lumpy. I hoped the train would come along while we were in sight of the track, so I could see it, but no such good luck. Soon we passed the "Brick Kiln,"

Kiln," a never-ending source of interest to me—how they dug the clay, mixed the mud by horse power, molded the brick, dried them in the yard, "hacked them up," covered them with "boards" to keep off the rain; then set them in the kiln, made the flues for the fire, burned them and at last opened the kiln. Here was the spot where Dr. Kemp brought some of his friends who wanted to see a "bat's nest."

Near town the rail fences were replaced by board ones along the road and we could read "S. B. Piper & Brother, Dry Goods, Hats and Caps, Boots and Shoes"—"H. Vance, Groceries and Queensware." At the east end of Main Street we passed the Masonic Hall with the queer sign, a big G with compass and square, over the door.

Once in town, the team began to put on city airs and grew a little "skittish," hunting for something at which "to scare" and sometimes succeeding. There was the office sign, "Drs. Williams and Judkins, Physicians and Surgeons"—Francis Davis lived there —Ely's Drug Store—The Bank—the Frazier House— the Enterprise Office—Reed's Shoe Store—Bradfields —then we turned down Chestnut Street, stopped at the railroad crossing to listen for "the cars," passed Reed's Tan Yard, that did not always smell good, saw the great piles of tan-bark; then "Smoky Row"— the Darkey Street—and there on the left was Hilles' Mill. It was a big square, four-story frame building with gambrel roof and a shed at the back with a square brick smoke-stack. We could hear the muffled rumble of the heavy gearing and see the clouds of black smoke roll away. There was a big beam projecting

from

from the top of the mill with a rope hanging down, and big double or "Dutch doors" on each floor.

We drove up under the rope and stopped. "Skip" Hilles came to an upper door, with his cheery, "Good morning, Eli." He pulled on a rope with his left hand and the rope from the beam, with chain and hook on the end, came slowly down. Father hooked the chain around a sack, "Skip" pulled on the other rope and the sack was taken up to the floor above. When a couple of sacks had been taken up, there was some delay, but soon "Skip" appeared again and asked father if he wished to sell the wheat, saying that he would exchange in flour, giving him flour from wheat just as good, and pay us a dollar ten for this when the regular price was a dollar. He said he wanted to sell our wheat for seed, because it was so plump and clean—no weed seeds, rye nor cockle. The exchange was accordingly made and the flour filled into our sacks and we did not have to wait for the wheat to be ground. Generally from the wheat that was delivered, the miller took out one-eighth toll for grinding, the remainder being ground and the flour put into sacks. The middlings and bran were put into other sacks and were taken home for stock feed along with the flour when the grist was called for a week later.

How well I remember "Skip"—short, stocky, dark hair, full beard of moderate length. He generally wore a neat, closefitting cap. He was always quiet, but inspired confidence—a pleasant man of known integrity with whom it was a satisfaction to have business dealings.

After

After we left the mill and drove up town, the team was tied to a hitch-rack in front of the store and the butter and eggs were traded for sugar and coffee and sometimes for goods to make clothing. I remember the stores had very small show-windows, and the inside was equally plain; some shelving along the wall, counters with inclined front, barrels of crackers, sugar, coffee, molasses and vinegar. All of the articles had to be weighed or measured out for you and the dry stuff wrapped in heavy brown paper, and liquids filled into vessels brought by the customer.

After we were through at the store, Father said, "Let's get the team and go home." This pleased me for my shoes pinched and my collar chafed my neck, and I was hungry and thirsty and wanted a drink from the big pump on the north porch.

And Now After Fifty Years—

I remember Father often took me to places of interest when we went to town, whether because he wanted to go or because he knew I wanted to see the machinery, I do not know.

One time we went to the McCartney Grist Mill and down into the engine room where there were four cylinder boilers being fired by two very black colored men. It was a hot day and this was a hot room full of noise and hissing steam. The fire doors under the boilers were red hot from such a furious fire in the furnace. I was glad to get out.

At another time we went to Watts' Foundry and Saw Mill. Their engine was one of the old type installed about 1850. The cylinder of this engine was seven inches in diameter with a thirty-six inch stroke. The

The connecting rod was made of wood, diamond shaped in section, with iron straps bolted on the edges, and ended in journal boxes at each end which were provided with gib and cotter. The steam chest was set off to the side of the cylinder with pipes running to the cylinder. This great length of port wasted much steam.

Many will remember the old woolen mill near Arch and Church Streets and its unusual engine exhaust. The engine was of similar design to the one at Watts, but the slide valve was not set properly and leaked very badly, so that instead of giving regular short puffs it let out great long and short wheezes that could be heard all over the neighborhood. They used two or three cylinder boilers and burned great quantities of coal.

The engine at Charles Kugler's Machine Shop— The Belmont Machine Works—was of much the same design, but had been rebuilt and was in good repair. The cylinder was, I think, eight by twenty-four inches. The piston was packed with platted hemp. I later on had two years' experience with it. I was chief engineer, oiler and fireman, too; when there was heavy work to be done, I would add an extra ring of hemp or screw up the "follower ring" as was needed. This was done by a long socket wrench and the square nut on the end of the piston rod. You can guess there was some "clearance," perhaps several inches. The cylinder head was held on by four one-inch left-hand thread bolts. The nuts were hand-forged. I was told of an old engine in the neighborhood tha wasted so much steam the boiler could not suppl enough, so they bolted a block of wood, eight inche thick, on the piston to fill some of the "clearance'
an

and then there was plenty of steam. "Charlie" Kugler's engine had a wooden "bed plate," the usual wooden connecting rod, a cast-iron shaft, octagonal in shape, and a crank. It was made of white iron and almost as hard as flint. The fly wheel consisted of a cast-iron spider, wedged on the shaft with wooden spokes bolted to it, and a cast-iron rim. This rim was made up of several sections and bolted on each side of the spokes. There was always a squeak about the wheel when running, so I suppose it was loose at some point. Fly-ball governor and butterfly throttle were used. The usual speed was about sixty revolutions per minute, which varied greatly according to the steam pressure and load.

I was not annoyed by oil or grease cups when working on the Kugler engine. Some of the old engines had to be stopped to oil the valves, but ours had a "lubricator" with bulb and two stop-cocks so that we could introduce oil when the stop-cocks did not leak enough to blow all the oil out. One kind of oil was used for both engine and cylinder. The boiler was of the single-flue type and was supposed to carry sixty pounds; with no insurance and "home-made" inspection. The lever safety valve was supposed to be set at sixty pounds; but one time, after several months, we found it "stuck with lime," so that it might have held down several hundred pounds. This was of small moment, as we generally ran at forty to fifty pounds. Only on special days did I carry sixty-pounds pressure when some of the big machines were in use.

It was a great old power plant—not very economical, to be sure, but it was reliable and gave no trouble. No one knew how old it was, but "Lev" Ellis said
it

it was old in 1844. Just recently I wanted to see the old engine, but could not find even a scrap of it.

When we think of these old engines and compare them with the modern turbine of some fifty thousand kilowatts or, say, over sixty-five thousand horse power, we can but wonder how it will be possible to make as great improvement in the next fifty or seventy-five years. Doubtless, however, the improvement will be beyond our imagination, for the future will hold even greater opportunities than marked the period between the present and the time when Father used to take me to these places that meant so much to me and the memory of which still lingers pleasantly in my mind.

Ridley Park,   WILLIAM HENRY STANTON.
Pennsylvania,
1921.

HAND-MADE BOTTLES
OF AMBER GLASS. PROBABLY BROUGHT FROM VIRGINIA
ABOUT 1810 BY MATTHEW BAILEY.

DEBORAH H. B. STANTON

DEBORAH H. B. STANTON

DEBORAH H. B. STANTON, daughter of Elijah and Eliza Hanson, was born on the Twenty-sixth of First month, 1839, at the old Hanson homestead about a mile and a half southeast of the present railroad station at Speidel, Ohio.

The Hanson family went to Goshen Meeting and belonged to that Preparative meeting. Their monthly and quarterly meetings were at Stillwater.

When Deborah was five years old she started to school, walking, in company with her brothers, about a mile to a little log schoolhouse. She particularly liked

289

liked spelling and always found it very easy. Al
through life she has memorized poems and from this
vast store often repeats very fitting lines, whatever the
occasion may be.

At the age of eighteen she attended Friends' Boarding
School at Mount Pleasant, Ohio. She then taught for
two years at "Flat Rock," a district school in Somerset Township. It was located not far from the
Friends' meeting house at "The Ridge."

On Third month Thirtieth, 1859, she married Caleb
L. Bundy, son of Ezekiel and Maria (Engle) Bundy.
This was a double wedding. Caleb's brother, Nathan,
married Anna Stanton, daughter of Joseph and Mary
Stanton.

Caleb and Deborah (Hanson) Bundy went to housekeeping on a small farm south of Barnesville, not far
from the district schoolhouse at "Sugar Grove." That
autumn Caleb Bundy bought from the Government
one hundred and sixty acres of land in Wyandotte
County, Kansas, and expected to move there the following spring.

On the Fifteenth of Twelfth month, 1859, Caleb
died of typhoid fever, a young man not yet twenty-
one years of age. The young widow went back to her
father's home and there on the Third of Second month,
1860, Mary Caleb was born.

In 1862 Deborah again taught school, her work this
time being in Warren Township, District No. 1, where
Chalkley Bundy was one of the directors. Six of his
children went to school to her. On the Sixth of Twelfth
month, 1864, she was married to Chalkley Bundy. His
youngest child, Mary E., was about four months
                                        younger

ounger than her daughter, Mary C., who was not yet
ve years old. These two little girls were treated in
he home as twins.

Chalkley Bundy died on the First of Twelfth month,
866, of typhoid fever. For the next four years Debrah kept the home together for his six children, her-
elf and little girl. In those years four had married
nd one entered boarding school. So, with Mary C.
nd Mary E., she went back again to her father's home
nd later taught school in District No. 2, where the
wo Mary Bundys went to school to her. Among her
ther pupils were William H., Sarah B. and Emma C.
tanton, the three children of Eli Stanton. On the
hirtieth of Seventh month, 1873, she was married to
li Stanton.

It is interesting to note that her own child and her
ine step-children had all been to school to her.

To her new home she took with her Mary C. and
Mary E., now about thirteen years old. On First
1onth Twenty-sixth, 1875, Nathan Eli was born. His
ntrance into the family circle made four families rep-
esented in one. This was a beautiful, happy home
ntil in 1885 Eli Stanton was called from works to
eward and Deborah H. B. Stanton was left, for the
hird time, a widow, her age at this time being forty-six.

Her three marriages were all solemnized in Still-
vater Meeting, and during her whole life, whether liv-
ng among Friends or people who knew nothing about
hem, she has lived in conformity with Friends' prin-
iples.

In 1891 and 1892 Deborah Stanton was nurse for
he boys of Westtown Boarding School, where her son
Nathan

PEWTER SPOON
MADE BY BENJAMIN HANSON OUT OF A PLATTER BELONGING TO
THE HANSON FAMILY.

Nathan was a student.   After leaving Westtown they
went to Iowa to join Mary C. and her husband, Thompson Smith.   From this time until Nathan's marriage in
1907, his mother made a home for him at different
points in Iowa where he was in business with Thompson Smith.

She was always a great lover of flowers and enjoyed
gathering, with the children, those which grew wild on
the prairies.

From the age of twenty on through life, Debora
H. B. Stanton has been unusually capable in nursin
sick people.   So many, many times she has been sen
for by relatives, neighbors and friends.   When sixt
years old she could count twenty-one cases of typhoi
fever she had nursed.   The number of children who
she was first to hold upon their entrance into life is to
numerous to count, but it can be stated that she is,
it were, godmother to four sets of twins, namel
Bernice and Beatrice Hanson, Edna and Ellen Stanto
Elma and Everett Hall and Elva and Melva Bundy.

From girlhood Deborah was a neat, compete
seamstress, and now at fourscore years she still cut
fits and makes her own clothing.

In spite of her eighty years, Deborah H. B. Stanto
having lived a useful, active life, is wonderfully pr
                                                    serve

erved.   The curly, wavy hair is white, but the mental
owers are clear and able.   All who meet her can but
eel the richness and beauty that have come through a
ong life of service to others.

anton,
hio,
920.

Mary C Smith

DICTIONARY
Owned by Elijah Hanson.

stown the
Thomp
marriage i
at differen
siness with Thomp

owers and enjoyed
ich grew wild o

ough life, Debora
capable in nursing
she has been sen
When sixt
ses of typhoi
children whom
life is to
ized that she is,
ins, namely
Ellen Stanton
Melva Bundy.

competen
she still cut

H. B. Stanton
fully pre
served

A JOURNEY IN A PRAIRIE SCHOONER

ON APRIL 10, 1896, my grandmother, Deborah H. B Stanton, together with her son Nathan and nephew Caleb Hanson, left Caledonia, Minnesota, in a prairie schooner for Esterville, Iowa, a distance of about two hundred and fifty miles. Grandmother insisted upon making the trip and Uncle Nathan only consented after she promised to take the train any time she became tired of the wagon. The greatest danger which might confront them during the journey was an encounter with a prairie fire. These fires were frequent and very dangerous, as the high winds, which were characteristic of the western prairies, rapidly spread the flames over a large area. Fortunately they saw no fires. Regular roads were scarce in that part of the country, and a wagon track or more often compass made by William H. Stanton was their guide across the unbroken prairie. At night the boys slept in the wagon, but always succeeded in finding a place for Grandmother in some farm house. Everyone was very kind to them along their line of travel, and Grandmother enjoyed the entire trip, which lasted about a week.

MARY AVICE S. WEBSTER.

CANDLE SNUFFERS

NOTES BY DEBORAH H. B. STANTON

MY Grandfather Hanson was a soldier in the Revolutionary War. He died soon after my father was
born in 1797. In 1805 grandmother moved with her
family from North Carolina to Belmont County,
Ohio. The mode of travel then was in covered wagons drawn
by horses. Their wagoners were hired and, as was customary,
had bells on their horses. Before entering the mountains the
bells were muffled and hidden in the wagon. Later they came
upon some other wagoners, who were stalled in the mountains;
they hauled them out and stripped them of their bells, that being
their trophy for the help given.

My mother came from Georgia and settled near Stillwater
Meeting, Ohio. My father and mother were married in that
meeting and lived in that neighborhood the remainder of their
lives

AN ARMY DISCHARGE
OF ELIJAH HANSON AFTER THE REVOLUTIONARY WAR.

295

lives. My father's wedding pantaloons were, as he called them, "buckskin breeches" and he made his shoes of what he called "upper leather." He wore no gloves, and I do not know of what material his coat and hat were made. Mother's wedding dress was of white material, and she wore a white shawl and white silk bonnet to match.

They went to housekeeping in the woods on the Leatherwood hills west of Barnesville. Mother had inherited forty acres of woodland and father cleared the land as fast as he could. They had a log house, barn, and other buildings. The floors of the house were split logs—puncheon floors, as they were called—one side as smooth as could be hewn with an ax. Nevertheless, mother often had to pick splinters out of the little boys' feet. The house was covered with clapboards.

The newly cleared cornfields, surrounded as they were by timber, were almost overrun with squirrels. In order that they should not have too big a share of the crop, cow-bells were tied to the little boys and they were sent around the fields to frighten away the squirrels and the birds. This was a combination of work and play for the boys. The woods, thick with pea vines and undergrowth, made it necessary also to "bell the cows," so that they could be located at milking time.

My father was a good marksman and often brought home wild turkey, squirrels, pheasants, and sometimes a doe or a buck.

In those early times much of the materials used were manufactured at home. They carded the wool on hand-cards and spun it on spinning wheels. My mother, who did not have a loom for weaving at home, walked a mile to a neighbor's to use her loom. In these trips she carried a baby on her arm and led little brother. They also grew much flax, which the men would break, scutch, and hackle all the coarse from the fine. The women would spin it on small spinning wheels into sewing thread or weave it on looms into linen for table and bed linen and for handkerchiefs. My mother was a good needlewoman and a very rapid knitter. She could knit a pair of men's socks in the twenty-four hours.

In order to clear the land for cultivation, the men cut splendid chestnut and walnut trees, split some into rails for fencing and rolled

THE DOUBLE STAKED AND RIDER FENCE

THIS TYPE OF FENCE WAS USED VERY GENERALLY IN BARNESVILLE NEIGHBORHOOD OR SEVENTY-FIVE YEARS AFTER THE ARRIVAL OF THE FIRST SETTLERS. THE MULE FENCE WAS SOMETIMES USED, IN WHICH THE STAKES AND DOUBLE RIDERS WERE REPLACED BY LONG POLES LAID LENGTHWISE OF THE FENCE AND HELD IN PLACE BY SMALL STAKES LOCKED IN THE CORNERS. THIS TYPE WAS NOT SO SUBSTANTIAL AS THE OTHER NOR WOULD IT STAND SO WELL ON SLOPING GROUND. AS DURABLE TIMBER BECAME SCARCE AND MORE VALUABLE, WIRE FENCES TOOK THE PLACE OF THE RAIL ONES.

SWEDE OR HILLSIDE FENCE

BUILT ON THE FARM OF PETER SEARS. CONDITION AFTER
FORTY YEARS.

olled the rest into piles and burned them to get rid of them. Today such would make very valuable lumber.

These

These kinds of employment were general in farm life then.
My parents were the next generation from pioneers. They
lived in comfortable homes in a simple way. I have heard my
mother say that she remembered when there were but three
houses in Barnesville, Ohio.

I remember when we had no cookstoves, only open fireplaces
with cranes attached to the side of the wall of the fire chamber.
A crane was pulled forward to hang our cooking vessels on
the hooks or chains suspended from its arm, and then swung
back over the fire. These cooking vessels were of three kinds,
kettles, skillets, and Dutch ovens, all of which had legs two or
three inches long on the bottom. In these we also baked our
wheat and corn bread, pies and cakes. We would mould our bread
dough into loaves and put it into the ovens and skillets to raise.
The lids, which fitted them as neatly as our sugar-bowl lids fit
today, were placed on the red-hot embers to heat. When the
bread was light enough and the lids the right temperature, they
were placed on the vessels and hot embers shoveled on top of
them. Today I can almost hear mother saying, "Lift the lid
and see how the bread is baking," for to me this was an actual
experience.

I have heard my father tell of a circumstance that happened
while he was yet a boy in his widowed mother's home:

A stranger stopped at his mother's door and asked for lodging
for the night. The request was granted and directions given
for the care of his horse. When he came to the door with his
saddlebags in hand he said, "Madam, take charge of my saddlebags until morning." Grandmother took hold of them and they
dropped to the floor with a bang. She then said to the stranger,
"I have a mind that I will not care for the bags and the contents."
He replied, "When you gave me leave to stay over night in your
house that was also a guarantee of protection to my belongings."
The bags were heavy with money with which to buy a new home,
for the man was a prospector. She was a frail woman, but she
picked them up, carried them across the room, took a key hanging
at her side, unlocked a large chest, dropped the bags into it,
locked it and went about her duties. The next morning when
the stranger was ready to depart, she presented the bags and
said, "Thee had better examine them and see if all is right."
He

He replied, "I have no need to, with you they were safe. You are a Quaker."

The early settlers often had wild turkey or venison, but in turn for these choice bits of meat procured from the forest, they had their enemy in the bears and wolves.

The bears molested the pig pens and the wolves the young calves and sheep.

Once Uncle Isaac Stubbs found, from tracks seen in a light snow, that a bear was molesting his premises. He and his dog started in pursuit with father close behind them. The latter lost sight of them after a half mile, but followed the tracks and found scattered along the way, first uncle's hat, then his "wammus" (blouse), his vest, and his shoes. Then he heard the report of a gun and soon came upon his brother and the dog with "bruin" lying dead at their feet.

DEBORAH H. B. STANTON.

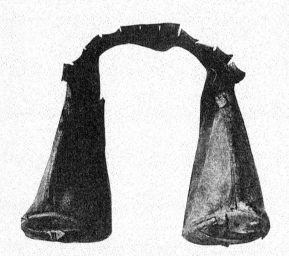

SADDLE BAGS

THEY WERE THE SATCHEL, SUITCASE AND TRUNK OF THE DAYS WHEN
EVERYBODY TRAVELED BY HORSEBACK.
PROPERTY OF JAMES WALTON.

EARLY SCHOOL LIFE

The following article was written by Deborah H. B. Stanton.
A modern building, called Goshen Schoolhouse, now stands a
mile farther south on the same road on which the schoolhouse
stood that she first attended.

ARLY in the Nineteenth Century when my parents were going to school they said the greatest concern of parents and those interested in education was to get a teacher for their children. After much attention was given to the subject, someone would finally report the name of a man or woman who for a small compensation would undertake to give lessons to the children for eight or nine weeks. Then another individual would decide that he would be able to take the school for a while, and so the task went from one to another.

Small children attended school in the summer and older boys and girls in the winter months. The school usually occupied a room in the home of some Friend's family who felt they could spare a room for that purpose. As time went on the interests of education demanded a building for a schoolhouse. The community joined together and erected a log schoolhouse. The cracks

300

cracks between the logs were chinked in with bits of timber and the space between filled in with mortar. In one side of the room there was built a very large fireplace. The men hauled with their oxen great logs and limbs of trees for the open fire. Father has said, "We boys thought it fine fun to cut this timber into lengths to burn in the big fireplace in our schoolroom."

In 1844 I started to school. The schoolhouse was half a mile from home and most of the distance I had to walk through the forest. I crossed the creek on a foot-log, which was a big oak tree cut down and trimmed of its branches. The top of the log was hewn off, making a flat surface on which to walk. When the water was low in summer I waded the stream, which performance I much enjoyed. The log schoolhouse had only one room, with five windows. The interior was lined with boards or paper and in the center of the room was a large stove. The room was kept, as I remember, at a very pleasant temperature in winter, and in summer with the door and five windows open we had plenty of fresh air.

On entering the schoolroom we girls turned to the right and hung our bonnets and shawls on wooden pegs driven into the wall. The boys disposed of their hats in a similar way. To the left of the door was the teacher's desk. Around three sides of the room were heavy boards fastened to the wall with the front edge supported by narrow boards reaching to the floor. This arrangement was called "the desks." Under the desks was a shelf on which we placed our books, copybooks, inkstands and slates. Around the front of this continuous huge desk was a birch bench on which the larger pupils sat during school hours and where we all went for our writing lessons. I remember for several years

years I was not tall enough for my feet to reach the floor when sitting at this desk to write. We faced the wall with our backs to the center of the room. The teacher passed around behind us giving instructions as to how to hold the pen and making copies for us. Our writing pens were made from goose quills. The teacher or some of the older boys shaped and sharpened them with a penknife. With these quills we did our best to become good penmen, imitating the copy our teacher made for us in our copy-books.

There were two or three rows of lower benches around the stove on which the younger children sat most of the time.

School work began at eight o'clock in the morning and closed at three in the afternoon. We had one hour for noon, but no morning nor afternoon recess. We had no blackboards in the schoolroom, so "ciphered" on our slates and carried them to the teacher to be corrected or approved.

The first book I used was a primer that was badly worn by older members of the family. From that I soon passed on to an Electric Speller. We spelled through this book a number of times. There were columns of words to spell and define; these we kept reviewing until we almost committed them to memory— really that was the object in the teacher's mind. Next we had what was called United States Reader. This was not easy to read. Then McGuffey's readers were introduced, also McGuffey's spelling-book and Webster's dictionary. McGuffey's readers were not difficult, and after them we had an English reader with a sequel. Frequently we had reading lessons from the Scriptures.

We

We had many handicaps in school life in those days, but, oh, the beauty of the surroundings of those old log schoolhouses which were mostly in the woods! In their season the wild flowers were at our feet and we were surrounded by the beautiful dogwood, wild cherry and crabapple trees. By the old fallen trees covered with lichen and green moss we built our playhouses and decorated them with the wild flowers and fruits around us. But time has moved onward and brought many changes. Our rustic surroundings, wild fruit, flowers and childhood pleasures are all things of the past.

CANDLE MOULDS

TO MAKE CANDLES, THE WICKS WERE TWISTED AND DOUBLED, THE ENDS WERE TAPERED TO A POINT AND RUN THROUGH THE SMALL HOLES IN THE LOWER CONICAL ENDS OF THE TUBES. A SMALL WOOD ROD WAS THEN RUN THROUGH THE LOOPS AT THE UPPER ENDS OF THE WICKS. THE WICKS WERE THEN SPACED IN THE CENTER OF THE UPPER ENDS OF THE TUBES AND DRAWN DOWN TIGHT. THE MOULDS WERE THEN FILLED WITH MELTED TALLOW AND SET OUT TO COOL. A GOOD COLD-WEATHER JOB TO BE REPEATED OFTEN.
USED BY NATHAN W. BUNDY.

A PIONEER SUPPER

I WAS born at a time when there were still remnants of pioneer days in our section of the country. At this interesting time much of the pioneer life was still well known and many of the tools, implements, and goods were yet in existence.

I shall never forget a visit I made, when a boy, to the home of Elijah Hanson, my step-grandfather, on his farm in Goshen Township, Belmont County, Ohio. All their children were married, and he and step-grandmother, Eliza Hanson, had given the use of their large frame house to their son Benjamin and they were living in a small house on the farm. It was a one-story frame house with three rooms joined end to end. In the first room and in the end of the house was an open fireplace, which would take wood about four feet long. This room was used as a living-room and as a kitchen. In

304

In it were several chairs, a stand, a cupboard, a table, and the bed which they used. The next room was a spare room with two beds. The third was a store room.

Their life here was simple, even primitive. They used many pieces of furniture and utensils that were similar to those used by their parents in pioneer days. Some of the household articles were the same ones that their ancestors had handed down to them. It was cold weather, but grandfather had a big wood-fire in the fireplace and as night came on there was plenty of light and cheer, but only on one side, as the corners were dark and cold and there were chills around the spine. It seemed one was never warm all over at once.

After a little while, when the fire had burned down and there were plenty of hot coals, grandmother lighted a tallow candle, with a splinter, at the fire, and proceeded to make biscuit. She cut them and placed a layer of them in the bottom of the old-fashioned baking skillet. Grandfather shoved the "fore stick" back and raked some hot coals forward and set the baker with an iron cover on it on them, then he raked some more coals, banking them up around it and on the lid. Grandmother got a "crock" of sausage, made some cakes, placed them in another skillet, and grandfather put it also on some hot coals.

The coffee was now put in the big tin coffee pot, and grandfather, swinging out the crane, hung the pot on one of the iron hooks, then pushed the crane back so that the pot would hang over the remainder of the fire. Soon it was boiling and set off on the hearth, and an iron teakettle of water put on to heat for dishwashing. Grandmother set the table and put on butter and jam. The sausage, "all pork," was browned, turned and taken

OPEN FIREPLACE WITH CRANE
In the home of Hezekiah and Elizabeth (Bundy) Bailey.
Built about 1848.

taken up and real gravy made in the skillet. Soon everything was ready and grandfather and I were asked to "draw up our chairs." The biscuits were taken from the baker nicely browned and cracked open "way deep" and the coffee poured "piping hot." I think I had been getting more hungry every minute since grandmother began to make the biscuit, and the fragrant odor of the sausage with "sage" in it only made matters worse.

Such a supper! The biscuit and gravy disappeared and the sausage followed suit, with never a thought of headache or indigestion. Supper over, grandfather put more wood on the fire. Grandmother soon had the dishes washed and the simple cooking things put in n order and had sat down to knit. Grandfather talked over some of the old days and lapsed into silence as the ire burned low.

Now it was bedtime and the same candle lighted ne to the next room. There was no heat, but a great, igh feather bed. No ceremony about undressing in his cold room, only a scramble to get up and in. Vhat a fine bed! The feathers came up on both sides nd the covers seemed to lie straight across. Only a ninute until I was good and warm and then dreamless leep.

W. H. S.

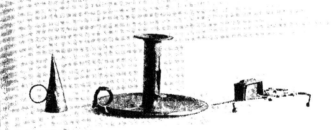

CANDLESTICK WITH EXTINGUISHER AND SNUFFER
FORMERLY IN THE HOME OF DEMSEY BUNDY.

PIONEER FOODS AND THEIR PREPARATION

ABOUT the time the State of Ohio was admitted to the Union our forefathers came from North Carolina to hew-out their homes in the unbroken forest of this new state. They built their houses of logs, sometimes hewn logs, but more often of the round timbers just as they were cut from the forest trees.

All around their homes there grew in abundance wild grapes, raspberries, plums, gooseberries and crab apples, all of which made excellent dishes when properly cooked. These were used and enjoyed by our ancestors not only while in season, but were preserved and dried by them for winter use.

In the course of fifty or sixty years splendid orchards of peaches, apples and many other fruits were grown. These fruits were also put away for winter use, sometimes by preserving, but more often by drying in the sun. Apples were cut in quarters, strung in long strings, and hung on a rack suspended from the ceiling or hung on pegs that jutted around the large open fireplace.

I

It was the custom in those early days to invite the neighbors to the various homes, and while the men gathered, cut and hauled many cords of wood, the women pared, cut and strung apples to be dried. These parties were known as "a wood hauling and an apple paring."

The log houses in these early days were all built with large fireplaces and the cooking was done over or by these open wood-fires. From the wall of the fireplace extended an iron crane upon which hung hooks and chains. The cooking pots were suspended by these over the fire. Meats were broiled or fried and the coffee boiled by drawing a mass of red-hot coals out on to the stone or earthen hearth and placing the cooking utensil on this red-hot bed.

To bake bread the "Dutch oven" was placed upon one of these beds of hot coals, the dough put into the oven and an iron lid placed over it, then live coals heaped upon the lid. If the first coals brought out on to the hearth or put on top the oven died out before the bread was sufficiently baked, more coals were brought from the fire with a long-handled shovel.

The griddle for pancake baking was a round, flat iron over twelve inches in diameter with short legs and a long bale with a hook and a swivel so the cakes could be turned and evenly baked.

The "Dutch oven" above mentioned was of iron about twelve inches in diameter and four inches deep. There was another oven which was also often called a "Dutch oven" or an "out-oven," or sometimes it was called a "clay oven." This oven was generally used for baking bread, pie and cake. It was built of stone or sometimes of brick and clay, either in one
corner

corner of the house or out of doors. Ovens of this
type are in use by some bakers today and occasionally
one is found in a private home. This kind of oven
is made very hot by building a fire in the oven itself,
and when sufficiently hot, the coals are drawn out
and the bread and pastry put in to bake.

MARY C. (BUNDY) SMITH.

THE OUTSIDE OVEN

NONE COULD BE FOUND ABOUT OUR OLD HOME IN OHIO, BUT THERE ARE MANY IN EASTERN
PENNSYLVANIA; SELDOM USED NOW, HOWEVER.
UPPER RIGHT—ONE PHOTOGRAPHED IN LOS ANDES, CHILI, S. A., 1912, BY W. H. S.
LOWER LEFT—BACK VIEW OF ANOTHER TYPE, SHOWING THE SHAPE AND THE "SQUIRREL TAIL" FLUE
LOWER RIGHT—ANOTHER TYPE, OF WHICH THE OWNER SAYS: "I'VE BAKED MANY A HUNDRED LOAVES
OF BREAD IN THAT OLD OVEN."
THE CHILI OVEN MORE NEARLY REPRESENTS THE OVEN BUILT AND USED
BY THE PIONEERS IN OHIO.

Anna Stanton

Nathan Bundy

NATHAN AND ANNA STANTON BUNDY

Anna Stanton Bundy, daughter of Joseph and Mary Stanton, was born at the old Stanton home a few miles north of Barnesville, Ohio, on Stillwater Creek, Eighth month Eighth, 1837. On the thirtieth day of the Third month, 1859, she was married to Nathan Bundy, son of Ezekiel and Maria Bundy. He was born Eighth month Twenty-second, 1837, at the old Bundy home about three miles east of Barnesville.

The following article was written by their daughter, Mary Bundy Colpitts, Eighth month Twenty-fourth, 1919.

FATHER and Mother were both educated at the Friends' School near Stillwater Meeting House and at Mount Pleasant, Ohio, Boarding School. Father also attended Westtown School, Westtown Pennsylvania. It is said by those who knew mother in her girlhood days that she was of an unusually gay and happy temperament, enjoying to the fullest the innocent pleasures of life. Father was a great student and lover of knowledge. At one time he was a surveyor, laying out the Barnesville and Somerton Pikes; the Warnock and St. Clairsville Pike; the plot of the Southern Cemetery at Barnesville, and much other work of the kind. He was an enthusiastic member of the Masonic Lodge, living according to the high principles for which it stands, a true Christian, unselfish,

311

HOME OF ANNA STANTON BUNDY
BUILT BY WILLIAM HOYLE.

unselfish, loving his fellow men to the extent that he was sometimes the loser in this world.

Father and Mother lived for a short time on Sandy Ridge in what was probably the first house built by Henry Doudna, for his home. When Grandmother Stanton died, they moved back to the old home. Here the following children were born to them: Joseph S. (1–19–1860); Caleb L. (12–12–1862); Mary M. (7–7–1864); and some years later, while living in Barnesville, Clara Elma (11–7–1871). Clara died at about eighteen months.

In 1865 we moved to the edge of Barnesville, where my father and his cousin, Chalkley Dawson, put down a coal shaft, which they operated for a few years. About 1870 we moved up on East Main Street when Father purchased a men's tailoring store. Not long after this his health began to fail. From young manhood

CUPS AND SAUCERS

LEFT—MARY P. (HODGIN) STANTON'S.
RIGHT—HER MOTHER'S (ELIZABETH HODGIN). PROBABLY BROUGHT FROM GEORGIA BY
STEPHEN HODGIN. THESE WERE SO MUCH ADMIRED BY ANNA STANTON BUNDY THAT
STEPHEN HODGIN GAVE HER THE SET AFTER HIS WIFE'S DEATH.

hood he had not been strong. In the fall of 1873 he went to Oregon, thinking that the change to that climate might be of benefit to one with lung trouble. It was only a temporary relief. While he was gone, Mother took us to the country to the home of her brother, Eli Stanton. Uncle Eli did so much for us then and a few years later. His was a home to which we always loved to go and in childhood we spent many happy hours there. Father returned in the spring and we went back to our home, but his health continued to fail until late in the summer of 1874 he passed quietly away at the age of thirty-seven.

Mother took us then to her sister's, Elizabeth Stanton Bailey. Uncle Lin and Aunt Lizzie were so good to us. We lived with them that winter and in the spring purchased a little home near them and close to Tacoma Station, near also to Uncle Will Stanton's.

We children went to District School No. 2, and each in turn taught there for a short time. We each attended Barnesville School and Lebanon, Ohio, Normal School. Joseph also attended Normal School at Valparaiso, Indiana.

He was an apt and studious scholar. Being the eldest, he soon developed manly traits, influencing and

encouraging

encouraging us so much for the good. Deprived of a father at the age of fifteen, he was the comfort and pride of a noble mother and loving brother and sister. After he had taught in Barnesville a year he wanted us to move back there. So we rented the William Hoyle property on South Lincoln Avenue and moved there the Spring of 1883. A few years later, Mother purchased this property and lived there the remainder of her life. Brother Joseph as a teacher was very successful, winning the hearts of his pupils by his kindly nature, generosity and forbearance. He taught several terms at No. 1 School and from 1880 to 1884 he taught in Barnesville High School. Later in the year 1884 he entered into a partnership with T. W. Emerson, for the purpose of furnishing abstracts of titles of Belmont County lands. At the same time, he attended to considerable surveying, which occupation he had followed for some time. He was Deputy County Surveyor at the time of his death. Stricken with typhoid fever when twenty-five years old, at the very beginning of a useful and prosperous life, his death seemed doubly sad. About two weeks before he came home from St. Clairsville, where he was engaged in business, he expressed a firm belief in the Christian religion and was willing to answer the call. His life was above reproach. Firm in purpose, always guided by a clear conscience, he set an example which others might well follow, thus illustrating "It is not how long, but how well we live."

My brother, Caleb L. Bundy, after teaching for a short time in our home district, decided to study telegraphy. About 1882 he went to Paralto, Iowa, where he studied with "Cade" Plummer. After holding positions as operator in various parts of the West, he was located

located at Sabula, Iowa, as operator and agent at the "Y," a responsible position. There he was married in 1890 to Miss Kate Snyder, a popular and worthy young lady of that place. She was so well suited to fight life's battles with him, but alas! in a little less than a year their happy home was broken up. He was taken with typhoid pneumonia and lived only a few weeks, passing away at the early age of twenty-eight years. Mother was with him. She had gone West for an extended visit about two months before, expecting to spend the winter with them. His was a character of worth, delighting in doing well that which he saw as his duty, and at all times ready to help a weaker brother, leaving all things to Him who is the just rewarder of good deeds.

Cale's wife came back and lived with us for a few years and was a great comfort to Mother. In the sad days that followed, her little grandson, my only son, who was then a babe of a few months, helped to occupy her

PEACOCK FEATHER BRUSH

BOUGHT BY JOSEPH S. BUNDY FOR USE IN HIS MOTHER'S HOME AND NOW IN POSSESSION OF HIS SISTER, MARY M. COLPITTS. THESE BRUSHES WERE IN COMMON USE IN 1875 FOR KEEPING FLIES FROM THE DINING TABLE. THIS ONE WAS MADE BY ABBY KENNARD.

WOODEN BUTTER BOWL

GIVEN TO ANNA STANTON BUNDY BY HER MOTHER WITH THE UNDERSTANDING THAT
HER OWNERSHIP CEASED IF SHE DID NOT KEEP THE BOWL SCOURED. SHE OWNED
AND USED THE BOWL THE REST OF HER LIFE.

her mind and alleviate her sorrow. Her home was with
us. My husband, John Colpitts, was as good and kind
to her as an own son could be, taking pleasure in
making her happy.

Mother's friends were numerous. To her

> "No life is so strong and complete
> But it yearns for the smile of a friend."

Our friends she was able to make her friends. Her
relatives were very dear to her. "To love and to be
loved is the greatest happiness of existence" to her
especially was true. She was good company, having a
gift of humor. Not being a good sleeper, she complained
of lying awake many hours in the night, but she would
get sleepy early in the evening. One evening after
trying in vain to keep awake, she suddenly arose from
her chair and said, "I'll go to bed, I know I can keep
awake there." Many times she had a witty answer
ready in conversation. A great lover of flowers, she
spent many happy hours in her flower garden. Another interest was in the culinary department. Sometimes she surprised us with new dishes, or she would
slip quietly to the kitchen and in a short time ask us
out to a nice meal with such delicious, flaky, hot
biscuits,

QUILT PIECED BY ANNA STANTON BUNDY
MADE ABOUT 1890 FROM MARY P. (BUNDY) STANTON'S DRESSES. NOW
IN THE POSSESSION OF SARAH B. (STANTON) HALL.

biscuits, along with other good things. She enjoyed these little surprises as much as any one. She was able to do this up to within a year or two of her death. It was her pleasure to have some interesting work to fill the spare moments. Sometimes it was knitting or crochet,

A CHAIR FROM THE
FIRST SET WITH WHICH
NATHAN AND ANNA
STANTON BUNDY BEGAN
HOUSEKEEPING. ELI
AND MARY P. STANTON,
WILLIAM AND JANE D.
STANTON, AND CALEB
AND DEBORAH H.

BUNDY ALL BEGAN
WITH THE SAME KIND
OF CHAIRS, AND NOW,
AFTER SIXTY YEARS OF
USE, THERE ARE MANY
OF THE CHAIRS WHICH
ARE IN USE AND AL-
MOST AS GOOD AS
WHEN NEW.

crochet, and many times piecing quilts. Of late years she pieced many quilts for the Needlework Guild, of which she was a director and very much interested member. She was never so happy as when doing something for someone who needed her help.

Her last sorrow, and in a way her greatest, because she was older and less able to bear it, was the passing from earth of her only grandson, Clifford B. Colpitts, on Ninth month Fifth, 1911, from tubercular meningitis. His life was a short period of twenty-one years. He had been in Cleveland, Ohio, where his aunts, the Misses Colpitts, had a millinery store. He was employed by Pike, Richmond & Company, a wholesale millinery firm, as city salesman. By pleasing and courteous manner and uprightness he was making a great success. He was a member of the First M. E. Church, joining when a child with his parents. We are speechless when we think that one so young and fair and so much wanted and needed to brighten up a little corner of this sad earth, has gone. Where are these loved ones?

> "I know not where His islands lift
>   Their fronded palms in air;
> I only know I cannot drift
>   Beyond His love and care."

Mother's grief was pitiful; even in her last years she was not to escape sorrow. It was not long after this great blow until she began to decline. She had been afflicted with asthma for many years. This caused heart trouble, and although she had been in poor health for two years, she did not become worse until within two weeks of her death, which occurred Tenth month Fifth, 1917. She was eighty years of age. In the fall time, when the flowers she loved so well lay down to
sleep,

sleep, she passed to the Great Beyond, and we laid her to rest in the Southern Cemetery, at Barnesville, beside her loved ones.

A lifelong member of the Society of Friends, she lived a life of simplicity, never wavering in her faith and striving to make each year of her long life more useful than the ones that had gone before. It was a pleasure to make her comfortable and happy. To me she was not only a mother—who in her patience and loveliness forgave so promptly all our errors—but many times filling the place of a sister.

"Mother! We all have known her. Not all of us in the same person, but the same glory framed each separate face in the aureole of its own divinity."

"Because thy loving kindness is better than life, my lips shall praise thee." *Psalm 63 : 3.*

Barnesville,
Ohio,
1919.

Mary Bundy Colpitts,

WATER PITCHER

FROM A SET OF DISHES IN THE HOME OF EZEKIEL BUNDY.
THE DISHES WERE USED AT THE DOUBLE WEDDING DINNER
OF NATHAN BUNDY AND ANNA STANTON AND CALEB BUNDY
AND DEBORAH HANSON. MARRIED 3-30-1859.

WAITERS AT THE MARRIAGE OF

Nathan Bundy
and
Anna Stanton

- 1st Hosea Doudna
       Hannah Clendenon
- 2nd Chalkley Dawson
       Martha Garretson
- 3rd William Stanton
       Eunice Doudna

WAITERS AT THE MARRIAGE OF

Caleb Bundy
and
Deborah Hanson

- 1st Robert Smith
       Rebecca Stanton
- 2nd William Hodgin
       Lydia Hanson
- 3rd William E. Bundy
       Rebecca Doudna

THE SONG OF THE COOKIES

Written by William Macy Stanton for his Aunt's (Anna
Stanton Bundy) Birthday, Eighth month Eighth,
1910.

Poets may sing of the babbling brook,
  Or the blue of the summer sky,
Or even more of the tempting look
  Of the crust of a country pie;
But this one song do I prefer,—
  A song so dear to me,—
Which now is sung alone for her
  Who today is seventy-three.

Others may sing of golden curls,
  And eyes of tempting blue,
Or the graceful forms of charming girls,
  Or drops of sparkling dew;
But in my mind the Muses stir
  To life a song so free,
A song of cookies baked by her
  Who today is seventy-three.

Each cooky's crust of brown was spread
  With sugar sprinkled fine;
And O more sweet than daily bread,
  Those cookies that were mine!
Oft in my memory does recur
  Those cookies baked for me,—
The cookies rolled and baked by her
  Who today is seventy-three.

                                        The

321

The taste was sweet, but sweeter yet
   The thought she always had;
For why should not an aunt forget
   What pleased a little lad?
Some pleasure though it did incur
   For some one else but me
Which twinkled in the eyes of her
   Who today is seventy-three.

So from my heart I sing this song
   For one to me so dear,
Who helped my youthful days along
   With cookies and good cheer.
And now to wish as I prefer,
   I wish that there may be
Still many happy years for her
   Who today is seventy-three.

Lansdowne,
Pennsylvania,
1910.

William Macy Stanton

William Stanton   Married First Month Twenty-seventh 1864   Jane S. Davis

WILLIAM AND JANE DAVIS STANTON

WILLIAM STANTON, son of Joseph and Mary (Hodgin) Stanton, was born Ninth month Fifteenth, 1839, in their Stillwater Creek home in Belmont County, Ohio. He was always a great lover of nature. As a boy he enjoyed fishing and hunting squirrels and rabbits, and he continued to be a good marksman as long as he could manage a gun. His business likewise showed the nature lover—nurseries, fruit growing, farming, and some dairying. The fruit was always carefully, even fondly, picked and packed, and his rare trees were admired by all who saw them. As an active member of the State Horticultural Society, he traveled to all parts of the State to attend the meetings. A close observer of atmospheric conditions made him a good weather-prophet. His wife, who depended upon his judgment in this matter, never had to take her clothes from the line on account of rain. He could tell fairly accurately the time of day by the position of the shadows of the house or trees.

When a boy he walked two miles to school and enjoyed watching the building of the first railroad—the Baltimore

323

THE RESIDENCE OF WILLIAM AND JANE
DAVIS STANTON
BUILT BY FRANCIS DAVIS.

VIEW OF STILLWATER VALLEY
FROM THE HOME OF WILLIAM AND JANE DAVIS STANTON, SHOWING THE
FORMER HOME OF ELI HODGIN AND THE LOCATION OF JOSEPH STANTON'S
HOME.

Baltimore and Ohio—to pass through that part of the State. When the station was opened at Tacoma, he was appointed the first Station Agent and Postmaster, which offices he held for nearly twenty years.

Mathematics was one of his strong points. Exceptional ability in that line enabled him to solve intricate problems without pencil or paper while conversation was going on about him, in which he often took part. He used many of the "short cuts," which have only recently been introduced into our schools.

Delicate and frail all his life, he was gentle and loving and beloved. He was an active member of the Society of Friends, serving as clerk of the meetings for about twenty years and for many years an Elder in Stillwater Monthly Meeting, of which he was a life-long member.

Until the death of his wife he lived within sight of the place where he was born. Then at the age of sixty-eight he went to live with his married daughter, Anna Stanton Palmer, at Westtown, Pennsylvania, where he attended the meetings for worship at the School.

He passed quietly away Fifth month Fifth, 1918, in his seventy-ninth year. His remains were laid beside his wife's in Stillwater Burying Ground, near Barnesville, Ohio.

Soon after his death, George L. Jones, Principal of Westtown School and a minister, spoke of him in their meeting. It was a fitting tribute, and as nearly as could be remembered at the close of meeting, what he said follows:

"There has recently been called from our midst one who was perhaps unknown to many of us, except as we saw him in our meetings. He came here and sat down

down quietly amongst us, but he had a real influence upon us. I feel that in a measure the words of our Saviour said of himself, apply to our aged friend, 'If I go not away, the Comforter will not come.' And so, though we will never again see him walk slowly into this room, never again have his kindly smile and his friendly handshake, he is here in spirit with us today. And as we gather here from time to time, we will feel his spirit as a benediction resting upon us. As we go to visit in the home where he lived and took such a keen interest in all that went on about him, we shall feel his spirit there as a benediction upon it and upon us, pointing us the way to higher things."

Jane Davis Stanton, daughter of Francis and Mary Davis, was born Seventh month Fifteenth, 1846, at Flushing, Ohio. She attended both Mount Pleasant and Westtown Boarding Schools, and many of the friendships formed while at these schools were life-long. She was a beautiful girl, with black hair, fair skin, delicate coloring, and regular features. She had a strong character and stood up for the right as she saw it, in spite of popular opinion. She was a devoted wife and mother, doing all a woman could for her delicate husband and large family of children.

Even though she had a large family, she was never too busy to minister to those about her. Her reputation for skill with babies was known for miles around and she had frequent calls, day and night, to come to a sick child. Her family physician said to his patients when a child was sick, "Better send for Mrs. Stanton, she knows more about babies than I do." She did not limit her ministrations to babies, however, but was always ready to lend a helping hand to any who needed it, whether white, foreign, or colored. There were whole

JANE S. DAVIS

TAKEN WHILE A STUDENT AT
WESTTOWN BOARDING SCHOOL.

whole families she looked out for for years, visiting them often, especially in the fall to see that they had what was needed for the winter.

Her guild garments were often boys' pants. "Because," she said, "others won't want to make them and the boys will need them." This was characteristic of her, never sparing herself, but doing what others did not want to do. She was particularly fond of boys and doing for them was a pleasure to her.

Her heart was greater than her strength and at sixty-three her health began to fail. Soon after the beginning of the year 1910 she left home and came to Philadelphia for treatment. While here she was taken
suddenly

suddenly ill and, after five days, died Third month Eighth, at her daughter's, Anna Stanton Palmer's, at Westtown, Pennsylvania. Her remains were taken back to Stillwater for burial, where they were laid beside those of her four children who had preceded her to the Land Beyond. She had expressed the hope that she might not outlive her day of usefulness. This wish was granted her, for she was active and doing for others until within a few weeks of her death.

When Jane was quite a young girl, her parents moved to Sandy Ridge, in the Stillwater neighborhood, where her father became active in the business interests of Barnesville, serving as president of the First National Bank of that place, and later took part in building construction. He superintended the building, in 1875, of Friends' Boarding School, near Barnesville, Ohio; Friends' Meeting House, at Stillwater, in 1878, and the Belmont County Children's Home, and lastly a large residence for himself at Tacoma, Ohio.

It was while living in the Sandy Ridge home that a young man called to see her brother John. He was not at home and Jane entertained William Stanton on the porch until John returned, thus meeting for the first time the man she married on First month Twenty-seventh, 1864. On her wedding day she was dressed in an ashes-of-roses silk dress, white silk bonnet, and white kid gloves. He wore a broadcloth coat, velvet vest, and high silk hat. Then, as now, emergencies had to be met at the last moment. William had depended upon a Barnesville merchant to get his gloves in Philadelphia. The time came for the marriage, but the gloves did not come, and he had to wear a pair of Jane's black kid ones. That morning it was also discovered that the man who was to have been first waiter,

waiter, Seth Shaw, had developed measles during the night.

They went to housekeeping about a half mile south of his birthplace. Jane Stanton's brother, John Davis, and his wife occupied half of the house. These two young married couples had lively times. One afternoon the girls went visiting and thought their husbands would come for them. It grew late afternoon and no sign of the men, so they walked home and then decided to play a joke on their husbands by hiding and not letting them know of their arrival. The men did the milking, came to the house, and not finding their wives decided to play a joke on them, and forthwith strained the milk into small bowls and cups and left them on the kitchen table. In the morning the girls

VIEW OF STILLWATER VALLEY

THE HOUSE IN WHICH WILLIAM AND JANE DAVIS STANTON STARTED HOUSEKEEPING IS SHOWN IN THE FOREGROUND. THE ARROW INDICATES THE LOCATION OF THE HOUSE IN WHICH WILLIAM STANTON WAS BORN—THE JOSEPH STANTON HOUSE.

girls strolled out of the guest room to surprise their husbands and were themselves surprised to find the milk.

The summer after they were married, William Stanton had a serious case of typhoid fever and was never very strong afterwards. He measured about five feet, ten inches and weighed one hundred and ten pounds. After living a few years in this valley home, they moved up on the hill where they lived in an old brick house, near the present Tacoma Station, until their family outgrew it about ten years later. From there they moved to a frame house only a few hundred yards away. In 1891, soon after the death of her father, they gave up their home and moved into the house he had built in order that they might care for her mother. This large house was in proportion to their hospitality and they entertained a great deal, especially at Ohio Yearly Meeting time when they have had as many as thirty-seven persons over night and to break-fast.

Shortly before Jane Stanton's death, plans were made to close the Tacoma home and move to Phila-delphia, because all their children had interests in this vicinity. A house was already rented in Lansdowne at the time of her sudden death. So the plans were promptly carried out, and all their possessions except some household goods were disposed of. The next day, after they left Ohio, the Boarding School took possession of the place in order to continue school for the rest of that session. The School building was burned Third month Thirty-first, 1910.

To William and Jane D. Stanton eleven children were born:

Eva T. (7–25–1868). She was a delicate child, slight

slight and dainty, but precocious. After completing her education, she remained at home, to aid her mother in rearing her large family. In 1898 she came to Philadelphia and was still here at the time of her mother's death in 1910. Then she made a home for the family in Lansdowne and generally took her mother's place. Now she has her own home in Lansdowne. Following the example of her parents, she is an active member of the Society of Friends, having her membership at Fourth and Arch Streets, Philadelphia, where she serves on many committees. She also takes an active interest in charitable organizations. She is a member of the Board of Managers for Aimwell School and has been for ten years on the Board for the Shelter for Colored Orphans. In 1897 she attended a reunion in Steubenville, Ohio, the birthplace of Edwin M. Stanton, and was the only person there whose name was then Stanton.

Mary Davis (4–24–1870). This second daughter's life on earth was a short one. At fourteen she was taken with typhoid fever and lived but a few days. She died Tenth month Fourth, 1884, and was buried at Stillwater. The last term she was at school she thoroughly enjoyed her work in Botany, tracing more than one hundred flowers.

Joseph E. (8–26–1872). He learned the nursery business from his father and followed that line of work after coming to Philadelphia. Of later years he has been connected with Westtown School, where he has aided in the direction of the mechanical upkeep and running of the school property. He is a well informed man, always having been a great reader. In 1900 he attended the Paris Exposition with his cousin Edmund C. Stanton.

Francis

Francis Wilson (4–5–1875). This unusual child had, like his father, marked mathematical ability, but his span of years was even shorter than his sister Mary's. When only eleven he, too, had typhoid fever, but apparently recovered and went to spend the day with his cousin Nate Stanton. They had been playing marbles in an upstairs room, and decided to go outside for some air. They went down and just as Francis reached the front door he fell over dead. Thus on Eighth month Eighth, 1886, he suddenly left his loved ones. He was laid beside his sister.

John Lindley (4–17–1877). Lin was a popular young man and a great lover of horses. He had them beautifully trained and could manage even the most spirited. He took great pride in a noble black stallion which he owned. No one else could manage "Sandy." His horses all knew him and loved him. A fine looking young man, tall, well built, and strong, he seemed the staff upon which his parents could lean as they grew older. But, alas! at twenty, with the brightest of prospects for the future, he was suddenly called from them Third month Twentieth, 1897, after a short illness from la grippe. His mother never ceased to mourn for this son.

Benjamin (3–16–1879). He lived but five days. His death on Third month Twenty-first, 1879, was the first break in the family circle.

"No little child has ever come from God and stayed a brief while in some human home—to return to the Father—without making glad that home and leaving behind some trace of heaven. A family had counted themselves poorer without * * * * that soft touch, that sudden smile. This short visit was not an

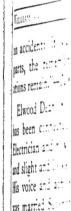

an accident: it was a benediction. The child de-
parts, the remembrances, the influence, the associ-
ations remain."—*Ian Maclaren.* So it was in this case.

Elwood Dean (8–20–1880). For twelve years Dean
has been connected with Westtown School, first as
Electrician and now as Business Manager. He is tall
and slight and looks much as his father did at his age.
His voice and actions are also much the same. He
was married Seventh month Twenty-eighth, 1909, to
Esther

**WILLIAM STANTON AND
EVA STANTON PALMER**
TAKEN AT WESTTOWN, PA.

Esther S. Fawcett, of Salem, Ohio. They now have four daughters: Jane Davis (9–27–1910), Sidney Fawcett (5-8-1912), Ruth Elizabeth (7–14–1915), and Katherine Macy (11–24–1919).

Anna Clara (4–9–1883). She did secretarial work and taught one year at Barnesville School before she married Charles W. Palmer, of Media, Pennsylvania, on Sixth month Twenty-fifth, 1908. He was for fifteen years a teacher at Westtown School and that is where they lived until this last year, when they bought a farm near there and moved on to it. In 1911 they traveled in Europe. Now they have two daughters— Eva Stanton (6–26–1912), and Mary Anna (10–20–1914). It was with this daughter that William Stanton made his home after his wife's death and her little girls helped to make the last years of their Grandfather's life more cheerful, and his influence over them has made them particularly gentle and thoughtful.

Edna Macy and Ellen Davis, twins (4–26–1886). Edna is a graduate of the University of Pennsylvania and has taught for a number of years. Ellen, after studying at the School of Industrial Art, married S. Howard Pennell, of Lansdowne, Pennsylvania, on Ninth month Fourth, 1915. He is a graduate of the University of Pennsylvania in Mechanical Engineering and is employed in Philadelphia. They are living in their new home, designed by her brother Macy, in Lansdowne, Pennsylvania.

William Macy (9–15–1888). This youngest child was born on his father's forty-ninth birthday. He was a delicate

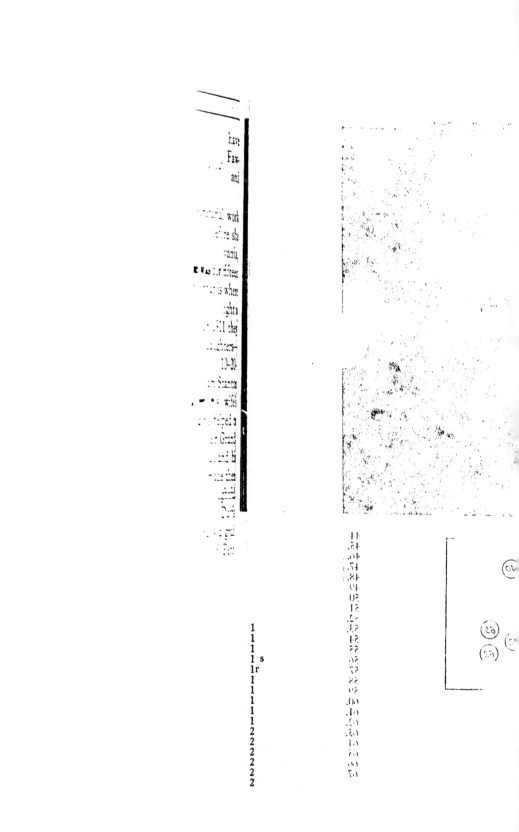

Our Ancestors—The Stantons

1. Charles W. Palmer
2. Anna Stanton Palmer
3. William Stanton
4. Jane Davis Stanton
5. Jane S. Warner
6. Beulah Palmer
7. T. Chalkley Palmer
8. H. Jane Palmer
9. Eva T. Stanton
10. Joseph E. Stanton
11. E. Dean Stanton
12. Edna M. Stanton
13. Ellen D. Stanton
14. William Macy Stanton
15. Edith L. Palmer
16. Walter Palmer
17. Louis Palmer
18. Anna S. Bundy

26. Mary Anna Bailey
27. Clarence R. Patten

35. Sarah B. Hall

44. Louisa Steer
45. Elizabeth Pickett
46. Henry Palmer, Jr.
47. Mary Negus
48. Wallace Doudna
49. Rose Doudna
50. Mary H. Thorpe
51. Ethel Blowers
52. Florence Hoge
53. Lydia Hoge
54. Phoebe Steer
55. Effie Beymer
56. Benjamin J. Thomas
57. Esther S. Fawcett
58. Thomas Branson
59. Rebecca Branson
60. Mabel Cameron

a delicate baby, but has developed into a strong man. He studied architecture at the University of Pennsylvania, where he took both a bachelor's and master's degree. He was traveling in Southern Europe in the study of architecture when the war broke out in 1914 and shortened his trip. He then taught architecture at the University of Illinois, and when our country entered the war, he taught for a while at the University of Pennsylvania and then worked for the Government in a shipyard, and later with the Emergency Fleet Corporation of the United States Shipping Board, where he is still employed. On Ninth month Second, 1916, he married Edith M. Cope, of Woodbury, New Jersey. To them two children have been born: Susanna Morris (7–23–1917) and William Macy, Jr. (5–31–1919). They now live in Lansdowne, Pennsylvania.

All this large family was educated entirely in private schools. All who lived to be old enough attended school at the "Little Brick" at Stillwater, and Barnesville Boarding School. Six also attended Westtown School

THE RESIDENCE OF S. HOWARD AND
ELLEN STANTON PENNELL,
LANSDOWNE, PA.

School and the four youngest are graduates of that
institution. All are members of the Society of Friends
and all who are married, married Friends.

William and Jane Davis Stanton lived happily together, surrounded by their children, for forty-six years.
The last wedding anniversary they celebrated together
was their forty-fifth. Before the forty-sixth Jane had
left home for the last time. The following is copied
from the "Barnesville Enterprise," January, 1909:

"The forty-fifth Anniversary of the marriage of
William and Jane D. Stanton will long be pleasantly
remembered by those who were so kindly entertained
at their home on the twenty-seventh inst.

"On

WILLIAM STANTON AND FAMILY

BACK ROW—ESTHER SIDNEY STANTON, EDITH COPE STANTON. WILLIAM MACY
STANTON.
MIDDLE ROW—ELWOOD DEAN STANTON, JANE DAVIS STANTON, WILLIAM STANTON,
RUTH ELIZABETH STANTON, JOSEPH ELI STANTON, EVA STANTON PALMER, MARY
ANNA PALMER, SAMUEL HOWARD PENNELL, ELLEN STANTON PENNELL, SIDNEY
FAWCETT STANTON.
LOWER ROW—EDNA MACY STANTON. EVA T. STANTON, ANNA STANTON PALMER,
CHARLES WARNER PALMER.
PHOTOGRAPH TAKEN IN 1916.

"On returning from the mid-week religious meeting, they were surprised to find that a few of their relatives and friends had preceded them and were comfortably seated in the living-room. Of a large family of children, only the youngest son, Macy, and Edna, one of the twin daughters, are at home at present.

"The dinner which was soon announced was still more of a surprise. So quietly and cleverly had it been managed in all its details, as to give no hint that anything unusual was forthcoming. While most bounteous, it was daintily served, and the young people had ample reason to believe that their efforts were appreciated by every one. That the absent children were all present in thought was shown in various ways. Reminiscences of days gone by frequently brought up the names of dear ones long since departed.

"Upon

AN OLD HODGIN CHAIR
IT WAS BROUGHT IN AN OX CART FROM GEORGIA TO BARNESVILLE, OHIO, BY STEPHEN HODGIN IN 1803. NOW IN THE POSSESSION OF JOSEPH E. STANTON.

"Upon request the marriage certificate was brough forth and the names thereon were read. Of the sixty five guests, who signed their names, only twenty wer living, and forty-five of the number had died withi the forty-five years."

It is the earnest desire of their surviving childre that they may so live as to be a credit to the parent who worked and sacrificed for them, and who set thei such an unquestionable example in uprightness an altruism that its attainment is a lofty aim.

EDNA MACY STANTON.

Lansdowne,
Pennsylvania,
1919

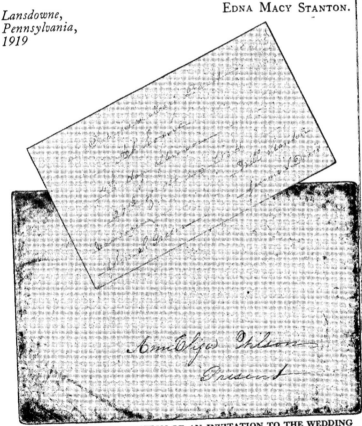

A FULL-SIZE REPRODUCTION OF AN INVITATION TO THE WEDDING RECEPTION AFTER THE MARRIAGE OF WILLIAM STANTON AND JANE S. DAVIS

WOOD POPPING

AS William Stanton sat before the open fire in our home at Westtown he was often annoyed by the wood "popping" and throwing sparks out on the carpet. Most people are satisfied with the use of a screen to overcome the difficulty, but in his characteristic way he set himself the task of finding out a better method than this. By long observation and repeated experiments he found that this "popping" always throws the sparks towards the center of the tree. If a split stick is placed in the fire with the heart toward the back of the fireplace, the sparks will all fly towards the back, and the difficulty is entirely overcome.

This seemed such an interesting discovery that I have sought an explanation from one of the professors in the Yale School of Forestry and from the head of the Botanical Department at the University of Pennsylvania, and I find it is a fact that they did not previously know, much less could they offer any explanation. It will remain, therefore, a scientific discovery to the credit of a man who throughout a long life schooled himself by his deep interest in and his keen observation of all that went on about him.

CHARLES W. PALMER.

MOUNT-PLEASANT BOARDING SCHOOL.

Wm Stanton

REGISTER OF RECITATIONS,

From 10 month 20 1859 to 11 month 19 1859

Studies.	LESSONS.			
	Very Well.	Well.	Indifferent.	Missed.
Mathematics. .				
Astronomy. .				
Arithmetic, . .	18	1	0	0
Spelling, . . .				
Etymology. .	13	5	0	0
Grammar, . .	9	2	0	0
Geography. .	12	4	0	0
Physiology, .				
Chemistry . .	19	0	0	0
History. . . .				
Philosophy, .				
Composition, .				
Botany. . . .				
Reading. . . .				
Writing. . . .				
Conduct	Satisfactory			

A MOUNT PLEASANT REGISTER

A REPRODUCTION OF A RECORD OF STUDIES OF WILLIAM STANTON WHILE A STUDENT
AT MOUNT PLEASANT BOARDING SCHOOL.

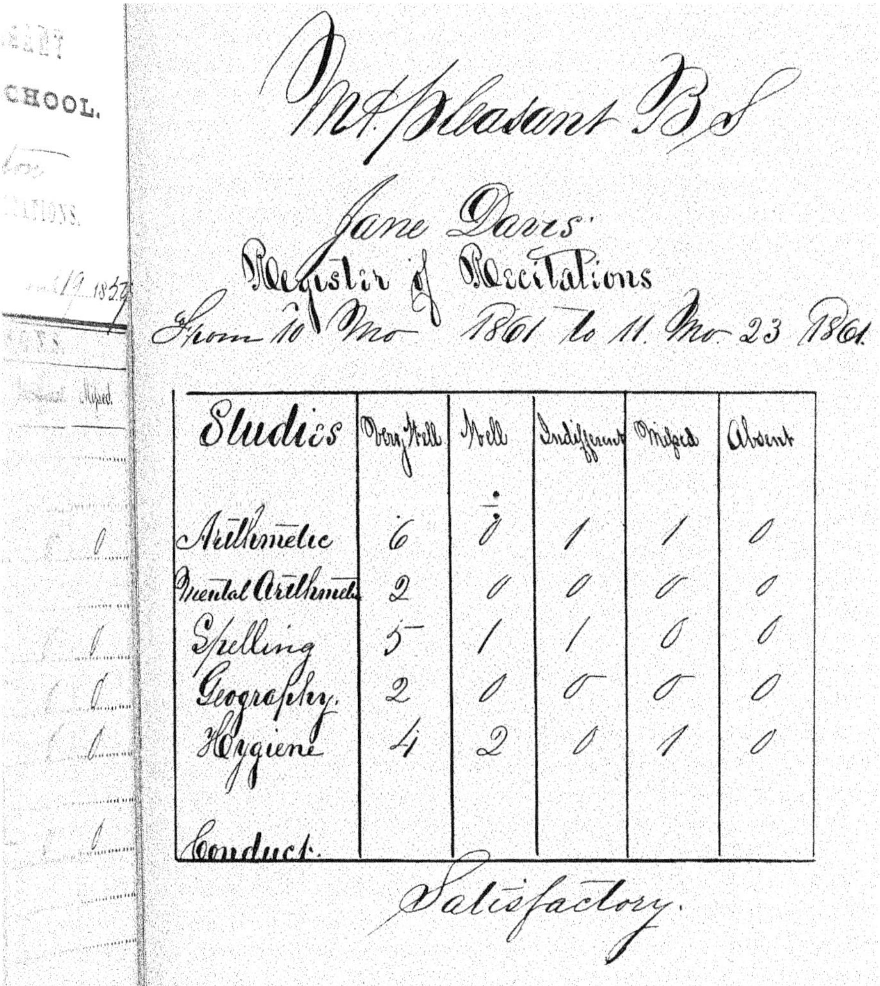

Mt. Pleasant B.S.

Jane Davis'
Register of Recitations
From 10 Mo 1861 to 11 Mo. 23 1861

Studies	Very Well	Well	Indifferent	Neglect	Absent
Arithmetic	6	0	1	1	0
Mental Arithmetic	2	0	0	0	0
Spelling	5	1	1	0	0
Geography.	2	0	0	0	0
Hygiene	4	2	0	1	0
Conduct.					

Satisfactory.

A MOUNT PLEASANT REGISTER
A REPRODUCTION OF A REGISTER OF JANE DAVIS STANTON.

PIONEER "SQUIRREL" OR LONG RIFLE AND POWDER HORN
THE KIND USED BY WILLIAM STANTON.

THREE GENERATIONS

ELWOOD DEAN STANTON, JANE DAVIS STANTON, WILLIAM STANTON.
PHOTOGRAPHED IN 1912.

IT was our parents' love which strengthened their guiding hands and gave to us a heritage upon which our characters formed and grew.

This parental love in turn dictates the course of our own development to build monuments that will sing for them their worthy praise and prolong the bright and lighting influence of their lives.

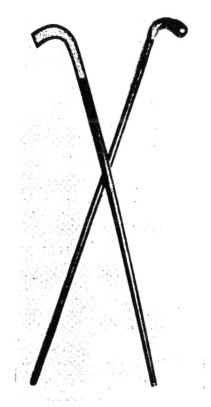

WILLIAM STANTON'S CANES

THE two canes used by William Stanton during his later life. The left-hand one was made by John Bundy from a cherry tree that grew in his yard in Barnesville, Ohio. The other cane was purchased in Rome, Italy, by his son, William Macy Stanton, and presented to his father in 1914. These canes were very much appreciated because they were strong and at the same time very light in weight.

AN APPRECIATION OF EDNA MACY STANTO]

Alice Clark Struck, the author of this article, was Edna's closest friend. They met while attending Teachers' College, Columbia University, New York City.

T IS indeed with pleasure that I welcom this opportunity to testify to the richnes of blessing which has been, and is, min through the friendship of that dear one Edna Stanton; and yet I undertake to d so with trepidation, for it takes a master-pen to expres at all adequately these deeper things of the heart while mine is all too halting even in ordinary matters.

Edna's character, as it was unfolded to me througl eight years of close friendship, was a constant sourc of admiration and inspiration. Although she suffered a constant strain upon her physical system througl ill health almost all the time I knew her, she neve: exhibited irritation or the effects of over-wrough nerves to those about her. She was always sympa thetic toward the troubles of her associates and family ready to give unselfishly of her time and energy (almost too much so for her own good), yet always hiding her own burdens from others and trying to bear them

as

344

as much as possible alone, in so far as mortal help was concerned. The last year, when she was so helpless and suffering so much, her chief worry was that she was causing anxiety and care to the members of her family. Her beautiful, pure, unfaltering faith was the source of her strength, and she accepted the misfortune that came time after time to her, as the chastening hand of God. She had much to bear that only those of us near to her realized. She shared with me, perhaps, more because I was strong and had so few worries of my own. She called me her "safety valve," because so often when her heart cried out for human sympathy it eased the tension to write me about it (for six years of our friendship we were separated by space but close in love). She knew I would understand—we seemed always in such perfect sympathy and talked so freely of the sacred, deeper things of life concerning which we found ourselves in wonderful accord with each other.

It always grieved me that I could not be nearer to Edna physically, to share with her a little of the blessings that came my way. Vain regrets arise to mock me now when I think that I might have helped her with more frequent letters. Our love and friendship, however, flowed on, independent of our letters. It is wonderful to have a friend like that. I feel as sure that she loves me still, although in that unknown land, as I am that my love for her can never die. I am most grateful to the Author of all blessings for this priceless pearl, Edna's love.

No matter how overwhelming her own troubles, Edna always considered others first. The measure of unselfishness which was hers was greater by far than that found in the average one of us. To be of
use

use or comfort to others, to be of use to Christ in the furtherance of His Kingdom, were the guiding desires of her life. In her college days she would go out of her way time after time to aid others. In her teaching, her heart and soul were wrapped up in the welfare of those under her guidance. Often she wrote me in those days of how she was suffering because some one of her charges must be punished. I am sure it was far more painful to her tender heart (and remembered longer) than to the youthful victim. It seemed as though the very strength of her yearning love should hold back the erring girl or boy from the wayward path, but she often felt discouraged—that the results were too meager and that it was all in vain. The loving Father alone knows what seeds for good were planted by her patient hands in those young lives. Many testimonials have come from parents of former pupils and from pupils themselves telling of the good influence she exerted upon their characters. In the last year and a half, when she was too ill to teach regularly, she was able to do quite a good deal of tutoring and she also did considerable work on this book. It comforted her, too, that she was able to knit for the soldiers; sweaters and scarfs, helmets and more sweaters her busy fingers turned out, and many and many a letter went out to cheer the far-away soldier boys of her acquaintance. When the war was over, there still were many things she found to do for others. I doubt if she was ever idle when her strength permitted her to be doing anything. Her skilful needle made many things of use for her family and friends. Her last Christmas gifts were all the work of her hands; for months previously she had been working on them. I wish I could remember

member how many she said she had made, her love going into each stitch. I feel sure no one was left out.

We cannot omit, in a testimonial of this kind, a word about Edna's unusual intellectual ability. Her instructors and classmates in secondary school and in college and her associates everywhere acknowledged her superior reasoning power. Her quick mind traveled surely and quickly to the conclusion or heart of a matter, to which the most of us arrived only after slow and arduous work. Not only was she quick in seeing through things, but she retained in her memory an enormous store of knowledge about many different subjects, always ready as needed to bring light to bear on some related matter which might come up. It was a pleasure for men, as well as for women, to converse with her; her quick-wittedness, her sweet consideration for others' opinions, her original and deep-probing thought about things made her companionship valuable to the most keen intellects. She won many honors in her school and college work, gaining the bachelor's degree at the University of Pennsylvania just the spring before her last illness began, but a good deal of her finest work went unacknowledged because of her modesty. She was never one to thrust herself or her opinions forward, and sometimes her work went unrecognized because its merit was not noted by the professor whose time and attention were monopolized by the more aggressive ones. This did not discourage Edna's indomitable spirit, however, but rather spurred her on to further effort.

And now I have left the most wonderful thing about Edna's personality till the last—at least it seemed to me the most wonderful characteristic. That was her
courage,

courage, her unsurpassed "grit," to use a common but expressive term. She often called to my mind the well-known lines, whose authorship I do not know:

> "It is easy enough to be pleasant
> When life flows along like a song;
> But the man worth while is the one who will smile
> When everything goes dead wrong."

I have seen Edna time after time in college days, going about her daily work and hiding behind her brave smile the suffering and pain from which she was so seldom free. Nothing could daunt her ambition. It was never the easier path she chose if the other offered more opportunity to help or to fit herself for future helpfulness in the world. And the tortures she suffered the last years, with teeth and treatments, operations and weakness! Her attitude through it all was expressed in a letter she wrote me just before she went to the hospital for the last operation. She did not shrink from it, thinking of the long time of suffering she had experienced only a few months before when for weeks following the operation she could not stir from the one position, flat on her back in bed. No, her thought was this: "I do not dread the pain so much—the thing that worries me is that it causes so much anxiety to my family, and expense." It eases the grief of our loss to know that our dear Edna is now where pain and sorrow cannot trouble her, and where, we feel sure, she is reaping the reward of her brave struggle while here. The thought and influence of her love, her beautiful faith, her unselfish life and her wonderful courage will continue to live on after her in the lives of those who knew and loved her.

ALICE CLARK STRUCK.

State College,
Pennsylvania,
1921.

OUR ANCESTORS

Our sires were filled with souls so free
That naught could bid them stay;
   No parent ties
   Or counsel wise
Could bar their westward way.

They sought the light of virgin lands,
They longed to live and be
   In nature's home
   Where they could roam
At will and with their God be free.

They pushed their way with spirits brave
Across the sea where they could live
   With fellow-kind,
   Who left behind
The reign that these restrictions give.

They paused near the coast of the western land,
They toiled at the trades they knew,
   They lived in the love
   Of the God above
And the grace of His servants, too.

The freedom they found was a lure so strong
That they faced the unknown west,
   And pushed their way,
   Like the night the day,
While their souls dreamed of the quest.

O'er

O'er mountain and river through forest dark,
O'er a road with a thousand thrills,
   By the light of day
   They led the way
To a ridge in the Belmont hills.

Their homes were hewn from the trunks of trees,
Their food was the hunted game,
   The soil was tilled
   And garners filled,
And thanks was said in the Master's name.

They lived and loved in the great out-doors,
They gave and received their share;
   The life they led,
   As the ancient said
Was sweet like a breath of heavenly air.

They lived and gave of life's sweetest dream
That our lives should be noble and strong;
   So let their memory cling
   As the phantom thing
That leads us on in the earthly throng.

But wherever we are or whatever we do
Let all praise and all credit go
   To the ones who gave
   Of their hearts to save
Us from the strife it was theirs to know.

Urbana,   WILLIAM MACY STANTON.
Illinois,
1921.

FRANCIS AND MARY DAVIS

FRANCIS DAVIS, son of John and Ann Sparrow Davis, was born on the Ninth of Seventh month, 1819, in Belmont County, Ohio, about three months after his parents came to this country. The parents of John Davis seriously objected to their eldest son leaving their comfortable home in the north of Ireland, but John and his wife being young and ambitious sailed away to America and gave up their families and their share of the family fortunes.

When they had been in this country but a few years John Davis died and left his young son Francis the sole support of his Mother and two sisters. Francis Davis thus came face to face early with the stern realities of life. He worked hard and denied himself a thorough education, never going to school more than three months in the year. He was genial, kind-hearted and of a cheerful disposition, winning the admiration and respect of his neighbors. Responsibility thrown upon him by necessity developed in him sound business principles and an unusual amount of executive ability.

At

FRANCIS AND MARY DAVIS

At the age of twenty-one Francis Davis married Mary Smith, daughter of Jesse and Anna Smith, of Smyrna, Guernsey County, Ohio. Their early married life was spent near Flushing, Ohio. Before the railroad was built Francis Davis did general hauling and made regular trips with a six-horse team from Wheeling, West Virginia, over the old National road to Cumberland, Maryland. He had many experiences that

FRANCIS DAVIS' WATCH AND CASE

Now in the possession of Eva T. Stanton.

THE WORKS OF FRANCIS DAVIS' WATCH

An old-style case and movement showing the crown wheel, cylinder escapement and the fusee. This chain, winding on a conical drum, was arranged to compensate for the varying strength of the mainspring and thereby secure more regular running. This watch was made before the invention of dead-beat escapement.

that were characteristic of those trans-mountain team
sters, and was well versed in their traditions.

After a few years they moved to a farm near Barne
ville, Ohio, and from there he went several times t
Iowa to take up Government land. He had to tak
the money in gold to pay for the land and I remembe
seeing the belt into which the money had been sewr
This belt was worn around his waist under his clothing
The land rapidly increased in value and his interest
were of such proportions that it was often necessary fc
him to go to Iowa, and frequently his wife accom
panied him. I remember hearing him say he had crosse
the Mississippi River forty-two times.

At one time be was interested in a planing-mill ii
Barnesville, and was engaged in the
wholesale grocery business with Milton
Lewis. With his business interests thus
located the family moved to town.
While living there Francis Davis was
active in the affairs of the town and was
President of the First National Bank for
many years. In 1874 they moved again
to the country, where building and contracting claimed part of his time. He
built the Friends' Boarding School and
the Stillwater Meeting House. He assisted with the building of the Belmont
County Children's Home and acted as its
superintendent for a few months.

For almost half a century Francis and
Mary Davis lived and labored together
and gave to the community the strength
that was theirs—serving as they saw and
understood

THE OPEN FIRE-
PLACE TONGS.

A DAVIS-STANTON SECRETARY

JOEL DAWSON HAD THIS SECRETARY MADE AND USED IT FOR A NUMBER OF YEARS. AT HIS SALE IT WAS PURCHASED BY FRANCIS DAVIS, WHO USED IT DURING HIS LIFETIME. IT WAS THEN USED BY JANE DAVIS STANTON AND NOW IS IN THE POSSESSION OF ELLEN STANTON PENNELL.

understood and striving ever to brighten the path of
their influence—and left a goal set up that has inspired and led forward lives that have followed. Both
were active members of the Society of Friends. Nine
children were born to them, only three of whom reached
maturity. While they lived on the farm near Barnesville their daughter Jane became acquainted with William Stanton, and on the Twenty-seventh of First month
1864, they were married at Stillwater Meeting, thus
connecting two of the prominent families of the community.

EVA T. STANTON.

Lansdowne,
Pennsylvania,
1921.

A DAVIS TEA POT
FROM THE HOME OF MARY (SMITH) DAVIS. IT IS
PROBABLY FROM HER FATHER'S FAMILY.

THE WEDDING CERTIFICATE OF JOHN DAVIS

Whereas John Davis son of Francis Davis, of Eumiscorthy in the County of Wexford, and Elizabeth his wife and Ann Sparrow, daughter of William Sparrow, late of Growtown, in said County, and Martha his wife, both deceased, having declared their intentions of taking each other in marriage, before the monthly meeting of Friends, commonly called Quakers of the County of Wexford, the proceedings of the said John Davis and Ann Sparrow after due enquiry and deliberate consideration thereof, were allowed by the said Meeting their intentions having been twice published in the Meeting to which they belong, and they appearing clear of all others and having consent of parents. Now these are to Certify that for the accomplishing of their said marriage this Ninth day of the Sixth month in the Year of our Lord, One Thousand Eight Hundred and Fourteen they the said John Davis and Anne Sparrow appeared at a publick Meeting for Worship of the aforesaid People in their Meeting House at Forest and he the said John Davis taking the said Ann Sparrow by the hand, declared as followeth: Friends, I take Anne Sparrow to be my wife, promising thro Divine assistance to be unto her a loving and faithful husband, until death shall separate us . . . and the said Anne Sparrow did then and there in the said Assembly declare as followeth: Friends, I take John Davis to be my husband, promising thro divine assistance, to be unto him a loving and faithful wife until death shall separate us and the said John Davis, and Anne—as a further confirmation thereof did then and there to these presents, set their hands as Husband and Wife

John Davis
Anne Davis

and we who were present at said Marriage, have also subscribed our names as witnesses thereunto the day and year above written

Elizabeth Cockarill	Margaret (Mar) tin	Francis Davis
Rebecca Goff	Elizabeth Gooch	Deborah Sparrow
John Brenam	Sarah Baker	Thos. Sparrow
Susan Diggin	Anne Baker	Sally Davis
	Mary Sparrow	Margaret Sparrow, Jr.
	Hannah Martin	Francis Bassett
Jacob Poole	Catharine Martin	Rich'd Poole
John Poole	Ebin Martin	Mary Goff
Mary Poole	Sam'l Martin	Sarah Davis
	Tane Davis	Mary Martin, Jun.
		Samuel Davis
		Williams Davis
		Hannah ———
		Deborah Davis

THE OTHA FRENCH HOUSE
BUILT BY OTHA FRENCH, SR., ABOUT 1844 AND OCCUPIED BY WILLIAM STANTON
FROM ABOUT 1867 TO 1877.

IT was on the front wall of this house that Otha French had written in large black letters on a white sign, "Hold on to the Maine law forever." It was his admonition for prohibition, and this proverb, emblazed on his dwelling place, was incised on his tombstone. Almost seventy years elapsed before the country came to the full meaning of his conviction.

THE CLAY PIKE

THE clay pike, as it was known, was a state road between Zanesville, Ohio, and the Flats of Grave Creek, West Virginia, built for the purpose of driving stock from the West to the markets of the East. The national road could not be used for this purpose because the McAdam or stone road made the animals' hoofs unfit for travel.

The clay pike passed through Senecaville, Salesville, Quaker City, and Spencer Station in Guernsey County and through Barnesville, Tacoma, and Burtons Station in Belmont County.

The road was sixty-six feet wide and all kinds of stock were driven over it, but cattle predominated. In the spring of the year the road would become very bad from the cattle ridging the mud from side to side of the road between their steps.

Many of the farmers along the pike made a practice of taking care of the droves over night and received a generous remuneration. Some interesting stories are told of these drovers by the people in whose homes they spent the night. An instance I have heard my father relate happened at Grandfather Thomas Webster's, one mile west of Quaker City. One spring day a large drove of mules came along about dark. The "boss" wanted to get lodging for the men and animals for the night. He applied to grandfather and was assigned a pasture separated from an oat field by a good, substantial eight-rail stake-and-ridered fence. The boss inspected the fence thoroughly and declared it would not turn the mules, so he detailed three of his men to sit on the fence and guard the mules all night.

Another instance happened at the home of John Hall, just west of Spencer Station. Among the drovers was a small boy. The women, thinking the boy rather timid and backward, had
taken

359

taken special care to see he was well helped at the table—driving gave them all a good appetite. When the pie was passed, the boy refused a second piece, the women insisted, and he said, "Well, if I stand up, maybe I can eat another piece," and suited the action to the word.

It is related in the History of Belmont County that in 1849 a drover called at the home of Otha French and asked to stay over night. Mr. French put his usual question, "Has any of your stock been fed at a still house?" and was answered in the negative. The drove was turned in and fed and the hands had all washed, ready for supper, which was on the table. Mr. French had found out by some means that the hogs, for the greater part, had been fattened at the Waverly distilleries. He instantly ordered the drove to be taken out of his field and would not let even the drover or his men have their supper.

Columbus,   WILLIS V. WEBSTER.
Ohio,
1920.

Lindley P. Bailey   *Married Seventh Month Twenty-ninth 1874*   *Elizabeth Stanton*

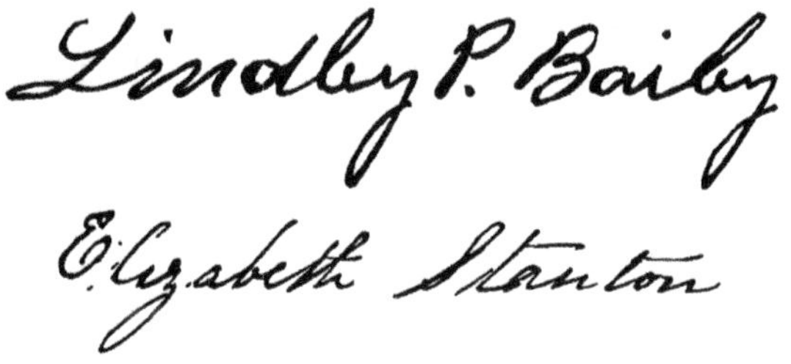

Lindley P. Bailey

Elizabeth Stanton

LINDLEY PATTERSON AND ELIZABETH STANTON BAILEY

ELIZABETH S. BAILEY, youngest daughter of Joseph and Mary Stanton, was born the Twenty-fourth of Twelfth month, 1846, on a farm a short distance northwest of her present home at Tacoma, Ohio. Her Uncle Eli Hodgin lived on one side of her home and on the other side was the home of her Aunt Amy Clendenon. Many happy times did the children of the three families have together. After a morning or afternoon spent at play, when her cousins started home Elizabeth would always "go a piece" with them—"to the beechnut tree" with Aunt Amy's girls and "to the apple tree" with Uncle Eli's. Those days have lingered

fresh

fresh in her memory and she loves to tell her children and her grandchildren of those happy times when she was a little girl.

Grief came early to little Elizabeth, for at the age of eleven years her invalid mother died. Her father's death followed two years later. Thus, at thirteen she was left without parents, but her brothers and sisters welcomed her to their firesides and were so good to her that she felt she had three homes. Most of the time until her marriage was spent with her sister Anna, who was always kind and thoughtful and helped her to feel less the loss of father and mother.

She was educated at Friends' Primary School at Stillwater and at Mount Pleasant Boarding School. In those days the rules of boarding-school life were very strict. Boys and girls were not allowed to mingle together. One day Elizabeth and one of her girl friends were out in the yard and, seeing some boys on the roof, stopped to see what they were doing. But, alas, a watchful teacher saw this "misdemeanor" and their registers were "marked." She had to explain to her sister Anna that her report was marked for "looking at the boys." After leaving school Elizabeth was invited to attend the wedding of Lindley Bundy and Ruanna Frame and to be a "waiter" with Lindley P. Bailey, almost a stranger to her at that time. This meeting was the beginning of a friendship that resulted in their marriage.

In 1871 she married Lindley Patterson Bailey, born Third month Eighth, 1850. He was the third son of Jesse and Asenath Bailey. His mother was a minister in the Society of Friends. Her life had been full of hardships, with very little education, yet she was possessed

JESSE AND ASENATH BAILEY
1815-1898　　　　　　1820-1905

possessed of a wonderful mind. While on a religious visit she spoke to the convicts in Iowa State Prison. So feelingly and so forcibly did she speak to those sin-hardened men, that there was scarcely a dry eye in the room when she finished. She was a woman full of energy and with a bright look ahead, giving to her sons her best in life. Knowing she had missed much by her lack of school training, she did everything she could in order that her sons should have as good an education as possible. Lindley lived with his parents on their farm about four miles east of Barnesville, Ohio, and attended the district school nearby. Being a great lover of debate, he was one of the leaders in

ers in organizing a debating club where they met ar
discussed the leading questions of the day. Often I
would go out on the farm by himself, get upon
stump, and speak to an imaginary audience. Th
practice gave the youthful orator a training that w:
useful to him in later life. After completing the cour:
at the district school, he attended Mount Pleasant Boar
ing School for four years, following this with a year ;
Normal School in Barnesville. He then started t
teach in his home district.

After their marriage on Seventh month Twenty
sixth, 1871, they lived for a while in "the weanin
house"—a little house on his father's farm. From th
home they went to an adjoining farm, where h
worked during the summer and taught school durin
the winter. While living on this farm their eldest sor
Edwin M., was born Seventh month Eighteenth, 187:
In 1873 they bought a farm of one hundred and si:
teen acres, which proved to be a heavy burden durin
the financial panic of 1873.[1]

Lindley continued the combination of farming an
school teaching during the six years that they live
on this farm, in which time three children were born
Oscar J., Twelfth month Fifth, 1874; Anna, Eight
month Sixteenth, 1876; Clara, Sixth month Twenty
fifth, 1878.

In 1878 they sold the home and fifty acres of the lan
and rented a farm near Speidel, Ohio, in 1880 and live
there for six years. While in this home their two younges
sons

---

[1] The rate of interest was eight to ten per cent., and prices of all farm product:
rapidly decreased. Wool dropped from sixty cents to twenty cents per pound:
hogs dropped down to two or three cents a pound; cattle, two and a half to four:
wheat at fifty cents a bushel; corn, twenty-three to thirty cents a bushel; butter, ten to twenty cents a pound. The best horses were selling for one hundre
dollars or less.

THE SQUIRE WHITE LOG HOUSE NEAR SPEIDEL, OHIO

IT WAS OCCUPIED FOR SIX YEARS BY LINDLEY P. AND ELIZABETH S. BAILEY. THEIR
SONS ALVA AND JESSE WERE BORN IN THIS HOUSE. IT IS KNOWN TO HAVE BEEN
STANDING IN 1845. THE CHIMNEY WAS OF BEAUTIFULLY DRESSED SANDSTONE. THERE
WERE WOOD FIREPLACES ON THE FIRST AND SECOND FLOORS.
ELIZABETH, HOLDING JESSE ON THE PORCH, ANNA AND CLARA ON THE STEPS, AND
ALVA, WITH THE LITTLE WAGON.

sons were born: Alva C., Fourth month Twenty-sixth,
1880; Jesse S., Fourth month Fifteenth, 1884.

These years were full ones for the family. Six
hearty children had to be fed, clothed and sent to
school. The nearest school was over a mile away.
They were taught to work as well as to play and many
happy days were spent here.

While living on this farm Elizabeth had a very
severe illness. For a few days her condition was
critical, but she had a mission yet unfilled and
was spared for her family. Dr. Kemp, the family
physician, attended her. He was a familiar figure
in those days as he rode along on his old gray horse,
humming a tune or talking to himself. Dr. Kemp
was an unusual character and many families owe him
a debt

a debt of gratitude for his services to their loved ones.

During the year 1883 Lindley engaged in a side venture and left the details of the business to a partner, only to find himself, as a result, under heavy financial obligations.

In the early spring of 1886 they rented the John Bundy farm, containing 181 acres, near Tacoma, Ohio, and in 1888 bought it, where they have since made their home. The farm having been rented for a number of years had lost much fertility and was in bad condition when they bought it. The barn was good, but the house poor. The kitchen and sitting-room chimneys had fallen down and the roof of the kitchen was broken in. Undaunted, they went to work to fix things up the best they could. One side of the kitchen roof did not leak. The table stood on this side, and with boards hung over the stove to keep out the rain, the good wife and mother managed to feed her flock until better things came.

Their children, after finishing at the district school, were sent to the Friends' Boarding School at Barnesville, Ohio. The boys each spent two years there, and if they chose they could have later had one year at agricultural or business college.

Elizabeth had a natural liking for cows. She made high-class butter, commanding a premium price in the village. Lindley had no natural inclination for dairy cows, preferring beef cattle and sheep, but he finally discovered that Elizabeth's cows brought better returns than the other farm interests. James Edgerton, a few years before, had imported from Rhode Island three registered Jersey cattle, said to be the first ever shipped across the Allegheny Mountains. Eliza-

beth

beth had a great desire to own some, so she persuaded Lindley to trade a threshing machine—which he was running somewhat against her wishes—for a Jersey bull, a cow and a heifer calf. Lindley soon became interested in dairying and especially in Jersey cows. Elizabeth's children feel they can justly call their mother the sponsor of the Jersey cattle interests in Ohio. Ohio now ranks highest in number of Jersey cattle of all the states in the Union except Texas.

Elizabeth made a twenty-pound tub of butter and sent it to the first National Dairy Show held in Madison Square Garden, New York City, in 1887, and placed it in competition there with over two hundred entries of famous New England and Eastern States' dairy butter. Lindley attended the show, mingling with the fancy buttermakers of the East and getting acquainted with their methods, but he did not let them know he had butter in the competition. When the awards were made, Elizabeth's little tub of butter, made on a rented farm in Ohio, came out third best, winning a thirty-dollar prize. Since then the farm has exhibited dairy products—milk, cream and butter—at nearly all the National Dairy Shows, universally winning a prize and many times "gold medals" and "First Prizes." A Second Prize was won with two thousand exhibitors on cream at the Panama-Pacific Exposition, 1915. The cream, shipped three thousand miles, from Ohio, arrived in good condition without re-icing on the way.

It is conceded now that Belmont Stock Farm, two miles east of Barnesville, Ohio, holds more medals and grand prizes for Dairy Products than any other farm in America. There is on this farm of two hundred and fifty acres an average herd of one hundred Registered Jersey cattle.

**THE HOME OF LINDLEY P. AND ELIZABETH STANTON
BAILEY**

FORMERLY THE HOME OF JOHN AND ANNA E. BUNDY. THE FRAME ADDITION TO THE
HOUSE, THE DAIRY BARN AND NUMEROUS OTHER BUILDINGS WERE BUILT BY
LINDLEY P. BAILEY.

cattle.. The three modern dwelling houses and two large
barns are supplied with city water and electricity. Here
in 1888 was built the first creamery in Belmont County.
Cream and milk from the neighboring farms were
brought in and the creamery was run on the co-opera-
tive plan. Thus, a dairy interest was started in the
community that has been gradually developing ever
since.

Lindley and Elizabeth adopted new methods whenever they believed them to be helpful to their interests.
Lindley allied himself with state and national organizations pertaining to agriculture, livestock and dairying. For eight years he was on the directory of the
American Jersey Cattle Club. He assisted in organizing the Ohio State Dairymen's Association in 1894,
then served as Secretary for six years and as President for ten years, and is now Honorary President.
During this time he became active in legislative
work, often being called to appear before Con-
gressional Committees in Ohio and Washington,
D. C., in the interest of agricultural legislation. He
was

was for five years a member of the State Board of Agriculture, serving as President in 1907, for five years a member of Ohio Live Stock Commission, for four years Vice-President of American Dairy Farmers' Association, for six years on the Agricultural Extension Lecture force of Ohio State University, active in lecture work for the American Jersey Cattle Club, and of the Ohio State Grange, calling him to different States of the Union.

At the Panama-Pacific International Exposition held at San Francisco, California, the summer of 1915, Lindley

LINDLEY P. AND ELIZABETH STANTON BAILEY AND FAMILY

TOP ROW—FREDERICK R. BUNDY, CLARA BAILEY BUNDY, CLARENCE R. PATTEN, ANNA BAILEY PATTEN.
CENTER ROW—EDWIN M. BAILEY, LILLIAN D. BAILEY, LINDLEY P. BAILEY, ELIZABETH STANTON BAILEY, OSCAR J. BAILEY, MARY ANNA BAILEY.
LOWER ROW—LAURA E. BAILEY, ALVA C. BAILEY, LYDIA H. BAILEY, JESSE S. BAILEY.

Lindley Bailey was one of the Commission chosen to have charge of Ohio's exhibition. He, accompanied by his wife, spent a month in the Ohio Building on the Exposition grounds. After leaving California they spent some time traveling in Oregon, Washington and Canada.

In 1917 Governor Cox of Ohio appointed Lindley Bailey Food Commissioner for Belmont County to serve during the war.

He was always Republican in politics, but actuated from principle rather than partisanship. While often solicited to become a candidate for office, he always refused, except twice—he was once a candidate for Congress and one time a candidate for Ohio Constitutional Convention. He was defeated both times.

In the summer of 1893 their oldest son, Edwin M., married Lillian M. Doudna, daughter of Josiah W. and Ruth B. Doudna, who lived on an adjoining farm. After their marriage Edwin managed a creamery near home, then went to Pittsburgh, Pennsylvania, where he has become one of the leading milk dealers of the city. They have one son, Herbert J. (6–8–1899).

Oscar J., the second son, married Mary Anna Brackin, of Colerain, Ohio, in 1896. To them five sons were born: Alfred L. (3–16–1897), Oliver B. (6–14–1901), Joseph O. (7–5–1903), Edward F. (1–30–1907), Lindley P., Jr. (8–9–1911). In 1914 Mary Anna died, leaving a motherless home where five boys and their father mourned the loss of one who had taken a high place in the hearts of the whole community and to whom everyone looked for counsel in those things that are high and noble. She was a devoted companion and a mother of the choicest love

LAVADA S. BAILEY

love and inspiring confidence for her children, and her memory lingers now in their hearts and the heart of their parent who has lived to carry on her life-giving parental message.

Three years later Oscar married Sara Lavada Stockdale, of Fairview, Ohio, a graduate of Mt. Union College. Oscar has a dairy farm at Tacoma, Ohio. In 1919 Alfred married Anna Bundy, of Tacoma, Ohio. To them one daughter was born: Dorothy L. (4–7–1920).

Anna, the eldest daughter, married Clarence R. Patten, of Whittier, Iowa. Their home is now at Tacoma, Ohio, where they manufacture Patten's Baby Nests. To them three children were born: Bertha E. (6–1–1903). Bertha graduated at Friends' Boarding School, Barnesville, Ohio, in 1920, at Westtown Boarding School, Westtown, Pennsylvania, in 1921. Beulah L. (2–23–1907). Oscar M. (3–20–1909).

Clara married Frederick R. Bundy. They have a home at Tacoma, Ohio, where they are giving special attention

attention to high-class poultry. Two sons came to bless their home: Willard L. (4–2–1906), J. Stanton (1–28–1911).

Alva married Laura E. Steer, of Colerain, Ohio, in the summer of 1901. To them were born seven children: Harmon E. (7–14–1902), Mary E. (9–20–1904), Raymond C. (6–28–1907), Rolland A. (6–28–1909), David B. (12–29–1912), Nathan C. (9–29–1914), Ralph W. (2–21–1921). They have a dairy farm near Fairview, Ohio.

Jesse, the youngest of the family, married Lydia M. Hoge in 1908. They live with his father and mother, sharing the care and management of the home and farm. They have four children: Elizabeth S., Jr. (5–16–1911), Florence E. (6–27–1913), Lester W. (11–22–1915), Charles Lloyd (3–20–1918).

This completes the circle of twenty-two grandchildren and one great-grandchild. All are ever glad to go to Grandfather's and are always sure of a welcome there.

Elizabeth has always been greatly devoted to her family interests. System in all things enables her to discharge her various duties timely and with ease, leaving her time to advise with her family, to have sympathy with all and to lend a helping hand to the needy. In community affairs she is an active leader; her counsel is often sought. Always has she been the confidant of her children, helping and guiding them in their most intimate affairs. This confidence and influence extends to her twenty-two grandchildren.

> "Who ran to help me when I fell,
> And would some pretty story tell,
> Or kiss the place to make it well—
> My mother."

Now,

Now, though Lindley and Elizabeth Bailey are past seventy years of age, they still have the confidence of the family. Never do their children or grandchildren take a step of importance without first asking their advice, being assured of receiving loving sympathy and sound judgment.

It is a great satisfaction to this couple that their children, except Edwin in Pittsburgh, are living near them and all have a common business interest. They frequently meet together in a family reunion, rejoicing as but few families can rejoice.

Tacoma,   ANNA BAILEY PATTEN.
Ohio,
1920.

A PIONEER LANTERN
MADE OF TIN AND BURNED A TALLOW CANDLE. IN THE HOME
OF LINDLEY P. AND ELIZABETH STANTON BAILEY.

GOLD, SILVER AND BRONZE MEDALS

WON ON DAIRY PRODUCTS, BY L. P. BAILEY AND SONS, AT NATIONAL AND INTER-NATIONAL
EXPOSITIONS 1907 TO 1918

THE STRAWBERRY REUNIONS

LONG IN 1900 AND FOR MANY YEARS AFTER, WHEN THE STRAW-
BERRY SEASON WAS AT ITS HEIGHT, IT WAS THE CUSTOM FOR
THE STANTON FAMILY CONNECTIONS AROUND TACOMA TO HOLD
A REUNION. THE FAMILIES ROTATED IN GIVING THE ENTER-
TAINMENT, BUT THE MENU WAS ALWAYS THE SAME—BELMONT
COUNTY STRAWBERRIES AND JERSEY ICE CREAM.
THE COMBINATION WAS NOT TO BE EXCELLED, AND THE PLEASANT
MEMORIES OF THOSE FEASTS PROMPTS THE WRITING OF THIS AND A LONG-
ING FOR THEIR RE-OCCURRENCE.

W. M. S.

SILVER CUPS—FIRST PRIZE

OHIO DAIRYMEN'S ASSOCIATION 1907, AWARDED L. P. BAILEY AND SONS
ON MARKET MILK AND MARKET CREAM

THE CIRCULATING LETTER

 A DESIRE TO BIND MORE CLOSELY THE SCATTERING FAMILIES, PROMPTED JANE DAVIS STANTON, IN 1900, TO START A CIRCULATING LETTER THAT CARRIED THE NEWS FROM ONE HOME TO ANOTHER IN REGULAR ROTATION. THE LETTER WAS A WELCOME VISITOR AND ITS READING AROUND THE FAMILY FIRESIDE BECAME AN ANTICIPATED OCCASION AND KEPT ALIVE A FAMILY INTEREST THAT WAS WHOLESOME AND WORTH WHILE.

W. M. S.

THE GUESTS AT THE FIFTIETH ANNIVERSARY WHO ALSO ATTENDED THE MARRIAGE OF LINDLEY PATTERSON AND ELIZABETH STANTON BAILEY

FRONT ROW—MARY M. (BUNDY) COLPITTS, CHALKLEY DAWSON, RUANHA (FRAME BUNDY) STEER, LINDLEY PATTERSON BAILEY, ELIZABETH STANTON

A FIFTIETH ANNIVERSARY

LOOKING forward, fifty years seems a very long time, but to those looking backward, only a little while, and yet what changes such a period brings, for when we gathered on Seventh month Twenty-sixth, 1921, for the fiftieth anniversary of the marriage of Lindley P. and Elizabeth Stanton Bailey, we traveled by automobile, some of us a two-days' trip over the mountains, covering a distance of four hundred miles. Fifty years ago horse-back riding was the popular mode of travel, but of the hundred and thirty-seven guests not one came in a horse-drawn conveyance. Messages of congratulation came by telephone, telegraph, and wireless telegraphy could have been used.

The day of the anniversary was beautiful, as was the wedding day fifty years before. It seemed the sunshine, the grass, the trees and the flowers alone were unchanged and that love that made this happy occasion was unchanged too, only broadened and deepened as it reached out and enfolded their little flock even to the fourth generation.

The bride and groom of fifty years were seated at the

ANNIVERSARY BOUQUET
A DUPLICATE OF THE BRIDE'S BOUQUET AT THE WEDDING. ARRANGED
FROM MEMORY BY WILLIAM H. STANTON.

the table with most of their original wedding guests
who were present this day. Many jests on their youthful frolics were passed and, too, the thought came of
faces that were missing.

It was a bountiful chicken dinner that was served,
similar to the one on the bridal day—but the bride
and groom no doubt were in a better position to enjoy
this one. Gold and white were predominant in the
decorations and in the preparation of the meal to the
point that there was white brick ice cream with a
golden heart, golden cake with white icing, white
cake with golden icing.

There

1. JOHN COLITTS
2. HILDA BOYD
3. S. OLIVE BOYD
4. SAMUEL BAILEY
5. BARBARA BAILEY
6. WILLIAM BOYD
7. FINLEY HOWELL
8. MILDRED BAILEY
9. VIRGINIA BAILEY
10. RUTH BAILEY
11. EDWIN STANTON
12. WILLIAM H. STANTON
13. LAURA S. BAILEY
14. LOUISE S. STANTON
15. WILLARD BAILEY
16. ROBERT SMITH
17. JOSEPH BAILEY
18. VIVIAN BAILEY
19. ERNEST BAILEY
20. ROSS BAILEY
21. RALPH W. BAILEY
22. NORA BAILEY
23. DELBERT BAILEY
24. BEULA C. WEBSTER
25. BEULAH L. PATTEN
26. EDNA B. TABER
27. ANNA B. PATTEN
28. MARY L. WEBSTER
29. RUABNA BUNDY STEER
30. HATTIE BAILEY

37. HELEN BAILEY
38. HERBERT BAILEY
39. CLARENCE R. PATTEN
40. EDNA B. TABER
41. PAUL TABER
42. EVA L. BAILEY
43. SARAH B. HALL
44. DAVID R. BAILEY

51. MARY E. BAILEY
52. JOSEPH M. BAILEY
53. CLARENCE J. BAILEY
54. CLARA B. BUNDY
55. JESSE S. BAILEY
56. C. LLOYD BAILEY
57. HARMON E. BAILEY
58. FREDERICK R. BUNDY

65. FREDERICK BAILEY
66. AMANDA B. BAILEY
67. EDWIN M. BAILEY
68. EDWIN M. BAILEY
69. ROLAND A. BAILEY
70. BERTHA E. PATTEN
71. OLIVER B. BAILEY
72. I. STANTON BUNDY

79. MARTHA CHANCY
80. AGNES B. CUNNINGHAM
81. DOROTHY L. BAILEY
82. ALFRED L. BAILEY
83. ELIZABETH S. BAILEY, IND.
84. EVA T. STANTON
85. LAVADA S. BAILEY
86. RUSSEL BUNDY

93. EVA S. PALMER
94. MARY ANNA PALMER
95. ANNA S. PALMER
96. WILBUR BAILEY
97. MARY M. COLITTS
98. LAURA B. CLARK
99. MARIA SMITH
100. JESSIE MILLER
101. JOSIAH W. DOUOMA
102. SUSSER F. STANTON
103. SUSSER F. STANTON
104. PAULINE STANTON
105. RUTH E. STANTON
106. KATHERINE M. STANTON
107. E. DEAN STANTON
108. RUTH DOUOMA
109. ABIGAIL SPEER
110. ABIGAIL SPEER
111. CHARLES CLARK
112. EARL CLARK
113. FLORENCE HOGE
114. MARY E. WATTERSON
115. MARY E. WATTERSON
116. CHARLEY DAWSON
117. EDITH C. STANTON
118. CORA HOWELL
119. DORIS HOWELL
120. ALMA B. STANTON
121. ARTHUR E. STANTON
122. W. MACY STANTON

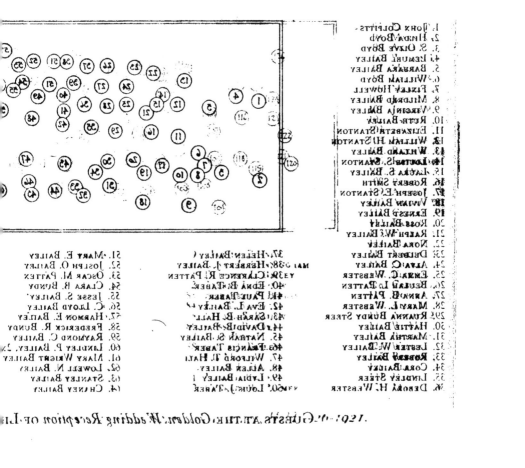

1. John Colpitts
2. Hiram Boyd
3. S. Olive Boyd
4. Lemuel Bailey
5. Barbara Bailey
6. William Boyd
7. Eliza Howell
8. Mildred Bailey
9. Veronia Bailey
10. Ruth Bailey
11. Elizabeth Stanton
12. William H. Stanton
13. Wiland Bailey
14. Loretta S. Stanton
15. Alvira S. Bailey
16. Robert Smith
17. Joseph E. Stanton
18. Vivian Bailey
19. Ernest Bailey
20. Rosa Bailey
21. Ralph W. Bailey
22. Nora Bailey
23. Delbert Bailey
24. Alva O. Bailey
25. Emma C. Webster
26. Beulah M. Patten
27. Anna B. Patten
28. Mary L. Webster
29. Ruanna Buddy Steer
30. Hattie Bailey
31. Martha Bailey
32. Lester W. Bailey
33. Robert Bailey
34. Cora Bailey
35. Lindley Steer
36. Denora H. H. Webster

37. Helen Bailey
38. Herbert J. Bailey
39. Clarence R. Patten
40. Edna B. Taber
41. Paul Taber
42. Eva L. Bailey
43. Sarah B. Hall
44. David B. Bailey
45. Natah S. Bailey
46. Francis Taber
47. Wilford T. Hall
48. Allan Bailey
49. Lydia Bailey
50. Louise J. Taber

51. Mary E. Bailey
52. Joseph O. Bailey
53. Oscar M. Patten
54. Clara B. Bundy
55. Jesse S. Bailey
56. C. Lloyd Bailey
57. Harmon E. Bailey
58. Frederick R. Bundy
59. Raymond C. Bailey
60. Lindley P. Bailey
61. Mary Wright Bailey
62. Lowell N. Bailey
63. Stanley Bailey
64. Chaney Bailey

Guests at the Golden Wedding Reception of Li... 1921.

There were flowers everywhere, both indoors and out. They varied from the bouquet of old-fashioned flowers in vogue fifty years ago to the large basket of roses in modern artistry. Fifty years ago the one bouquet had to be moved from the table, as one Friend felt it was too frivolous.

In the afternoon we gathered on the lawn and had our pictures taken and listened while anecdotes were told of the days that are gone. A song was sung and Uncle Lin gave a little appreciation of the love and service of his helpmate.

Lansdowne,   EDITH COPE STANTON.
Pennsylvania,
1921.

FOUR GENERATIONS

LINDLEY P. AND ELIZABETH STANTON BAILEY, OSCAR J. AND LAVADA BAILEY, ALFRED L. AND ANNA BAILEY AND DOROTHY LOUISE BAILEY. PHOTOGRAPHED AT THE GOLDEN WEDDING ANNIVERSARY.

FOR FIFTY YEARS

The bleak cold breath of winter's winds,
  Whipped snow flakes through the dell,
The stars stood out in the wintry sky,
The giant oak-trees wreathed a sigh—
  The country-folk slept—and all was well
    As a child was born.

A maid it was, who came to bless,
  The home that winter's night,
Just as the bells of Saint Nicholas rang—
After the carols the children sang,
  Just as a ray of Bethlehem's light,
    The babe came to dwell.

For years she lived with girlish glee,
  Four seasons of child-like joy,
When over the hills, not far away—
In another home one warm spring day,
  Life first breathed in a little boy,
    And he joined the march of years.

They lived in their spheres with each one apart,
  Nor saw what the future held,
They learned in school the laws of man,
They learned to live in Him who can
  The hearts of two forever weld,
    The twain as one.

That

That spark of their love first shone on the day,
That another was wed of the folk:
Of the joy of love to give and grow
Their hearts left always an overflow,
To lighten the sting of another's yoke,
As through toil the world has passed.

They gave to the world of their precious kind,
And filled each heart with love,
That came of toil they won through prayer,
That they be helped to do their share,
To give them life.   All praise above,
Where dwells the Master.

The childish love for each has grown
More pure as the years have fled,
The rays of youth have changed to gold,
And days of life sweet pleasures hold,
As silvery strands bedeck each head,
Once of a youthful hue.

They live in light that all should know,
The light of precious life,
The years have fled to fifty now
Since love sealed firm the wedding vow,
But strong of heart and staunch in strife,
They now live on.

The years will bring them work to do—
His task is not yet o'er,
So may they stand in azure bright
With us, until that golden light
Shines on their souls, as those before
And calls them home.

WILLIAM MACY STANTON.

*Lansdowne,
Pennsylvania,
1921.*

QUAKER WEDDINGS OF YESTERYEAR

RIENDS' weddings during the Nineteenth Century were conducted much the same as they are today, except that some of the practices accompanying them were typical of that period.

The bride and groom were attended by three couples of their friends called "waiters." After the marriage at the Meeting House a reception was held at the home of the bride's parents and the following day another reception was given at the home of the groom's parents. There was usually a serenade the evening following the marriage. After the noise was stopped by the appearance of the bride and groom, a general good time was enjoyed.

After the serenaders had gone and it was bedtime the custom was for the bridesmaids to put the bride to bed, then the groomsman or first waiter to accompany the groom to the room, enter with him carrying the oil lamp and place it on the old bureau, then to aid him in taking off his coat and pulling off his boots.

When I was first waiter for Benjamin Stanton when he

he married Elizabeth Plummer in 1870 the bridesmaids played a joke on us and had much fun at our expense. When bedtime came Benjamin and I went to the room designated. There we found a large feather bed with the covers as smooth as the carpet on the floor and the pillows standing up unruffled. We backed out and went into several other rooms thinking they had purposely misdirected us. The members of the wedding company downstairs were having a good laugh, but finally Rachel Frame called to us, from the foot of the stairs, that Elizabeth was in the big feather bed in the first room. We found out later that the girls had made a hollow in the feather bed, put Elizabeth in, smoothed the covers out straight and put the pillows over her face so the bed gave an undisturbed appearance. It was a long time before we heard the last of that experience.

So far as I can learn, Ruanna and Elizabeth Stanton were the two girls who decided to break this custom in 1870 and since that time it has not been practiced.

The wedding company always had such good times that it was said jokingly that one wedding always caused a second one and this proved true with Lindley Bundy and Ruanna Frame's wedding, for a year later Elizabeth Stanton, who was my company at their wedding, became my wife.

Tacoma,   LINDLEY P. BAILEY.
Ohio,
1921.

THE PIONEER'S FUN

DURING the pioneer days of the nineteenth century the country folks were a hard-working, industrious people. The clearing of the forests, the preparing for farms, and the plowing and cultivating the land, among many stumps and stones, developed a sturdy manhood and womanhood. This strenuous labor increased rather than weakened their desire for amusements and entertainments. There developed, therefore, combinations of work and play that were very delightful, such as the "husking bee," the "apple cutting," the "quilting" and "sewing" parties for the women, and "log rollings" for the men. The "taffy pulling," the "spelling school," the "literary and debating society," and "sled riding" party were functions of a more purely social nature.

Most prominent among the country people during the fall season was the "husking bee." When the corn was ready to be gathered the farmer, with the help of his neighbor, "jerked" the ears from the stalk, hauled them to the barn and piled them in a row a hundred or more feet long on the large floor or just outside the barn.

384

barn. Then a general invitation was given to all the neighbors. In the evening when they arrived the men and women alternating lined up on one side of the long pile of corn. They pulled the husks from the ear of corn, threw the husks behind them and the ears over the pile, as jokes and laughter filled the air. It was a most hilarious company.

"The red-ear privilege" was a custom prevailing at these "husking bees." When a young man found a red ear of corn he was privileged to kiss the girl next to him—a custom it is said that was allowed among married folks as well as single. If a young lady found a red ear she slipped it over to the young man next to her and it is said that the young men often searched their fathers' corncribs for red ears and if they found any they hid them in their capacious hunt-shirts—outer garment common in those days—and pulled them out at the husking bee and demanded a forfeit.

Refreshments consisting of pie, cake, fruit, sweet cider and sometimes a popular non-intoxicating drink called "spruce beer" were served. Apple cuttings were common and came next in order of popularity. The young people of the neighborhood assembled at some farm house, where a good supply of apples had been gathered for drying or for apple butter. The young men took off the peelings and some of the young women quartered and cored the apples, while some strung the quartered apples on a twine string with a darning needle and hung them near the stove or the open wood fire to dry. After about an hour of this kind of work the floor was cleared by removing the tables and placing the chairs and benches around the outside of the room. The fun for the evening now began. It consisted of the various games that were

popular

popular at that time. A common play was for one
couple to start marching around the room singing

> "We are marching down to old Quebec,
>   Where the drums are loudly beating,
> The Americans have gained the day,
>   And the British are retreating,
> So we'll take another roar;
>   He that delights in a pretty little wife,
> Go bring her on the floor."

This was responded to by other couples joining until
the room was filled with couples marching. Then the
singing would suddenly change to some song, considered appropriate for suggesting the closing scene, as:

> "The higher up the cherry tree,
>   The sweeter grows the cherry,
> The more you kiss a pretty girl,
>   The more you want to marry."

Every young man was privileged then to kiss his
partner. There was no dancing or card playing, but
many games similar to the one given were enjoyed.

Spelling schools, literary and debating societies were
common during the winter season. Most of the young
people attended and took part. These societies main-
tained a high standard of work and were beneficial in
developing the talents of the young people.

When it came time to go home after the meetings, a
common practice was for the young men to line up
near the door where the young ladies would pass out.
Each young man stood with the left arm akimbo and
when the girl of his choice was passing he would say:

> "The moon shines bright,
>   Can I go home with you tonight?"

If she wished to consent she would say:

> "The stars do, too,
>   I don't care if you do."

If

If unwilling, she would lightly slap him in the face and he dropped out of line and was laughed at by all.

Log rollings and quiltings were enjoyed by the older people. These were mostly held at the same time—the women doing the quilting and preparing the refreshments, while the men were in the clearing piling logs and brush, preparing the land for plowing. The leading timber was oak, sugar, beech, poplar, ash and walnut. Those pioneers were no respecters of timber, all kinds were consigned alike to the log heap to be burned.

During the long winter evenings, when snow was on the ground, there was much "bedtime" visiting. A whole family would start out huddled down in the straw in the sled-bed, all covered with tanned animal skins and comforts and go to visit friends. Sometimes two or more families would go together. No invitation had been received and no notice sent to the family visited, yet it was understood that all should have supper.

Sled-riding parties were very popular. Often fifteen to twenty young people would go in one large sled. When the snow was deep the driver often delighted in upsetting the whole load of people into the snow.

I cannot recall any young man of my acquaintance owning a buggy up to 1870, so when there was no snow, people went on horseback or walked. The young people became expert riders. Great numbers of boys and girls would go on horseback, always in couples. Often the boys preferred, when taking their "best girls" for a ride, to take only one horse. Then the girl would ride behind. The men wore large spurs on the heels of their boots, with which they goaded the horse in the

the side to make it move faster and sometimes to try to make it kick, and then how the girl would hold on! The modern boy's hold of the "wheel" is not to be compared with the pioneer boy with spurs on his heels.

I am sure all will agree that the young people of the pioneer days had plenty of fun. With their simple forms of amusements, they experienced all the thrills and genuine pleasures that are needed to round out a wholesome, happy life.

LINDLEY P. BAILEY.

Tacoma,
Ohio,
1921.

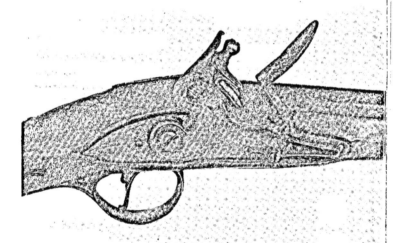

FLINT-LOCK GUN

WHEN LOADING THE GUN A CHARGE OF POWDER WAS PUT IN WITH BALL OR SHOT. THEN A LITTLE POWDER WAS POURED IN THE PAN, THE GUN ROLLED TO ONE SIDE TO FILL THE TOUCH-HOLE, THE HAMMER DRAWN BACK ONE NOTCH AND THE STRIKER OR ANVIL PULLED DOWN, COVERING THE PAN AND PREVENTING THE POWDER FROM SPILLING OUT. WHEN READY TO SHOOT, THE HAMMER WAS DRAWN BACK TO THE SECOND NOTCH AND ON PRESSING THE TRIGGER THE FLINT IN THE HAMMER STRUCK THE ANVIL A GLANCING BLOW, KNOCKED OFF A HOT SPARK OF STEEL WHICH DROPPED INTO THE PAN, SET OFF THE POWDER AND THROUGH THE TOUCH-HOLE EXPLODED THE CHARGE IN THE GUN.

MANY OF OUR PIONEER QUOTATIONS CAME FROM THIS INSTRUMENT, FOR INSTANCE TO "GO OFF HALF-COCKED," REFERRING TO THE ACTION OF THE HAMMER BEFORE SUFFICIENTLY READY; TO "FLASH IN THE PAN" AND NOT SET OFF THE CHARGE IN THE GUN.

THIS ALSO PROMPTED CROMWELL'S FAMOUS SAYING: "TRUST IN GOD, BUT KEEP YOUR POWDER DRY." VERY NECESSARY WHEN USING FLINT-LOCK GUNS. ANOTHER SAYING, "QUICK ON THE TRIGGER," REFERRED TO A GUN WHICH WAS DISCHARGED BY A VERY SLIGHT PRESSURE ON THE TRIGGER.

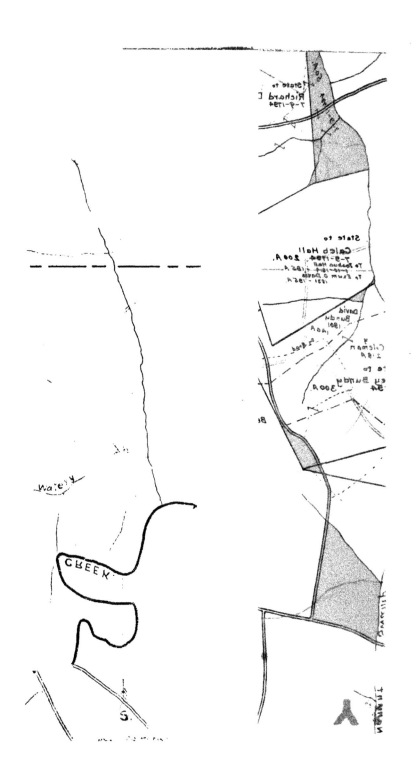

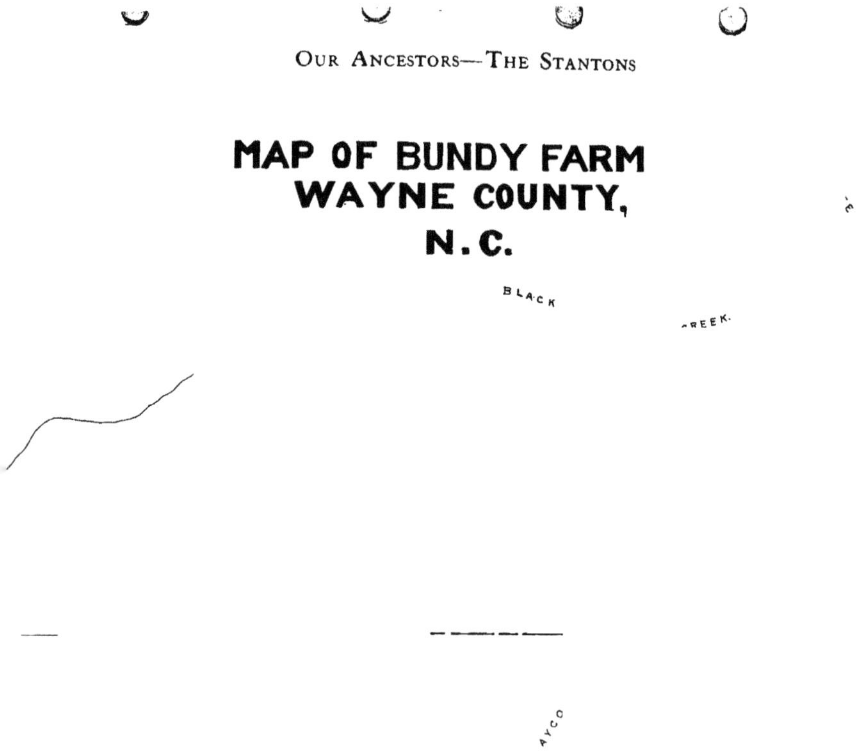

MAP OF BUNDY FARM
WAYNE COUNTY,
N.C.

BLACK

CREEK.

AYCO

THE BUNDY FAMILY

THE Bundy family, from its close and many connections with the Stanton family, is one of special interest.

It is hoped that some one will make a thorough investigation, and record the full history and genealogy of the Bundy family, which cannot be attempted here.

Tradition indicates that the family was in France in the Eleventh Century and probably takes its name from, or gave its name to the Forest of Bondy; and that some members came to England in 1066, with the Normans under William the Conqueror, as the name Bandy appears on the battle rolls of some of the chiefs. It is probable that due to carelessness or difference of pronunciation, the spelling was changed to Bundy.

It appears they settled first in the rugged hills of Wales and later moved to Yorkshire, England. Tradition also says that five brothers emigrated from York, England, and landed on the coast of Virginia or North Carolina, and that one of these brothers became dissatisfied and moved north to what is now known as New York State, and never returned. A family of Bundys now located there resembles those from North Carolina and seems to confirm this tradition.

While some of the early members were fierce warriors and while several members volunteered for service in the Rebellion, the large majority of the family has followed agriculture and the members earned their living in peaceful ways.

The family has generally occupied the middle walk of life—no great wealth and no members in poverty. The industry and thrift practiced and their artistic, well-kept and substantial homes, seem to point to a French ancestry, or at least to a strong admixture of that blood.

Compiled largely from notes
by Thomas Clarkson Bundy.

CABIN ON BUNDY LAND, NORTH CAROLINA

WILL OF DEMSEY BUNDY

1st my will and desire is that all my just debts be paid in due time after my decease.

Then I give to my loving wife Mary Bundy all the land and plantation whereon I now live above that given to my son David Bundy during her life and after her decease for my son Wm. Bundy to have the above mentioned land and Plantation to him and his heirs forever.

I give to my son Zadock Bundy a piece of land bounded as follows—beginning at the head of my son Wm's land is my son David's line thence with his line to Joseph Hollowell's line thence with his line to the corner a post oak thence along a line of marked trees to a black gum is Forts line thence up Forts line to my son Wm's line and with his line to the beginning to him and his heirs forever.

I give to my son John Bundy the remainder part of my land to him and his heirs forever.

I give to my loving wife Mary Bundy all the movable part of my estate to her disposal.

Lastly I nominate and appoint Mary Bundy Exec. and my two sons David and Zadock Bundy Execs. of this my last will and testament 9th 4 mo. 1798.

David and Zadock Bundy qualified as Exec.—April term 1798.

The Inventory of Demsey Bundy

1 horse
8 head of cattle
30 hogs
3 geese
1 chest
2 tables
10 chairs
1 couch
3 pots
1 skillet
1 frying pan
1 pr. fire tongs
1 set of flatirons
1 pr. iron wedges
1 frow
1 set coopers tools
7 axes
3 grubbing hoes
4 weeding hoes
3 plows
1 scythe
2 quart bottles
3 reap hooks
2 hammers
1 hand saw
1 whip saw
3 augers
2 chisels
2 gimlets
1 curry comb
1 saddle & bridle
1 case knives & forks
1 pr. sheep shears
1 pr. cloth shears
1 set cart wheel boxes
1 flower tub
6 gums

2 bbls.
1 hhd.
1 parcel bbl. timber
2 drawing knives
1 pepper box
3 porringers
A parcel of pu—?
1 knife box
Some packed pork
Some flax tow
1 tablecloth
Some salt, pepper & ginger
2 pr. pot hooks
1 spooling wheel
Also his wearing apparel the
  day & date first mentioned

1 case and bottles
1 griddle
1 coffee mill
2 pr. steelyards
1 loom & gear
2 flax wheels
1 wool wheel
3 basins
20 plates
3 dishes
4 cups
3 bowls
1 coffee pot
1 milk pot
8 spoons
1 tub
3 piggins
1 half bushel
3 wheat seives
6 baskets
1 chamber pot
1 glass tumbler
1 dram glass
1 looking glass
1 pr. traces & other gear
3 pr. cords
13 books
3 pamphlets
1 x saw file
1 candlestick
1 cart & wheels
2 combs, a parcel of cotton
1 stack of fodder & some loose
Some corn
1 bucket
1 cowhide
2 sides of leather & some
  pieces of leather
A parcel of hogs lard
A parcel of bacon
1 cann
1 reel
10 yds. cloth
Some spun cotton
1 rope
1 ox yoke
Small quantity of iron and
  steel
1 killing hoe
1 iron spoon
1 meal sifter
3 joiners planes
  £7-1 s-3d
  in and —?

April Term
1798

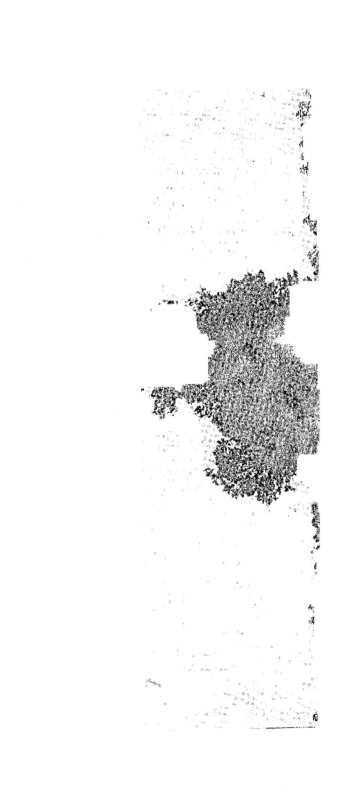

WILLIAM BUNDY, SENIOR

ILLIAM BUNDY, Senior, was born probably in Wayne County, North Carolina,
First month First, 1780. He was the sixth
child of Demsey and Mary Bundy. He was
a man of much energy and ability and very
careful and exact in all his business methods.

In 1804, when twenty-four years old, he settled his
mother's estate. Six years earlier, his older brothers,
David and Zadock, had, with their mother, settled their
father's estate.

In 1806, two years after his mother's death, he
moved to Belmont County, Ohio. He first lived on
Captina Creek, under government permit, in the
southeast quarter of Section Six, Somerset Township,
where he built a small cabin and made some improvements. Eighth month Second, 1806, he entered the
northwest quarter of section thirty-six. This piece of
ground was the first of his several purchases of land
from the government.

The land office which issued the grant for this land
in Somerset Township, was located at Marietta, Ohio,
about seventy-five miles south, to which he rode on
horseback through the almost unbroken forest. He
carried

BRICK RESIDENCE BUILT BY WILLIAM BUNDY IN 1824

LATER THE HOME OF HIS SON EZEKIEL.

WILLIAM BUNDY'S GREAT-GRANDDAUGHTER, MARY CAKES BUNDY, STANDING IN THE YARD.

**LAND OFFICE OF THE OHIO LAND COMPANY
MARIETTA, OHIO**

WILLIAM BUNDY CAME HERE TO ENTER LAND IN SOMERSET TOWNSHIP. THE BUILD-
ING WAS ERECTED IN 1788 AND WAS STILL STANDING IN 1921. THE OLDEST HOUSE
IN OHIO.

carried the silver in his saddle bags with which to pay for the land. He left his young wife and small children in the cabin home on Captina Creek, expecting to be gone two weeks, but there was a full month of waiting and suspense before he was heard of or seen again.

For land in Warren Township, he had to go to the office at Steubenville, Ohio. We cannot easily understand the hardship of such trips. There were no roads, scarcely trails, no hotels and but little protection from the weather. Food would have to be carried for several days at a time and the progress would be very slow over the rough ways and in the primeval forest.

As we have no record of permits, except for one year, he probably moved to one of the parcels of land bought, and between the years 1811 and 1815, built the famous "Red House." Thomas Marshall greatly admired this
property,

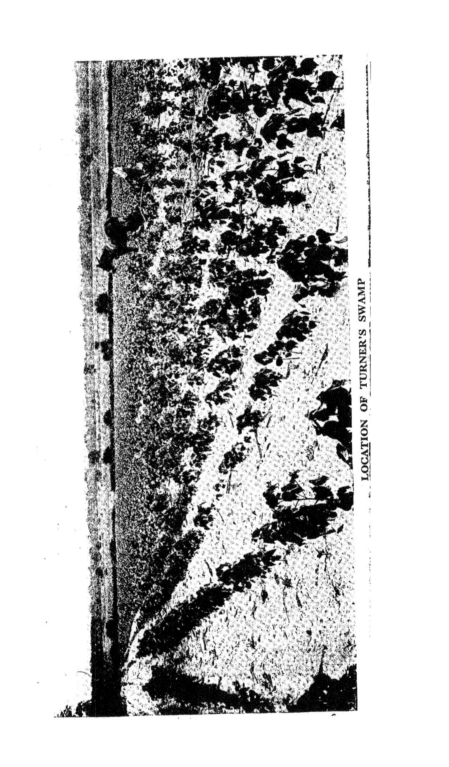

LOCATION OF TURNER'S SWAMP

LAND-OFFICE AT MARIETTA,

Decem 3, 1804

IN conformity with the provisions of the Act of Congress, entitled "An Act to prevent Settlements being made on Lands ceded to the United States, until authorized by Law," permission is hereby given to *William Bently* now settled on a certain Tract of Land belonging to the United States, lying in this District, it being *the South East* Quarter of Section No. *6* in Township No. *7* and Range No. *6* containing 160 acres, to remain thereon as Tenant at Will, on condition of doing no Waste or Damage on the Land, and on the other condition expressed in the Act above mentioned.

Ebenezer Tug

David Edwards
Acting for the Register.

(FRONT)

I DO hereby declare, that I do not lay any claim to the within described Tract of Land; and that I do not occupy the same by virtue of any claim, or pretended claim, derived or pretended to be derived from any other person, or persons who *----*

In presence of

William Munday

(BACK)

STATE of NORTH-CAROLINA.

By the Justices of the County Court of Pleas and Quarter-Sessions for Wayne Wayne *County,* August *Term,* 1804

IT having been certified to us that Mary Bundy *Wm Bundy* late of the said County, is dead, and hath not made any Last Will and Testament; and having applied to us for Administration upon the Estate of the said Deceased, and having entered into Bond, with Security, as the Law in such Case directs: These are therefore to authorise and empower the said William Bundy to enter into, and upon all and singular the Goods and Chattels, Rights and Credits, of the said Deceased, and the same into h possession take wheresoever in this State, to be found, and an Inventory thereof to render, and all the just Debts of the Deceased to pay, and the Residue thereof to distribute as the Law in such Case directs.

Witness, JAMES SASSER, Clerk of said Court, at Waynesborough the 2 2 Day of August A.D. 1804

"RED HOUSE" IN 1920

WILLIAM BUNDY built this house and moved to it from his "squatter permit" on Captina Creek, about three miles southeast.

The house was torn down, moved to the farm of William McCoy in 1865 and re-erected. It seems the weather-boarding was left off, and also only the main part of the building rebuilt. The near view shows the good state of preservation of many of the logs. Note how nicely the logs are hewn and how accurately they are notched at the corner. Note also the large "gain" near the left where the wall of an additional room or rooms has been joined to the main building and fastened to it by two wood pins through each log. Vertical rows of smaller pin holes will be noticed on each side of the corner and again two or three feet distant. These were no doubt to secure the vertical "nailing strips" to which the weather-boarding was fastened and which was painted red, giving the house its name.

The notching or dovetailing of the corner, which is generally used in this section of Ohio, is more difficult, but better than often seen in the eastern section of the country.

THE ORIGINAL LOCATION OF THE "RED HOUSE"

IT WAS LOCATED AS SHOWN BY THE ARROW IN THE PICTURE AND ABOUT FIVE HUNDRED FEET
EAST OF THE WEST LINE AND 1150 FEET NORTH OF THE SOUTH LINE OF THE WEST ONE-HALF
OF THE NORTHWEST, ONE-QUARTER OF SECTION THIRTEEN, TOWNSHIP EIGHT, RANGE SIX OF
CONGRESS LAND, WARREN TOWNSHIP, BELMONT COUNTY. OHIO, ABOUT TWENTY FEET SOUTH
OF THE PRESENT ROADWAY AND FRONTING THE PRESENT RESIDENCE OF ALBERT McGILL.
THE FRONT ENTRANCE GATE WAS HUNG BETWEEN TWO TREES USED AS POSTS.

property, and in 1815 William Bundy sold it to him,
and bought from him for twenty-seven hundred dollars the north half of Section Four, Township Eight,
Range Six. Here he erected a log cabin. When the
big brick house was built, the foundation of which
was laid in 1824, this cabin was moved and used as a
"loom shop" where cloth was woven for the family use
from home-grown wool and flax.

He died suddenly Sixth month Twenty-first, 1828, of
apoplexy or heart failure. In company with his wife,
he was attending Friends Quarterly Meeting held at
this time at Chesterfield, Morgan County, Ohio. He
died as he was seated at the breakfast table of his
daughter, Mary French. He was buried at Elliott's
Crossroads Burying Ground, six miles west of Chesterfield.

His wife Sarah (Overman), who had accompanied
him on horseback, had to ride the lonely three-day
                                                      trip

ILLIAM BUNDY.

James Madison, President of the United States of America,

TO ALL TO WHOM THESE PRESENTS SHALL COME, GREETING.

Know Ye, That William Brady of Belmont County, Ohio

having deposited in the *General Land Office* at Steubenville whereby it appears that

full payment for the North East quarter of Township

Eight of Range Twenty seven

... Steubenville ... by the act of Congress ...

... Territory north-west of the Ohio, and above the mouths of

... the United States ... William Brady ...

... section ...

There is therefore ... patent,

In testimony whereof ... Land Patent, ... the Seal of the ...

**Given ... at the City of Washington the twenty fourth day of Mass

... one thousand eight hundred and Nine and of the Independence of the

... the thirty third.**

BY THE PRESIDENT:

Jas: Madison

Secretary of ...

THE CHALKLEY BUNDY HOUSE

RESIDENCE OF CHALKLEY AND SARAH (DOUDNA) BUNDY AND CHALKLEY AND DEBORAH (HANSON) BUNDY AND LATER OF HIS SON, LINDLEY BUNDY. PHOTO. 1584, WILLIAM H. STANTON. BUILT 1811 BY WILLIAM HODGIN AND BELIEVED TO HAVE BEEN THE FIRST BRICK HOUSE IN WARREN TOWNSHIP. THE DATE 1811 WAS CUT IN ONE OF THE BLACK WALNUT JOISTS OVER THE SECOND STORY AT THE TOP OF THE STAIRWAY. IT WAS TORN DOWN IN 1901.

CHALKLEY AND SARAH (DOUDNA) BUNDY

trip back to her home, leading the riderless horse. Her younger children, Chalkley and probably Demsey and Elizabeth, played under the shade of a big tree and watched for the return of their parents. We can think of the delight with which they recognized the familiar figure of their short, plump little mother, riding her horse; and the race down the road to meet her; and the query as to the riderless horse; then no doubt reading in their mother's face the first sad news of their father's death.

Her son, Ezekiel, who was now twenty-one, led in the care of the farm, and with his mother, settled his father's estate and later occupied the brick home.

Sarah (Overman) Bundy is described as short, stout, with dark complexion, gray eyes, low forehead, black hair and large nose, possibly the original of the "Bundy Nose." She stood erect, walked briskly, was hospitable and was greatly beloved by all who made her acquaintance. She lived twenty-five years after her husband's death. She died Fifth month Eighth, 1853, age sixty-eight, and was buried at Stillwater.

Compiled largely from notes
by Dillwyn C. Bundy.

A PIONEER STONE JUG.

EZEKIEL BUNDY
1807-1866

SARAH (HOYLE STANTON)
BUNDY, 1821-1885

ELIZABETH BUNDY, BAILEY
1826-1891

MARY CALEB (BUNDY) SMITH
GRANDDAUGHTER OF EZRRIEL BUNDY.

WHITE WOOLEN BOOTEES

WHITE WOOLEN BOOTEES KNIT BY SARAH (OVERMAN) BUNDY IN 1850 FOR LUCINDA (BUNDY) HANSON. THEY WERE ALSO WORN BY HER ELDEST DAUGHTER, CORA (HANSON) VON HOFSTEN. THE OUTSIDE BANDS ARE BLUE—THE CENTRE, ORANGE.

CRADLE

CRADLE MADE BY STEPHEN DOUDNA, SON OF JOEL AND REBECCA, PROBABLY ABOUT 1840. THE WOOD IS BLACK WALNUT. ORIGINALLY QUITE FANCY IN DESIGN, HAD CORNER POSTS AND HOOD. THE YOUNGER CHILDREN OF JOEL AND REBECCA DOUDNA WERE ROCKED IN IT AND ALL THE CHILDREN OF CHALKLEY AND SARAH (DOUDNA) BUNDY. IT WAS REPAIRED IN ABOUT 1852 AND ALTERED TO ITS PRESENT FORM. NOW OWNED BY NATHAN W. BUNDY.

Articles of agreement made & Concluded upon this twenty second day of first month Eighteen hundred & twenty three Betwen Elias Williams of Belmont County of the one part & William Bundy of the same place of the other party as follows to wit — —

The s^d Elias Williams for the Consideration hearafter mentioned hath agreed to do in a good & workman like manner & according to the best of his art & skill the following describd work viz. to lay the wall of a Cellar forty feet by twenty two with a stone partion through the middle thereof make one fire place in the Cellar & ais Butmans sufficiat for fire above. lay the foundation of a Kichen twenty two feet by twenty. the Cellar wall to be seven feet high & the kichen foundation to be four feet & a half high from the bottom. the whole front to have three ranges of stone at the top each Eight inches high. Also to Cut four door sills & four door heads of Common size also twenty sills & twenty heads for fifteen light windows. sills to be of a Convenient length & five inches thick the heads to be nine inches broad & Eight inches thick & a Convenient length to put in four small rough sills in the Cellar windows. to Cut six sills for gable end windows. to Cut & lay twelve out door steps & twelve peaces for the tops of the Chimnys. the steps to be eight inches by twelve. & the Chimny tops to be at least four inches thick & to rough Cut & lay Eight Cellar door steps rais walls thereto & finish it with slanting Cheeks. s^d Williams to split all the peaces for s^d Cut stone & the s^d

the second hundred lbs of flax to be paid next Fall or fore part of winter provided the stone are all Cut & the money to be paid when the work is all Compleated. the flax to be delivered at s^d Williams hous..

for the true & faithful performance of the foregoing Covenants & agrements we bind our selves in the sum of one hundred and forty dollars in witness whereof we have hereunto set our hands and seals the day and year before written.

Signed and Sealed in presence of
Stephen Todd
David Smith

Elias Williams (seal)
Wm Bundy (seal)

the 200 lbs flax named in the above article is paid

HOLLOW ROCK

MENTIONED IN THE CONTRACT OF WILLIAM BUNDY AND CHRISTOPHER RIVERS.
NOTE THE PIPE FROM THE SPRING AND THE WATERING TROUGH.

PEWTER TEAPOT

BOUGHT EARLY IN THE 19TH CENTURY BY SARAH (OVERMAN)
BUNDY.
NOW IN THE POSSESSION OF DILLWYN C. BUNDY, WHO
REMEMBERS USING IT WHEN A SMALL BOY TO INHALE STEAM
FROM HERBS TO CURE A COLD.

COPY OF A RECEIPT

18th of 4th Mo., 1806 Recd of Joseph Cox William Bundy & John Colyer the sum of two hundred & fifty Dollars in full for the carriage of their property from Carolina to the State of Ohio in Belmont County I say recd by us for Edmund Lane.

Test   Hedar Nutt
James Edgerton.   his
                          Eldred   x   Allum
                                  mark
                                       Waggoners.

COPY OF CONTRACT FOR WORK

Article of Agreement made & concluded between Wm. Bundy and Giles Brooks both of the County of Belmont & State of Ohio —Witnesseth—that the said Brooks for & in consideration of the property hereafter mentioned doth agree to do the carpenter & joiner work of a house for said Bundy which he is preparing to build in a good & workman like manner & in every respect as the said Bundy shall dictate. the said Bundy is to furnish all the materials for said work & board & lodge said Brooks & what hands he may have employed during the time he is doing the same which is to be completed in two years from this date provided the material is found as fast as said Brooks is able to go on with the work. but it is understood if the said Bundy should fail in providing the materials the said Brooks is to have a reasonable time to complete the work after they are provided for which work when completed the said Bundy binds himself his heirs & assigns to make or cause to be made to said Brooks or Assigns a good and lawful deed of conveyance for the East half of the Northwest quarter of Section No. Twenty Seven Township No. Eight in range•Six in the Steubenville distric. but if the work when done shall amount to more than Five Hundred Dollars according to what is called the old prices the said Bundy is to pay to Brooks the overplus in trade at the old price but it is likewise understood that if the work doth not amount to Five Hundred Dollars that the said Bundy agrees to take it as full satisfaction for the land. in witness whereof we have hereunto set our hands & seals this Twentyeth day of the First mo. 1824.

Witness   William Bundy (se)
    Isaac Stubbs   Giles Brooks (sed)

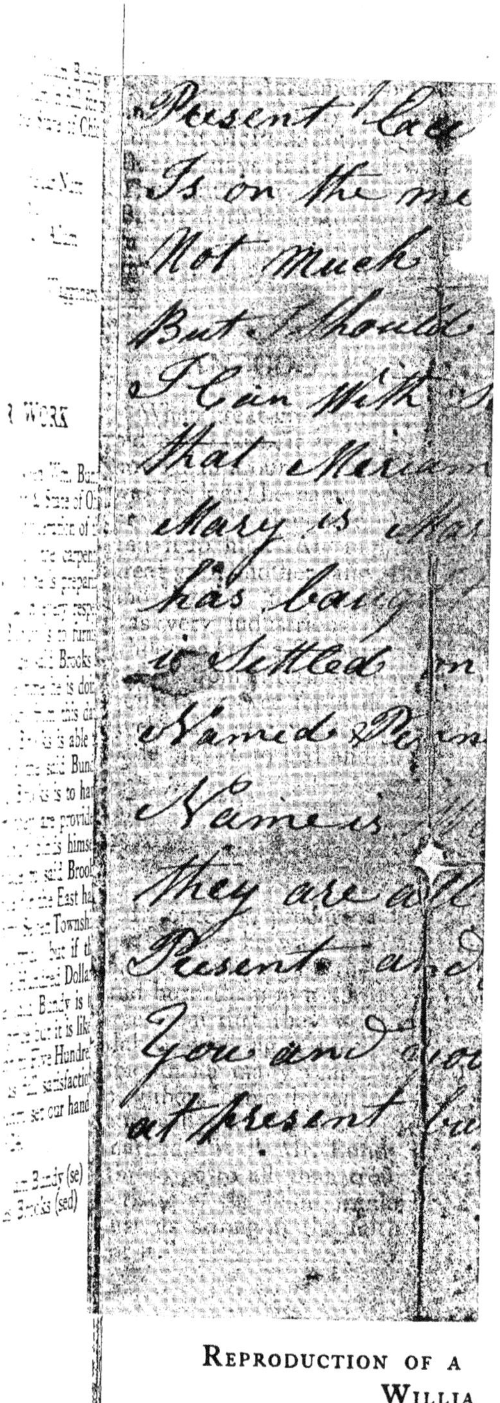

Present [...]
Is on the me[...]
Not Much
But I should
I Can with [...]
that Maria[...]
Mary is [...]
has bang[...]
is settled on
Named [...]
Name is [...]
they are all
Present and [...]
You and you[...]
at present [...]

REPRODUCTION OF A
WILLIA

COPY OF A RECEIPT

No. 1806 Rec'd of Joseph Cox William Bundy [...] One Hundred & fifty Dollars in full for the [...] property from Carolina to the State of Ohio [...] hauled by us for Edmund Lane.

Hedar Nutt
his
Eldred x Allum
mark
Waggoters

COPY OF CONTRACT FOR WORK

This contract is concluded between Wm. Bundy [...] the County of Belmont & State of Ohio [...] the said Brooks for & in consideration of [...] doth agree to do the carpenter [...] for said Bundy which he is preparing [...] him when he marries & in every respect [...] the said Bundy is to furnish [...] him with a bed & board & lodge said Brooks [...] and employ him during the time he is [...] two years from this date [...] as fast as said Brooks is to [...] but it is understood if the said [...] furnish the materials the said Brooks is to [...] complete the work after they are prepared [...] the said Bundy binds himself [...] of conveyance for the East [...] the New Twenty Seven Town [...] district, but if [...] Five Hundred Dollars [...] we give the said Bundy the [...] the old price but if he [...] agreement to Five Hund [...] as to work doth pertain [...] the said Bundy agrees to take it in [...] we have hereunto set our [...] day of the First mo. 1824.

William Bundy [seal]
Giles Brooks [seal]

COPY OF AGREEMENT

Article of Agreement between Richard McPeak of the one part and William Bundy of the other part witnesseth, that the said Richard McPeak doth agree to work one year for the said William Bundy, days that the law requires excepted, and to begin the Thirteenth day of the First month next, and the said William Bundy doth agree to give the said Richard McPeak Fifty Dollars in specie and ten in Davenport's Store at the expiration of the time—28th of 12th mo 1822.

:   *   *   *

ANECDOTES OF THE BUNDY FAMILY

When great-grandfather, William Bundy, became owner of the old home farm, it was almost an unbroken forest and the wolves howled all around. When he was building the first house, which was of logs, he came over from Somerton to work at it and brought his daughter, Mary, and son, Ezekiel, to cook for and help him. At night great-grandfather would go back to great-grandmother and the smaller children and leave Mary and Ezekiel to guard the new (to be) home. Aunt Mary was very industrious and would sit till late at night to knit, while she kept a fire burning all the while so as to keep the howling wolves from entering the room. Part of the time they only had a quilt to answer for a door shutter. Grandfather Ezekiel was a lively boy and would play and romp around his sister till she bade him go to bed and to sleep.

East Canton,   MARY C. (BUNDY) SMITH.
Ohio,
1920.
               *   *   *   *

In order to procure a fine white lime to finish the plastering for a house he was building William Bundy, Sr., had men haul mussel shells from the Ohio River, twenty-eight miles away, and burn them in a kiln made of logs. In order to keep the shells free from dirt they were picked out of the ashes by hand and slaked, yielding a yfinish for the walls that remained hard and smooth for many years. While this work was in progress one of the neighbors came by on an errand and stopped to talk as neighbors will, and began to help pick out shells. After a time he remarked, "Well, Mr. Bundy, you are stronger in the faith than I am to go to all that trouble." William Bundy's reply, characteristic of the blunt frankness of the man, was, "George, thee is just as strong in the faith as I am, but thee is too lazy to work for it."

Some of William Bundy, Sr.'s, boys found a fawn in the woods near the house, so they took it home and fed it. It grew to be a great pet, but it would trespass on the neighbors' gardens. Finally, a man shot it, causing great grief among the children. The man became quite abusive and told them he would have shot the fawn if it had been in their own dooryard. Among other things he spoke of the mother as "a dirty squaw." Grandmother said afterwards, "I expect I was dirty, as I was digging potatoes."   *   *   *   *

A favorite way of catching wild turkeys was to build a rail pen, provided with a sliding door in one side held up by a trigger to which a string was attached. The hunter would hide behind a log to leeward and wait until the turkeys followed the trail of corn into the pen. He would then pull the string and catch the birds at his leisure. Ezekiel Bundy one time caught so many turkeys that the family had to divide with the neighbors in order to get them used before they spoiled.

*   *   *   *

WILLIAM BUNDY
"BLACK BILL." 1819-1905.

William Bundy, Jr., has said that he never shot at any game in his life, except at a pheasant sitting on a limb, and that he did not think he came anywhere near hitting his mark that time

OUR ANCESTORS—THE

School Exami
Wilmington, Clin

M

Mr. *William Bundy* This day made appl

Examiners of *CLINTON COUNTY*, for a CERTIFICATE

SCHOOL, and said BOARD being fully satisfied that M r:

is competent to teach READING, WRITING, ARITHMETIC, ENGLISH

satisfied that *he* possesses a good moral character, a CERTIFI

Mr William Bundy to tea

Learning for the term of *Two Years* from the d

Given Under my Hand. J. F. Pa

Of the B

S. B. DRAKE, Pr.—*Whig Office*.

REPRODUCTION OF A *Certificate to Teach School* GRANTED
(SON OF WILLIAM AND SARAH BUNDY). Date

School Examiner's Office,
Wilmington, Clinton Co. Ohio.

March 26th 1840

Mr. William Bundy This day made application to the BOARD OF School Examiners of CLINTON COUNTY, for a CERTIFICATE to teach a COMMON ENGLISH SCHOOL, and said Board being fully satisfied that Mr. William Bundy is competent to teach READING, WRITING, ARITHMETIC, ENGLISH GRAMMAR, GEOGRAPHY, and are also satisfied that he possesses a good moral character, a CERTIFICATE is accordingly granted said Mr. William Bundy to teach the above named branches of Learning for the term of two years from the date above written.

Given Under my Hand. J. H. Patton CLERK, Of the Board of School Examiners.

S. P. Drake, Pr.—Whig Office.

REPRODUCTION OF A *Certificate to Teach School* GRANTED TO WILLIAM BUNDY (SON OF WILLIAM AND SARAH BUNDY). Dated 3-26-1840

One time the Bundy boys had cleaned and oiled their guns ready for a hunting trip, when a great flock of turkeys came and settled in the dead trees of the clearing, but the boys had put so much tallow in the locks of their guns that they could not shoot. and before the locks could be cleaned the turkeys had all taken flight and did not return.

* * * *

Sarah (Overman) Bundy was a woman of strong character, even though her education was extremely meager when measured by modern standards, but she bravely took up the work, after her husband's death, of conducting the home and caring for her brood of eleven children, though some of them were grown men and women. Her home was noted for its hospitality. In the slavery controversy she was no neutral figure. Her stable loft more than once concealed runaway slaves on their way to Canada and freedom.

It was not strange that sons who grew from such stock and in such surroundings were ready to take their part in the public affairs of the community and state. One of the sons, William Bundy, Jr., was especially active in the anti-slavery agitation. He was for a number of years a conductor on the underground railway by which runaway slaves traveled. There was no regular station on the farm and his duty was to take the passengers after dark, from the next man to the south, and conduct them as far north as he could, and yet return before daybreak. He would be found the next morning in the harvest field, it might be, as though he had been in bed all night. To be discovered by the officers of the law would draw a heavy penalty, not only of fine but also of imprisonment. The infirm slaves and children were conveyed in vehicles and the others marched after the conductor. In this work William Bundy, Jr., claims never to have lost but one passenger and that one strayed away in the dark and became lost. One bright moonlight night he passed a country church just as the worshipers were coming out. The road was full of men and women who knew him, but so general was the sentiment against slavery that no one reported him. On account of the long distance they had to travel, parallel to the Virginian shore of the Ohio River, most of the runaways were taken by a route further west, but some of the old hiding places in Belmont County may still be seen.

* * * *

There appears to have been some special affinity between the Bundy and Doudna families, as three Bundy brothers married Doudna sisters at first or second marriages, and two nephews

. For any one especially interested in the escaping slaves, the book "Bonnie Belmont," by John S. Cochran, contains many interesting anecdotes and incidents.

and two nieces married Doudnas. Joel Doudna boasted at one time that he had three William Bundys for sons-in-law and four daughters and two sons who married Bundys. The fact that this family was once so numerous in Stillwater Meeting illustrates the changefulness of nature, as only five of the grandchildren of William and Sarah Bundy are now identified with Stillwater community at Barnesville, Ohio.

Dillwyn C. Bundy.

*　　*　　*　　*

Grandmother Sarah (Overman) Bundy lived about twenty-five years after grandfather's death. She had a favorite old riding horse named Jack. She was very short and stout and when perched in her side saddle reminded me of a snow ball. She rode old Jack wherever she went, and often visited her youngest daughter Elizabeth, who married Hezekiah Bailey. Frequently on such occasions she would take the saddle from old Jack and he would run back home, a distance of some four miles, but one time he must have run too hard, for next morning he was found dead in the field.

Chalkley Dawson.

*　　*　　*　　*

When William Bundy, Sr., and his wife Sarah were leaving home to attend Quarterly Meeting at Chesterfield, Demsey and Elizabeth went out to the gate with them. Sarah said to her son Demsey, "Be a good boy until I come back," but William said, "I cannot say that—Till I come back."

He died while on this visit in Morgan County.

*　　*　　*　　*

COPY OF A RECEIPT

Received Twenty Five Cents of William Bundy Treasurer of Stillwater Meeting for Paper for the Clerk.

1st Mo., 27th, 1828.　　　　　　　　　　　　Henry Stanton.

*   *   *   *

The following poem was composed by Demsey Bundy about
1870, on the occasion of accidently killing a snow bird while
moving a shock of corn.—*Eunice H. Henderson.*

Poor little bird, I mourn thy early fate,
   An inadvertent stroke of mine deprived thee of thy mate.
Sweet warbler! Oh, I truly sighed,
   When I perceived thy mate had died.

With poignant grief, I viewed thy dead,
   When I perceived that life had fled,
I smoothed his wings, arranged his crest,
   And stroked the down upon his breast.

With heartfelt grief and tearful eye,
   I saw thy dear companion die,
And now, my friend, don't censure me
   For all the pain I brought on thee.

This is a world of grief and woe,
   Where dearest friends must part we know,
Submit thyself and be resigned,
   Thou mayst yet sweet comfort find.

Thine is a bitter cup of woe,
   I drank it many years ago,
Though months have past and years gone by
   As yet my breast doth heave a sigh.

For memory still recalls to view
   The friends I mourned with sorrow true,
But lenient time hath eased the wound,
   And round my heart new friends are found.

ANNA (EDGERTON) BUNDY

JOHN BUNDY

JOHN BUNDY

THE fifth child of William and Sarah (Overman) Bundy, was born Second month Seventeenth, 1813, most probably in the "Red House." He was only a small boy when the brick home was being built. He has said that he and his little brothers used to run up and down the inclined runways like squirrels, also that he had a small board on which he carried a few bricks at a time to the masons. He naturally felt he had quite a little part in the building of the house.

He has related how his parents came over the mountains from Wayne County, North Carolina, in a cart; how the goods were hauled by wagoners—how his father brought with him a "piggin" of silver, principally Spanish quarters and halves, with which to buy the land. The "piggin," he said, was a small wooden bucket or dipper without a bail but with one long stave projecting above the others to use as a handle and held about as much as an old-fashioned bell-crown hat.

He married first, Tenth month Thirtieth, 1833, Ruth Patten, daughter of William and Sally Patten.

So

411

ASHER MOTT   SARAH (BUNDY) MOTT

Daughter of John and Ruth Patten Bundy and twin sister of William P.
Bundy and sister of Mary P. Stanton.

So far as can be learned, John and Ruth went to house-keeping in a small log house which stood about three hundred yards west of "Number Two" district school on the farm of William Patten. To John and Ruth were born five children, Sarah and William P., twins; Mary P., Martha and Charity. Sarah married Asher Mott, William P. married Tabitha Doudna, and Mary P. married Eli Stanton, Twelfth month Ninth, 1857. Martha and Charity died young.

John Bundy's daughter, Doctor Elizabeth B. Frame, says: "Soon after they were married, father was going to have a corn husking and a company of men to dinner and there was no meat in the house. He did not know where any was to come from, but he started out early in the morning with his gun, and in a big tree, not far from the house, he sighted a large wild turkey.

He

WILLIAM P. BUNDY   TABITHA (DOUDNA) BUNDY
TAKEN ABOUT 1865.

He took aim and fired, the turkey fell to the ground and they had all the meat they needed. I recall hearing him say that he felt that the turkey was 'providentially provided' for him.''

At the time of William Patten's death, he bought the farm and took care of the "blind mother" Sally, until she died. He says of Sally Patten: "She was a very hale and hearty woman, but was blind the last sixteen years of her life. I cannot remember her exact age, but it was between eighty and ninety years. She died of old age. Ruth Bundy died at the age of twenty-seven, from disease consequent of childbirth. She was a strong woman, although of slender build.'"

John Bundy married second, Sidney (Wood) Tipton. Their children were Thomas W. and Ephraim, the latter died young.

His

RESIDENCE OF JOHN AND ANNA E. BUNDY

House built about 1825 and the barn in 1854. Photographed in 1891 by W. H. S.

46 5:35 -

OUR ANCESTORS

THE

STANTONS

10-30-1833

John Bundy of Belmont County and State of [Ohio] Son of William [...] County and State aforesaid and Sarah his wife [...] former [...] and Ruth [daughter] of William Patten of the County and State aforesaid and [...] his wife having [...] intentions of marriage with each other before a [...] of their religious society held at Stillwater and having [...] of parents their said proposals of marriage [...] said meeting [...] it may concern that for the full [...] of their said intentions this [...] day of the tenth month [...] the year of our Lord [...] hundred and thirty three they [...] John Bundy and Ruth Patten [...] a publick meeting of the said [...] held at Stillwater aforesaid and the [...] Bundy taking the said Ruth Patten by the hand declared that he took her [...] to be his wife promising with divine assistance [...] unto her loving and [...] until death should separate them and then the said Ruth Patten did [...] declare that she took him the said John Bundy to be her husband promising [...] assistance to be unto him a loving and faithful wife until death should [...] [...] moreover they the said John Bundy and Ruth Patten (she according [...] of marriage adopting the name of her husband) did [...] confirmation [...] to these presents set their hands

John Bundy
Ruth Bundy

names are hereunto subscribed being [...] present at the [...] of said marriage [...] set our hands they day and year above written

	Relatives	Relatives
	Zachar Scholfield	Mary Jones	William Patten
	Gerrard Patterson	Thomas Smith	Sarah Patten
	Joseph Jones	Nathan Bundy	
	Linsey Middleton	John Smith	Sarah Bundy
	Jane Dawson		
	Mahlon Scholfield	Charity Bundy	Aaron Overman
	Sarah Bailey	Robert Plummer	Aaron Morris
	Henry Doudna	Nathan Morris	Phebe Morris
	Henry Stanton	Isaac Morris	Mahlon Patten
	Rachel Engle	Eli Bundy	Sarah Bundy Jun
	Elizabeth Rodgers	Joseph Smith	Leah Hoover
	Stephen Hodgon		Elias Bundy

ficate OF JOHN AND RUTH (PATTEN) BUNDY   Married 10-30-1833

His third wife was Anna Edgerton, who survived im several years. Their children were Ruth, who aarried Josiah W. Doudna; Jesse, who moved to the rest coast and married; Elizabeth, a graduate in steopathy, who married Ira S. Frame and with him has racticed that profession for many years; Rebecca nd Wilson, who died young.

John Bundy took great interest in whatever kind of ork in which he was engaged. We find that his farm ad no superior in Belmont County. He used "up-to-ate" methods, and endeavored to have each thing rst-class of its kind. He thoroughly enjoyed devoting me and energy to bringing about these results.

In 1854–55 he built a very remarkable barn for that me. It was sixty by seventy feet. The outside was nished as nicely and painted as well as a dwelling. aiah Fields was the head carpenter, and Mason homas made the iron work in his country blacksmith 1op. Wilford T. Hall states that it was generally orted that all the iron work was made for one indred dollars and that the long timbers were pur-rased, hewn and hauled from near Dora, about four i les southeast. The inside was well planned and jually well built. The carpenter work is admired by J who see it.

He will be remembered as a man rather below average ight and weight, who stood erect, walked with a ick, firm step, had blue eyes and black hair. He ways shaved smooth and cut his hair around even id combed down straight. He had a characteristic ibit when he removed his hat, of stroking his hair wn with both hands.

Many

Many of his sayings were likewise characteristic of him, as when he was sure of something, he would often say, "Di-pend upon it," or when something was not fully disclosed, "There's something behind the curtain," and when something did not go right, he would exclaim "Tut! tut!"

He thoroughly enjoyed mechanical work of almost every

INTERIOR OF JOHN BUNDY'S BARN
SHOWING ONE OF THE LONG HAND-HEWN OAK TIMBERS SPANNING THE BARN IN ONE PIECE.

every kind, and usually succeeded in whatever he undertook, but was very ready to concede a point to others when such action was deserved.

In 1876 he gave up the management of the farm and built a new home on East Main Street, Barnesville. John Colpitts relates that he wanted a slab of sawed sandstone for a hearth and bought one from Colpitts Brothers. The slab had to be cut to size. This he tried to do, but broke the stone. He bought another and borrowed the proper tools for cutting such stone, but this stone broke also. He bought a third one and said: "I guess thee had better cut it—I cannot get the proper 'wiggle' to the chisel." Those who know the motions of mallet and chisel will understand how apt was his expression and how difficult a job he had undertaken.

He died Ninth month Twentieth, 1898. During his life of more than fourscore and four years, he had seen the country change from almost unbroken forest to one of very well-tilled farms with comfortable homes. He had seen modern transportation, public schools, government mail, electric lights, telephones and other modern conveniences come into use, and had taken great interest in these changes.

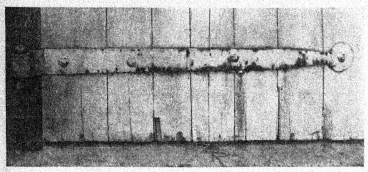

BARN-DOOR HINGE FROM JOHN BUNDY'S BARN
MADE BY MASON THOMAS.

A SHEEP-SHEARING

A NEIGHBOR. boy, "Si" Doudna, and I went over to "Uncle John" Bundy's, two miles away, to shear sheep. There were one hundred sheep to be sheared at eight cents "a head." We each sheared fifty and went home before night. "Uncle John" paid us four dollars each and remarked, "Boys, this is making money pretty fast." And it was for those days, when a day's work on the farm was from sun to sun and the pay fifty cents a day. My father paid one dollar a day for mowing grass and a little more for cradling wheat and oats.

HENRY S. DAWSON.

SAMPLER MADE BY RUTH PATTEN
SHE MARRIED JOHN BUNDY IN 1833.

JOHN BUNDY'S POCKET KNIFE
PRESENTED TO HIS GRANDSON, WILLIAM H. STANTON.

KNIFE USED BY JOHN BUNDY
PRESENTED BY HIM TO HIS GREAT-GRANDSON, HARLAN
WEBSTER, IN 1892.

FOLDING RULE USED BY JOHN BUNDY
PRESENTED BY HIM TO HIS GRANDSON, WILLIAM H. STANTON.

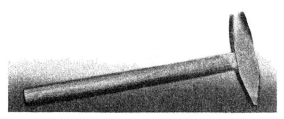

HAMMER USED BY JOHN BUNDY
PRESENTED BY HIM TO HIS GREAT-GRANDSON HARLAN
WEBSTER, IN 1892.

BASKET USED BY ASENATH (DOUDNA) BUNDY

THIS KIND OF BASKET WAS USED ABOUT 1860 AS A TRAVELING BAG IS USED TODAY.

CANDLESTICKS USED BY WILLIAM AND ASENATH BUNDY IN 1869

TYPICAL OF THE BETTER TYPE OF CANDLESTICKS USED BEFORE THE DAYS OF KEROSENE LAMPS. NOW IN THE HOME OF DILLWYN AND ELIZABETH (STEER) BUNDY.

WOOD KNOT MAUL

MADE BY JOHN BUNDY BEFORE 1898. NOW IN THE POSSESSION OF REBECCA W. HALL.

THOMAS W. BUNDY   ABIGAIL (DOUDNA) BUNDY

THOMAS W. BUNDY

THOMAS W. BUNDY enlisted in the Civil War the twentieth of December, 1863, in Company F, Fiftieth Regiment of New York Engineer Volunteers. He was with Grant's Army of the Potomac much of the time that he was in the service. The greater part of his work was in the construction and laying of pontoon bridges. The Fiftieth New York Regiment had the record of constructing a pontoon bridge across the Anticosta branch, three-quarters of a mile in length, in just seventeen minutes and fifteen seconds by the watch. Once in a violent storm on Chesapeake Bay their company was the only one that got through. The brigade had shops in Washington where one company or more always remained for building new pontoons. Such a company was always taken from the Fiftieth Regiment. During the war, under the direction of Captain M. H. McGrath, Company F, Fiftieth Regiment, the engineer troops built a little church near Meade's headquarters. It was in the Gothic style, and was constructed entirely of poles with the bark on, placed vertically like a batten house. The badge of the engineer brigade was a castle and it was worked in the front of the church about the center of the second story of the steeple.

A picture of the church came out in the National Tribune, February twenty-seventh, 1890, and was at once recognized by Thomas Bundy as the one he had helped to build. He was discharged from the service of the United States the thirteenth day of June, 1865, at Fort Barry, Virginia.

ABIGAIL (DOUNDA) BUNDY.

HOUSE BUILT BY HENRY DOUDNA ABOUT 1810
The First Home of Wilford T. and Sarah B. (Stanton) Hall.

THE DOUDNA FAMILY

THE earliest history we have of the Doudna family is of Henry and Elizabeth Doudna living in England. Their son John, when a little boy, was kidnapped and kept on shipboard until he was about twenty-six years old. The ship was wrecked and John, with two companions, reached a small barren island on pieces of the ship. After eight days without food and very little water they succeeded in signaling a sailing vessel and were taken on board. The vessel in three or four days landed them on the coast of North Carolina. John determined he would never go to sea again and started out to find work. He met a little girl, Sarah Knowis, on her way to school, who told him that her father could probably give him work. She was the first girl he met in this country and her kindness made a deep impression on him. He worked for the Knowis family for two years, then married Sarah; he was twenty-eight years old and she fourteen. He and his young wife settled in Edgecomb County, North Carolina, where
they

422

they lived in peace and happiness. In 1804 they, with most of their children, moved to Belmont County, Ohio, where they lived the remainder of their days. John Doudna probably helped to build the first Friends' Meeting House in Warren Township.

It is said that while on shipboard John Doudna was not allowed to acquire an education, so when he married he did not know his A B C's. In later life he acquired a wide knowledge of the Scriptures and was said to have no equal in this respect in the neighborhood. His wife survived him several years; both were buried in Stillwater Burying Ground. At her death in her ninety-ninth year she had four hundred and fifty children, grandchildren and great-grandchildren.

One of their sons, Henry, lived two and a half miles east of Barnesville, a few hundred yards north of the Sandy Ridge Road. Here he built a very remarkable barn. It was of good size and yet no power was used in the preparation of the lumber. All the large timbers were hewn out by hand. The braces and weather-boarding were split from large logs; the chestnut shingles were pinned on with wooden pegs. Nails were not used about the building except to fasten the weather-boarding, and these he made by hand. The barn was blown down about 1902.

He also built a residence somewhat nearer the road. The space between the weather-boarding and plaster in the frame construction was filled with brickwork, adding greatly to the warmth of the building. The doors were furnished with big "strap" or "barn-door hinges." The "pins" were provided with a square

HOSEA DOUDNA, SR.

HE CAME WITH HIS PARENTS, JOHN AND SARAH (KNOWIS) DOUDNA, FROM NORTH CAROLINA IN 1804.

a square shank which was driven into the door post, while the strap hinges were riveted to the door by several hand-made flat-head rivets.

So far as is known, Henry came to Belmont County with his father in 1804 and probably had the building completed by 1810. After Henry's death the farm was owned and the house occupied by Peter Sears, Sr., whose grandson, William H. and wife, Mary (Naylor) Sears, have very kindly given me the above data regarding the work of Henry Doudna and the remarkable buildings he erected. The farm was later owned by George Tatum and sold to Thomas P. Hall. His son, Wilford T., and wife, Sarah B. (Stanton) went to housekeeping in the house in 1890.

A small house stood about twelve rods northeast from the barn. This was probably the first house built on this site and used by Henry Doudna during the time he was building the new barn and house. In this older house Nathan and Anna Stanton Bundy began housekeeping in 1859. The well which they used may still be seen.

Hosea Doudna, Sr., a younger brother of Henry, was a familiar figure to many persons of Stillwater neighborhood. Many remember the broad-brimmed, light-gray silk hat, the gray suit and heavy cape that he wore and the dun horse he rode for so many years. Late in life he was quite deaf, but all who knew him remember his kindly greetings, which showed plainly that he realized the handicap of dull hearing. He died in 1888 at the age of ninety-five years.

W. H. S.

ALL THAT IS LEFT OF THE FIRST HENRY DOUDNA HOME—THE WELL
The house was occupied by Nathan and Anna Stanton Bundy when they first went to housekeeping on Sandy Ridge in 1859.

TWENTY-FIVE CENT POSTAGE

THOSE WHO DEMAND ONE-CENT POSTAGE SHOULD CONSIDER THE POSTAGE OUR AN-
CESTORS HAD TO PAY AND THE SCARCITY OF MONEY IN THOSE DAYS.

RESIDENCE OF WILLIAM E. AND REBECCA (DOUDNA) BUNDY

ERECTED ABOUT 1855 BY JOEL DOUDNA. IT IS BUILT OF ONE-BY-SIX-INCH BOARDS LAID FLAT
WITH EDGES OVERLAPPING NEARLY AN INCH ALTERNATELY, AND EACH COURSE OF BOARDS
NAILED TO THE ONE BELOW. THE CORNERS WERE INTERLOCKED. IT WAS HIS INTENTION TO
COVER IT WITH STUCCO OUTSIDE, BUT LAP WEATHER-BOARDING WAS USED INSTEAD. IT WAS
PLASTERED INSIDE. PHOTOGRAPHED IN 1884 BY W. H. S.

CANDLE BOX

THIS BOX WAS MADE BEFORE 1850 BY STEPHEN DOUDNA FOR HIS SISTER, SARAH (DOUDNA) BUNDY. DURING THE CIVIL WAR AT THE TIME OF "MORGAN'S RAID" CHALKLEY BUNDY PLACED HIS MONEY AND VALUABLE PAPERS IN IT AND BURIED IT IN HIS TOBACCO HOUSE.

MARY P. DOUDNA'S TEAPOT

IT BELONGED TO HER MOTHER, JANE PLUMMER. ONE EVENING IT WAS LEFT ON THE HEARTH TOO CLOSE TO THE FIRE AND ONE LEG MELTED OUT OF SHAPE, NEVERTHELESS IT STOOD MANY YEARS OF SERVICE.

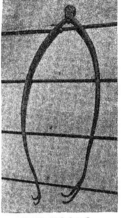

POT HOOKS

WHEN THE COOKING WAS DONE OVER THE OPEN FIRE, THE BAILS OF THE POTS WOULD GET TOO HOT TO TAKE IN HAND, AND A PAIR OF HINGED HOOKS WERE USED TO LIFT THE POT OR KETTLE FROM THE FIRE. THESE WERE FOUND AT THE FORMER HOME OF ROBERT PLUMMER NOW THE HOME OF CARVER AND EVELYN (PLUMMER) BUNDY. THEY ARE OF UNKNOWN AGE.

PLUMMER SPOONS

THEY WERE WEDDING PRESENTS GIVEN TO ROBERT, SR., AND RACHEL PLUMMER AT THEIR MARRIAGE IN CALVERT COUNTY, MARYLAND, IN 1793. NOW IN THE POSSESSION OF MARY PLUMMER DOUDNA.

BACK COMB

IT BELONGED TO ANNA DOUDNA SEARS AND WAS WORN BY HER WHEN A GIRL BEFORE COMING FROM NORTH CAROLINA IN 1804.

NECK HANDKERCHIEF
BELONGING TO SARAH (DOUDNA) BUNDY.

CAP WORN BY REBECCA (HODGIN) DOUDNA
SHE WAS THE WIFE OF JOEL DOUDNA.

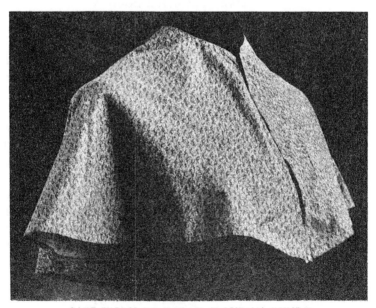

CAPE WORN BY SARAH (DOUDNA) BUNDY
SHE WAS THE WIFE OF CHALKLEY BUNDY. THE CAPE IS OF THE SAME MATERIAL
AS THE LAST DRESS SHE WORE.

MARY PLUMMER DOUDNA

ROBERT PLUMMER'S FIRST STOVE

ALL our cooking was done on the open fire until about 1845. We used the crane, iron pots, the long-legged and long-handled skillets, the Dutch oven and other pioneer cooking utensils. One day, when I was about eight years old, a man drove up to the house with a stove in his wagon, which he wanted to sell to father. Father did not feel inclined to buy, but just then I had to go on an errand to Polly Warricks', who lived a short distance west of us. I was much interested in the stove and made the trip as quickly as possible, but when I returned the stove was setting on the hearth. It was a Buck's Patent. At first it seemed very strange to cook on it, but soon we learned to like it very much.

Tacoma,
Ohio,
1920.

Mary P Doudna

ROBERT PLUMMER'S SMOKE HOUSE

A Pioneer Smoke House

IN the early days it was generally necessary at the approach of winter to provide, store and preserve the family food. The hogs were butchered, lard rendered, sausage ground, and the hams, shoulders and some of the side meat hung in the smoke house, which was usually a small building separated from the main house. When early spring came a small fire of green wood was kept burning in the smoke house for several days. The surface of the meat absorbed the creosote from the wood smoke, which thoroughly preserved the meat until used. The smoke-cured ham with its gravy was too delicious to be soon forgotten.

Mary Plummer Doudna says that the smoke house here illustrated, located on her father's farm, was built by her Grandfather Robert Plummer, Sr., before 1840. The logs are of split chestnut and show how well they have weathered all this time, and look now, in 1920, capable of lasting several more years.

W. H. S.

AN INDIAN STORY

THOSE of our ancestors who were early settlers came in close touch with the Indians, and the tales of these people were of great interest to pioneer children.

There has come down to us one of these stories, of which there are several versions. Lucinda (Bundy) Hanson, a daughter of Chalkley and Sarah Bundy, relates the following:

STOLEN BY THE INDIANS

"My great-grandmother, Agnes Childrey Hodgin, I think, was born in Georgia. When a little girl five years old, she, with her sister, who was seven years of age, went in search of a cow. They did not return. After a long search their parents gave them up for lost, thinking some wild beast or the Indians had killed them. But the Indians had only stolen them and carried them off to their camp. A council was held by the Indians to consider what to do with the girls and the old chief decided to adopt them as his own. The Indians took good care of them, so far as Indian care goes, and kept them fifteen years. The sisters knew they were not Indians and, as they grew older, they became dissatisfied and longed for their own people, so they planned to run away and try to find their family. For days the girls wandered in the woods, living on berries and roots, until they came to a white settlement. Here no one knew them nor did they know any one. They did not even know their names, only the names the Indians called them. The white people in the settlement took them in their homes and did all they could to help them find their own people. The older sister, a few days after they reached the settlement, died, no doubt from exposure in the woods. Agnes finally found her relatives, but not until after her mother's death. Agnes married William Hodgin and moved to Ohio, where, in 1811, he built the brick house in which I was born. William and Agnes Hodgin were my great-grandparents. Joel and Rebecca (Hodgin) Doudna my grandparents and Chalkley and Sarah (Doudna) Bundy my parents. I have grandchildren now and am am writing this so they may know and remember a little of the history of one of their relatives."

*   *   *   *   *   *

Mary C. (Bundy) Smith writes concerning this story: "Agnes, the younger of the two girls, was of a happy disposition, while her sister fretted and worried. Agnes played jokes on the Indians and they thought she liked them, so they trusted her. Sometimes, when she had cooked her meat on a sharp-pointed stick before the fire, she would hold the sharp point near the cheek of an Indian and call to him, so when he turned his head he would jab his cheek on the stick; then she and the other Indians would laugh at him. So they thought she was happy to be with them. When it came time for the tribe to move, they put Agnes on a pony with her sister on behind her. They followed along with the Indians until they came to a stream, when Agnes stopped to let her pony drink. As soon as the Indians were out of sight, she rode in another direction and at last found a white settlement."

*   *   *   *   *   *

T. C. Bundy, a great-grandson of Agnes, writes: "Great-grandmother was stolen by the Indians in about 1790. In Georgia the Indians raided the settlement and killed all the family except Agnes and one sister, girls of about twelve and fifteen years of age, whom they carried into captivity. Their father was killed in the yard and fell across the path where the girls had to step over his dead body. After traveling a while, some of the Indians wanted to kill the girls and some wanted to save them. Finally they seated them on a log and drew their bows to shoot them, when one Indian, who was determined to save the girls' lives, knocked the arrows out of the bows. The Indians then decided to keep them and take them to their town. On the whole, they were well treated until they were grown. Then the Indians decided it was time for them to marry. The girls made no objections to this, but told the Indians it was customary for the white people to make certain preparations for marriage, such as storing fruit and berries. The Indians assented to this preparation and the girls went out into the woods to gather and dry berries. Every day they would go a little farther and stay a little longer, until finally they made the break and ran away. After traveling many days, they met two young white men on horseback; the young men put the girls on their horses and started for the settlement, but

but before reaching home the younger girl was taken sick and died. One of the young men was William Hodgin. He later married Agnes, my great-grandmother, and moved to Ohio in 1803. In 1811 he built the Chalkley Bundy brick house, probably the first brick house in Warren Township."

*   *   *   *   *   *

Mary B. (Sears) Niblock writes concerning the Indian Story and Agnes Childrey:

"As I remember what her daughter Aunt Rebecca Doudna and also my grandmother Sears told me as a child she, Agnes Childrey, was playing in and near a big hollow stump when she saw some Indians coming. She hid in the stump till they left, so escaped being found and carried away as her sisters were. I do not remember clearly what she did afterwards nor in regard to her parents. I have a faint recollection that aunt and grandmother said the girl's parents were from home. I well recall how sister Sarah and I wondered what the stump was like and how she could see the Indians taking her sisters away without the Indians seeing her. There was a large, hollow chestnut stump on our home place that we decided must be similar to the one where she hid and we would play around and in it with that idea in mind, of course I know we may have had the wrong thought, but it is the one that has stayed with me."

It is not surprising that the story should vary when repeated so many times, and we can readily believe that when told to small children, certain portions were wisely omitted. There seems little doubt that all the stories refer to the one occurrence.

The principal settlement of Friends in Georgia was near Wrightsborough, McDuffie County. This settlement was made in 1770 and ended in 1803. Although they tried to live peaceably with the Indians, there was much trouble experienced, and finally the Friends moved away.

William Hodgin was born in 1766. He, with William Patten, visited Ohio in 1802. In 1803 they returned and brought their families. William Hodgin died in North Carolina in 1820 when on a visit.

THE FOX SKIN

WHEN I was a boy going to school, about 1857, I often noticed fox tracks in the snow. At a certain place in the road the tracks showed where two foxes had crossed and recrossed it many times going from one ridge to another. Oh, how I wanted to catch those foxes! I thought if only I had a gun I could hide nearby and watch for them. But I had no gun, so that thought was abandoned. I had a fine shepherd dog, but I knew he couldn't catch them, so that method was also abandoned. Then I had a happy thought, "I will borrow a neighbor's steel trap and set it in their path and maybe one will step on it." I did this, but the sly foxes walked around my trap instead of stepping on it.

I knew that foxes were fond of chicken, so I decided to take one of my mother's chickens and bait the trap with it. So I killed the chicken, took it over to the trap, built a pen by driving sticks in the ground close together in a circle about three feet across, leaving an opening on one side just large enough to fit the trap, set the trap in the opening and placed the chicken in the pen. The foxes could not get the chicken without passing over the trap. For several mornings as I went to school I would peep over to see if the fox was there. Everything was just as I had left it and I began to get discouraged, when one morning, to my surprise, there he stood with one foot fast in the trap! I at first thought it was our neighbor's big yellow dog, but when he saw me he jumped the length of the chain and then I got a glimpse of his big bushy tail and knew I had the fox all right.

I ran

I ran home in great excitement and shouted to everyone I met, "I've caught a fox! I've caught a fox!" They just laughed at me and said, "I'll bet Henry has caught someone's yellow dog." "No," said I, "he has a great bushy tail." Whereupon grandfather, Henry Stanton, remarked, "Now, maybe the boy has a fox." I called Frank, my dog, and we started for the trap. As soon as Frank caught sight of the fox, he jumped upon it and killed it. It was, indeed, no yellow dog, but a genuine large, red fox. When I got it home, with some effort, I'll grant, everyone wanted to see it. Grandfather and I took it into the old washhouse and skinned it, then tacked the skin up on the outside to dry. I think I went hundreds of times to see if it was drying all right. After a long and impatient wait, I pronounced it ready for market. I took it down, rolled it up, and started for town.

Now, Isaac Hawkhammer, a Jew of the type who never paid a cent cash for anything if he could help it, kept a large miscellaneous store and bought furs, such as fox, mink, skunk, and muskrat. I was surprised at the pile he had and wondered how so many were caught. When I went in he said, "Well, son, what have you there?" "A fox skin for sale," I replied. He took it, unrolled it, examined it and said, "I can't buy that. You let the dog kill it. Here is a hole and a part of the tail is gone." He showed me some beautiful ones for which he had paid a big price—three dollars. I felt discouraged and began wrapping mine up, when he said, "I will take it and give you a due bill for fifty cents. You can bring it in next time and I'll pay you." Disheartened, I took the due bill which, by the way, I could not read.

I went from there to the shop where I had left my shoes to be mended and they asked me there how much I got for the skin. I told them the whole story and they said it was just like him to beat a boy out of fifty cents.

I took the due bill home, put it in a drawer and promptly forgot it until I heard of his death some time later. Then I gave it up as lost. Nearly two years later, I was again in the shoeshop, when one of the shoemakers asked, "Well, did you ever get your fox skin money?" He asked if I still had the due bill and when I told him I had, he said to take it to Squire Meeks, who was administrator for the Hawkhammer estate, and he would pay me.

The

The next time I was in town I took it and handed it to Squire Meeks. He read it and asked why I had not presented it sooner. I told him that I knew Mr. Hawkhammer had died and thought that ended it, until I was recently told to take it to him and I would be paid. He then said he would have to write out an affidavit and for me to come in again in a few days, when he would be ready for me to sign and be sworn to the affidavit before he could pay me. I tell you I was scared when he said I would have to swear to something, for mother had always told me never to say a swear word and I could not remember that I ever had. However, the next time I went to town I took my due bill, with fear and trembling, back to the Squire. When I handed it to him for a second time, he re-read it, walked over to his desk, opened it and took out a roll of foolscap paper, perhaps three or four sheets, all closely written over. How well I remember to this day how I wondered what this all meant and how I was to swear. Then he said, "Son, I have here a written affidavit in regard to that bill which you hold against the Hawkhammer estate. You will have to swear to it." (How scared I was!) "Please hold up your right hand." I did it quickly and he read the affidavit and then said a lot about it and finally said, "Is this the truth, the whole truth," etc. I told him it was and he said, "That is all," and I had not said a bad word! He then opened a drawer, took out fifty cents and gave it to me. I hurried to the shoemaker's shop and told them all about it and one said, "Didn't I tell you you could get it that way!"

Thus, after much work, long waiting, a persistent effort, and a big scare, I got my fifty cents for a genuine red fox skin.

Columbus,   HENRY S. DAWSON.
Ohio,
1919.

THE OLD STILLWATER BRICK MEETING HOUSE

RESTORATION DRAWN BY WILLIAM MACY STANTON IN 1921 FROM DESCRIPTION AND DATA FURNISHED BY ROBERT SMITH, WILLIAM H. STANTON AND OTHERS. THE BUILDING WAS THIRTY-FOUR FEET BY NINETY-SEVEN FEET AND HAD A TWELVE FOOT STORY. IT WAS BUILT IN 1811–12 AND LENGTHENED IN 1823-24, AND TORN DOWN IN 1878. THE LARGER YEARLY MEETING HOUSE WAS BUILT ON THE SAME SITE.

FRIENDS' MEETINGS

THE first Friends' meeting for worship in Warren Township was held in 1803 in a log cabin erected by James Vernon near the present location of the "Township Graveyard." In the spring of 1804 the Friends of the neighborhood erected a log meeting house near the middle of "Section Nine" on ten acres of land purchased later of Richard and Ann Croy. The location of this meeting house was within the boundaries of the present Stillwater burying ground and near the northeast corner. This was the first building erected in the township for the purpose of holding religious meetings. Another room was added to this building in 1805, in which business meetings were conducted.

This log house was replaced about 1812 by a brick building which was enlarged in 1823 or 1824 to a size about thirty-eight feet wide by ninety-seven feet long with a twelve-foot story. This building remained in constant use until the spring of 1878, when it was demolished, so the present meeting house, measuring sixty by one hundred feet, could be built on the same location. This new house cost nine thousand dollars.

In

In the spring of 1805 a Preparative Meeting was established at Stillwater, followed on the twenty-ninth of Third month, 1808, by a Monthly Meeting. On Eleventh month Twenty-eighth, 1821, there was established by an order of Ohio yearly meeting, Stillwater Quarterly Meeting, to be composed of Plainfield, Stillwater, Alum Creek (Delaware County, Ohio), and Somerset Monthly Meetings.

The following information concerning the establishment of other meetings under Stillwater Monthly Meeting was taken from the minutes of that Meeting and establishes the fact that: In Sixth month, 1808, an "indulged meeting" was granted to Friends "living down Captina Creek," which privilege was continued until the establishment of Captina Preparative Meeting in 1816.—In Second month, 1809, a request was granted for an indulged meeting for Friends "living down Leatherwood Creek," which continued until the establishment of Richland Preparative Meeting in 1816.—In 1811 Ridge indulged meeting was granted and the Preparative Meeting established in 1815.— In 1818 Somerset Monthly Meeting was established and consisted of Somerset and Ridge Preparative Meetings.

Thus many meetings were established within a comparatively short period of time and shows the rapid spread of the established Friends' families throughout the western part of Belmont County soon after Ohio was admitted to the Union. Most of these meetings continue today, some with increased membership, while others report a decreasing attendance.

Barnesville,   MARY B. NIBLOCK.
Ohio,
1921.

THE OLD MEETING HOUSE
STILLWATER, OHIO

By SARAH D. (DOUDNA) SEARS
Barnesville, Ohio
9-17-1878.

Our dear old meeting house is gone;
　　We've torn it all away:
The walls, which stood the storms of years,
　　Were levelled in a day;
We've built a new one in its place,
　　'Tis nicer, well we know:
With longer aisles and easier seats,
　　And ceiling white as snow.

We do not doubt but it is best
　　The new was built, and yet
We think upon our dear old house
　　With feelings of regret:
For there in childhood's early years
　　Were many family bands
Into the house of God first led
　　By loving mothers' hands.

While more than threescore years rolled by,
　　Through man and womanhood,
To this same house their steps were bent
　　To seek the Fount of good.
And when gray hairs have silvered o'er
　　Each once-fair, youthful brow,
Some laid them down in peace to sleep,
　　Some see our new house now.

And holy influence there was cast
　　Upon the hearts around,
Until it seemed we almost deemed
　　That spot was hallowed ground.
Oh! could those walls a record give
　　Of all the truths there heard,
How would "our hearts within us burn"
　　At holy memories stirred.

But let us leave our treasured house,
　　And trust that in the new
Will fall upon our waiting hearts
　　Refreshing Heavenly dew.

The New House

I am thinking of the new one,
  Now as from the old I part;
And with longings for our welfare,
  I have questioned in my heart:

Will we be more true and faithful,
  When within the new we meet?
Will we be as meek disciples,
  Sitting at the Saviour's feet?
Will our meeds of praise rise sweeter
  Than they did within the old?
Will each heart in deep contrition
  Seek the depths of Love untold?

Can we yield earth's dearest treasures?
  Lay its "weights and burdens down?"
Will we count no cross too heavy
  For the gaining of a crown?
Can we yield our all, in reverence,
  To the Holy Spirit's power?
Will the sleepers learn to waken?
  Can we "watch with Him one hour?"

Will we imitate more closely
  Quakers of the olden time—
"Sons and daughters of the morning,"
  Children of a faith sublime?
And, should God see meet to prove us,
  Could the aged and the youth
Suffer cruel persecution,
  To procure the cause of Truth?

Well we know, the new house never,
  One stained heart can make more pure,
And God's mercy is not greater
  Just because our house is newer.
But I would, oh, Heavenly Father,
  That we might more faithful be;
That "this house which we have builded"
  We might dedicate to Thee.

Not with formal words and phrases,
  Not with worldly pride and show;
But that, from each heart, sweet praises
  Daily to Thy throne might flow;
That we might when there assembled,
  Bow more meekly 'neath Thy rod;
Strive to be more humble followers;
  More a people serving God.

A Bench from the Old Stillwater Meeting House

THE benches from the old meeting house which was torn down in 1878 were apparently entirely hand-made. The top, bottom and front rails were dovetailed to the end piece in addition to secure nailing. The top rail is held by a hand-made rivet through a diamond-shaped washer. Both are characteristic of the old days of hand-wrought hardware. All of the benches were of poplar wood.

STILLWATER MEETING HOUSE—EAST SIDE

THE MACHINE WORK ON THE IRON SUPPORTS OF THE BACKS OF THE SEATS WAS DONE BY WILLIAM H. STANTON.   HE ALSO HELPED WITH MUCH OF THE MILL-WORK, WHICH WAS DONE AT THE BELMONT MACHINE WORKS, BARNESVILLE, OHIO.   THE MEETING HOUSE WAS BUILT IN 1878.

MEMBERS ATTENDING OHIO YEARLY MEETING

AT STILLWATER MEETING HOUSE, 1921

PORCH POSTS ARE BLACK WALNUT, FROM THE INTERIOR OF THE OLD MEETING HOUSE.

STILLWATER MEETING HOUSE—VIEW FROM NORTH SIDE

LOCATION OF FIRST LOG MEETING HOUSE, BUILT IN THE SPRING OF 1804, IS SHOWN BY THE
WHITE SQUARE IN THE NORTHEAST CORNER OF THE PRESENT BURYING GROUND.

HORSE SHED USED BY ELI STANTON

IT PROTECTED HIS TEAM DURING MEETING HOURS. THE SHED WAS
BUILT BEFORE 1860 AND TORN DOWN IN 1921.

MOUNT·PLEASANT YEARLY MEETING HOUSE
BUILT IN 1815–16. IT IS SIXTY-TWO BY NINETY FEET.

MOVEABLE SHUTTER
MOUNT PLEASANT YEARLY MEETING HOUSE.

MACHINERY FOR RAISING AND LOWERING SHUTTER
Mount Pleasant Yearly Meeting House.

THE shutter separating the men's and women's rooms of the Mount Pleasant Yearly Meeting House was of large dimensions and was arranged to be wound up on a drum located above the ceiling. This drum had five sides, and the shutter was hinged so that as it revolved and increased in size the panels between the hinges were increased a corresponding amount; on the end of the drum was a large wheel carrying several coils of heavy rope; this rope in turn was attached to a vertical shaft with hand-bars by which it was turned as the men walked around the circular track; the windlass was provided with a ratchet wheel and pawl. The design is very ingenious and the workmanship on the wood parts very well done. The iron work may be considered good when we remember the very primitive tools and supplies which they had in 1815 and 1816.

GOSHEN MEETING HOUSE
ALL THAT IS LEFT OF A ONCE WELL-FILLED MEETING HOUSE.

DETAIL OF GOSHEN MEETING HOUSE
SHOWING THE WAY LOG HOUSES IN GENERAL WERE "CHINKED AND DAUBED." THE
BLOCKS OF WOOD WERE SAWED AND SPLIT AND FILLED INTO THE SPACE BETWEEN THE
LOGS WITH A LAYER OF CLAY MUD—IN THE BETTER HOUSES LIME MORTAR—BETWEEN
THEM. THE INTERIOR WAS FINISHED BY PLASTERING ALMOST FLUSH WITH THE SUR-
FACE OF THE LOGS. ON THE OUTSIDE THE PLASTER WAS APPLIED AT A SLIGHT ANGLE
TO CATCH LESS WATER AND DIRECT THE WATER OUT OF THE JOINT.

SITE OF CAPTINA MEETING HOUSE
STONE BASE OF CHIMNEY IS ALL THAT REMAINS. AARON AND THOMAS DEWEES
STANDING IN THE GRAVEYARD.
PHOTOGRAPH TAKEN IN 1907.

SHUTTERS FROM SHORT CREEK MEETING HOUSE
HENRY STANTON AND CLARY PATTERSON WERE MARRIED IN THIS HOUSE 3-30-1809.

STILLWATER MEETING HOUSE IN WINTER
Photographed about 1910.

**FRIENDS' MEETING HOUSE,
LANSDOWNE, PENNSYLVANIA**
Built 1830.

LITTLE BRICK SCHOOL HOUSE

THE LITTLE BRICK SCHOOL HOUSE

THE little brick school house was built some time prior to 1833 and was in continuous use from that time until 1899, when it was torn down and the new frame school house erected. During these years, many generations of Friends in Stillwater neighborhood attended school in this almost primitive brick structure that has endeared itself to all who have started their life's education within its walls.

SAMPLER OF MOUNT PLEASANT BOARDING SCHOOL
MADE BY MARY SMITH (DAVIS) ABOUT 1837 OR '38. NOW IN THE POSSESSION OF
ELLEN STANTON PENNELL.

MOUNT PLEASANT BOARDING SCHOOL
BUILT 1835–36.
FROM A WATER-COLOR DRAWING BY J. HERVEY BINNS, 1872.

ING SCHOOL

THE POSSESSION OF

1. ANNA C. STANTON
2. RACHEL BINNS
3. ELLEN D. STANTON
4. EVERETT G. HALL
5. EMILY FRAME
6. IDA STANTON
7. ELMA HALL
8. LEWIS J. TABER
9. E. DEAN STANTON
10. LURA FRAME
11. ELSIE HALL
12. SELMA TABER
13. WILLIAM TABER

THE SCHOLARS A

OUR ANCESTORS—THE STANTONS

1. ANNA C. STANTON
2. RACHEL BINNS
3. ELLEN D. STANTON

14. CHALKLEY BUNDY
15. ALICE EDGERTON
16. ESTHER EDGERTON

A LAMP FROM MOUNT PLEASANT
BOARDING SCHOOL
Now in the possession of Anna Stanton Palmer.

FRIENDS' SCHOOLS

SINCE the foundation of the Society, Friends have been systematic and thorough in education, and as they moved and settled in new sections of the country, the school house was among the first buildings to be erected. In some cases school was held in the Meeting House until it was possible to construct a separate building.

The Friends who settled the western part of Belmont County chose Samuel Barry as their first teacher. The

451

WESTTOWN SCHOOL—1810
FROM A CRAYON DRAWING.

The school was taught in the Stillwater Meeting House in the winter 1805–1806. The following summer the first school house in Warren Township was erected by Friends in Section One on the Ridge between the Hezekiah Bailey farm and the present Number One District School. As this school house was a little distance from the Meeting House, school was also held in the Stillwater Meeting House for a number of years until some time prior to 1833 a school house called "The Little Brick" was built near the Meeting House. In 1899 "The Little Brick" School House was torn down and replaced by a frame building.

On account of the scattered population due to the rural districts in which Friends lived, it became necessary that the higher branches of education should be taught in a centrally located school. The limited modes of travel necessitated a school at which the pupils could live. Therefore, in 1836, a large brick boarding

WESTTOWN SCHOOL, 1870
BOYS' BUILDING.

WESTTOWN SCHOOL, 1870
GIRLS' BUILDING.

NEW WESTTOWN SCHOOL
GIRLS' END.

boarding school was completed at Mount Pleasant in Jefferson County, Ohio, near the Ohio Yearly Meeting House.

After the separation in the society in 1854, Mount Pleasant Boarding School remained under the control of the Wilbur branch, but in 1874 the courts ruled that the property rightfully belonged to the other branch. The Wilburs accordingly gave up the property and decided to build a boarding school at Stillwater. The necessary funds were raised by popular subscription and the building erected and opened for school on New Year's Day, 1876. The school was known as "Barnesville" or "Olney Boarding School" and continuous sessions were held in the building until the Thirty-first of Third month, 1910, when the building was destroyed by fire. The brick walls of the burned building

FRIENDS' BOARDING SCHOOL, BARNESVILLE, OHIO
As originally built in 1875 and opened 1-1-1876.

FRIENDS' BOARDING SCHOOL, BARNESVILLE, OHIO
Rebuilt after the fire on 3-31-1910.

building were found to be in perfect condition after the conflagration, so that a new structure was erected within the walls similar to the former building with the exception of the reduction in the number of stories to comply with the State school law. Separate cottage dormitories were constructed, together with other buildings, forming a modern school plant.

After the middle of the nineteenth century many of the young Friends, after attending Mount Pleasant or Barnesville, continued their studies at Westtown Boarding School in Pennsylvania.

The many families which made their homes in that section of Ohio, of which Stillwater is the center, have sent their children to some of these schools in which they were taught the fundamentals of education that fortified them against the problems of daily life and fitted them better to live that the community felt the influence of their lives.

MARY B. NIBLOCK.

Barnesville,
Ohio,
1921.

**VASE MADE FROM RAFTER
OF LITTLE BRICK SCHOOL**

IN 1804 there came from North Carolina to Ohio a colony of Friends, most of whom settled in Belmont County, Ohio. Among these was Richard Edgerton, whose daughter Anna was the third wife of John Bundy. He settled on a tract of land some five miles southeast of Barnesville, Ohio. This farm was known for many years as the Archie Cole farm.

After becoming settled in his primeval home, Richard Edgerton built a grist-mill on the north side of Captina Creek. This stream of water flowed through his land and furnished an abundant supply of water to fill the long race that conducted the water to the old-time overshot water-wheel.

Isaac Patten, a half-brother of Ruth Patten, the first wife of John Bundy, bought, probably about 1825, the farm and mill of Richard Edgerton and made many changes in the building, also improving the mill-race; but he was not content until he had the old mill torn down and a larger structure erected in which he installed the best equipment of those days for making choice buckwheat flour, corn meal and wheat flour. He

457

He also put in a sawmill which did good work in sawing out boards of various dimensions, frame timber, studding, etc., as well as hundreds of cords of fire wood, as late as the year 1882.

The carpenter work on this new mill was done or overseen by Joseph Williams, who also directed the putting in of all of the machinery, he being in the full sense of the word a "millwright."

After Isaac Patten's death his son, Mahlin Patten, controlled and operated the mill until it was bought and run by a Mr. Bierd. It was then known as Bierd's Mill until about 1864, when it was purchased by Archibald Cole, Senior, who owned it the remainder of his life or until about 1910.

Cole's Mill, as built by Isaac Patten, was a five-story building one hundred feet by sixty feet. The overshot water-wheel was twelve feet in diameter and eight feet across its rim. It was a good wheel and did excellent work until that day in 1883 when a workman turned the full volume of water on to it at a time when not only the wheel itself, but all of the machinery, was standing still. The sudden great demand on the wheel to move all the machinery caused it to break.

A. G. Cole, a grandson of Archie Cole, says:

"This was one of the best—in fact, the best built mill that I ever saw in eastern Ohio. The frame was made of select white oak, hewed with broadax as smooth as the average carpenter would dress today with a plane. The building showed that it was the work of an expert. It was five stories high, counting the upper part where there was quite a little machinery.

"The part of the old mill that is still standing was what we called the wagon shed—in fact, it was not used
for

for any of the machinery, it was just the north end of the old mill.

"When I was a small boy the water-wheel broke, and grandfather Cole did not think that it would pay him to rebuild it, owing to the fact that he could only run the mill very little of the time because of the lack of sufficient water. After the white oak forests were cut the water soon ran off those old hills and the dam would not hold water enough to run very long at a time. I just remember seeing the old mill run and can remember seeing the people come on horseback with their two-bushel sacks of wheat or corn to be ground, and I can see the old miller taking out one-eighth for what he called "toll," then dumping the remainder of the grain into the hopper and grinding out the grain that the customer brought. Each man got flour from the grain that he brought.

"The mill-dam was three-quarters of a mile west of the mill and there was always quite a little trouble in keeping the race in shape. The dam also gave a great deal of trouble, and soon after they quit using the mill the channel of the creek changed and made it almost impossible to bring the water back into the race.

"There was also a sawmill, which was about one hundred feet west of the mill. A great deal of lumber was sawed at this mill. I can just remember seeing Thompson Smith sawing there when he was a young man.

"I am very sorry that these properties were not kept up, for they were built so well that they would have lasted centuries if they had been kept properly roofed. I have never seen such foundations as were under both these mills—all built of the best of cut stone."

East Canton,
Ohio,
1921.

MARY C. (BUNDY) SMITH.

COLE'S MILL
THE OLD WAGON SHED—ALL THAT NOW REMAINS OF THE MILL.

HOW I wish we could again drive down the winding road into the old mill, receive the hearty greetings of the dusty miller, feel the cool shade of the big building, hear the mighty splash of the water— the rumble of the great gears and the whir of the machinery—but the dam is dry, the race filled up, the miller gone to his long home and not a sound in the little that remains of "Cole's Mill."

W. H. S.

"BOBBIE" PETERS, COOK

WHEN Friends, leaving the South on account of slavery came to Ohio, many of them brought with them freed colored people, among whom was "Bobbie" Peters, who came with Jesse Bailey, Sr., from Dinwiddie County, Virginia, in 1811.

Evidently this same "Bobbie" Peters occupied a cabin, later part of the tobacco house which stood across the hollow south of our old log house, for Father told me that an old colored man of that name once lived there. The cabin was probably erected by Jesse Bailey, Sr., and occupied by him while he was building the hewed log house that many years later became our home. There were four apple trees planted near this cabin, one of which had blown down but still bore apples—a variety that was green and flat, very hard in the fall, and a very late keeper.

"Bobbie" was a small man and wore a "spade tail' coat which came down almost to his boot tops. It is said that he was the only colored man who was ever a member of Stillwater Quarterly Meeting. At one time he lived on the farm of Robert H. Smith, Sr., and "kept" the Meeting House. He was a famous cook and cake baker as well. No wedding dinner was quite right unless "Bobbie" cooked it.

Robert Smith says, "He kept his cooky box well filled for the boys of the neighborhood and if he was not on hand when they called they would sometimes climb down the stick chimney of his cabin to get them, though they knew the door was never locked, just to hear him scold about them 'ornery' boys that would steal his cookies; but it pleased him and was just what he wanted and expected them to do." It is surmised that Robert Smith was a competent judge of good cookies when he was a boy.

At last, no longer able to work, "Bobbie" went to live near Stanton and Ann (Nancy) Bailey Bundy and was cared for by them and their family while he lived, the meeting paying something towards his support. He died sometime in the forties and was laid to rest in Stillwater burying ground by those whom he had faithfully served, far from his sunny south, but in a land of peace and freedom.

W. H. S.

PIONEER CLOTH

THE present generation knows but little of the inconvenience and hardships our forefathers had to endure while making their homes in the wilderness and clearing up our now beautiful land, once the home of Indians, wild beasts and venomous reptiles. In these days, when we are in need of food and raiment we may step into a store and be supplied with them ready for immediate use, but in pioneer days many of our forefathers had to prepare the grain for food by grinding it on hand-mills or horse-mills or by cooking it whole, until water-mills could be provided, and had to raise flax and wool and make it into clothing and bedding by hand—a slow process, since the spinning was done on a machine with one spindle and the weaving on hand-looms.

Flax was grown for its seed and fiber—the seed being used to make linseed oil and the fiber for thread, clothing, linen table cloths, etc. After the seed was cleared off, the flax was laid out on the ground, somewhat as grain is laid from the grain cradle, in swaths to rot in order to make the woody part of the stems tender as a preparation for the break. The fall of the year

FLAX NEEDLES

THE NEEDLES WERE HAND-MADE FROM HARD WOOD BY
JOSEPH W. DOUDNA'S GRANDFATHER ABOUT THE YEAR
1812 AND WERE USED IN MAKING HARNESS FOR LOOMS USED
TO WEAVE FLAX.

year was considered the best time for this work. The breaking process broke and loosened the woody part of the stems for the swingling process, which in turn took out any part of the woody substance left by the break. And lastly came the hackling or combing, which prepared the long fiber and tow for spinning. The long, straight fiber was wound on the distaff; the tow was not wound on the distaff, but was spun from a bunch lying on the lap of the operator.

The wool was carded into rolls, either by hand or at the woolen mills, and the rolls spun into yarn for filling the web on the large woolen spinning-wheel. Stocking yarn was made in the same way except that the strands were doubled and then twisted again on the same wheel. This wheel required the operator to be all the time on foot and do much walking to and fro, while the flax spinning-wheel could be operated only in a sitting posture.

Let

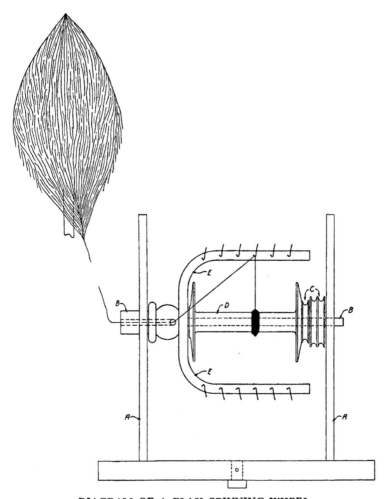

DIAGRAM OF A FLAX SPINNING-WHEEL

SHOWING DETAIL OF "PLIERS" AND THE COURSE OF THE THREAD.

Let A represent the uprights upon which the fliers are supported, B the spindle, C the fliers, D the spool, E the whirl. On the right end of the spindle is the whirl with two or three channels for one of the bands to run in. At the right end of the spool there is another channel a little smaller in diameter than the channels on the whirl for the other band to run in. The band, which should be of wool and about $\frac{1}{8}$ inch in diameter, is made just long enough to reach from the wheel to the spindle twice. The channel on the spool is a little smaller in diameter than the channels of the whirl, thereby making the spool run the faster, and that is the reason it winds the thread on the spool while twisting. If it inclines to take up the thread too fast it is an easy matter to hold on to the thread until it is twisted enough, and while the spool is not allowed to run any faster than the fliers, the band running in the spool channel slips until the spinner slackens her grip on the thread, when it immediately begins to wind upon the spool.

The flax fiber, after it is nicely combed or hackled out, is taken in one hand and the distaff in the other; the fiber is placed sideways to the distaff and is wound on with the ends of the fiber parallel to the distaff, with the ends hanging down. Spinning is begun by pulling out just the right amount while twisting to make the thread the proper size, and this operation continues until all is spun off the distaff or the spool is filled. When the spool is full the band running in the spool channel is lifted off to one side in order that the spool may run free and the thread is reeled off the spool.

The end of the spindle where the thread is fed in is hollow, with an opening in the side near the point where it enters the fliers, through which the thread comes

comes out and runs along over the hooks on the fliers
and down to the spool. In order to ensure an even
filling of the spool from end to end the thread has to
be moved back and forth along the hooks as the spinning goes on.

The spinning-wheel for flax could also be used for
spinning wool after the wool was carded into rolls,
and for spinning long fiber wool into stocking yarn
right out of the fleece; this last could not be done
on the large wool spinning-wheel unless the wool was
first carded into rolls. The chief use of this wheel,
however, was for spinning flax—the long, straight,
strong

FLAX · BREAKER
BUILT BY JOSEPH W. DOUDNA IN 1859, AND HAS BEEN IN HIS FAMILY
EVER SINCE.

HACKLING FLAX

TO COMB OUT
THE TANGLED
THREADS

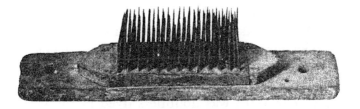

FLAX HACKLE
USED BY
MARY DAVIS,

THE MOTHER
OF JANE D.
STANTON

JOSEPH W.
DOUDNA

SCUTCHING
FLAX

strong fibers into thread for sewing, and thread or yarn for weaving into cloth for linen handkerchiefs, towels, cloth for clothing and household use. It was used also to spin the tow or coarser, weaker fiber of the flax plant into a thread or yarn usually a little coarser than the flax thread. This tow thread or yarn was used as a woof or filling with linen warp or chain and made the cloth for the tow linen shirts and pants of pioneer days.

History tells us that as soon as Abraham Lincoln saw his parents and their children comfortably settled in their new home in Illinois, and had struck out for himself, the first thing he did was to split three thousand rails for enough walnut-dyed jeans for a suit of clothes. This same jeans was doubtless dyed in the very same kind of dye the writer of these lines (now in the eightieth year of his age) used to help prepare. The bark was stripped from white walnut trees and an ooze made with which the woolen yarn was colored after it was spun and ready for weaving.

> "How wondrous are the changes
> Since one hundred years ago,
> When the girls wore linen dresses
> And the boys pants of tow!"

Barnesville,
Ohio,
1921.

Joseph W. Doudna

FLAX READY PREPARED FOR SPINNING INTO THREAD

FLAX READY FOR BREAKING

FLAX READY FOR SCUTCHING

TOW MADE BY HACKLING OR COMBING FLAX
READY TO BE SPUN INTO FILLING.

JOSEPH W. DOUDNA
COVERING A DISTAFF WITH FLAX
PREPARATORY TO SPINNING.

FLAX SPINNING-WHEEL

SPINNING FLAX IN THE HOME OF
JOSEPH W. DOUDNA

FLAX THREAD READY FOR USE

An Old Wool Wheel

HO made the wheel? Who used it? Maybe grandmother or a great aunt. And now, as I look, who is the spinner whose sturdy figure is at the wheel? She is plainly clad in material somewhat heavy and coarse but simply cut and made. Her face is strong but very kindly—one you could trust. Her hands are muscular and hardened, but how many things they know how to do!

With what pleasure she showed her new wheel to the visitor, and the neat rolls of yarn she had made and colored—the skeins twisted, then doubled and one end slipped in the loop of the other. How they admired the simple colors, the soft texture and the evenly spun and twisted thread.

Where is the yarn spun on the old wheel—and the cloth—the coverlets—the stockings—mitts—pulsewarmers? All are gone, not a single piece is definitely known. Gone, too, is the musical tone of the wheel—beginning so low, then increasing under each impulse of the hand, and dying down again, then a few revolutions backward; and several forward to wind upon the spool the length of yarn spun and twisted.

All are gone, and even memory fails us. How we would prize some samples of her handiwork, or her picture—what pleasure to hear the kindly sayings of this lovable ancestor of ours!

472

LAP-SHINGLE ROOF

THIS STYLE OF ROOF WAS USED BEFORE THE DAY OF SHAVED
AND JOINTED SHINGLES, BUT PERHAPS NOT QUITE SO EARLY
AS THE CLAPBOARD ROOF.
FROM THE HORSE SHEDS AT STILLWATER MEETING.

EARLY SHINGLE ROOFS

SINCE part of the purpose of this history is to inform the younger generation concerning the events of pioneer days, and to turn the mind of the older back to pleasant memories of the past, a few details might be added in regard to the roofing of the cabins and early homes.

Three kinds of shingles came into use, and which were preferred and required hand-work about in the order named—clapboard, lap-shingle, and jointed shingle. The clapboard was easiest to make, but the jointed shingle made a roof more nearly tight, especially against fine, driving snow, and is the one in general use now.

In

473

In those days the settlers had no difficulty in getting plenty of roofing material, for there was the greatest abundance of all kinds of good timber. They were generally provided with the hand-tools to work this timber into the kind of shingle wanted. Ax and saw to cut the tree down and saw the trunk into "cuts" the length of the shingle, then maul and wedges to split the cuts into the blocks, and frow and drawing-knife to split the blocks into shingles and to shave them.

The clapboards were usually cut three to four feet long. The manner of laying the clapboard was to begin the course by laying two boards with their edges together, then one over the joint, continuing in this way until that course was finished. Each course that followed covered the joints in the course already in place. In the new country nails could not be bought, so many roofs were pinned on with wooden pegs.

Another kind of wooden roof which came into use soon after the clapboard, was the lap shingle. These shingles were generally made twenty-eight inches long, with one edge thick and the other thin. They were laid showing twelve inches to the weather, and in courses of three or four shingles in width from the eaves to the comb, instead of horizontally from end to end of the roof.

Jointed

AN AX HANDLE PATTERN
THE PIONEERS SOUGHT OUT THE BEST SHAPE AND MADE PATTERNS FROM THEM WHICH
THEY KEPT AS GUIDES.

Jointed shingles were made about eighteen inches long, of equal width and about one-half inch thick at one end and tapered down to a feather at the other. They were laid edge to edge across the roof showing about five, or six inches to the weather and making the roof three courses in thickness.

Clapboard and lap-shingles were usually made from white oak; the jointed shingles were made from chestnut, walnut, cedar, and poplar. Both kinds of roof have been known to last about fifty years.

Barnesville,   JOSEPH W. DOUDNA.
Ohio,
1921.

CLAPBOARD ROOF
ONE OF THE EARLIEST KINDS OF ROOF USED BY THE PIONEER.
FROM A BUILDING AT THE HOME OF URIAH BAILEY.

EFORE the days of power saw mills and good roads, our ancestors used small tools to make many articles of wood. The ax, saw, frow, and drawing-knife were most essential. After the tree had been cut down and trimmed up by the ax, short sections were sawed off, and these split into smaller blocks. Jesse I. Doudna is here shown splitting a block into clapboards to be used as shingles.

The frow is driven into the center of the block by the mallet, and the piece split in two. When the block has been reduced so thin that there is a tendency of the crack to run out of center, making one side thin and the other thick, the block was inserted in the forks of a log, the thicker part down.

Then the operator, by springing the lower half with his weight, at the same time bearing down on the handle of the frow, would draw the crack toward the center of the block, thus making the two pieces of equal size and uniform thickness.

These early workers possessed very great skill in the use of their simple tools and by means of them made very beautiful clapboards, palings, lath, tobacco sticks and many similar articles, which were later made on the power saw mills.

The good work of those days depended on the skill of the workman, and he took great pride in doing fine work, whereas today much of the best work is due to the excellence of the machinery and tools used in its manufacture.

HAND-SPLIT PLASTER LATH

THE WAGONER

THE old-time wagoner has crossed the last ridge and gone down out of sight. About all we know of him is what "father said" or what may be learned from a few things he left, now treasured as relics of the early days. His was a sturdy manhood; his faithful, willing horses were of good blood, and his wagon strong and dependable. Truly an outfit to challenge our admiration.

To learn something of these old-time wagons let's drive over to W. F. Gibbons', a mile or so west of Somerton, Ohio, whose father, William Gibbons, was one of the old-time wagoners and lived in that big

brick

LEVER BRAKE AND CHAIN
USED ON THE OLD WAGONS.

brick farm house on the hill. William's father, Homer Gibbons, born in Loudon County, Virginia, was a wagoner also, and William began driving for him when seventeen years old.

The wagon he bought and used when in business for himself had been built in Winchester, Virginia, for a man by the name of Williams for use in through hauls from Baltimore and the east to as far west as civilization extended. The rear wheels were six feet four inches high, the tires four inches broad. It was fitted with the old English or "scoop" bed and with the top box would hold one hundred bushels of ear corn.

The regular outfit consisted of two full feeds of grain for six horses, a heavy wool blanket for each horse, feed trough, water buckets, body chains, ice cutters, tar bucket and two jack-screws. As there were six horses to pull and only two that could hold back it was very necessary to have reliable "rubbers" or "brakes." For moderate grades and bare roads the lever brake was pulled down and the chain hooked over a pin in the brake bar, but on steep grades and on icy roads the ice cutters were set under the wheels and held by chains so that they would cut into the ice and prevent slipping.

The

The jacks were used to raise an axle when greasing the wheels and at night were placed one under the center of each axle, to take the heavy weight off the axles and wheels. Such an outfit traveled hundreds of miles from home, carrying all kinds of freight and in all kinds of weather.

Six horses were always driven to the wagon; outfitted as above, it weighed 4,400 pounds and carried a load of 10,000 pounds on the National Road and a smaller one on country roads, the number of pounds depending on the condition of the road. It was generally used on hauls about Barnesville, as they paid better than the long hauls from the east. Its last use was in hauling stone to build the Baltimore and Ohio Railroad arch under Main Street in Barnesville.

But who shall tell us about the Wagon Maker of the early days—that "white-oak artist"—and his "wagon studio" decorated about the door with splotches of "red lead," green, blue and yellow paint? Often an unpretentious building, time had trimmed the inside in harmonious tones of brown and gray. Along the wall stood the bench with straight, solid, heavy, wood top; there was the wooden screw and lever, both polished smooth by long use, and such a heavy vise!

On the wall the racks for tools—and such a lot

ICE CUTTER AND WAGON LOCK
Used on steep grades.

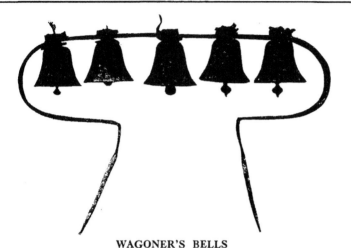

WAGONER'S BELLS

THE PRIZE GIVEN TO THE RESCUER WHEN A TEAM HAD TO BE PULLED
OUT OF THE MUD, IN THE DAYS OF LONG WAGON HAULS. THE BELLS
WERE WORN ATTACHED TO THE HORSE'S HAMES.
OWNED BY WILLIAM F. GIBBONS.

lot of them: planes, saws, chisels, bits of all sizes, draw knives, spoke shaves, gauges, squares and many more. All showed signs of long use, but were bright, well ground and sharp; it would have been less dangerous to strike the wagon maker's child or kick his dog than to "nick" one of those tools. Farther along were wood patterns for hounds, fellies, bolsters, axles, spokes and the various parts of the wagon. Out on the floor was the chopping block, a section of a log set on end, with a hand-ax sticking in it—no one ever laid a hand-ax down! Farther toward the rear was the old round stove with cracks in the fire bowl and the crooked pipe that seemed ready to fall down.

Then there was the wagon maker himself—a man of medium height, all bone and muscle; dressed in gray, with gray beard and gray hair, too, but a clear, sharp eye nevertheless; and a soft felt hat, one time black, but now gray with dust, the right brim rolled
up

up from many handlings, the band soaked many times with honest sweat; and such hands—horny palms and knotty knuckles, but no matter, they fitted the tool handles and that was all that was necessary.

He did not talk much unless you said "wagon," then the words just rolled along in endless procession. For the small boy he ran out his choice conundrum, "Over the hills and over the hills and always has its tongue out?" He went to church on Sunday because he wanted to do right, and he roused up when the minister mentioned "chariots and horses" or the "oaks of Bashan"; anyhow it helped to fill in the time until Monday morning when he could live his normal life and carve out those wooden works of art in his shop. He knew wagons, could see one around the corner and tell who made it before it came in sight! He knew timber, too, thought God never made a better tree than the white oak and he would not have cared if He had not made any other. He picked out his timber "on the stump," chopped the tree down, cut off the logs, and had it sawed in great thick boards or slabs, then "stuck them up" in the yard on good foundation with sticks between and shaded from the sun so they could dry or "season" slowly and not crack. A year or two later they were brought into the shop for the finishing course in seasoning.

When the timber was ready for use a piece was carefully selected, and here the "cub" or apprentice was called in—that husky boy of undeveloped mind who was expected to have a well-developed back, a boy ready to work and anxious to learn. Here he was allowed to do a man's part and carry one end of the heavy plank to the stout trestles on the floor.

floor. Several layers of dust were swept off and the piece very carefully inspected. Then the patterns were laid down and placed to cut to the best advantage. Around each pattern the wagon maker cut a mark with a gouge scribe, which made a little round groove which he could see plainly. The patterns were then laid aside, and now his interest began to grow, for though the plank was dark and unattractive he knew the beauty on the inside and was impatient to get it out. The rip-saw and meat rind came down and he began. Think of sawing by hand a dry, hard plank some three inches thick; but evidently he enjoyed the work and each time he moved his trusty saw he sent it just that much farther through the wood. Generally he chewed tobacco—if the wood was extra hard more was required. Soon that piece was out and turned over to the "cub" to chip off some parts with the hand-ax, and woe betide him if he cut "below the line."

AN OLD WAGON HUB
SHOWING THE NOTCH FOR TAKING OUT THE LINCH PIN.

Over on the bench, the side from which to lay out the work was planed down straight and out of "wind"—no need for a straight-edge or square, he had them both in his clear eye, and when he held the piece up to get the proper light and took a "squint" at it even his critical exactness could find no need for a tool.

Then the piece was carefully and accurately "laid off" and other sides were worked down; much of the work was done with "draw" knives of various sizes. As a surface

face was finished what beautiful "grain" was exposed, and such delicate tints—it was genuine white oak, not red oak, nor chestnut, nor Spanish oak, nor any other one of the two dozen varieties that now pass for "oak," neither was it "dead" and worm eaten—worms do not work in "live" timber! It was tough, very tough, and hard and had the peculiar satin gloss that indicates great strength and long life.

How the wagon maker enjoyed his chosen task! He

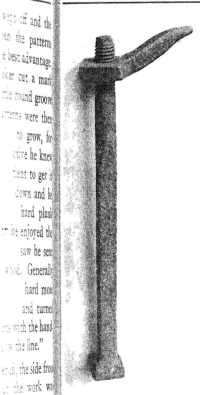

TAIL NUT

BEFORE TOOLS WERE SO COMMON IT WAS CUSTOMARY TO MAKE NUTS FOR BOLTS WITH A TAIL OR HANDLE, SO THAT THEY COULD BE TIGHTENED OR LOOSENED WITH ANY CONVENIENT HAMMER.

knew the timber was reliable and he put into the work the best skill he possessed. He rounded out the most beautiful curves, circles and ovals and tangents to them—every cut he made seemed so easy, the piece just changed shape as a flower develops in a movie picture.

WING NUT

WITH LEFT-HAND THREAD·

picture. How he enjoyed his work! It was all good, honest labor. The "fits" were all fits,—"glue joints" that would "pinch a hair." What did he care for "more wages, shorter hours, and better working conditions," work was pleasure and the consciousness of work well done was good pay.

So one piece after another was carved out. Now a new pleasure—to fit these pieces together to make the whole complete. The wheel was given the proper "dish"—an arch effect, the tire was the "shew back" and the hub the "keystone," thus giving greater strength to the wheel to carry the greater strain when on the low side of the road; the axles were tapered so that the spokes would stand vertically from the hub down and carry the load and all the angle given from the hub upward; also the wheels were given sufficient "lead" to prevent the hubs from running hard against either the collar or the linch pin. When all was complete, the wagon maker with many fears trusted his treasure to the blacksmith to be "ironed." There was a perennial quarrel on between the two—the ironwork was not so good as the woodwork, and the woodwork was not so good as the ironwork, but an impartial judge would have admired both. The iron in the hands of the blacksmith seemed to turn just the way he wanted it to, or to flatten out and round itself off at the corner; he did not "beat" it into shape, but just tapped a little here and there and trimmed it off a little, patted it "easy like" with his hammer and behold the pieces were fitted for the woodwork, in size and curve nicely matching the parts of the wood. The tires were bent and welded after careful trials with his "traveler" wheel to get their them just the right size, not too loose nor yet too tight, as this would injure the fellies. They were then heated in a circular wood-fire in the yard and when just hot enough were slipped on the wheel and quickly cooled—to burn the fellies was the "unpardonable sin" in the mind of the wagon maker. There was indeed a friendly rivalry as to who should do the best work, and make a heavy edition of that famous one-horse shay, every piece of which you remember was made equally good and strong so that no one part gave out before the other.

At

TAR BUCKET

EVERY WAGONER CARRIED A WOODEN BUCKET FILLED WITH TAR FOR GREASING HIS WAGON. IT WAS USUALLY HUNG ON THE COUPLING POLE UNDER THE WAGON. PINE TAR WAS IN GENERAL USE AS A LUBRICANT. FOUND AT THE HOME OF ROBERT PLUMMER, NOW OWNED BY CARVER BUNDY.

At last the wagon was finished; then came the painting—the best of linseed oil and "red lead" for the running gears, with the body finished in green or blue and the name, maybe, Isaac Perry, or Uriah Bailey, plainly painted on the side. Every effort was made to make the best; neither labor nor material was spared to secure this result. And when one day some farmer drove away from the shop with "the best wagon ever made" the artist heaved a sigh and felt as if he had parted forever from his long-time friend, but he wisely hid his sorrow, and—began carving out another masterpiece.

Ridley Park,   WILLIAM H. STANTON.
Pennsylvania,
1921.

COBBLER'S TOOLS

SHOEMAKING AND REPAIRING TOOLS USED FOR KEEPING THE FAMILY FOOTWEAR IN REPAIR AND SOMETIMES MAKING A PAIR OF BOOTS OR SHOES, AND MENDING THE HARNESS AS NEEDED. USED IN THE HOME OF PETER SEARS.

"CAMEL-BACK" FREIGHT ENGINE

DESIGNED FOR MOUNTAIN GRADES ON THE BALTIMORE AND OHIO. SOME OF THESE
ENGINES WERE LATER USED ON THE CENTRAL OHIO DIVISION THROUGH BARNESVILLE.
ENGINEERS LIKED THIS DESIGN BECAUSE OF ITS HEIGHT AND BECAUSE THEY COULD
EASILY SEE THE TRACK AHEAD. NOTICE THE BOILER FEED-PUMP CONNECTED TO THE
REAR WHEEL. CALEB STARBUCK STANDING ON STEPS.

RAILROADS

THE first acquaintance of many of our relatives about Barnesville with railroads was with the Baltimore and Ohio. A half century has made a great change in the Central Ohio Division of this road, one of the early roads in the Middle West.

Father told me that in 1856, when the road began running trains, they would sit on the porch at his home and listen for the whistle as the train passed the numerous grade crossings. There were almost no factories in those days and the sound of a steam whistle was very rare.

It must have been about ten years later when I saw the first locomotive that I can remember. Father took me to the "depot" at Barnesville. I recollect holding his left hand as we walked out the wood platform to the engine. The train was headed east. The engine seemed as high as a house, with its boiler covered with gray sheet iron, the joints of which were re-covered by brass bands

487

bands about three inches wide. There was much brasswork on the engine and all was kept beautifully polished, and the whole engine was kept neat and clean. The enginemen of those days took great pride in their work and in the machine in their care; it was a thing of life to them and they cared for and ran the same engine for years. There are numerous instances where a man has quit the railroad because his engine was wrecked or because he was asked to run any engine the company wanted to take out the train. Under such circumstances, we may be sure, the engine was kept in repair and handled carefully.

Wood was generally used for fuel. The smoke-stacks were made conical, about thirty inches in diameter at the top, and covered with fine wire screen to prevent the light wood sparks from being blown out and setting fire to the cars and material along the roadway. At each station there were long ricks of cordwood, and it was a common sight to see the engine uncouple and run on a siding to take on a supply of fuel. The passenger cars were small in proportion to the engine, perhaps one-third to one-half the capacity of the coaches used now. They had little windows almost square, no vestibule or automatic coupler, no gas or electric light, no air-brakes, steam heat, or water-cooler. There were no chair, dining or sleeping-cars; just the simplest kind of accommodations, which included coal-oil lamps, and few of them; wooden cars that too frequently took fire in case of accident; and a little stove in one end of the car—when you were too hot or too cold, you changed your seat if you could.

Water tanks to supply the engine were located at points along the road where water was easily available. When the engine stopped for water, the brakeman brought in a supply in a can like a florist's watering pot, without spray nozzle, but with four drinking glasses in a rack in front, and he proceeded to water the passengers, and you waited for a fresh drink until the engine got thirsty again.

There were no air-brakes, so on approaching a station the engineer whistled a long blast for the station and, if the train was to stop there, ended with two short ones for "down brakes," and the brakeman ran through the car to set the hand-brakes to stop the train. Generally he carried a stout club to give him greater leverage on the hand-wheel. In the case of freight trains you

you may guess that running over a string of cars on a windy, sleety night to set the brakes was not exactly a soft job; but the brakemen were a husky lot of fellows, perhaps because they got so much exercise and fresh air.

Instead of automatic couplers, the old link and pins were used, and many a brakeman lost a first finger while lifting one end of the link to enter the coming coupler and not getting out quickly enough. The little freight cars carried about ten or twelve tons, while now our standard cars have a capacity for fifty-five tons.

The roadbed was a mixture of the best and the poorest. The ballast was broken stone, and the cross-ties, while not "quarter sawed," were of fine native white oak. The rails were about one-half as heavy as the ones in use today and they were wrought iron, not steel. The splice bars consisted of a small flat bar about two feet long placed on the inside of the rail, and a wooden bar, about three by five inches, six feet long for the outside; there were four bolts through both the iron and wood splice and two through the rail and wood bar. This wooden piece was spiked down to the ties on which it lay. Any schoolboy who has walked the ends of the ties barefooted will remember the sharp threads and the ragged corners of the big square washers of the splice bolts.

Many slivers of iron were mashed off the ball or top of the rail by the flange of the wheels, and sometimes the ball would be mashed down on each side of the web, which very soon necessitated taking the rail out for repair. The joints or ends of the rails naturally gave out first.

Repairs were made in a blacksmith shop which stood on the southerly side of the track a little east of the "depot" building. Here a flat bar of iron, usually from six inches to two feet long, was shaped to fit the depression in the rail, then laid in place and both subjected to a welding heat in a big blacksmith's coal fire; then raised out of the fire and run on an overhead trolley to an anvil, sometimes out of doors, and four men with sledges beat it into place, welding it thoroughly and shaping it similar to the other parts of the rail. Blowing the fire and handling the rail, in fact, all the work was done by hand. You may readily believe that anyone who was constitutionally opposed to perspiring was not eligible for this job. That "one-armed" pest, the cigarette smoker, had not arrived. Workmen were men. They expected

to

to work and knew how to work; they took pride in whatever they did, and the operation of the road and development of the equipment, considering the tools and material at their command, shows the mechanical ability they possessed and the effort they made to develop the business in which they were engaged.

Many of the engines were not provided with the "Stevenson link" to reverse the motion, but used the "V." The "forward" and "reverse" eccentrics were each provided with an inverted V, one of which was dropped on the valve rod connection and ran the engine forward or backward at the will of the engineer. There was no "variable cut-off" and much steam was wasted.

Injectors and steam pump boiler feeders had not come into regular use. The boiler feed-pump was attached to the crank of the rear drive wheel and could not be used except when the locomotive was running. It was no unusual sight to see an engine stop at the depot after coming up the heavy grade from the west, cut loose from the train and run out to the "Rocky Cut" and back a few times to pump sufficient water into the boiler to last until the train was ready to go on.

Uncle William Stanton related some years ago that some of the early engines were named for towns on the line—the "Zanesville" ran on the Central Ohio Division. Others were named for animals, such as "Lion," also "Barney," "Buck" and "Berry," the names often given to a yoke of oxen. We may readily believe that such names created a very personal interest in the machines which were so far in advance of the times in that new country and which gave a quick and easy communication with the outside world.

Ridley Park,   WILLIAM HENRY STANTON.
Pennsylvania,
1921.

THE LOCOMOTIVE OF 1922

THE MAKING OF THE BOOK

WITH the book almost finished, let us look back over the time in which the material has been gotten together. Let us in a light vein picture the methods used and the hardships endured, so that in years to come the reader can look back and realize the conditions under which this book was conceived. In order that a true portrayal may be given, strict conventionalities will be waived, and intimate and familiar terms used.

Early in the winter of 1918–1919 "Cousin Will" came to Lansdowne for a visit, saying he had a "concern" that he wished to talk over with us. It was then that he made known his life-long desire to record, in a permanent way, some of the instances and anecdotes connected with the Stanton family. He feared with the passing of the present generation much would be forgotten of the old folk-lore and traditions which had been told and retold around the open fires of our parents and grandparents. During the conversation concerning the possibilities of enough material so many tales were told and remembered and things brought to light, that he was encouraged and believed that there

would

would be enough of interest, if each would only tell a story or two.

The regret was felt generally that a similar under-taking had not been started one generation further back so that we might profit for ourselves and the coming generations by the wealth of information that could have been supplied by our grandparents. But, with the firm conviction that an undertaking is better late than never, "Cousin Will" resolved to begin the collection of what material he could find.

At first the process was slow and the work moved on with but few tangible results. As time went on, how-ever, and the interest of various members of the family increased, material of the greatest interest came to light—facts and things not known to exist uncov-ered themselves and came to join the then ever-accumulating wealth of material.

The vision of the little pamphlet that "Cousin Will" had in mind at first now came up to a volume com-parable to Webster's Dictionary for size and to a volume of Æsop's Fables for interest. So much mate-rial poured in that he now felt encumbered by the magnitude of this treasured story and asked my sister, Edna Macy Stanton, and me to help him with the assembly and compilation of his "Stanton History," as it was then called.

Through the following months Edna busied herself with the bringing together of the actual family line and charting the genealogy of our family, from Robert of Newport to William Macy Stanton, Junior, of Lans-downe; while I investigated the possibilities concern-ing the physical appearance and makeup of the book.

Many visits were made by "Cousin Will" to Lans-downe and many hours of consultation were very

happily

happily spent by the three of us, in which we discussed and formulated the whole conception of "the
book" and of what would be of interest. No one but
"Cousin Will" and myself will ever know the profound
and genuine pleasure that the three of us enjoyed,
gathered as we did in the very atmosphere of our forefathers and seeing again the pure and unpretentious
lives they led and breathing again a breath of that life
that did all for them in their contented sphere and
made them and their lives the glorification of our ideal,
that has led us in the past, and now, with this touch
of dynamic love that was ours by this re-living, as it
were, for a brief period, their lives will billow us on with
a power that remains untold because it is so manifold.
It was a joy to Edna, it is a joy to us, and our fondest
hope is that you who read the pages we have made
may feel the pulse of love they had for us and that you
also will feel the joy.

In order to secure and bring together the material
for the book, letters were written to all we thought
would be likely to have any interesting information.
The recipients of these letters were not confined to the
Stanton family, but were to be found among the members of all of the families with which our ancestors came
in contact while they were establishing themselves in
pioneer days in the neighborhood where their descendants are now found.

The responses to the letters were most gratifying;
everyone contributed all that was asked for and a
large part of the book is made up of these contribu-
tions, which were brought together and edited by us
to bring them into the style or trend which had been
adopted for the book. We took great care to preserve
as

as much as possible the contributor's own handiwork, but to make the book a finished, comprehensive and co-related one, certain adaptations were necessary.

At first we concentrated our work around the ancestors and children of Joseph and Mary Stanton; and most of the articles concerning their ancestors and several other members of the family had been prepared or edited by Edna, when she died. Her death caused us to lose interest, and to hesitate to take up the unfinished work of the book that she had so carefully and ably started. But to stop would be to defeat a well-established undertaking and to destroy her conception of the whole proposition.

Within a few weeks, therefore, the work was resumed and "Cousin Will" asked Edna's twin sister, Ellen, to go on with the work that our sister had undertaken. Ellen felt some hesitancy in undertaking the work, but it was felt that a twin sister was the nearest one to Edna and the logical one to finish her task.

The collection of material and the preparation of the articles were well under way before any thought was given to the title; we just referred to it as "the book." "Cousin Will" in time made a list of suggested titles and we debated for some time which we should adopt. Strange to say we agreed on the last on his list. Some of the others considered were:

> "A little history of the Stanton family, for the relatives,"
> "Personal reminiscences of the Stantons, for our relations,"
> "Our ancesters—a little history and anecdotes for the relatives."

When we were assured of the book's reality, the next question was—What kind of book and who should we get to print it? After considerable investigation

we

we selected the firm of Innes & Sons, of Philadelphia, to print the book under the direction of Austin C. Leeds. We soon decided on the size of the page and the consequent size of the printed page form. By this time photographs were available of heirlooms and we soon had some of the engravings made. The first cut for the entire book was the one shown on the bottom of page 186, the last cut, the lighthouse shown on back of cover. We decided that all illustrations were to be zinc etchings, half-tones or photogravures. We have held to this and the majority of the illustrations are half-tone engravings on copper plates, having been made through a 133-screen. The eight portraits showing the children of Joseph and Mary Stanton are photogravures, and were made in Boston, Massachusetts. All the cuts that are in "line" are zinc etchings. One ton

THE PRINTING HOUSE

THE OFFICE OF INNES & SONS, PRINTERS, TWELFTH AND CHERRY STREETS, PHILADELPHIA, WHERE THE BOOK WAS PRINTED.

ton of 90-pound Alexandra Japan paper was required. The folded paper is the finest grade imported Japanese Vellum and is especially tough and suited to a folded sheet. The type selected is the Caslon, and is as near like old letters as we can find in modern printing. The majority of pages are printed in 12-point type. The type was set on a machine that moulds each letter separately and is known as a monotype machine.

When a photograph was obtained that we desired to insert in the book we discussed the size that would be desirable for the finished illustration and marked it with lines showing the portion of the view to be retained and the size to which it was to be reduced or enlarged. The photographs thus marked were sent to the printers, who, in due time, sent us a proof of the cut to which was attached the original photograph. These proofs were numbered so that we could identify them and not lose track of any during the period of collecting the material, as the cuts were not all made at the same time, but covered a period of almost three years. In point of size, the cuts varied from the smallest line engraving, one-half by three-quarters of an inch to the largest half-tone engraving, eighteen by eighteen inches.

When the written articles were finally revised they were typewritten and four copies made; the original was kept as a permanent file, the second copy for the printer, the third copy for the person writing the article and the last for the office copy. The printer's copy was sent and the type set, the galley proofs of the type were presented to us. These were corrected and cut up into the pages and pasted on a "dummy" showing the location of the cuts in the respective printed pages. This "dummy" was given to the printers

printers and they submitted a page proof which
showed the pages as they would appear. When this is
corrected the book will be ready for the final printing.

The family charts were made up from the information obtained, and arranged in a preliminary way,
after which the charts were carefully lettered by hand
on "tracing linen," from which the zinc cut was made.
The frontispiece, title page, dedication and record
pages in the back of the book were arranged and
hand-lettered, after which zinc plates were made. The
family

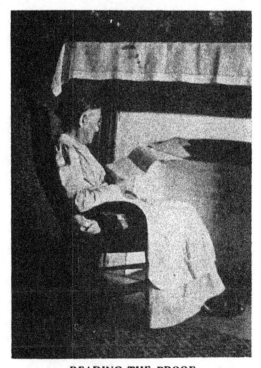

READING THE PROOF

"AUNT LIZZIE" (ELIZABETH STANTON BAILEY) READING SOME SHEETS OF
THE GALLEY PROOF IN HER HOME AT TACOMA, OHIO, THE NEXT DAY AFTER
THE FIFTIETH ANNIVERSARY OF HER MARRIAGE.

THE PRINTING PRESS

The cylinder press of Innes & Sons on which the book was printed. Sixteen book pages were printed on one side of a sheet of paper. The large sheet were then cut and folded makes two sixteen-page "signatures."

family groups were also separately hand-made, the pictures inserted and a half-tone made from which the printing will be done. The sample pages of cloth were made by having the card printed with the titles and guide lines, several months before the rest of the book, and the little samples cut on a trimming machine. When these were ready "Cousin Will" glued by hand each separate piece to the card. We calculated that he made over one million separate motions in order to accomplish the task.

There have been many pleasant experiences that have gone hand in hand with the real work of getting up "the book." In the Fall of 1920, "Cousin Will" and Ellen went to Ohio, in an automobile, and carried on a "collecting campaign" among the different families. They visited many of the old places. This visit aroused

"OLD DOBBIN"
"COUSIN WILL'S" BUICK AUTOMOBILE IN WHICH MANY TRIPS WERE MADE, INCLUDING THREE TO OHIO, TO GATHER MATERIAL FOR "THE BOOK."

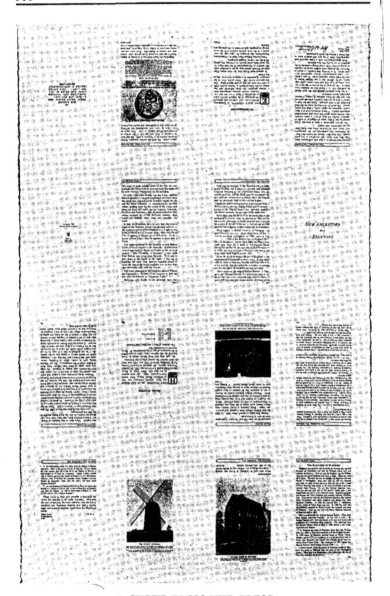

A SHEET FROM THE PRESS

THE FINAL PRINTED SHEET WHICH FOLDS INTO THE BOOK SIZE AND MAKES
TWO "SIGNATURES" OF SIXTEEN PAGES.

aroused still further interest in "the book" among the relatives in Ohio, and the material which came in during the following winter and spring, added greatly to the completeness of the undertaking.

During the winter, I was in Illinois and many letters were sent back and forth between Ridley Park and Urbana.

In order to exhaust all sources of the early information the Friends' Meeting and County records in North Carolina and Rhode Island were carefully examined by Sara W. Heston, Germantown, Pennsylvania, who secured much valuable data and many pictures.

Willis V. Webster, and his son Thomas, undertook to look up the land titles in North Carolina and Ohio,

A SHEET FROM THE "DUMMY"

EACH PAGE WAS ARRANGED IN THIS WAY BY CUTTING THE GALLEY PROOF INTO PAGES AND FITTING THE ILLUSTRATIONS TO THE PAGES. DIRECTIONS FOR THE PRINTER WERE WRITTEN ON EACH SHEET. THE "PAGE PROOF" WAS MADE FROM THIS.

THE HOME OF WILLIS WEBSTER
Columbus, Ohio.
Where all the maps were made.

Ohio, and to prepare the maps. They also made many photographs. While examining old records they unearthed the original will of Benjamin Stanton, of Beaufort, and the inventory of his property, signed by the executrix, his wife, Abigail Stanton. This was indeed a great find—a photographic reproduction is shown.

The greatest care was given to the proof-reading to make sure that there were no mistakes in the text.

AT WORK ON "THE BOOK"
"Cousin Will" and myself busy at our desk. Taken during the summer of 1921 in the office at 1310 Arch Street, Philadelphia.

text. A great portion of this work was done by Sarah G. Yocum, of Ridley Park, Pennsylvania.

It was decided early in the formative period that photographs of all the descendants of Joseph and Mary Stanton would be published in family groups. This has been followed out with all pictures that are available, which have been arranged to show the families, or descendants, of Grandfather Joseph.

Where no photographs of buildings that had been of especial interest to the family existed, reconstructed drawings of them were prepared and presented; with the

WHERE "THE BOOK" WAS MADE

OUR OFFICE WAS ON THE TOP FLOOR OF THE WHITE STONE BUILDING, 1310 ARCH STREET, PHILADELPHIA. THERE WAS NO ELEVATOR AND WE TOOK MANY STEPS IN GIVING YOU "THE BOOK."

the thought that, although not exactly accurate, they will give the best possible idea of the building, the record of which is forever lost.

When the summer of 1921 came, we decided to combine the trip to Ohio to celebrate Uncle Lin's and Aunt Lizzie's Golden Wedding Anniversary with the final collection of the remaining material in Belmont County. While in Ohio many interesting side trips were made to collect material and many photographs taken of things that were of interest to our family.
No

BOOKBINDING

Sewing the "signatures" together by hand, in the bindery of Alfred Smith & Company. The best linen thread was used and the binding is linen buckram imported from England.

STARTING UNDER THE MEETING HOUSE

OSCAR PATTEN HALF-WAY UNDER TO LOOK FOR THE STUMP. CLARENCE BUNDY GUARDING THE ENTRANCE. THE STUMP WAS NOT FOUND, BUT THE REWARD WAS PAID ANYWAY.

No stone was left unturned to find some of the old relics that were very much wanted, and pictures of which we had not so far succeeded in obtaining. We went to many extremes to secure photographs and information. An example of this is shown by our desire to locate a stump over which it was said the first Stillwater Meeting House was built (1811-12) and now covered by the second Stillwater Meeting

"ALL ABOARD"

ONE OF THE TRAINS UPON WHICH WORK WAS DONE ON "THE BOOK." THE BRIEF CASE CARRIED BOOK MATERIAL MANY MILES.

Meeting House. Rewards were offered and a thorough investigation was made, but no remnant of the stump was found. It had boubtless been removed when preparing the site for the present house, erected in 1878.

The last winter of the preparation, I was again in Illinois doing considerable traveling. While on the trains I did a great portion of making the "dummy" and correcting the page proofs. I worked under all conditions and with all kinds of environment, from a comfortable writing desk in the observation car of the "Panama Limited" out of Chicago to a single seat in a stuffy Big Four day coach running out of Indianapolis. But whether I worked to the tune of crying babies or to the incoherent conversation of my intoxicated western seat mate I have enjoyed it all and as the pages are read perhaps another interest will be added when some of the conditions under which "the book" was made are realized.

This semi-technical dissertation is given as a record of how "the book" was published and may be of interest to small boys as well as large ones in years to come, when this book is read, and the conditions and ways of book-making are greatly changed and the methods we used have joined many things herein shown, now so interesting to us.

Urbana,
Illinois,　　　　　　　　　　　　WILLIAM MACY STANTON.
1922.

WHEN NOW THE PAGES ALL ARE TURNED
AS ON THE SUNSET SLOPE OF LIFE WE FIND
OUR CANDLE BURNING LOW WITH ONLY
MEMORIES TO LIGHTEN AND TO CHEER.

AND NOW WITH STORY
TOLD WE TURN TO

THINGS OF RECORD

IN CHART AND
TYPE AND IMAGE

PHOTOGRAPHIC RECORD OF THE
DESCENDANTS OF JOSEPH AND MARY
(HODGIN) STANTON. THE PHOTO-
GRAPHS ARE ARRANGED IN FAMILY
GROUPS WHERE THE DESCENDANT
WAS MARRIED AND HAD CHILDREN.

A SCHOONER
1796

OF THE
ND MARY
PHOTO-
FAMILY
NDANT
HILDREN.

ELI STANTON
1835 — 1885

MARY P STANTON
1837 — 1871

LOUISE SMITH
STANTON — 1869

WILLIAM HENRY
STANTON
1860

1869
WILFORD T. HALL

186'
SARAH B. HALL

GUY WOODWARD
1891

EVA H. WOODWARD
1891 - 1919

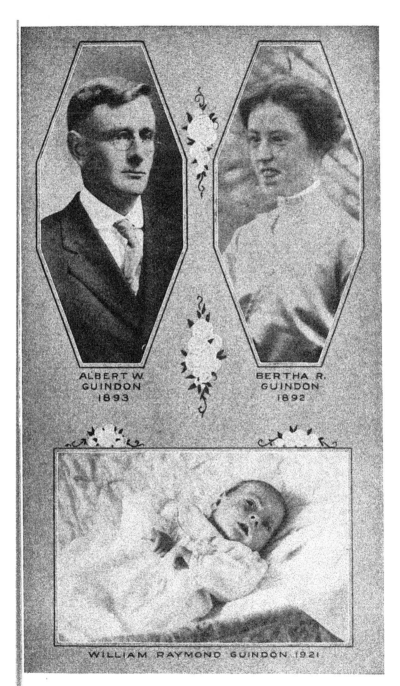

ALBERT W. GUINDON 1893

BERTHA R. GUINDON 1892

WILLIAM RAYMOND GUINDON 1921

HAROLD
HOLLOWAY
1895

HELEN H.
HOLLOWAY
1899

PAUL W. HOLLOWAY 1919

HARLAN STANTON WEBSTER
1889

MARY AVICE
WEBSTER
1891

WILLIS WILLIAM WEBSTER
1914

516

NATHAN ELI
STANTON
1875

SARAH E.
STANTON
1873

EDITH REBECCA
STANTON

1908

1910
MERVIN DANIEL
STANTON

1914
WILLIAM HANSON
STANTON

518

WILLIAM
STANTON
1839-1918

JANE DAVIS
STANTON
1846-1910

FRANCIS
WILSON

STANTON
1875-1886

1877-1897
J. LINDLEY
STANTON

1870-1884
MARY DAVIS
STANTON

521

ANNA STANTON
PALMER
1883

CHARLES WARNER
PALMER
1879

EVA STANTON
PALMER
1912

MARY ANNA
PALMER
1914

ELWOOD DEAN
STANTON – 1880

ESTHER SIDNEY
STANTON – 1882

JANE DAVIS
STANTON – 1910

CENTRE BELOW
SIDNEY FAWCETT
STANTON – 1912

KATHERINE MACY
STANTON – 1919

RUTH ELIZABETH
STANTON – 1915

EDITH COPE STANTON   WILLIAM MACY STANTON
1888   1888

1917   1919
SUSANNA MORRIS STANTON WILLIAM MACY STANTON JR.

525

EDWIN M. BAILEY
1872

LILLIAN D. BAILEY
1874

HERBERT J. BAILEY
1899

OSCAR J.
BAILEY
1874

OLIVER P.
BAILEY
—1901

MARY ANNA
BAILEY
1876
1914

1907
EDWARD
F. BAILEY

1903—
JOSEPH O.
BAILEY

191
LINDLEY
P. BAILEY

DOROTHY LOUISE BAILEY 1920

ALFRED L. BAILEY
1897

ANNA B. BAILEY
1894

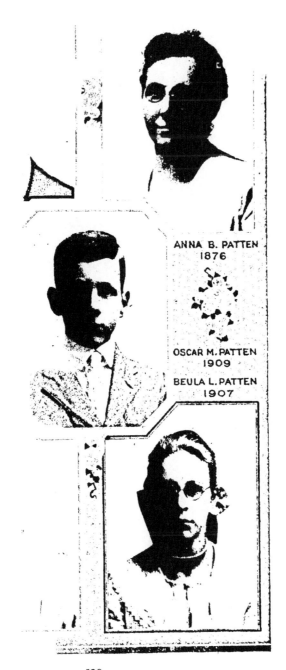

ANNA B. PATTEN
1876

OSCAR M. PATTEN
1909

BEULA L. PATTEN
1907

ALVA CALEB BAILEY
1880

LAURA ELIZABETH BAILEY
1877

1902
HARMON EUGENE BAILEY

1904
MARY ELIZABETH BAILEY

1907
RAYMOND
CALEB BAILEY

1909
ROLLAND
ALVA BAILEY

RALPH WARREN

BAILEY 1921

DAVID BRANSON
BAILEY
1912

NATHAN CHESTER
BAILEY
1914

FREDERICK R. BUNDY
1873

CLARA BAILEY BUNDY
1878

1906
WILLARD BUNDY

1911
JOSEPH STANTON BUNDY

JESSE S.
BAILEY
1884

ELIZABETH
STANTON BAILEY JR.
1911

FLORE
BAIL
191

CENTRE
LESTER W.
BAILEY
1915

BELO
CHARLES
BAIL
19

"*ARRIVED TOO LATE*
FOR *CLASSIFICATION*"

MARY AGNES BAILEY
DAUGHTER OF ALFRED L. AND ANNA B. BAILEY.
5-6-1922.

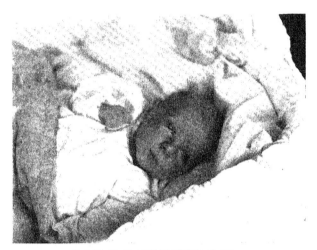

ELWOOD DEAN STANTON, JR.,
SON OF ELWOOD DEAN AND ESTHER SIDNEY STANTON.
5-8-1922

EDNA STANTON PENNELL
DAUGHTER OF S. HOWARD AND ELLEN STANTON PENNELL.
9-22-1922.

INTRODUCTION TO
OUTLINE FAMILY CHARTS

Connected and Related Families.

I N making a little record of our branch of the Stanton family, there are so many other families closely connected in relationship, association or business that it seems best to give a brief outline of some of these for a better understanding of their connections with our family. We are not attempting to make a complete record, but only to show a few of those families closely connected with our direct line, and of the ones shown, generally the older members. To include all is entirely beyond the scope of the present work.

The complex relationship existing among the families of Stillwater neighborhood was caused by the settlement there early in the Nineteenth Century of many Friends' families from Virginia, North Carolina and Georgia. The rules of the Society of Friends discouraged marriage with non-members, which virtually encouraged intermarriage to perhaps an undesirable degree.

When tracing the history of the families more directly connected with the Stanton family, it is seldom possible to get definite information farther back than that they came from a certain state about a given year. There is a rare opportunity for each family to work up and record its history as far back as possible, before any more has been forever lost.

THE STANTON FAMILY

SO much has been said of this family in the preceding pages that suffice it to say that the folded chart gives the descendants and Stanton ancestors of Joseph and Mary (Hodgin) Stanton.

The chart was completed by Edna Macy Stanton in 1919 and has been brought up to 1922 since her death.

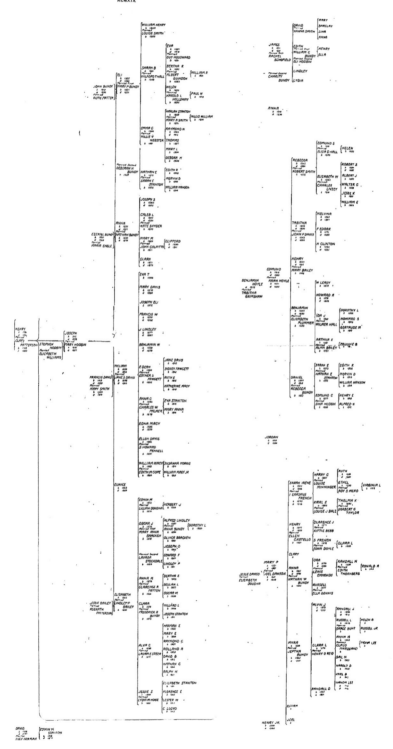

IT seems clear that Edmund and Elizabeth Bailey (maiden name not known) came from England to America, perhaps near the middle of the Eighteenth Century, and settled in Virginia, probably in Dinwiddie County.

Tradition tells us that all their children were born in Virginia and the records of Stillwater Monthly Meeting, which was established 3–29–1808, state that a certificate of membership was received on 7–28–1808 for Stephen Bailey of Dinwiddie County, Virginia, and in 1811 (month not known) certificates were received for Jesse Bailey, his wife, two sons and four daughters from Dinwiddie County, Virginia. No certain knowledge as to when Micajah, Matthew and James Bailey, Sr., came to Warren Township, but evidently before 1808, as all were members of Friends, and Micajah's name occurs as a member of a committee in one of the first Monthly Meetings held at Stillwater. I have the above information relative to the Meeting Minutes from an article written by Jonathan Schofield for the "History of Belmont County, Ohio," published in 1880.

THE BAILEY FAMILY

An excerpt from the genealogy of this
family showing its connections with

THE STANTON FAMILY

EDMUND
b 10-2-1794
d 4-8-1873
Married
MARGARET
DOUDNA
b 8-26-1799
d 5-18-1873

LYDIA
Married
GEORGE
STARBUCK

JESSE
Married
MARY JANE
BUNDY

CALEB
J CLINTON
CLYDE
CLARA
ADELBERT
EDITH

DANIEL
Married
ANN STRAHL

SARAH
Married
DEMSEY BAILEY

TABITHA
b 10-3-1831
d
Married
ELI PATTERSON
b
d

ELLEN
Married
BENJAMIN
STANTON SEARS

DELITHA
b 4-9-1803
d 1870
Married
BENJAMIN
BUNDY
b
d

ANN
Married
ROBERT W
HAMPTON

EDGAR C
Married
AGNES BUNDY

CHARLES
Married
MARGARET
NAYLOR

FRED R
Married
CLARA BAILEY

WILLARD L
Married
J STANTON

MATILDA
b 3-28-1807
d
Married
WILLIAM
PIERPONT
b
d

LYDIA
Married
RICHARD
PATTEN

CLARENCE R
Married
ANNA BAILEY

BERTHA E
BEULAH L
OSCAR M

JESSE
b 2-2-1764
d 7-15-1844
Married First
PHARIBA
JOHNSON
b
d 7-17-1820

EDWIN M
Married
LILLIAN DOUDNA

HERBERT J

OSCAR J
Married First
MARY ANNA
BRACKEN

ALFRED L
Married
ANNA BUNDY
OLIVER B
JOSEPH O
EDWARD F
LINDLEY P

JESSE
b 1-1-1815
d 5-14-1898
Married
ASENATH
PATTERSON
b 7-4-1820
d 11-29-1905

LINDLEY P
Married
ELIZABETH
STANTON

ANNA M
Married
CLARENCE R
PATTEN

BERTHA E
BEULAH L
OSCAR M

CLARA
Married
FRED R BUNDY

WILLARD L
J STANTON

ALVA C
Married
LAURA E STEER

HARMAN E
MARY E
RAYMOND C
ROLLAND A
DAVID B
NATHAN C
RALPH W

EDMUND
BAILEY
b
d 12- 1806
Married
ELIZABETH
b
d

JESSE S
Married
LYDIA M HOGE

ELIZABETH
STANTON
FLORENCE E
LESTER W
C LLOYD

538

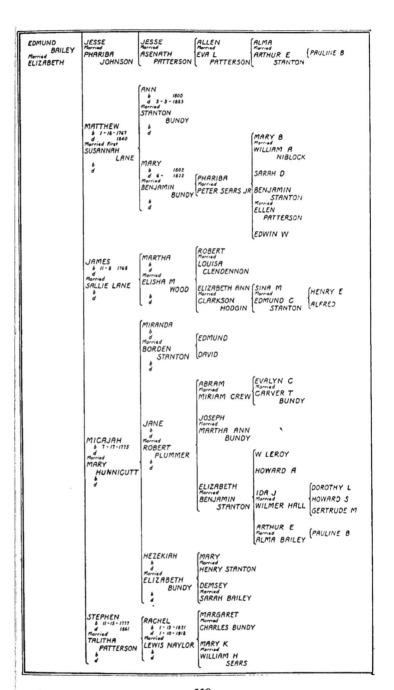

EDMUND BAILEY
Married
ELIZABETH

JESSE
Married
PHARIBA JOHNSON

JESSE
Married
ASENATH PATTERSON

ALLEN
Married
EVA L PATTERSON

ALMA
Married
ARTHUR E STANTON

{PAULINE B

MATTHEW
b 1-18-1767
d 1840
Married First
SUSANNAH LANE
b
d

ANN
b 1800
d 3-3-1863
Married
STANTON BUNDY
b
d

MARY
b 1802
d 6- 1822
Married
BENJAMIN BUNDY
b
d

PHARIBA
Married
PETER SEARS JR

MARY B
Married
WILLIAM A NIBLOCK

SARAH D

BENJAMIN STANTON
Married
ELLEN PATTERSON

EDWIN W

JAMES
b 11-8 1768
d
Married
SALLIE LANE
b
d

MARTHA
b
d
Married
ELISHA M WOOD
b
d

ROBERT
Married
LOUISA CLENDENNON

ELIZABETH ANN
Married
CLARKSON HODGIN

SINA M
Married
EDMUND C STANTON

{HENRY E
{ALFRED

MICAJAH
b 7-17-1775
d
Married
MARY HUNNICUTT
b
d

MIRANDA
b
d
Married
BORDEN STANTON
b
d

EDMUND

DAVID

JANE
b
d
Married
ROBERT PLUMMER
b
d

ABRAM
Married
MIRIAM CREW

EVALYN C
Married
CARVER T BUNDY

JOSEPH
Married
MARTHA ANN BUNDY

W LEROY

HOWARD A

ELIZABETH
Married
BENJAMIN STANTON

IDA J
Married
WILMER HALL

DOROTHY L
HOWARD S
GERTRUDE M

ARTHUR E
Married
ALMA BAILEY

{PAULINE B

STEPHEN
b 11-15-1777
d 1861
Married
TALITHA PATTERSON
b
d

HEZEKIAH
b
d
Married
ELIZABETH BUNDY
b
d

MARY
Married
HENRY STANTON

DEMSEY
Married
SARAH BAILEY

RACHEL
b 1-13-1821
d 1-10-1918
Married
LEWIS NAYLOR
b
d

MARGARET
Married
CHARLES BUNDY

MARY K
Married
WILLIAM H SEARS

THE BUNDY FAMILY

WILLIAM BUNDY, SENIOR, with his wife, Sarah (Overman), and daughter, Mary, came from Wayne County, North Carolina, in 1806 and settled temporarily on Captina Creek, in Somerset Township, Belmont County, Ohio.

THE BUNDY FAMILY

An excerpt from the genealogy of this
family showing its connections with
THE STANTON FAMILY

EZEKIEL
b 7-26-1807
d 11-22-1846
Married First
MARIA
ENGLE
b
d

NATHAN
b 8-22-1837
d 8-20-1874
Married
ANNA
STANTON
b 8-24-1837
d 10-5-1917

MARY M
Married
JOHN
COLPITTS

(GLIFFORD

ELI
b
d
Married
SARAH
VERNON
b
d

WILLIAM C
b
d
Married
EDITH
STANTON
b
d

ELLA
HENRY

CHARITY
b 3-2-1811
Married
JAMES
STANTON
b 8- 1811
d 1-20-1851

(No Children

WILLIAM H
Married
LOUISE SMITH

JOHN
b 2-17-1813
d 9-20-1896
Married First
RUTH
PATTEN
b
d

MARY P
b 12-18-1837
d 12-6-1871
Married
ELI
STANTON
b 2-12-1835
d 3-25-1885

SARAH B
Married
WILFORD T
HALL

EVA
Married
GUY WOODWARD

BERTHA R
Married
ALBERT W
GUINDON

WILLIAM
RAYMOND

HELEN
Married
HAROLD L
HOLLOWAY

PAUL W

EMMA G
Married
WILLIS V
WEBSTER

HARLAN
STANTON
Married
MARY AVICE
SMITH

WILLIS
WILLIAM

RAYMOND NATHAN
THOMAS

MARY LYDIA

DEBORA HARRIET

JOHN BUNDY
b
d 2-22-1731
Married
ELIZABETH
b
d 3-17-1731

CALEB
b 5-12-1721
d
Married
ELIZABETH
b
d 5-11-1762

DEMSEY
b 4-16-1746
d 4-10-1796
Married
MARY
b
d 3-21-1804

WILLIAM
b 1-1-1780
d 6-21-1828
Married
SARAH
OVERMAN
b
d 5-8-1853

DEMSEY
b 8-3-1821
d 4-26-1877
Married Second
ANN CREW
b 4-4-1826
d 7-10-1854

JEPTHA
b 4-14-1850
d 3-9-1920
Married
MYRA
DAWSON
b 8-29-1856
d

ALVIN J

CLARA L
Married
HENRY D
REID

RANDALL J

RUSSELL L
Married
GRACE BUNT

HELEN G
RUSSELL JR

ANNA M
Married
CLAUD MARQUAND

(MONA LEE

GAIL M

HAROLD D

KARL B

RANDALL D

WANDA LEE

CHALKLEY
b 2-24-1823
d 12-1-1866
Married
SARAH
DOUDNA
b 9-16-1824
d 8-1-1862

REBECCA
b 12-11-1853
d
Married
DANIEL
STANTON
b 8-26-1853
d 4-25-1918

SARAH E
Married
NATHAN E
STANTON

EDITH REBECCA

MERVIN DANIEL

WILLIAM HANSON

EDMUND C
Married
SINA
HODGIN

HENRY EDMUND

ALFRED HODGIN

ELIZABETH
b 5-26-1826
d
Married
HEZEKIAH
BAILEY
b
d

MARY
b 11-16-1843
d
Married
HENRY
STANTON
b 6-25-1847
d 5-23-1912

No Children

541

THE CLENDENON FAMILY

ISAAC and Hanna (Worral) Clendenon came to Stillwater neighborhood, Barnesville, Belmont County, Ohio, from Pennsylvania, probably the southeastern part, about 1803.

THE CLENDENON FAMILY

An excerpt from the genealogy of this family

showing some related connections with

THE STANTON FAMILY

ISAAC
CLENDENON
Married
HANNA WORRAL

BENJAMIN
Married
AMY HODGIN

SARAH
Lived Single

LYDIA
Married
ELISHA T
SMITH

AMY
REBECCA F
SARAH
ELLA
NETTIE

STEPHEN
Married first
MATILDA DAWSON
daughter of
Joel Dawson

SARAH LOUISA
Married
ROBERT WOOD

MATILDA JANE
Married
SMITH H MOTT

ISAAC WILSON
Married
NELL BARNES

MARY L
Married
GARRETT PIM

Married Second
ELIZABETH F
BRANSON

SMITH
Married
MAY COOPER

HANNA
ELIZABETH

AMY HODGIN
Married
LEVI GREEN

LYDIA E
Married
EDMUND BAILEY

HANNA
Married
ISAAC E STANLEY
In Iowa

THE DAVIS FAMILY

JOHN and Anne Sparrow Davis left the north of Ireland in the spring of 1819 and settled in Belmont County, Ohio, in order to secure better business opportunities. Here Francis Davis was born Seventh month Ninth, 1819.

THE DAVIS FAMILY

An excerpt from the genealogy of this

family showing its connections with

THE STANTON FAMILY

FRANCIS DAVIS
Married
ELIZABETH

{ JOHN
Married
ANNE SPARROW
daughter of
WILLIAM
and
MARTHA
SPARROW

{ FRANCIS
b 7-9-1819
d   1889
Married
MARY SMITH
b 8-25-1820
d   1910
daughter of
JESSE
and
ANNA SMITH

JOHN F
Married
TABITHA
STANTON

MELVINA

F EDGAR

H CLINTON

ANNE

JANE S
Married
WILLIAM
STANTON

EVA T

MARY DAVIS

JOSEPH ELI

FRANCIS WILSON

JOHN LINDLEY

BENJAMIN W

ELWOOD DEAN
Married
ESTHER SIDNEY
FAWCETT

JANE DAVIS

SIDNEY FAWCETT

RUTH ELIZABETH

KATHERINE MACY

ANNA CLARA
Married
CHARLES W
PALMER

EVA STANTON

MARY ANNA

EDNA MACY

ELLEN DAVIS
Married
S HOWARD
PENNELL

WILLIAM MACY
Married
EDITH M COPE

SUSANNA
MORRIS

WILLIAM MACY JR

HANNAH

JOSIAH

LINDLEY

SMITH

WILLIAM
Married
SARAH GIFFIN

545

THE DAWSON FAMILY

ERY little is known of the ancestors of this family. They left New England on account of religious persecution and settled in North Carolina. When Friends left that section to live in free territory they came to live in Stillwater neighborhood. Jesse Dawson married Elizabeth Doudna who was born in North Carolina 12-17-1784.

THE DAWSON FAMILY

An excerpt from the genealogy of this
family showing its connections with

THE STANTON FAMILY

			MARY		
			WILLITS		
		CHALKLEY *Married First* MARTHA GARRETSON	MELVINA *Married* ELISHA GAMBLE		
			CALEB		
			SINA		
	JOEL *Married First* SARAH BUNDY *daughter of* WILLIAM BUNDY	*Married Second* ANNA BRANSON [MARTHA			
		Married Third THERESSA HOPPER			
		Married Fourth MRS LOAR			
		MATILDA			
		ELI			
		JESSE			
JESSE DAWSON *Married First* ELIZABETH DOUDNA *daughter of* JOHN *and* SARAH KNOWIS DOUDNA		SARAH IRENE *Married* ISRAEL ERASMUS FRENCH	HARRY CLIFFORD *Married* LOUISE MINNINGER	RUTH ETHEL *Married* ROY S MEAD	VIRGINIA LOUISE
			KARL ERASMUS *Married* LOUISE J BALZ	THELMA KATHERINE *Married* HERBERT L TAYLOR	
		HENRY *Married* ELLEN CASTELLO	CLARENCE J *Married* KITTIE BEBB		
			STANLEY FRENCH *Married* EDNA DOYLE	CLARA LOUISE	
	Married Second MARY P STANTON *daughter of* HENRY *and* CLARY STANTON	CLARY	ORA *Married* LEWIS EMMONDS	RANDALL N *Married* EDITH THORNBERG	RONALD ALBERT
		ANNA *Married* NATHAN W BUNDY	RUSSELL *Married* ELLA DENNIS		
			ALVIN J		
				RANDALL J	
				RUSSELL L *Married* GRACE BUNT	HELEN G RUSSELL JR
		MYRA *Married* JEPTHA BUNDY	CLARA L *Married* HENRY D REID	ANNA M *Married* CLAUD MARQUAND	MONA LEE
				GAIL M	
				HAROLD D	
Married Second JANE [VERNON] BRYANT	TAMER JANE *Married* DANIEL HODGIN	ELVIRA		KARL B	
		JOEL	RANDALL D	WANDA LEE	

547

THE DOUDNA FAMILY

An excerpt from the genealogy of this family

showing some related connections with

THE STANTON FAMILY

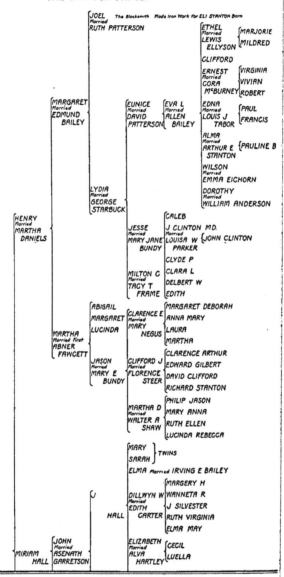

		RUSSEL J
JOSEPH H Married		CHESTER E
NORA E		ALFRED M
HARTLEY		DELBERT H

		BEULAH M
JOHN A Married		
MARY E		STANLEY J
CARTER		KENETH LLOYD

ROSETTA B

ELISHA Married First   ABBY Married THOMAS W BUNDY
MARY   MATILDA Married AMOS HODGIN
PICKETT

JAMES

MARY Married ISAAC HALL

KNOWIS Married HANNAH WEBSTER

SARAH Married _ _ _ _ _ _ FARMER

ELIZABETH   JOEL Married First SARAH BUNDY   See DAWSON Chart
Married   Married Second MARY P STANTON
JESSE DAWSON

ANNA Married PETER SEARS   See SEARS Chart

PEGGY

PENIAH Married JOHN LYLE

HOSEA   JOSEPH   JOSIAH W   ALBERT Married BLANCH HALL
Married   Married First Married   LILLIE Married EDWIN M BAILEY
MARY   BELINDA   RUTH BUNDY   ERNEST Married GERTRUDE KIRK
FARMER   HOBSON   ALICE Married EARL SMITH

                         MARY Married SIMEON HOYLE
           Married Second EDWIN Married LIZZIE PLUMLEY
           ANNA ELIZA
           WILSON   RUTH Married _ _ _ _ _ _ HIBBS

ZILPAH Married JOHN EDGERTON

ASENATH Married BENJAMIN BOSWELL

SARAH Married CHALKLEY BUNDY   See BUNDY Chart

                    PRUDENCE

                                     HOWARD
                    CLARKSON   WILLIAM
                    Married
                    RACHEL   MARY
                    CREW   ELVA
       ASENATH   MELVA
       Married
       WILLIAM
       BUNDY   JOEL

                    ALMEDA

                    EVALINE

       JOHN   CHARLES
       Married   CHARLES ELLIS
       MARY   AMY
       BUNDY   DILWYN   WALTER ALONZO
                    Married
       ROBERT   ELIZABETH   MARY E
JOEL   Married First STEER   MARGARET A
Married ESTHER   ANNA REBECCA
REBECCA BUNDY
HODGIN Married Second
       RACHEL
            WOOD   REBECCA Married JOHN CADWALADER

       TABITHA   SARA LOUISA
       Married First Married
       WILLIAM P   LOUIS STEER
       BUNDY

       EUNICE

       STEPHEN

       WILLIAM Married MARY JANE DAVIS

       REBECCA   ELMER E
       Married
       WILLIAM E   AGNES M
       BUNDY   BERTRAM

       AGNES

       JOEL

549

THE DOUDNA FAMILY

THIS family, of English ancestry, after stopping several years in Edgecomb County, North Carolina, came to Warren Township, Belmont County, Ohio, in 1804. It was a large family and there were many marriages into the Bundy family and several into other families connected with the Stantons.

THE HODGIN FAMILY

THIS family with many others came to Warren Township, Belmont County, Ohio, from Georgia in 1803. They had experienced much trouble in that state from the Indians and all were anxious to live in a free country and away from the evil influence of slavery.

THE HODGIN FAMILY

An excerpt from the genealogy of this
family showing its connections with

THE STANTON FAMILY

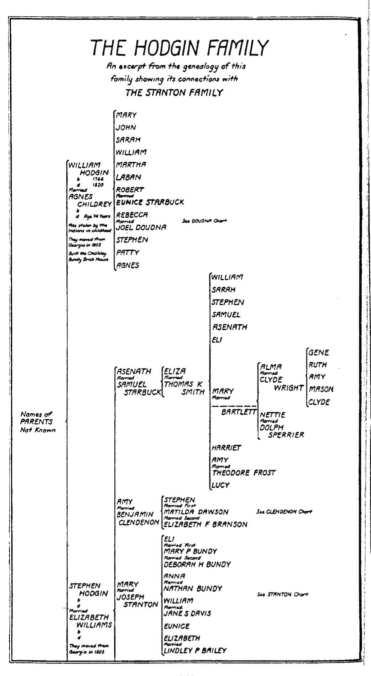

WILLIAM
HODGIN
b   1766
d   1820
Married
AGNES
CHILDREY
b
d   Age 74 Years
Was stolen by the
Indians in childhood
They moved from
Georgia in 1803
Built the Chalkley
Bundy Brick House

MARY
JOHN
SARAH
WILLIAM
MARTHA
LABAN
ROBERT
Married
EUNICE STARBUCK
REBECCA
Married
JOEL DOUDNA   See DOUDNA Chart
STEPHEN
PATTY
AGNES

WILLIAM
SARAH
STEPHEN
SAMUEL
ASENATH
ELI

ASENATH
Married
SAMUEL
STARBUCK

ELIZA
Married
THOMAS K
SMITH

MARY
Married
———
BARTLETT

ALMA
Married
CLYDE
WRIGHT

GENE
RUTH
AMY
MASON
CLYDE

NETTIE
Married
DOLPH
SPERRIER

HARRIET
AMY
Married
THEODORE FROST
LUCY

Names of
PARENTS
Not Known

AMY
Married
BENJAMIN
CLENDENON

STEPHEN
Married First
MATILDA DAWSON   See CLENDENON Chart
Married Second
ELIZABETH F BRANSON

STEPHEN
HODGIN
b
d
Married
ELIZABETH
WILLIAMS
b
d
They moved from
Georgia in 1803

MARY
Married
JOSEPH
STANTON

ELI
Married First
MARY P BUNDY
Married Second
DEBORAH H BUNDY
ANNA
Married
NATHAN BUNDY   See STANTON Chart
WILLIAM
Married
JANE S DAVIS
EUNICE
ELIZABETH
Married
LINDLEY P BAILEY

552

STEPHEN
HODGIN
Married
ELIZABETH
WILLIAMS

WILLIAM
Married
HARRIET
MOORE

THOMAS
Married
ADALINE
ARNOLD

LIZZIE
Married
OSBORNE
SMITH

HARRY
Married
ELLA
HOPKINS

(LOIS

DIENA
Married
SYLVANUS
SMITH

THOMAS
Married
— — — — —
WILLIAM

(I FRANK

ROBERT
Married
JENNIE VANLAW

FRANK
Married
MAMIE L CREW

(EARL FLEMING

ELZA

ROBERT
Married
LIZZIE
VERNON

ELISHA

BETSY ANN

ASENATH
Married
JOHN EDGERTON

ANNA MARY
Married
WILLIAM PATTERSON

STEPHEN
Married First
SARAH
MILLHOUSE

CLARKSON
Married
ELIZABETH
WOOD

SINA
Married
EDMUND C STANTON

CHARLES EARL
Married
RACHEL HEALD

CLARKSON EMLIN
Married
MILDRED PATTON

Married Second
REBECCA
[BRIGGS]
SMITH

WILSON Married MARIA BRIGGS

MARY ESTHER Married JOSEPH BRANTINGHAM

AMY Married CARSON JAMES

ELI
Married First
MARY ENGLE

JOHN E
Married
TAMER D
VERNON

MARY E
Married
THOMAS
THOMASSON

JESSE
Married
ALTHEA
THOMAS

HESTOR

ROY

LILLIAN G

WALTER

ELLWOOD

SIMEON

FLORENCE L
Married
DEAN
HAWORTH

PAUL

WILFORD

VERNE

RACHEL
Married
BARTON D
COPPOCK

ADA J
Married
ANDREW
BOWLES

ELSIE R

HELLEN E

JESSE

ALFRED

ELZA Married SARAH POLLARD

EDGAR
Married
MAY MAQUIRTER

HELLEN

JOHN EDGAR

WILLIAM

HARRIETT Married EGBERT C COLLAR

DANIEL W
Married
TAMER J
DAWSON

ARTHUR

ALONZO A Married FLORA BLANCHARD

EDWIN
STANTON

Married First CLARA BICHWELL

Married Second IDA WOODWORTH

CARRIE Married GEORGE JOHNSON

WILLIAM
Married
MIRIAM BALDERSTON

JENNIE
Married
CLARENCE LAMB

Married Second
SARAH
[VERNON]
BUNDY

ELI
Married
MARY MORRIS

ALICE
Married
WILLIAM ROBINSON

AMOS
Married
MATILDA DOUDNA

ERNEST

EARL

553

THE PATTEN FAMILY

ILLIAM PATTEN came from Georgia to Belmont County, Ohio, in 1802 with William Hodgin, and returning brought out his family in 1803, and settled in Stillwater neighborhood.

THE PATTEN FAMILY

An excerpt from the genealogy of this
family showing its connections with
THE STANTON FAMILY

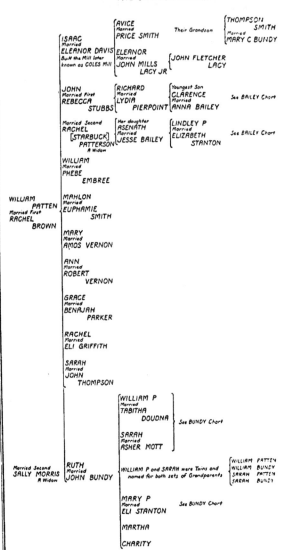

EN came
Belmont
in 1802
gen, and
to cut his
in Still-

WILLIAM
PATTEN
Married First
RACHEL
BROWN

ISAAC
Married
ELEANOR DAVIS
Built the Mill later
known as COLES Mill

AVICE
Married
PRICE SMITH

Their Grandson

THOMPSON
SMITH
Married
MARY C BUNDY

ELEANOR
Married
JOHN MILLS
LACY JR

JOHN FLETCHER
LACY

JOHN
Married First
REBECCA
STUBBS

RICHARD
Married
LYDIA
PIERPOINT

Youngest Son
CLARENCE
Married
ANNA BAILEY

See BAILEY Chart

Married Second
RACHEL
[STARBUCK]
PATTERSON
A Widow

Her daughter
ASENATH
Married
JESSE BAILEY

LINDLEY P
Married
ELIZABETH
STANTON

See BAILEY Chart

WILLIAM
Married
PHEBE
EMBREE

MAHLON
Married
EUPHAMIE
SMITH

MARY
Married
AMOS VERNON

ANN
Married
ROBERT
VERNON

GRACE
Married
BENAJAH
PARKER

RACHEL
Married
ELI GRIFFITH

SARAH
Married
JOHN
THOMPSON

Married Second
SALLY MORRIS
A Widow

RUTH
Married
JOHN BUNDY

WILLIAM P
Married
TABITHA
DOUDNA

SARAH
Married
ASHER MOTT

See BUNDY Chart

WILLIAM P and SARAH were Twins and
named for both sets of Grandparents

WILLIAM PATTEN
WILLIAM BUNDY
SARAH PATTEN
SARAH BUNDY

MARY P
Married
ELI STANTON

See BUNDY Chart

MARTHA

CHARITY

555

THE PATTERSON FAMILY

WILLIAM and Kaziah Patterson came from North Carolina to Belmont County, Ohio, in 1805.

THE PATTERSON FAMILY

An excerpt from the genealogy of this

family showing its connections with

THE STANTON FAMILY

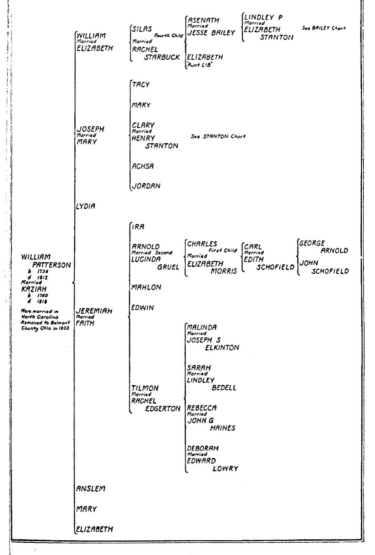

WILLIAM
PATTERSON
b 1734
d 1812
Married
KAZIAH
b 1740
d 1818
Was married in
North Carolina
Removed to Belmont
County Ohio in 1805

WILLIAM
Married
ELIZABETH

SILAS
Married
RACHEL
STARBUCK

Fourth Child

ASENATH
Married
JESSE BAILEY

ELIZABETH
"Aunt LIB"

LINDLEY P
Married
ELIZABETH
STANTON

See BAILEY Chart

JOSEPH
Married
MARY

TACY

MARY

CLARY
Married
HENRY
STANTON

See STANTON Chart

ACHSA

JORDAN

LYDIA

JEREMIAH
Married
FAITH

IRA

ARNOLD
Married Second
LUCINDA
GRUEL

MAHLON

EDWIN

CHARLES
First Child
Married
ELIZABETH
MORRIS

CARL
Married
EDITH
SCHOFIELD

GEORGE
ARNOLD

JOHN
SCHOFIELD

TILMON
Married
RACHEL
EDGERTON

MALINDA
Married
JOSEPH S
ELKINTON

SARAH
Married
LINDLEY
BEDELL

REBECCA
Married
JOHN G
HAINES

DEBORAH
Married
EDWARD
LOWRY

ANSLEM

MARY

ELIZABETH

THE SEARS FAMILY

An excerpt from the genealogy of this

family showing some connection with

THE BUNDY FAMILY

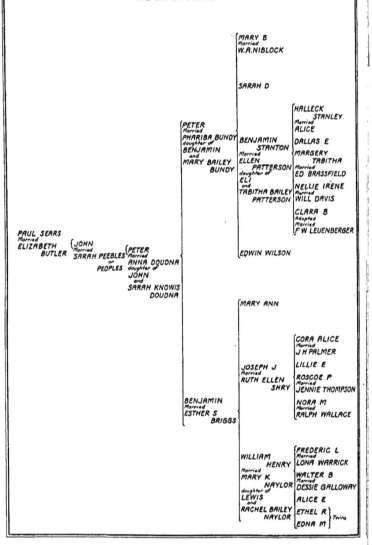

FOUR sons of Paul Sears (name of his wife not known), named Paul, Richard, Reeder and Daniel, came to America from France early in the eighteenth century. Settled in Prince George County, Virginia; the land records show that Paul bought land there in 1730. Paul and Richard married. Reeder went to the Indian War, and was gone a long time; returned to Virginia, stayed awhile, went West again and was not heard of afterwards. Daniel bought land in Prince George County, Virginia; served in the Revolutionary Army, and was not heard of after.

Peter Sears, Senior, came to Warren Township, Belmont County, in 1806; spent the summer; returned to Virginia; came again in 1809; was married the following spring to Anna Doudna. They located in Somerset Township, made three separate improvements, each time selling out to a newcomer; they moved, then, to Warren Township, located first near "Slab Town," where he operated a sawmill; from there to what used to be Chalkley Bundy place (the brick house); from there to Henry Doudna's place (the old house below W. H. Sears).

THE VERNON FAMILY

THE Vernon Family is believed to have come from Louden County, Virginia, in 1805, and settled near Barnesville. James Vernon erected a cabin about two miles northeast of Barnesville and a few rods from the township, or French graveyard. In this cabin was held the first Friends meeting in Warren Township.

THE VERNON FAMILY

An excerpt from the genealogy of this
family showing its connections with

THE STANTON FAMILY

JANE
Married First
————————
BRYANT

Married Second
JESSE
    DAWSON

TAMER JANE
Married
DANIEL W
    HODGIN   *See HODGIN Chart*

THEODATE
Married
WILLIAM
    McLAIN

WILLIAM
Married
PENINA
    STANTON

ELIZABETH
Married
BARACH
    BAILEY

AMOS
Married
JANE WAY

ASA

JAMES
Married
ELIZA
    STEWART

CHARLES
Married
ABBIE
    THOMASSON

JAMES

Names of
PARENTS
Not Known

JAMES
    VERNON
Married
TAMER DAVIS
5-5-1796

Married at Friends
Meeting House
Chestnut Creek Va

JESSE

TAMER D
Married
JOHN E
    HODGIN   *See HODGIN Chart*

RACHEL S
Married
WILLIAM
    WORRALL

DEBORAH H
Married First
ISAAC
    MONROE

JOHN
JANE
IDA
SARAH
WILLIAM

Married Second
STEPHEN
    BALLIETTE

JESSE

ELI
Married
ELIZA
    HANSON

JANE W
Married
DANIEL
    SHELHAMMER

ELIZABETH
WILLIAM
RACHEL
JOSEPH
BENJAMIN

562

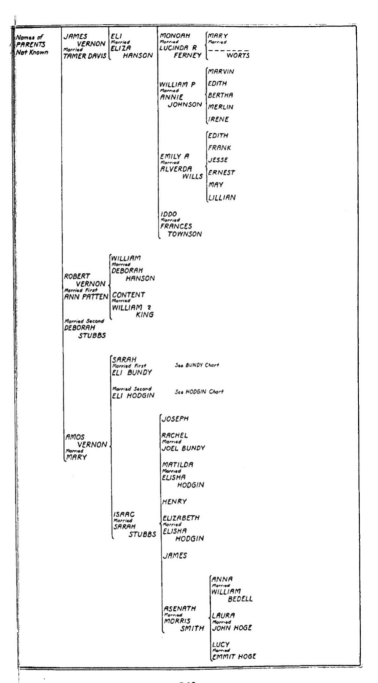

As the water of the stream falls without
ceasing and flows away, so the life of man
turns on in generic cycles.

GENEALOGIES

CHILDREN OF
NJAMIN AND ABIGAIL STANTON

DESCENDANTS OF
HENRY AND CLARY STANTON

PARTIAL GENEALOGY OF THE
BUNDY FAMILY

lctified the fabbath y, lanctified it.
12 ¶ ᵐ Honour thy father and thy mother :
that thy days may be long upon the land which
the LORD thy God giveth thee.
13 ⁿ Thou shalt not kill

THE FIFTH COMMANDMENT. A PHOTOGRAPHIC REPRODUCTION
FROM THE OLD STANTON BIBLE.
Exodus 20.12.

CHILDREN OF BENJAMIN AND
ABIGAIL (MACY) STANTON

Copied from Byron Stanton's notes
on the Stanton Family.

David   b. 11- 3-1774 died in infancy.
Elizabeth b. 12-24-1775 m. Joshua Scott. '
Sarah   b. 1-12-1778 m. Richard Williams.
Avis   b. 12- 1-1779 m. Jesse Thomas.
Anna   b. 6-12-1782 m. Aaron Brown.
Henry   b. 2-25-1784 m. Clary Patterson.
Abigail   b. 3-23-1786 m. Benj. Mitchner.
David   b.. 5- 1-1788 m. Lucy Norman.
Lydia   b. 10-11-1790 m. William Lewis.
Benjamin b. 7-28-1793 m. Martha Townsend.
Joseph   b. 1- 2-1797 m. Mary Townsend.

Benjamin Stanton, married, first, Elizabeth
(Carver) Jorden, the daughter of James and Elizabeth Carver, and the widow of Robert Jorden.
They had one son, James, born 10-9-1770, who
married Rebecca Craddock. They had no children.

Elizabeth Stanton, married Joshua Scott in North Carolina.
They moved to Ohio about 1802 or 1803 and lived for some years
near Mt. Pleasant, Ohio, in Jefferson Co. They afterwards moved
to Logan Co., Ohio, where many of their descendants now live.
She and three of her sisters (Avis, Anna, and Abigail) are buried
in the Friends' burying-ground near Zanesfield, Logan Co. Their
children were—Job, who married Meriba Straught; Jesse, who
married Hannah Watson; Hannah, who died, aged 8 years; Anna,
who married John Hall; Rebecca, died unmarried; Stanton, who
married Esther Edmundson; Enoch M., who married Rebecca
Brown (*nee* Rea); Elizabeth W., married John Fuson or Fewson;
Joshua, who married Sarah Harris; Benjamin S., who married
Eliza Ann Harris—ten in all.

Sarah

Sarah Stanton, married Richard Williams in North Carolina, removed to Jefferson Co., Ohio, in 1802. I remember Uncle Richard as a bright, jovial old man, fond of jokes and full of anecdotes. Their children were—Robert, who died in childhood; Eliza, who married, 1st, Micajah Dillingham, 2nd, Axia Jonston; Abigail, who married, Jehu Fawcett, of Salem, Ohio, and died 10-10-1835; Dearman, who married Mary Farmer; Deborah, who married Daniel Osborn; Asa, who married Edith Cadwallader; Mary, who married Joseph Emmons; Benjamin, died unmarried; Lydia, married Joseph Stanley; David, married Hannah Young; Edward, married Hanna Bruff—eleven in all, of whom all are deceased.

A son of Micajah and Eliza Dillingham died some years since in the Tennessee penitentiary, to which he had been sentenced for assisting a fugitive slave. The descendants of Richard and Sarah Williams are scattered throughout the West, chiefly in Ohio and Iowa.

Avis Stanton, married Jesse Thomas in North Carolina, removed to Ohio about 1802. He was one of the persons I remember to have seen who wore knee-breeches; he wore to the last the costume worn by Friends at the close of the last century and wore his broad-brimmed hat even at the table. He died at Mt. Pleasant, Ohio, (about 1845), and Aunt Avis went to live with one of her children in Logan Co., where in the burying-ground of Goshen Meeting House, near Zanesfield, she lies buried. Their children were—Abigail, who married, 1st, Nimrod Hogue and, 2nd, Joseph Lawrence and died at Bellefontaine, Ohio, aged some years over eighty; William, died in childhood; Nathan M., married Pamela Brown, died at Schoolcraft, Michigan, his wife was from New England, he is the author of the memoir of Abigail Stanton cited above; Jonathan, married Sarah Cowgill; Gulielma, died unmarried; Jesse, married Minerva D. Hollenback; David, unmarried; Ann Eliza, married Joseph Roff; Joseph, married Minerva Roff—nine children in all. Some of the descendants of Jesse and Avis Thomas live in Logan Co., Ohio, others in and about Schoolcraft, Michigan.

Anna Stanton, married Aaron Brown in North Carolina. They came to Ohio with grandmother Stanton in 1800 and lived for some years in or near Mt. Pleasant, Ohio, removing afterwards to Logan Co., Ohio. Their children were—Benjamin S., who was a physician in Bellefontaine, Ohio, who married Rebecca Shaw. Their only daughter died soon after arriving at maturity. Mary, who died unmarried; Zaccheus, married Hannah Marmon; Ira, married Rebecca Rea, who, after his death, married his cousin, E. M. Scott; Ezra, twin brother of Ira, died in infancy; Asa, married Hannah Sands, he is deceased, she and her children live near Zanesfield, Ohio; Anna, married John Outland; James, married Elizabeth Ann Willis; Davis, married Susanna Marmon; Martha died

died unmarried; Elma, married Edward Kenton—eleven children in all. Many, perhaps most, of their descendants reside in Logan Co., Ohio.

Henry Stanton, married Clary Patterson, of Mt. Pleasant, Ohio, 3–30–1809. They lived on a farm in the southern part of Belmont Co., Ohio, not far from Barnesville, where Clary died, May 25, 1860, in the 73rd year of her age. She was born in North Carolina, probably in Guilford Co.

Their children were—James, who married, 1st, Rachel Schofield, 2nd, Charity Bundy; Joseph, married Mary Hodgin; Anna died unmarried; Edmond, married Sarah Hoyle; Jordan, died unmarried; Mary, married Joel Dawson; Henry, died unmarried; David died, aged 17 years. Some of their descendants live in Belmont Co., Ohio, others in Iowa and Nebraska. All of the children of Henry and Clary Stanton are deceased except Mary Dawson, who lives (1885) in Barnesville, Ohio, and who writes in June, 1897— "I have been the lone and only surviving one of father's children for 34 years and I can truly say that goodness and mercy have followed me through a long and chequered life."

Abigail Stanton, married Benjamin Michener. She is buried at Goshen Meeting House near Zanesfield, Ohio. Their children were—Levi, who died young; Susanna, who married John Brown and died June 24, 1888, at Zanesfield, aged 78 years and 38 days; John, married Mary Ann Brown; Lydia, married Kersey Graves; Henry, married Lydia Warner; David married Elizabeth Michener; Isaac, married Martha P. Gause; Edwin, married Eliza Anne Smith; Martha, married 1st, William Taylor, 2nd, Allen Williams; Elma, died unmarried. Many of their descendants live in Logan Co., Ohio.

David Stanton, married Lucy Norman. He was a physician in Steubenville, Ohio. She was from Virginia. She was a daughter of Thomas and Mildred Tutt Norman.

Children:

Edwin McMasters	b. Dec. 19, 1814
Darwin Erasmus	b. July 17, 1816
Lucretia	b. Nov. 30, 1818
	died Aug., 1820
Lucy	b. Apr. 13, 1820
	lived only one day
Oella	b. May 4, 1822
Theophilus	b. Nov. 27, 1824
	lived 12 hours
Pamphila	b. Feb. 20, 1827
	died Feb., 1899

David Stanton came with his mother to Ohio when a boy of 12 years. With his brothers Benjamin and Joseph he studied medicine

medicine in Mt. Pleasant, Ohio, with Dr. Hamilton, married and went to Steubenville, where he practiced his profession.

In 1897 his daughter Pamphila writes: "Their first home was on the south side of Market St., above Fifth. Here their sons Edwin and Darwin were born. The house on the south side of Third St., between Market and Washington."

David Stanton was greatly loved and admired both as a physician and as a man. His son Darwin is said to have resembled him in appearance.

Lucy Norman came to Ohio with friends of her mother by the name of Starr, whose daughter was her intimate friend, and a widow of the Rev. David McMasters. They probably arrived not earlier than 1813. Lucy Norman was a Methodist and the marriage was opposed by the Friends and was the cause of David Stanton leaving the Society. They were married by the Rev. David McMasters, a warm personal friend for whom they named their eldest son, but substituted the name of Edwin for David.

The day Dr. Stanton was buried the schools were dismissed that the children might attend the funeral as a mark of the respect in which he was held.

Lydia Stanton, married William Lewis of Washington Co., Pa. They had six children, five of whom died in infancy.

Children:

Morris, died aged 3 years.
Mary Anne, m. ——— Burns and had one daughter.
Essie, who married ——— Marsh.
Lucinda, died aged 5 years.
Susanna, died aged 3 years.
Lucinda Susanna, died aged 1 year.
David, died an infant.

William and Lydia Lewis lived for many years on a farm in Hennipen Co., Ill.

Benjamin Stanton, married Martha Townsend, who was born in Washington Co., Pa., 4–18–1794, died 1–12–1885, aged 91 years.

Children:

Rebecca b. 1– 9–1819 m. Chas. Weaver.
Laura b. 9–20–1820 m. Barnaby.
Oliver b. 7–26–1822 unm., d. 11–1–1898.
Joseph b. 5–30–1824 m. Mary H. Fry, died 1885.
Caroline b. 6–28–1826 m. Geo. W. Addams.
David b. 6– 9–1829 m. Lydia M. Townsend.
William b. 8–28–1832 m. Ellen Irish.
Dalton b. 8–14–1834 d. aged 10 years.
Byron b. 8–14–1834 m. 1st, Edith M. Weaver,
                  2nd, Harriet Alice Brown.
Benjamin Lundy b. 10–19 1839, d. 2–0–1841,
                  aged 16 months.

Joseph Stanton, married Mary Townsend. If related to Martha Townsend, who married Benjamin Stanton, the relationship was distant.

Children:

Thomas Townsend, unm. Died 1857.
Joseph Stanton was a physician and lived in Springboro, Warren Co., Ohio.

About 1832 or 1833 he went as one of a committee of the Warren Co. Medical Society to Wheeling, Va., to investigate the nature and treatment of Asiatic Cholera then prevailing there. He took the disease and died, leaving a widow with one son, Townsend. The latter, after his mother's death, went to California, where he died unmarried.

DESCENDANTS OF HENRY STANTON, 1784–1863, AND CLARY PATTERSON, 1788–1860

Married 3–30–1809.

1. James, b. 1811, d. 1–20–1851.
   m. 1st, Rachel Schofield, 2nd, Charity Bundy.
2. Joseph, b. 1–19–1812, d. 7–26–1859,
   m. 9–26–1832 Mary Hodgin, b. 4–10–1810, d. 9–27–1857, daughter of Stephen and Elizabeth Hodgin.
A. Eli, b. 2–12–1835, d. 3–25–1885,
   m. 12–9–1857 Mary P. Bundy, b. 12–18–1837, d. 12–6–1871, daughter of John Bundy and Ruth Patten.
   1. William Henry, b. 8–2–1860,
      m. 6–15–1898 Louise Smith, b. 1–11–1869.
   2. Sarah, b. 11–23–1861,
      m. Wilford T. Hall, b. 8–29–1869.
     (*a*) Eva, b. 9–26–1891, d. 2–26–1919,
        m. Guy Woodward, b. 2–5–1891.
     (*b*) Bertha R., b. 12–16–1892,
        m. Albert W. Guindon, b. 5–7–1893.
       (1.) William Raymond Guindon, b. 4–14–1921.
     (*c*) Helen, b. 6–30–1899,
        m. Harold L. Holloway, b. 12–28–1895.
       (1.) Paul W., b. 12–21–1919.
   3. Emma Clara, b. 10–5–1864,
      m. 8–23–1888 Willis Veil Webster, b. 3–1–1861.
     (*a*) Harlan Stanton, b. 9–6–1889,
        m. 9–3–1912 Mary Avice Smith, b. 11–12–1891.
       (1.) Willis William, b. 7–8–1914.

(*b*) Raymond Nathan, b. 7–27–1893, d. 9–5–1912.
(*c*) Thomas, b. 6–25–1897.
(*d*) Mary Lydia, b. 6–11–1904.
(*e*) Debora Harriet, b. 7–6–1906.
Eli Stanton m. 7–30–1873. 2nd, Deborah Hanson
          Bundy, b. 1–26–1839.
4. Nathan E., b. 1–26–1875,
          m. 6–20–1907 Sarah E. Stanton, b. 8–4–1873.
  (*a*) Edith Rebecca, b. 4–15–1908.
  (*b*) Mervin Daniel, b. 2–13–1910.
  (*c*) William Hanson, b. 1–8–1914.
B. Anna, b. 8–8–1837, d. 10–5–1917,
          m. 3–30–1859 Nathan Bundy, b. 8–22–1837, d. 8–20–
          1874, son of Ezekiel and Maria Bundy.
1. Joseph S., b. 1–19–1860, d. 12–20–1885.
2. Caleb L., b. 12–12–1862, d. 11–28–1890, m. Kate Snyder.
3. Mary M., b. 7–7–1864,
          m. John Colpitts, b. 7–12–1851.
  (*a*) Clifford B., b. 7–5–1890, d. 9–5–1911.
4. Clara Elma, b. 11–7–1871, d. 4–19–1873.
C. William, b. 9–15–1839, d. 5–5–1918.
          m. 1–27–1864, Jane S. Davis, b. 7–15–1846, d. 3–8–
          1910, daughter of Francis and Mary Davis.
1. Eva T., b. 7–25–1868.
2. Mary Davis, b. 4–24–1870, d. 10–4–1884.
3. Joseph E., b. 8–26–1872.
4. Francis Wilson, b. 4–5–1875, d. 8–8–1886.
5. John Lindley, b. 4–17–1877, d. 3–20–1897.
6. Benjamin W., b. 3–16–1879, d. 3–21–1879.
7. Elwood Dean, b. 8–20–1880,
          m. Esther S. Fawcett, b. 9–23–1882.
  (*a*) Jane Davis, b. 9–27–1910.
  (*b*) Sidney Fawcett, b. 5–8–1912.
  (*c*) Ruth Elizabeth, b. 7–14–1915.
  (*d*) Katherine Macy, b. 11–24–1919.
  (*e*) Elwood Dean, Jr., 5–8–1922.
8. Anna Clara, b. 4–9–1883,
          m. Charles W. Palmer, b. 8–9–1879.
  (*a*) Eva Stanton, b. 6–26–1912.
  (*b*) Mary Anna, b. 10–20–1914.
9. Edna Macy, b. 4–26–1886, d. 2–24–1920.
10. Ellen Davis, b. 4–26–1886,
          m. S. Howard Pennell, b. 8–17–1891.
11. William Macy, b. 9–15–1888,
          m. Edith M. Cope, b. 8–16–1888.
  (*a*) Susanna Morris, b. 7–23–1917.
  (*b*) William Macy, Jr., b. 5–31–1919.
D. Eunice, b. 10–19–1843, d. 9–6–1849.

E. Elizabeth, b. 12–24–1846,
    m. 7–26–1871 Lindley P. Bailey, b. 3–8–1850.
  1. Edwin M., b. 7–18–1872,
      m. Lillian M. Doudna, b. 6–22–1874.
    (a) Herbert J., b. 6–8–1899.
  2. Oscar J., b. 12–5–1874,
      m. 1st, Mary Bracken, b. 2–5–1876, d. 1–24–1914.
    (a) Alfred L., b. 3–16–1897,
        m. Anna Bundy, b. 8–24–1894.
      (1) Dorothy Louise, b. 4–7–1920.
      (2) Mary Agnes, b. 5–6–1922.
    (b) Oliver B., b. 6–14–1901.
    (c) Joseph O., b. 7–5–1903.
    (d) Edward F., b. 1–30–1907.
    (e) Lindley P., b. 8–9–1911.
  3. Anna, b. 8–16–1876,
      m. Clarence R. Patten, b. 6–27–1881.
    (a) Bertha E., b. 6–1–1903.
    (b) Beulah L., b. 2–23–1907.
    (c) Oscar M., b. 3–20–1909.
  4. Clara, b. 6–25–1878,
      m. Frederick R. Bundy, b. 9–30–1873.
    (a) Willard, b. 4–2–1906.
    (b) Joseph Stanton, b. 1–28–1911.
  5. Alva C., b. 4–26–1880,
      m. Laura E. Steer, b. 11–1–1877.
    (a) Harman E., b. 7–14–1902.
    (b) Mary E., b. 9–20–1904.
    (c) Raymond C., b. 6–28–1907.
    (d) Rolland A., b. 6–28–1909.
    (e) David B., b. 12–29–1912.
    (f) Nathan C., b. 9–29–1914.
    (g) Ralph Warren, b. 2–21–1921.
  6. Jesse S., b. 4–15–1884,
      m. Lydia M. Hoge, b. 9–13–1883.
    (a) Elizabeth Stanton, b. 5–16–1911.
    (b) Florence E., b. 6–27–1913.
    (c) Lester W., b. 11–22–1915.
    (d) Charles Lloyd, b. 3–20–1918.
3. Anna, b. 4–1–1814, d. 12–2–1836.
4. Edmond, b. 10–14–1816, d. 12–14–1850,
      m. 7–1–1840 Sarah Hoyle, b. 1–11–1821, d. 1–16–
      1885, daughter of Benjamin Hoyle and Tabitha
      Grimshaw.
  A. Ephraim, b. 8–2–1841, d. 8–15–1841.
  B. Rebecca, b. 7–5–1842, d. 4–18–1904,
      m. 9–26–1860 Robert Smith, b. 3–11–1838.

1. Edmund S., b. 9–18–1861,
        m. Eliza D. Hall, b. 4–23–1853.
    (a) Helen R., b. 9–23–1893.
2. Elizabeth W., b. 1–7–1863,
        m. Charles Livzey, b. 3–7–1861.
    (a) Robert S., b. 11–27–1894, d. 3–7–1895.
    (b) Albert J., b. 3–6–1897.
    (c) Walter C., b. 1–24–1899.
    (d) Jesse K., b. 1–31–1901.
    (e) William E., b. 8–11–1903.
3. Maria H., b. 1–9–1868.
C. Tabitha, b. 3–13–1845, d. 2–13–1920,
        m. John F. Davis, b. 1–0–1842, d. 12–12–1899.
1. Melvina, b. 4–2–1865, d. 1867.
2. Francis Edgar, b. 12–12–1871, d. 8–27–1889.
3. Henry Clinton, b. 8–26–1884, d. 5–21–1885.
D. Henry, b. 6–25–1847, d. 5–23–1912,
        m. Mary Bailey, b. 11–16–1848.
E. Benjamin, b. 4–22–1849, d. 8–6–1898,
        m. Elizabeth Plummer, b. 9–17–1850.
1. Wilford LeRoy, b. 12–10–1872.
2. Howard A., b. 2–24–1876, d. 11–1–1898.
3. Ida Jane, b. 1–26–1881,
        m. Wilmer Hall.
    (a) Dorothy L., b. 2–2–1906.
    (b) Howard S., b. 8–26–1908.
    (c) Gertrude M., b. 2–22–1912.
4. Arthur, b. 9–6–1891,
        m. Alma Bailey, b. 9–14–1892.
    (a) Pauline B., b. 12–23–1917.
F. Daniel, b. 8–28–1850, d. 4–25–1919,
        m. Rebecca Bundy, b. 2–2–1844.
1. Sarah E., b. 8–4–1873,
        m. Nathan E. Stanton, b. 1–26–1875.
    (a) Edith Rebecca, b. 4–15–1908.
    (b) Mervin Daniel, b. 2–13–1910.
    (c) William Hanson, b. 1–8–1914.
2. Edmund C., b. 9–17–1877,
        m. Sina M. Hogdin B., 3–11–1883.
    (a) Henry E., b. 7–22–1910.
    (b) Alfred H., b. 10–15–1912.
    Jordan, b. 12–0–1818, d. 12–16–1839.

6. Mary Patterson, b. 5–8–1821, d. 3–23–1901,
        m. Joel Dawson, b. 2–27–1814, d. 2–10–1859.
A. Sarah Irene, b. 12–18–1844, d. 1–13–1906,
        m. Israel Erasmus French, b. 5–7–1843, d. 5–8–1876.

1. Harry Clifford, b. 1–28–1867,
    m. Louise Minninger.
  (*a*) Ruth, b. 9–22–1891, d. 3–12–1892.
  (*b*) Ethel, b. 12–24–1895,
      m. Roy S. Mead.
    (1.) Virginia Louise, b. 12–3–1918.
2. Karl Erasmus, b. 9–19–1868,
    m. Louise J. Balz.
  (*a*) Thelma Katherine, b. 3–5–1893,
      m. Herbert L. Taylor.
B. Henry Stanton, b. 3–19–1847, d. 1–10–1920,
    m. Ellen Castello, b. 9–18–1851.
  1. Clarence J., b. 1–18–1871,
      m. Kittie Bebb.
  2. Stanley French, b. 12–12–1876,
      m. Edna Doyle.
    (*a*) Clara Louise, b. 8–19–1900.
C. Anna, b. 6–26–1852, d. 6–6–1879,
      m. Nathan W. Bundy, 10–6–1869, b. 6–11–1848.
  1. Ora, b. 7–10–1870, d. 6–22–1898,
      m. 1–26–1893 Lewis Emmonds.
    (*a*) Randall N., b. 1–23–1894,
        m. Edith Thornburg.
      (1.) Ronald Albert, b. 8–19–1918.
  2. Russell C., b. 8–22–1877,
        m. 3–17–1904 Ella Dennis.
D. Myra, b. 8–29–1854,
      m. Jeptha L. Bundy, b. 4–14–1850.
  1. Alvin J., b. 4–5–1873, d. 7–1–1873.
  2. Clara L., b. 7–18–1874,
      m. Henry D. Reid.
    (*a*) Randall J., b. 5–7–1894, d. 7–20–1918 (in action a
        Soissons, France, Co. B., 28 Inf., 1st. Division).
    (*b*) Russell L., b. 8–19–1896.
        m. Grace Bunt.
      (1) Helen G.
      (2) Russell Jr.
    (*c*) Anna M., b. 2–14–1899.
        m. Claud Marquand.
      (1) Mona Lee.
    (*d*) Gail M., b. 2–10–1902.
    (*e*) Harold D., b. 6–12–1905.
    (*f*) Karl B., b. 11–28–1912.
    (*g*) Wanda Lee, b. 2–13–1918, d. 11–27–1918.
  3. Randall D., b. 9–5–1883, d. 8–1–1901.
7. Henry, Jr., b. 8–0–1824, d. 10–16–1844.
8. Daniel, b. 6–0–1827, d. 11–16–1844.

A PARTIAL GENEALOGY OF THE BUNDY FAMILY

John Bundy—Parents unknown.
Born ———,   died 2–22–1731.
Married, date and place unknown.
Elizabeth ———, born ———, died 3–17–1731.

Their children were—
Joshua Bundy, born 4– 4–1717.
John   "   "   1–12–1719, died 2–8–1745.
Caleb   "   "   5–12–1721.
William   "   "   1–21–1723.
Joan   "   "   1–12–1725, died 1–30–1735.
Benjamin "   " 12–12–1729.

Caleb, son of John Bundy, and Elizabeth, his wife.
Born 5–12–1721,   died ———.
Married ———,   date ———.
Elizabeth ———,   born ———, died 5–11–1762.

Their children were—
Demsey Bundy, born 4–16–1746, died 4–10–1798.
John   "   "   11– 1–1747, "   2–14–1762.
Miriam   "   "   8– 1–1749, "   2–13–1762.
Samuel   "   "   3–28–1756, "   2–22–1762.
Sarah   "   "   1– 9–1759.

Demsey, son of Caleb Bundy, and Elizabeth, his wife.
Born 4–16–1746,   died 4–10–1798.
Married about 1767   ———
Mary, ———. Born———, died 3–21–1804, (about the 50th year of her age).

Their children were—
Millicent Bundy, born 12–11–1769.
Marian   "   "   3–15–1771.
Ruth   "   "   8–22–1773.
David   "   "   8–11–1775.
Zadock   "   "   9–20–1777.
William   "   "   1– 1–1780, died 6–21–1828.
John   "   "   5–22–1782.
Ruth (the 2nd)   "   7– 4–1784.
Mary   "   "   7–31–1786.

William, son of Demsey Bundy, and Mary, his wife.
Born 1–1–1780, died 6–21–1828.
Married ——— 9–22–1803, at Turner's Swamp, North
Carolina.
Sarah Overman, born probably in 1785, died 5–8–1853 (age
68 years).
Their children were—

Mary	Bundy, born	2–25–1805.
Ezekiel	" "	7–26–1807, died 11–21–1866.
Eli	" "	3–13–1809.
Charity	" "	3– 2–1811.
John	" "	2–17–1813, " 9–20–1898.
Nathan	" "	10–16–1814.
Sarah	" "	1–29–1817.
William	" "	10–10–1819, " 5–10–1905, delegate to First National Republican Convention.
Demsey	" "	8– 5–1821, died 4–28–1877.
Chalkley	" "	2–24–1823, " 12–1–1866·
Elizabeth	" "	5–28–1826, " 12–14–1891:

The children of William and Sarah Bundy married as follows:
Mary Bundy married William French, their children were—

Eli	Cassandra
Sarah E.	Emma
Otho	Martha
William	

Ezekiel Bundy married Maria Engle, their children were—

Sarah	William E.
Elizabeth	Mary Jane
Nathan	Martha Ann
Caleb	Anna Maria

Ezekiel Bundy married, second, Sarah Stanton (formerly Hoyle,
Edmund Stanton's widow) in 1852. Their children were—

John	Chalkley C.
Hannah	Sarah Alice
Ezekiel	

Eli Bundy married Sarah Vernon, their children were—

William C.	Ruthanna
Mary	Esther

Charity Bundy married James Stanton (no children).
John Bundy married, first, Ruth Patten, their children were—

Sarah } twins	Mary P.
William P. } twins	Charity
Martha	

Married, second, Sydney Tipton (formerly Sydney Wood),
their children were—

Thomas	Ephraim

Married, third, Anna Edgerton, their children were—

Ruth	Wilson
Rebecca	Elizabeth
Jesse	

Nathan Bundy married Sarah Doudna, their children were—
Milton—in early days went to California, became wealthy and settled there.

Martha	Chalkley
William H.	Nathan
Clarkson	

Sarah Bundy married Joel Dawson, their children were—

Chalkley	Eli
Matilda	

Jesse—went to Colorado, studied medicine, was physician of Colorado Penitentiary and Surveyor General of the State.

William Bundy married Prudence Wood, they had one child—
Allen S.

Married, second, Asenith Doudna, their children were—

Prudence	Evaline
T. Clarkson	Charles
Joel	Dillwyn C.
Almeda	Rebecca H.

Demsey Bundy married Ann Wood, their children were—

Emily	Amanda

Married, second, Ann Crew, their children were—

Jeptha	Jefferson
Melvina	

Married, third, Rebecca Smith, no children.

Chalkley Bundy married Sarah Doudna, their children were—

Lindley	Rebecca D.
Joel D.	Emma
Nathan W.	Mary E.
Lucinda	Chalkley

Married, second, Deborah H. Bundy (widow of Caleb Bundy, deceased; Caleb Bundy was the son of Ezekiel Bundy.) No children.

Elizabeth Bundy married Hezekiah Bailey, their children were—

Sarah	Almeda
Mary	Adaline
Dempsey	Lucinda
Melvina	

The children of Ezekiel Bundy and Maria Engle (his first wife) married as follows—
Elizabeth to John Hoyle, their children were—

Simeon	Nathan
Ezekiel	

Nathan to Anna Stanton, their children were—
    Joseph S.   Mary M.
    Caleb L.   Clara E.
Caleb to Deborah Hanson, their child—
    Mary Caleb
William E. to Rebecca Doudna, their children were—
    Elmer E.   Bertram
    Agnes M.
  Married, second, Eunice Tallman, no children.
Mary Jane married Jesse Starbuch, their children were—
    Caleb   Clara
    J. Clinton   Adelbert
    Clyde   Edith
Martha Ann married Joseph Plummer, no children.
Anna Maria married Stewart Watt, their children were—
    Forest   William
    Olga   Walter
    Daisy
Ezekiel Bundy and Sarah Stanton (his second wife)—child—
  John H. married Mary Doudna, their children—
    Clinton   Ezekiel
    Alice   Chalkley } all deceased
    Hannah, deceased   Sarah Alice }
Children of Eli Bundy and Sarah (Vernon) married as follows—
  William C. married Edith Stanton, their children were—
    Henry   Ella
  Mary married John Doudna, their children were—
    Eli   Charles
    Clarissa   Ada
    Eva   Walter
  Ruthanna married Gersham Mott, their children were—
    Sarah   Eleanor
    William   Hester
  Hester married Robert Doudna, their children were—
    Rebecca
Children of John Bundy and Ruth Patten (his first wife) married as follows—
Sarah married Ashur Mott. They had no children.
  William P. married Tabitha Doudna, their children were—
    John   Wilson
    Eddie (who was drowned)   Harvey
    Sarah
          (All of above died young)
    Louisa married Louis C. Steer.
  Mary P. married Eli Stanton, their children were—
    William H.   Emma C.
    Sarah B.
Children of John Bundy and Sidney Tipton (his second wife)—

Thomas W. married Abigail Doudna (their children were—
three sons, who died while young).

| Mary E. | Edith, died in infancy |

Children of John Bundy and Anna Edgerton (his third wife)—
Ruth married Josiah W. Doudna, their children were—

| Albert | Ernest |
| Lillian | Alice |

Jesse married a woman from California.

Elizabeth married Ira Frame. They have no children.

Children of Sarah Bundy Dawson—
Chalkley married, first, Martha Garretson, their children
were—

| Mary | Caleb | Melvina |
| Willits | Sina | |

Married, second, Anna Branson, their child—
Martha

Married, third, Theresa Höpper. They had no children.

Married, fourth, a Mrs. Lohr.

Matilda married Stephen Clendenon, they had one child—
Louisa

Eli married Hester Tipton (daughter of Sidney Wood Tipton,
the second wife of John Bundy), their children were—

Jesse, went to Colorado, married and had one child—
Clyde

Children of William Bundy and Prudence Wood (his first wife).
Allen died while a young man.

Children of William Bundy and Asenith Doudna (his second
wife) married as follows—
Clarkson married Rachel Crew, their children were—

| Howard | Edith Merle | Mary |
| William | Elva and Melva (twins) | |

Dillwyn Bundy married Elizabeth Steer, their children
were—

Ellis	Mary
Amy	Margaret
Walter	Anna

Rebecca married John Cadwallader. They have no children.

Children of Demsey and Ann Wood (his first wife) married as
follows—
Emily married Thompson Frame, they had one child—
Mary

Amanda married Samuel French, their children were—

Melvina	Emily
Fred	John
Laura	Albert
Josephine	Anna

Children of Demsey Bundy and Ann Crew (his second wife)—

Jeptha married Myra Dawson, their children were—

Alvin J.

Clara L.

Melvina—died, aged 5

Randall D. (Randall fell from the top of a windmill tower, to which point he had climbed to oil the machinery, and was killed.)

Jefferson Bundy married Jennie Smith, their children were—

Ross

Fred

Othol

Walter

Cecil

Everest—six sons

Children of Chalkley Bundy and Sarah Doudna married as follows—

Lindley married Ruanna Frame, their children were—

Sarah

Carver   Tacie

Chalkley

Bertha

Joel D. married Mary Ellen French, they had one child—Emma.

Nathan W. married, first, Anna Dawson, their children were—

Ora   Russell

Married, second, Agnes P. Hanson, their children were—

Warren C.   Anna M.

Lucinda married Benjamin H. Hanson, their children were—

Cora S.   Mary E.

Alva E.   Caleb L.

Maude E.   Herman B.

Rebecca married Daniel Stanton, their children were—

Sarah E.   Edmund C.

Mary E. married Jason Fawcett, their children were—

Clarence E.   Clifford J.   Martha D.

Children of Elizabeth Bundy and Hezekiah Bailey married as follows—

Sarah (did not marry.)

Mary married Henry Stanton, they had no children.

Demsey married Sadie Bailey, their children were—

Elmer E.   Daniel   Anna

Bernard   Edmund   Rose

Melvina married Joseph Garretson, they had one child—Ora.

Melvina deceased and her sister Almeda married Joseph Garretson, their children were—

Ross   Eva

Isabel   Myrtle   Everett

Adaline married Robert H. Smith, their children were—

Lucinda   Tacy

Lucinda died when about twenty years of age, being employed as teacher at Friends' Boarding School, Barnesville, Ohio, at the time of her death.

A GENEALOGICAL REVERIE

WHEN father told me a little about our ancestors, I was glad I was a Stanton, but let me see, mother was a Bundy, therefore I am only—

½ each

Eli Stanton	Mary P. Bundy

¼ each

Joseph Stanton	Mary Hodgin	John Bundy	Ruth Patten

⅛ each

Henry Stanton	Stephen Hodgin	William Bundy	William Patten
Clary Patterson	Elizabeth Williams	Sarah Overman	Sally Morris

1-16 each

Benjamin Stanton	——— Hodgin	Demsey Bundy	———— Patten
Abigail Macy	*Unknown*	Mary ———	*Unknown*
Joseph Patterson	——— Williams	Aaron Overman	——— Morris
Mary ———	*Unknown*	*Unknown*	*Unknown*

1-32 each

Henry Stanton	——— Hodgin	Caleb Bundy	——— Patten
Lydia Albertson	*Unknown*	Elizabeth ———	*Unknown*
David Macy	*Unknown*	*Unknown*	*Unknown*
Dinah Gardner	*Unknown*	*Unknown*	*Unknown*
William Patterson	——— Williams	——— Overman	——— Morris
Kaziah ———	*Unknown*	*Unknown*	*Unknown*
Unknown	*Unknown*	*Unknown*	*Unknown*
Unknown	*Unknown*	*Unknown*	*Unknown*

1-64 each

John Stanton	——— Hodgin	John Bundy	——— Patten
Mary Clark	*Unknown*	Elizabeth ———	*Unknown*
Esam Albertson	*Unknown*	*Unknown*	*Unknown*
Unknown	*Unknown*	*Unknown*	*Unknown*
John Macy, Jr.	*Unknown*	*Unknown*	*Unknown*
Judith Worth	*Unknown*	*Unknown*	*Unknown*
Solomon Gardner	*Unknown*	*Unknown*	*Unknown*
Anna Coffin	*Unknown*	*Unknown*	*Unknown*
——— Patterson	——— Williams	——— Overman	——— Morris
Unknown	*Unknown*	*Unknown*	*Unknown*
Unknown	*Unknown*	*Unknown*	*Unknown*
Unknown	*Unknown*	*Unknown*	*Unknown*
Unknown	*Unknown*	*Unknown*	*Unknown*
Unknown	*Unknown*	*Unknown*	*Unknown*
Unknown	*Unknown*	*Unknown*	*Unknown*
Unknown	*Unknown*	*Unknown*	*Unknown*

1-128 each

Robert Stanton	——— Hodgin	——— Bundy	——— Patten
Avis ———	*Unknown*	*Unknown*	*Unknown*

Jeremiah Clark	*Unknown*	*Unknown*	*Unknown*
Francis Latham	*Unknown*	*Unknown*	*Unknown*
—— Albertson	*Unknown*	*Unknown*	*Unknown*
Unknown	*Unknown*	*Unknown*	*Unknown*
Unknown	*Unknown*	*Unknown*	*Unknown*
Unknown	*Unknown*	*Unknown*	*Unknown*
John Macy	*Unknown*	*Unknown*	*Unknown*
Deborah Gardiner	*Unknown*	*Unknown*	*Unknown*
John Worth	*Unknown*	*Unknown*	*Unknown*
Miriam Gardner	*Unknown*	*Unknown*	*Unknown*
Richard Gardner	*Unknown*	*Unknown*	*Unknown*
Mary Austin	*Unknown*	*Unknown*	*Unknown*
Stephen Coffin	*Unknown*	*Unknown*	*Unknown*
Mary Bunker	*Unknown*	*Unknown*	*Unknown*
—— Patterson	—— Williams	—— Overman	—— Morris
Unknown	*Unknown*	*Unknown*	*Unknown*
Unknown	*Unknown*	*Unknown*	*Unknown*
Unknown	*Unknown*	*Unknown*	*Unknown*
Unknown	*Unknown*	*Unknown*	*Unknown*
Unknown	*Unknown*	*Unknown*	*Unknown*
Unknown	*Unknown*	*Unknown*	*Unknown*
Unknown	*Unknown*	*Unknown*	*Unknown*
Unknown	*Unknown*	*Unknown*	*Unknown*
Unknown	*Unknown*	*Unknown*	*Unknown*
Unknown	*Unknown*	*Unknown*	*Unknown*
Unknown	*Unknown*	*Unknown*	*Unknown*
Unknown	*Unknown*	*Unknown*	*Unknown*
Unknown	*Unknown*	*Unknown*	*Unknown*
Unknown	*Unknown*	*Unknown*	*Unknown*

OBI

But the biologist tells us that we do not inherit our ability or characteristics with any such regular or mathematical exactness as shown above, but that we may receive much from one ancestor and little or nothing from others. If we examine our talents we may estimate with some accuracy from whom we receive certain ability or traits. Then do I receive my love of the beautiful from the old French ancestry—my love for the solid and substantial from the English, and the fondness for ships and sails and salt water from the early American Stantons, the Macys, Coffins, Gardners, and old Nantucketers? But on whom shall I blame my undesirable qualities?

But of one thing we are very sure, each should exert himself to the utmost to live an honorable life and, if possible, be a worthy descendant of such ancestors.

WILLIAM HENRY STANTON.

OBITUARIES

JORDAN STANTON

son of
Henry and Clary Stanton.
Born 11–25–1818 (probably.)
Died 12–16–1839.

From an old copy:

The following was extracted from a letter written by James Stanton to a distant relation dated 1st Month 8th, 1840, to be preserved by the family for its historical contents:

"When the storms of adversity and affliction are permitted to assail, and drive us from our downy nests of earthly ease, like as the eagle stirreth up or destroyeth her nest, when all her wooings are tried in vain to entice her young away, and taketh them and beareth them on her wings, we are brought by Divine Love into a nearer union with Himself, and attachment one towards another. Of the uncertainty of terrestrial things and all human calculations we have of late had abundant evidence.

"Dear Brother Jordan, who joined me in my ride but a few weeks ago, and visited your parts in full health and vigor of strength, has, alas! bid us a final adieu, and left his place here to know him no more forever. He was taken ill about the Eighth of last month, the disease which was the typhus or winter fever, made such rapid and even progress, baffling all medical skill applied, that in only eight days, on the evening of the sixteenth, his sufferings were closed, we trust forever. During the whole of his illness there was such a calmness and serenity of mind manifested by him, as to render his chamber a place of instruction. In the morning of the last day, when it became evident that his stay here could not be much longer, he signified to some of us, that although he had searched, he could not feel any condemnation, nor yet could he feel so sensibly an evidence of Divine acceptance as he wished, and that he knew no better way than to try to keep his mind composed, and see if anything would arise. In the course of the day he said in effect that the only convictions he had felt were for not having been more watchful and ardent in spirit in meetings for Divine Worship. In the evening he repeated in a clear and melodious voice the following passage: 'Great and marvellous are thy works, Lord God Almighty, just and true are all thy ways thou King of Saints.' A little after this he repeated a few detached or unconnected Scripture passages, which served to show what had been the occupation of his mind, although the organization of it was much broken; after this he said but little, and scarcely moving hand or foot, he quietly breathed shorter and shorter to the last, about seven o'clock. Aged 21 years and 21 days."

RUTH (PATTEN) BUNDY

Mary P. Doudna found the following paper among her Mother's (Jane Plummer) letters. "Some expression to Jane Plummer by Ruth (Patten) Bundy when on her death bed."

Born 3-10-1814.
Died 2-17-1841.

Advised her to seek and serve the Lord—that she had a family coming on—so that she might be prepared to bring them up to serve Him—that he was a merciful Father, she loved him so much she could not help expressing something of it, though it was inexpressible—she advised her to attend Meetings and to seek and serve Him while there and she would return with peace of mind which was of more value than all the world could give—and by so doing she might be a help to society for it needed her—she believed trials were coming in society—and she wanted her to stand faithful and if she would but serve and obey the Lord with full dedication of heart—although trials may be permitted to come they will be made easier than she had an idea of. (All that could be remembered by the one who wrote it down for her.)

DANIEL STANTON

Born 6– –1827.
Died 11–16–1844.

Barnesville, Ohio, 11/27/1844.

Dear Brother:

Father received thy letter of last First Day informing that thee had not heard from here since thee left. I wrote a letter on First Day the Seventeenth and mailed it so as to leave on the next morning. Informing of Brother Daniel's disease, there was no important change in him after thee left except he grew weaker until Seventh Day morning, * * * from that time he rapidly sank, but the fever rising and running to the head he became more restless and flighty all the day, yet not so, but that he at times made some sensible and touching expressions. About one or two o'clock he supplicated to the Lord to forgive him for he was a poor creature and be with him and go before him through the Valley and Shadow of Death and receive him into a better world. Then or soon after, turning to father, said, "I am prepared to go now." He said considerable more through the afternoon, but not being able to speak clearly, much of it could not be gathered. About four o'clock father, going to his bed (having been a few minutes absent), he looked earnestly at him and seemed to try to bid him farewell, then turning his eyes from him he fixed them nevermore to move and gently breathed shorter and easier to the last, about twenty minutes. He was buried the next day, leaving the house at three o'clock.

Father and Mother are about as well as usual, seem lonesome, but as cheerful as could be expected. Their colored woman being nearly sick with cold, cough and pain in her side, left them on the sixteenth and has not returned and doubtful whether she will, although she has got better.

We are in usual health except Lydda's eye which is worse this week than ever.

I remain, with love,
Thy brother,

JAMES STANTON.

MARY STANTON

Deceased the Twenty-seventh of Ninth month, 1857. Aged
forty-seven years, five months and seventeen days.
Compiled from notes written by her husband, Joseph Stanton.

Mary Stanton enjoyed almost uninterrupted good health all
her life until about the beginning of her last year, when her strength
began to fail. The weakness was first perceptible in her knees
and ankles which increased by such slow and almost imperceptible
degrees, that she gave attention to her domestic concerns and
attended religious meetings until about the First of Sixth month.
By this time the weakness had so increased that she was unable
to walk alone, but spent most of her time, until the day before her
death, in an easy chair. She suffered little or no pain from the
disease. Her appetite and general health were mostly pretty good
so she was able to enjoy the family circle and the company of her
friends who called to see her. She often spoke of this as a great
favour. But felt her greatest privation was her inability to
assemble with her friends for divine worship.

The weakness continued to increase to such an extent that for the
last six or eight weeks of her time she was unable to turn herself
in bed at night. This necessitated frequent attention and caused
many wakeful hours, which were often made truly heart rendering
seasons. At these times she expressed her apprehensions that she
should not continue long with us, and we were unitedly made
willing to resign the event to Him who knows best what is best for
us, and who will require no more of the humble and contrite ones
than He will enable them to bear.

About the Twentieth of the Ninth month, she took a cold which
settled in a cough. This condition reduced her strength more
rapidly, and on the Twenty-sixth she did not think she could
last many days longer and said, "I can see nothing in my way, but
I am afraid I have not searched every corner of my heart, as with
a lighted

587

a lighted candle. I have craved that I might be favoured with an assurance of divine acceptance before the time arrives. I fear I have not been as attentive to my duty, while strength and ability were afforded, as I ought to have been. O! for one of the lowest mansions in His kingdom." On the morning of the Twenty-seventh, after spending a worrisome night with her cough, she said that she thought she could not spend another such night. The same morning, she said: "I am almost gone and I see nothing in my way. I have endeavoured to search every corner of my heart as with a lighted candle and I trust the sincere endeavours of the humble and contrite ones will be accepted. My complaint has come on very gradually. I have had a great while to think of these things and I trust I have not been unmindful of them."

Shortly after it appeared evident to those about her that she could not survive much longer and while her children were standing around the bed weeping, she looked at them and said: "Dear children, do not fret, we have to part some time and it cannot be in a better time. I want you to be good children, to live in peace, and in the love and fear of the Lord, and try to help your father." A little later when it was thought by some present that she was not conscious of what was going on around her, someone proposed to lower her head, which had been raised on account of her cough, which had now entirely subsided. On hearing this, she shook her head and when asked if she did not want it lowered, said, "No." When other friends came in and wished to adjust her pillows, they were requested to just be quiet, to which she responded, "Yes, be quiet." Very soon her sister came in, whom she had not seen that morning. She went to the bed and stood awhile and was about to turn away, not apprehending our dear one was conscious of her presence, when we heard from a clear voice, "Farewell! farewell! my dear and only sister. Don't hold me, I am going to the mansions of rest and peace." These were the last words she spoke. She passed quietly away about 11 o'clock, A. M., just twenty-five years to the day and hour since we were united by the marriage covenant, which I trust has been mutually and faithfully fulfilled; a retrospect of which affords peace and satisfaction.

JOSEPH STANTON.

JOSEPH STANTON

Born 1–19–1812.
Died 7–26–1859.

Some account of the last illness and death of my dear friend, Joseph Stanton, who departed this life the 26th of 7th Month, 1859, aged 47 years, 6 months and 7 days. He was taken unwell about the 14th of the 7th Month and on the 16th a physician was called in and pronounced his disease an inflammation of the stomach and bowels. From this time to the 20th, some hope was entertained of his recovery, though his sufferings were very severe at times. His disease which had appeared to have been partially arrested, now became more alarming and it was not thought that he could survive long. At which time I was sent for and reached his residence on the 21st, found him very low, but thought to be some better. Soon after my going in to see him he said, "What poor shortsighted creatures we are;" and remarked, "That he had not been able to see how it might terminate, but felt resigned to the Divine will, believing that He doeth all things well." At another time speaking of the uncertainty of his recovery he said, his sufferings were so great he hardly had time to think a sober thought, and felt as though he would have to depend on the mercies of his Creator and the prayers of his friends, adding, "I want the prayers of the righteous for I feel myself such a poor frail mortal." 22nd and 23rd some hopes were entertained of his recovery though he continued to suffer most of the time. On my telling him the Doctor thought he was better, he said, "Well, it may be so, I may be spared to thee awhile, and who knows but thee may be an instrument in the Divine hand in raising me up. I am willing for thee to do all thee can. I have not been able to see how it may terminate and it is right that I should not, but if I judge from my own feelings, from the extreme pain, weakness and oppression, I doubt very much of my recovery," and added, "Oh!

"Oh! that I may never have to suffer over again," and prayed for patience and faith to hold out to the end.

His sufferings were so great he could not converse much, but being at times tried with great poverty of spirit such expressions as the following were frequently uttered: "Oh! wretched man that I am," and at other times, "Lord, what is man that thou art mindful of him or the son of man that thou visitest him. Surely nothing but a merciful Creator could deign to notice such a poor frail mortal." At another time he said: "Oh! if I should become impatient at last." Though he did not manifest anything like impatience or murmuring, often when his sufferings seemed almost more than human nature could bear, he would say, "Oh! dear Lord, have mercy," and "Oh! Lord Jehovah." He frequently expressed thankfulness for favors received, saying at one time, "Oh! I always have been favored more than I deserved, I have had an agreeable and beloved companion, one in whom I could confide, who would sympathize with me and feel for me, but she was taken away and I doubt not but she is gathered to her everlasting rest. And now thee is here to take her place and I know thee will do all thee can to help me bear my burdens, for I believe there is that feeling between us that goes beyond bounds or limits," and referred to the Scripture where it says, "For this cause shall a man leave his father and mother," etc. And father said, that no one could have kinder children than he had, that they always had been, that it was a great comfort to him that it was so and what a favor it was that he had them all around him, as well as his parents and sister and good kind nurses, and all was done that could be done for him, he always complied with their wishes, saying he was not fit to be trusted. The 24th, a friend going into his room, he inquired what sort of a morning it was; being told it was very bright and clear, he said, "What a pretty morning it would be to go to Heaven." Towards evening his sufferings from extreme pain, restlessness and oppression together with the hiccoughs or spasms of the stomach became almost unsupportable. After a season of great conflict he very expressively said (as if already beginning to enjoy the foretaste), "Oh! what a happy release to be free from all the sufferings and cares and trials and perplexities of this troublesome world, and be admitted into rest and peace." At another time, being asked if he wanted anything, replied, "Yes, I want to go to Heaven." A near relative saying to him she hoped he felt resigned, he said, "Yes, I believe I have no choice, but I am willing for you to do all you can," and requested her to pray for him that his faith and patience might hold out to the end. Afterwards speaking of his approaching dissolution he said, "I want thee to be resigned." I replied that I would try to be, but it seemed hard to give him up; he said, "I know what it is. I have had the trial myself, and I can feel for thee, I have parted with all my dear brothers and a dear sister and a beloved companion. Oh!

Oh! that was more than all the rest, my tears seemed all bottled up for the occasion."

About midnight the conflict of mortality appeared to be about to terminate; the family being called up, he inquired if they were all present; being answered in an affirmative, he said he had greatly desired that he might have a little ease before he died, and it was now mercifully granted, that he had never felt so comfortable in all his life. Then addressing himself to his children, he said to this effect, "that he had never seen anything more completely carried out, than their dear Mother's advice to them had been towards him in helping him along, and naming Elizabeth said she knew how to behave herself, and she was one he always thought a great deal of. That he did not want one of them to covet the settling of the estate, get the money into their own hands and keep it, that the two oldest knew what they had, and he wanted the other two to have as much, and the balance to be equally divided; that there would be nothing worth quarreling about, and he wanted them to remember his dear friend who was then at his left hand, for you feel to me as though you were all bound up in one bundle. · Use her liberally and care for her as long as she lives," and added, "Oh! I do feel for thee." After which he wished to know if we thought he was saying too much, said he thought his head was clear, and had been all the time. But the dear sufferer revived again and said, "I thought I was going, but my time has not yet come." He prayed for faith and patience to hold out to the end. Some time after this he underwent another season of apparent desertion, and speaking to a friend said, "Oh, we have often taken sweet counsel together, have we not." The friend assenting, he said, "Oh, I am so poor and weak, if thee can do anything for me in this extremity I want thee to do it, I want my friends to pray for me." The friend speaking encouragingly to him, he said, "Oh, I feel myself such a poor worm of the dust." On his taking leave of him, he said, "Pray for me."

After which he appeared to be comfortable in his mind and entirely sensible of his situation, saying at several different times, that the damps of death were on him now. The 25th, in the evening after giving him some wine he queried whether we thought he would "sup the new wine of the Kingdom, with his Heavenly Father against morning," and being very thirsty, "Oh, for that water whereof if a man drink he shall never thirst again." His physician coming to see him he told him to tell him just what he thought of him for he thought he should die, and he was willing, and if he thought so, not to give him anything to keep him here suffering, but let him go. Two friends going into his room he said to them, "You are old people and have seen a good many sicken and die." He wanted to know what they thought of him, saying they need not be afraid to tell him. Upon taking leave of him, one of them remarked that it had felt comfortable to be wit him

him; he replied, "I have had deep wadings." He remained during the day without much apparent change, but evidently growing weaker, and several times spoke of the approaching night, earnestly desiring that he might not see the dawning of another day, and requesting that some of his regular attendants should stay with him through the night.

In the evening his sufferings being extreme he exclaimed, "This is passing through Jordan," and some time after, "Oh! dear Lord Jesus, come and receive me." At another time, "Oh! death, where is thy sting, Oh! grave, where is thy victory." On asking him if he was willing I should lie down a while, he said "Oh! yes, dear, I know thee needs rest, try to compose thyself and get some sleep. I have nothing to do but to die, and that will not be much." I replied that I would; he then said, "Yes I know thee will," and bid me an affectionate farewell, twice repeating it, "Farewell dear." After this he became drowsy and did not appear to take much notice of what was passing around him, but knew all his friends and remained sensible (except at some short intervals) throughout all his sickness. He continued to suffer till within a few minutes of the last, when he quietly departed like one falling into a sweet sleep, about eight o'clock in the morning.

Composed by Achsah Smith.

AMY (HODGIN) CLENDENON

Born 1800.
Died 12–1–1868.

A short account of the death of Amy Clendenon, who departed this life the 1st of 12th Month, 1868, in the 68th year of her age. She was a member of Coal Creek Monthly Meeting of Friends.

This dear friend had from youth been a diligent attender of our religious meetings, attached to our principles and testimonies and the right maintenance of the discipline. She bore a long and painful illness with exemplary patience, and left her friends with the belief that to die was to gain.

HANNAH CLENDENON STANLEY

Born
Died 11–14–1868.

Died on the 14th of the 11th Month, 1868, at her home in Keokuk County, Iowa. Hannah C., wife of Isaac E. Stanley and daughter of Benjamin and Amy Clendenon, in the 33rd year of her age. A member of Coal Creek Monthly Meeting of Friends.

She bore a short but very severe illness with much patience. In the early part of her sickness, being queried with respect to her prospects, she replied: "I have lived under the crucifying, sanctifying power of Christ, which alone can save." Towards the latter part of her sickness she was frequently engaged in supplication. In conversation with her husband, she said with great tenderness: "I know I leave thee heart-broken and alone." Earnestly requesting him to do right, she said: "I feel that I am going home to an excellent Father and my sweet babe." She soon quietly passed away, leaving her friends the comfortable belief that her end was peace.

ELI STANTON

Born 2–12–1835.
Died 3–25–1885.

From "The Republican":

"Eli Stanton, one of our Leading Friends, a Progressive and Christian Citizen, has passed away.

"The startling news (we call it so because his serious illness was not generally apprehended) of the death of Eli Stanton was brought to town early Monday forenoon, which sad event occurred at three o'clock that morning. His complaint was chronic abscess of the kidneys, which had in different stages been troubling him for twenty years, but had been rapidly developing the last year and, in the past four weeks, took serious form, and resulted in his death. Dr. Kemp was the physician whose opinions were affirmed by the autopsy made Monday night. The patient's life had been wonderfully prolonged.

"Eli Stanton was about two months past fifty years of age, and had been married twice—the father of three children by the first wife, and one by the second wife, all living. His first wife was the daughter of John Bundy of East Main Street, and his widow is the daughter of Elijah Hanson. He was born on the old Henry Stanton farm, about three and one-half miles east of town, his mother was the daughter of Stephen Hodgin, his father was Joseph Stanton, his grandfather was Henry Stanton and was a cousin of Edwin M. Stanton, the greatest Secretary of War this country ever had. He is a brother of William Stanton, Mrs. Anna S. Bundy and Mrs. Lindley P. Bailey, all of this section, and who are mourners of a great loss.

"The deceased was a farmer living about two miles east of town. He made a special business of thorough-bred cattle, in which line he was one of the earliest movers, and won a reputation not merely local. Of his accumulations we are not prepared to say. He had a beautiful farm of about 100 acres, well improved and elegantly stocked. We feel as though the Republican had lost one of its best friends.

"He was a quiet, industrious man; strictly honest and unassuming and one of those who do not accumulate rapidly. Eli Stanton was a friend to everything that was right, a social sunlight that dealt out, intuitively, happiness and content on all sides.

"The Society of Friends has lost an influential member, one that was a power of good and one that created a Christ-like influence everywhere. The remains were taken to Stillwater burying ground this (Wednesday) afternoon at two o'clock, where they were quietly, prayerfully, and tearfully laid away forever."

JOSEPH S. BUNDY

Born 1-19-1860.
Died 12-20-1885.

Local Paper:

"A popular and esteemed Barnesville boy yields to the demands of the Great Conqueror. He dies, but leaves footprints on the sands of time.

"The death of Joseph S. Bundy occurred at his Mother's residence on South Lincoln Avenue, Sabbath morning at three o'clock. The startling news was like an electric shock to the entire community. Scarcely two weeks before his death he came home from St. Clairsville, where he had been engaged in business for the past year, suffering with what he supposed to be a heavy cold, but which soon developed into an alarming case of typhoid fever. On Thursday of last week, he was taken with a hemorrhage, which was followed by several more on the two following days, terminating in his death early Sabbath morning. He bore his sickness with remarkable fortitude, never uttering a murmur.

"He seemed to realize from the first that this was his last sickness, and expressed himself as being entirely ready to go, if the Lord so willed, and was perfectly satisfied with the hereafter. During his sickness he would have repeatedly read to him Isaiah 1-18. The blessed promise contained therein gave him much comfort. He expressed a firm belief in the Christian religion, and was desirous the people should so understand. Of his character and habits, nothing can be said, but that which is of the highest praise. Few young men were so well and favorably known. Noble, generous, cultured and agreeable, he has won and sustained the esteem and admiration of all who knew him. His life was above reproach, he undertook nothing which he did not accomplish. Firm in purpose, positive in action, always guided by a clear conscience, he set an example which others would do well to follow. He began his school life in the public schools here, afterwards attending the Friends school and the College at Lebanon, Ohio, Valparaiso, Ind., for several terms, and was always an apt and studious scholar. From 1880 to 1884 he taught in the high schools at this place, winning the hearts of his pupils by his kindly nature, generosity and forbearance.

"In November, 1884, he entered into a partnership with J. W. Emerson, for the purpose of furnishing abstracts of title of Belmont County

595

County lands, at the same time attending to considerable survey-ing, which occupation he had followed for several years, he being Deputy County Surveyor at the time of his death. This partner-ship has been dissolved by his untimely death.

"Deprived of a father at the age of fifteen, he had been the com-fort and pride of a noble Mother and a loving brother and sister. Stricken down at the age of twenty-five, at the very beginning of a useful and prosperous life, his death was doubly sad. We being only finite, may be unable to see the justice in his death, but believing in the divine wisdom of the Infinite, we bow in humble submission to His will, and content ourselves with the thought that one great day, when all sorrows are at an end, we will be enabled to see and understand.

"The bereaved family have the heartfelt sympathy of the entire community in their great affliction. The funeral services and burial were conducted by Friends' ceremony at Stillwater Meeting House, Monday afternoon at two o'clock and was one of the largest ever held in that Church. An affecting discourse was preached by Hannah Stratton and the ceremonies throughout were appro-priate and impressive."

CALEB L. BUNDY

Born 12-12-1862.
Died 11-28-1890.

From local paper:

" 'Death loves a shining mark,' and while the King of Terrors is always an unwelcome guest, his visitations at times are particu-larly sad. It was especially so in the case of Mr. Caleb Bundy, of Sabula, Iowa, a young man about twenty-eight years of age, just married, and with an apparently bright future before him. He was taken with typhoid pneumonia about three weeks ago, and notwithstanding all the care that loving hands could bestow, he rapidly sank into that sleep that knows no waking. His mother, Mrs. Annie Bundy, was with him, having gone west on an extended visit about two months ago, and intended making her home with her son during the coming winter. When it was found that the end was approaching, his brother-in-law, Mr. Jack Colpitts, was sent for, who started at once, and arrived on Friday, a few hours after the spirit had fled. The remains were brought to his old home and laid to rest in the Southern Cemetery on Monday afternoon. 'Cale' was a most excellent young man, and held in the highest esteem by those who knew him best. He was married only last March, and life to him seemed filled with love and happiness. But his plans, whatever they may have been, were not finished, his aspirations were not realized. The sadly bereaved young wife, as well as the Mother and sister, have the sympathy of the community in their affliction. Funeral services were held Monday afternoon.''

FRANCIS WILSON STANTON

Born 4-5-1875.
Died 8-8-1886.

From local paper:

"Sunday afternoon Frankie Stanton an 11 year old boy, of William Stanton, the well known Nurseryman two miles east of town, while on a visit to his aunt Deborah Stanton, who lives about a mile from the Friends Church, fell dead while standing in the doorway of the house. He had, as was thought, about recovered from a spell of typhoid fever and was allowed to go over to visit his relatives. He ate a hearty dinner, after which, in a boyish way, he amused himself at play with his little cousin, a boy about the same age in an upstairs room. About three o'clock his Aunt passing where the boys were playing, pleasantly asked if they were having a good time, and received an affirmative answer. Shortly after this at the suggestion of his cousin the boys came downstairs, Frankie in the lead. He had just descended the stairs and stepped to the front door when he was noticed to stagger against the door frame, and then to suddenly fall to the portico floor. He was quickly reached by his aunt, who raised him up, but one gasp was the only sign of life noticed, and the boy was gone. The Doctor gives it as his theory that death was caused by a rupture of the heart, brought on by over-exercise, the boy being still in a weakened condition from the fever.

"The sudden death of this bright boy is a peculiarly sad blow to the family, who it seems are sorely afflicted with disease. His father is just convalescing from a long spell of sickness, and was quite prostrated at the news of his son's death.

"Funeral services were held Tuesday, and the remains of the boy interred at Stillwater.

"The afflicted family have the greatest sympathy of the community."

JOHN LINDLEY STANTON

Born 4–17–1877.
Died 3–20–1897.

From Local Paper:

A PROMISING LIFE ENDED

"It is with an unusual feeling of sadness that we chronicle the death of John Lindley Stanton, son of William and Jennie Stanton, which occurred at their home at Tacoma, last Saturday morning. He had been suffering for some weeks with the prevailing grip, but was much improved and attended the Commencement exercises at the close of Friends school at Olney and probably contracted an additional cold, developing into pneumonia. The disease was severe from the first, but there was thought to be a decided improvement for a day or two before his death and his parents were very much encouraged. A sudden relapse came on Sunday night and death resulted in a few hours.

"Nearly every one in the community knew Lindley Stanton— knew him because he was a boy out of and beyond the ordinary. In early life he developed those manly traits that marked him among his playfellows and made him a favorite with all. At a very tender age he voluntarily took upon himself life's burdens, and applied himself to the tasks before him with a diligence and perseverance that were remarkable in a boy of his years. He was one of the most industrious boys it has ever been our good fortune to know, and it seems peculiarly sad that just as he was entering upon the threshold of a life of usefulness and promise he should so suddenly be taken away. His death is a sad blow to his parents who had come to depend upon him in an unusual degree for one of his years and his going out will cause a gloom and a sadness in the home that the years will never efface. Funeral services were held at Stillwater meeting house on Monday afternoon. The family have the deepest sympathy of their relatives and friends in their bereavement."

JOHN BUNDY

Born 2-17-1813.
Died 9-20-1898.

Father had never been sick in bed but once since I can remember, except for little attacks of what I suppose a physician would have termed "Petit Mal." These attacks seemed always to be associated with digestive disturbances, and as father would say, "My liver is out of order" and would proceed at once with "Todds Pills." I often used to laugh at father about him always thinking when any thing was the matter with any one, that "their liver was out of order," but I have come to the conclusion, with my own experience and that of many other people, that he was about right; for I know the liver is where we do most of our "living" or "dying" as the case may be.

A few days before father's last sickness, he and mother walked to Meeting. It was a beautiful September Sabbath morning, and as they came home, they rested by the way on some of the neighbors' doorsteps. We always had a man, who drove a public carriage, come take them to Meeting when the weather was inclement or they did not feel equal to the walk, but that day they seemed to feel well and wanted to walk. On Second day, father was out about as usual and after supper in the evening he walked across the street to George Wilson's and spent some time on their doorstep, talking and playing with their little children, of whom he was very fond. Third day morning he had very little appetite but ate a little breakfast. At dinner time he just tasted his food and pushed his plate away and remarked, "he guessed he would go and lie down," which he did. About the middle of the afternoon, nature gave way and he realized his condition, so mother and I put him to bed and I telephoned to Dr. Ely. When he came and examined him he said, "This is the beginning of the end, just make him as comfortable as possible." Father seemed never to want anything to eat after that, but would take some liquid nourishment as we gave it to him, and he lingered on, growing weaker till the following First day morning, just as the church bells were ringing, his sweet child-like spirit took its flight for "one of the many mansions prepared for those who love and serve the Master." I had so often heard father say "he hoped he would never live to be a burden to anybody." I felt so thankful for him that his wish was granted. It was just a "quiet going to sleep here, to awaken in that country where sickness and sorrow are no more."

Pasadena,
California,
1921.

ELIZABETH (BUNDY) FRAME.

CLIFFORD B. COLPITTS

Born 7–5–1890.
Died 9–5–1911.

From local paper:

"Clifford Colpitts, the only son of Mr. and Mrs. John Colpitts, died at the family home at Lincoln Avenue, Tuesday morning. He had been a sufferer for over two months with tubercular meningitis, that disease being the direct cause of his death. Clifford Colpitts was born in Barnesville, July 5, 1890, and grew to manhood here. He was a young man of exceptional business ability. For quite a while prior to his sickness, he was connected with the Pike-Richmond Company, wholesale milliners, of Cleveland. In the capacity of city salesman he was giving most excellent service to his firm, was unusually popular with the trade, and had his life and health been spared, would no doubt in the years to come, have filled a prominent position in business circles of the town. Although quiet and unassuming, he was very popular with his companions and the young people of the town generally, and was recognized by everyone, as a young man who took life seriously, and tried to do his duty as he saw it. Only twenty-one years of life were granted him, but these years were not useless ones, and he leaves behind him a record of honor and true worth that will be an enduring memory and comfort, while life shall last, to those who loved him. For the saddened parents, the way will now be lonely, and the once unbroken family circle shadowed and desolate, but those who sorrow, realize that the Master doeth all things well, and that some day we will be united with our loved ones. Funeral services will be held Thursday afternoon, conducted by Dr. Battelle McCarty, of the First Methodist Church, the deceased being a member of that denomination for a number of years. Burial in Southern Cemetery."

MARY ANNA (BRACKEN) BAILEY

Born 2-5-1876.
Died 1-24-1914.

From local paper:

"It is with sad hearts we record the death of Mary Anna Bailey, First Month, 24, 1914, the beloved wife of Oscar J. Bailey of Tacoma, Ohio. She was born at Colerain, Ohio, Second Month 5, 1876, daughter of Lindley M. and Anna S. Brackin. Fifth Month 20, 1896, she was united in marriage with Oscar J. Bailey. She leaves five boys between the ages of two and seventeen years to mourn the loss of a devoted mother.

"Only a few days ago she was taken to a hospital at West Chester, Pa., where she underwent an operation for gall-stones. Everything that skill and loving hands could do was done, but the summons came and late in the evening of the 24th, she was called Beyond. She was a faithful and consistent member of the Society of Friends, a loving and devoted wife and mother, a true home maker.

"Funeral services were held at Stillwater meeting house First Month 27th, attended by a large number of relatives and friends.

"She was one of seven children and she leaves besides her husband and five boys, her parents and two brothers and four sisters to mourn her loss. Her death was the first break in the two families. It is hard to let her go, but we can but quote from the pen of Jesse Edgerton:"

"As I weep o'er buried hopes,
    With tears which I may not restrain,
A vision, beautiful and bright,
    Dawns gently on my aching brain.

A glimpse of beauty, far away,
    In that bright city of the blest,
Where toil-worn feet no longer stray,
    And weary souls forever rest.

And there before the throne of God,
    With spotless robes and seraph wings,
Thy hand attunes a golden harp,
    Thy voice with angel sweetness sings.

God grant us faith to look above
    And see the glory thou hast won,
And through our sighs and tears to breathe,
    From bleeding hearts, 'Thy will be done.'"

ANNA STANTON BUNDY

Born 8-8-1837.
Died 10-5-1917.

From Local Paper:

"Mrs. Anna S. Bundy, an aged and beloved woman of this place, died Friday, at the home of her daughter, Mrs. John Colpitts, with whom she had lived several years.

"Mrs. Bundy was eighty years of age, and although she had been in poor health for two years, she did not become worse until two weeks prior to her death, which resulted from heart trouble, caused by asthma.

"The decedent was one of the pioneer women of the town, having lived her entire life here. Her maiden name was Anna Stanton, she being a member of the family that has held an honored and prominent place in this region throughout the years. She was married in 1859 to Nathan Bundy, who died in 1874.

"Mrs. Bundy was a member of the Society of Friends. She lived a life of simplicity, never wavering in her faith, and striving to make each year of her long life more useful than the ones that had gone before. Although called upon to bear more grief and sorrow than comes to many, she met each trial bravely, feeling that her duty to those about her called for cheeriness and the subjection of her personal troubles. During the sunset of her life she was most tenderly cared for by the devoted daughter who with her other relatives and loving friends did all that was possible to make her comfortable and happy.

"Besides the daughter, she is survived by one sister, Mrs. L. P. Bailey, and one brother, William Stanton, of Westtown, Pa.

"The funeral was held Monday afternoon at two o'clock. Burial in the Southern Cemetery."

BENJAMIN STANTON

Born 4-22-1848.
Died 8-6-1898.

From Local Paper:

"The death of Benjamin Stanton, a prominent resident of this vicinity, occurred at his home east of town last Saturday evening. He had been complaining for a long time, but had not been confined to his home until about two weeks before his death, when typhoid fever developed which with other complications resulted in his death. Mr. Stanton was born in 1848, his father, Edmund Stanton, being a first cousin of the great War Secretary Stanton. He was married to Elizabeth Plummer, in 1870, who with four children, three boys and one girl, survive him. Mr. Stanton was a highly esteemed member of the Society of Friends and while not of an aggressive type, yet he worked faithfully and honestly for what he deemed to be the right and had the confidence and esteem of all who knew him. His early years were devoted largely to the raising of fine sheep, an industry in which he was eminently successful. In later years his attention was more particularly directed towards the creamery business and Jersey cattle. He leaves a most estimable family who have the sympathy of every one in their bereavement. Funeral services were held on Monday afternoon. Interment at Friends' burying ground at Stillwater."

TABITHA STANTON DAVIS

Born 3-13-1845.
Died 2-13-1920.

From Local Paper:

"Tabitha S. Davis, a beloved woman of this neighborhood, died at her home east of town Friday, February 13, from complications arising from injuries caused by a broken hip.

"The decendent was seventy-three years of age, and practically her entire life was spent in this neighborhood, where she was born. Her maiden name was Tabitha Stanton, and she was the widow of the late John F. Davis, who died in 1900.

"Mrs. Davis was a grand, good woman, and noted for her cordial hospitality and kindness of heart. Throughout her life she was loving and kind and in going leaves the richest legacy earth affords, a pure and blameless life.

"With a birth-right in the Society of Friends, throughout all the years allotted her, she remained a true and faithful Christian, and when the summons came was ready to go and be forever at rest with Him in whom she had implicit faith.

"Services conducted in accordance with the custom of Friends, were held Tuesday. Burial in Friends' burying ground.

"Mrs. Davis was the last to be called of her immediate family, and is survived only by an adopted daughter."

FRIENDS' BURYING GROUND

PORTSMOUTH, RHODE ISLAND. THE FIRST RE-
CORDED HOME OF ROBERT STANTON. TYPICAL
OF MANY SUCH GROUNDS—NO EARLY RECORDS,
NO NAMES, AND FEW MARKERS.

RECORDS

THE recorded information given in the foregoing pages will not be perpetuating and must stop with the locking of the last page in the printing press. But the hope is held that with interest aroused in the history and genealogy of our ancestors each person possessing a copy of the book will record facts for future generations.

The following space provides for several families and it is hoped that each book will be handed down from one family to another, more cherished as it grows older and more complete as each family adds its contribution in the pages for record.

RECORD

OF THE CHILDREN

NAME	MO·DAY·YEAR

RD OF BIRTHS

HILDREN OF _____ ,

DAY-YEAR   PLACE   WEIGHT

RECORD OF

OF THE CHILDREN

NAME   TO   NAME

MARRIAGES

OF _____ ,

PLACE	MO.·DAY·YEAR
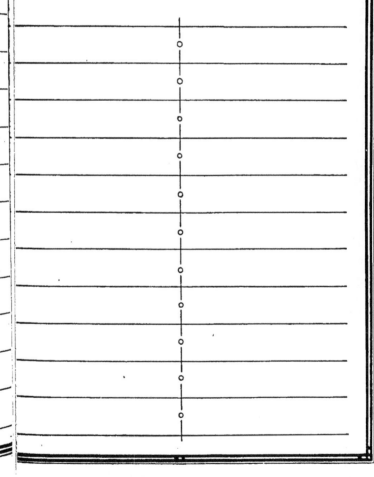

RECORD

OF THE CHILDREN

NAME	MO·DAY·YEAR

OF DEATHS

REM OF _____

PLACE	CAUSE

RECORDS OF

IN THE FAMILY OF___

TRAVELS AND
VISITS

PERSONAL
ATTAINMENTS

BUILDIN
IMPROVEN

RDS OF INTEREST

FAMILY OF _____

PERSONAL
AINMENTS

BUILDINGS~
IMPROVEMENTS

MISCELLANEOUS
ITEMS

RECORD OF

OF THE CHILDREN OF ____

NAME	MO·DAY·YEAR	PLACE

OF BIRTHS

OF _____

YEAR	PLACE	WEIGHT

RECORD OF

OF THE CHILDREN

NAME   TO   NAME

MARRIAGES

OF _____ ⸍

PLACE	MO.·DAY·YEAR

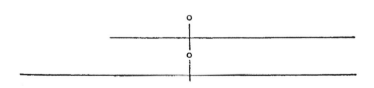

RECORDS

IN THE FAMILY

TRAVELS AND · PERSONAL
   VISITS   · ATTAINMENTS

OF INTEREST

OF _____

BUILDINGS~ IMPROVEMENTS

MISCELLANEOUS ITEMS

RECORD OF

OF THE CHILDREN

NAME   TO   NAME

MARRIAGES

OF _____

PLACE	MO.·DAY·YEAR

RECORD

OF THE CHILDREN

NAME	MO·DAY·YEAR

OF

OF____

PLACE

OF DEATHS

OF_____

PLACE	CAUSE

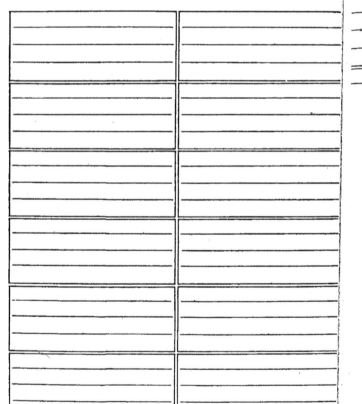

RECORDS OF

IN THE FAMILY

TRAVELS AND PERSONAL
VISITS ATTAINMENTS

IMPROVE

OF INTEREST

OF _____

BUILDINGS~ ·MISCELLANEOUS
IMPROVEMENTS· ITEMS

RECORD OF B

OF THE CHILDREN OF

NAME	MO·DAY·YEAR	PLACE

OF BIRTHS

OF _____

PLACE	WEIGHT

RECORD OF

OF THE CHILDREN

NAME	TO	NAME

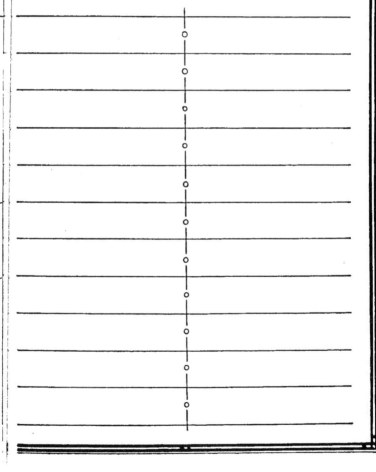

MARRIAGES

OF _____

PLACE	MO.·DAY·YEAR

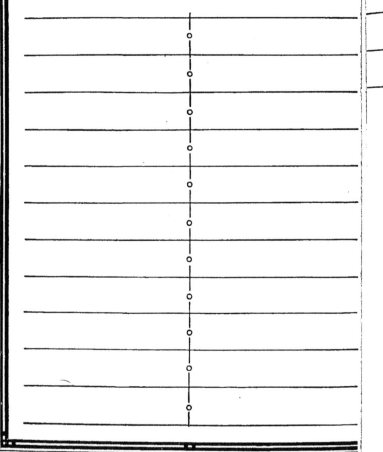

RECORD OF

OF THE CHILDREN

NAME	MO·DAY·YEAR

OF DEATHS

OF _____

PLACE	CAUSE

RECORDS OF

IN THE FAMILY

TRAVELS AND PERSONAL
VISITS   ATTAINMENTS   IMPROVEM

OF INTEREST

OF _____

BUILDINGS~ ·MISCELLANEOUS
IMPROVEMENTS·   ITEMS

FINIS

INDEX

A BRIG

FROM *A* CUT PRINTED IN *1796*

EXPLANATORY NOTES

The border at the top and bottom of the title page was copied from the New Testament title page of the Stanton Bible, a reproduction of which is shown on page 61.

*　*　*　*

The candle stick shown at the beginning and end of the book, with the long and short candles, belonged to Eli Stanton and was used in his home for many years. A larger illustration of the same candle stick is shown on page 218.

*　*　*　*

The kettle and crane shown on page 82 is now in use at the home of Joseph W. Doudna, Barnesville, Ohio.

*　*　*　*

The poem by Mary P. (Stanton) Dawson, printed on pages 164 to 166, has been illustrated from the actual articles referred to in the poem. The doorway is the one of her childhood home—the cup and plate are the ones her parents used—the Bible is the one from which her father read to the family. (The Bible is shown in detail and described on pages 58 to 64.)—The chair is the one used by her father and the gravestone marks her grave in Stillwater Burying Ground.

*　*　*　*

The poem about the cookies, printed on pages 321 and 322, has been illustrated according to references in the poem. The apple pie was baked by Edith Cope Stanton—the cookies by Mary B. Colpitts, daughter of Anna Stanton Bundy—the little girl is Susanna Morris Stanton—the little boy, William Macy Stanton, and the last is Anna Stanton Bundy, to whom the poem was dedicated.

*　*　*　*

The poem on pages 380 and 381, entitled "For Fifty Years," was written just previous to the fiftieth anniversary of the marriage of Lindley P. and Elizabeth Stanton Bailey, and was read to the guests on Seventh month Twenty-sixth, 1921.

*　*　*　*

The waterfall, shown on page 564, is located in the Pocono Mountains, in eastern Pennsylvania. The photograph was taken by William Macy and Edith Cope Stanton while on their "motor-trip" honeymoon in 1916.

Ellen Stanton Pennell

Abstracts from Minutes
  Meeting, 55-57
Agreement, Copy of, 465
Albertson, Lydia, m., 175
"All-aboard," illus., 465
Ancestors, poem, 349-50
Anecdotes, 91-92, 107, 117,
  154, 172-3, 405-06
Anniversary, Fiftieth, 380
Appreciation of Edna May,
  48
Arms, Coat of, illus., 13
Army discharge, 525
At work on "The Book,"
Ax handle pattern, 474

Bailey, Alfred L., 532-33
  370; m., 371, 372
Alva C., b., 369; m., 369
  530
Anna, b., 364; m., 371
Anna B., poem, 526
Asenath, 362; poem, 363
Charles Lloyd, b., 370
Clara, b., 364; m., 371
David B., b., 371-72
Dorothy L., 371; poem
Edward F., b., 370
Edwin M., b., 364
Elizabeth Bundy, poem
Elizabeth Stanton, Anna
  185, 187, 263; biog.,
  497, 525
Elizabeth Stanton, Jr.,
  533
Family, 533; chart, 534
Florence E., b., 370
Harmon E., b., 371
Herbert J., b., 370
Jesse and Asenath, 533
Jesse S., b., 364; m.,
  533
Joseph O., b., 370
Laura E., poem
Lavada S., poem
Lester W., b., 370
Lillian D., poem
Lindley P., article,
  384-88, poem, 525

INDEX

Abstracts from Minutes of Core Sound Meeting, 53-57
Agreement, Copy of, 405
Albertson, Lydia, m., 32; ch., 33
"All-aboard," illus. 505
Ancestors, poem, 349-50
Anecdotes, 91-2, 107, 128, 145, 147-48, 154, 172-3, 405-08
Anniversary, Fiftieth, 377-79
Appreciation of Edna Macy Stanton, 344-48
Arms, Coat of, illus. 12
Army discharge, 295
At work on "The Book," illus. 502
Ax handle pattern, 474

Bailey, Alfred L., appreciation of, 10. b., 370; m., 371; port. 528
  Alva C., b., 365; m. and ch., 372. port 530
  Anna, b., 364; m., 371
  Anna B., port. 528
  Asenath, 362; port. 363
  Charles Lloyd, b., 372; port. 533
  Clara, b., 364; m., 371; port. 532
  David B., b., 372; port. 531
  Dorothy L., 371; port. 528
  Edward F., b., 370; port. 527
  Edwin M., b., 364; m., 370; port. 526
  Elizabeth Bundy, port. 401
  Elizabeth Stanton, Articles by, 175-80, 185, 187, 265; biog. 361-73; port. 179, 497, 525
  Elizabeth Stanton, Jr., b., 372; port. 533
  Family, 537, chart, 538-39
  Florence E., b., 372; port. 533
  Harmon E., b., 372; port. 530
  Herbert J., b., 370; port. 526
  Jesse and Asenath, 362; port. 363
  Jesse S., b., 365; m. and ch., 372; port. 533
  Joseph O., b., 370; port. 527
  Laura E., port. 530
  Lavada S., port. 371
  Lester W., b., 372; port. 533
  Lillian D., port. 526
  Lindley P., articles by, 267-74, 382-83, 384-88, port. 525

Bailey, Lindley P. and Elizabeth S., biog. 361-73. Fiftieth wedding anniversary, 377-79; family group 369. Golden wedding, group portrait, facing 372; port. facing 361
  Lindley P., Jr., b., 370; port. 527
  Lizzie, 252
  Lydia H., port. 533
  Mary Agnes, b., 534
  Mary Anna, d., 370; obituary, 601; port. 527
  Mary E., b., 372; port. 530
  Nathan C., b., 372; port. 531
  Oliver B., b., 370; port. 527
  Oscar J., b., 364; m. and ch., 370-71; port. 527
  Ralph W., b., 372; port. 531
  Raymond C., b., 372; port. 531
  Rolland A., b., 372; port. 531
Barn, Eli Stanton's, 231-42
  John Bundy's, illus. 414, 416
Barnaby, Laura, port. 127
  Loretta, story about, 128
Barn-door hinge, illus. 417
Basket, illus. 420
Bear story, 191
Beaufort, oldest house, illus. 44
Bed spreads, illus. 250, 251
Bells, wagoner's, illus. 480
Belvoir castle, 13; illus. 14
Bench from Meeting House, 441; illus. 441
Bibles, Stanton desc., 59-64; illus. 58, 60-2, 153, 177, 565
"Bobbie" Peters Cook, 461
Bogue Banks, illus. 47
Bonnet, illus. 181
  Stolen, 96
Bookbinding, illus. 504
Bookcase, illus. 200
Book plate, illus. 192
Book, Reader, illus. 212, 225
  Where made, 503
Bootees, White Woolen, illus. 402
Bottles, Hand made, illus. 288
Bouquet, illus. 378
Bowles, Ada J., port. 188
  Elsie R., port. 188
Bracken, Mary Anna, m., 370

Brake, lever, *illus.* 478
Branson, Rebecca Ann, m., 171
Brig, preceding Index
Broadax, *illus.* 235
Brown, Aaron, m., 41, 78
Brown, Anna, 78
  Harriet A., m., 134
Bullet mold, *illus.* 211
Bundy, Abigail, article by, 421; *port.* 421
  Agnes H., 158
  Anna, m., 371
  Anna Stanton, biog. 311-19; m., 179;
    obituary, 602; *port.* 179, 322, 518
  Caleb, m., 179, 290; waiter, 201
  Caleb L., b., 312; m., 314; obituary,
    596; *port.* 518; teacher, 314
  Chalkley, director, 290
  Chalkley and Sarah, residence, *illus.*,
    port. 399
  Charity, b., 412
  Clara B., *port.* 532
  Clara Elma, b., 312
  Clarence, *illus.* 505
  David and Zadock, settled estate, 393
  Deborah H. B., biog. 208; 290-93
  Demsey, inventory, 391; poem by, 409;
    will of, 390
  Demsey and Elizabeth, anecdote, 408
  Demsey and Mary, 393
  Elizabeth, biog. 415
  Elva and Melva, twins, 292
  Ephraim, b., 413
  Ezekiel, 290; *port.* 401
  Family, 389; anecdote of, 405-08, 540;
    chart, 541; partial genealogy, 575-80
  Farms, *Map facing* 388
  Frederick R., m. and ch., 371; *port.* 532
  Jeptha, *port.* 159
  Jesse, b. and m., 415
  John, biog. 411-17; marriage certificate,
    facing 414; obituary, 599; *port.* 410
  Joseph S., b., 312; obituary, 595-96;
    port. 518; teacher, 314
  J. Stanton, b., 372; *port.* 532
  Kate S., *port.* 518
  Lindley, m., 362, 383
  Maria, 290
  Martha, b., 412
  Mary C., 208, 290
  Mary E., 208, 290
  Mary M., b., 312
  Mary P., m., 179, 201, 412
  Myra, 157; *port.* 159
  Nathan, biog., 311-19; coalshaft, 171;
    312; m., 179, 290; *port.* 518; waiter,
    201
  Nathan and Anna Stanton, 311-19; *port.*
    facing 311
  Nathan W., 158
  Rebecca, b., 415

Bundy, Ruth; obituary, 585
  Ruth, Jr., b. and m., 415
  Sarah, (Doudna); handkerchief and
    cape, *illus.* 427; *port.* 399
  Sarah, (Hoyle, Stanton); *port.* 401
  Sarah, (Overman), 398; 400-408
  Sarah, m. and *port.* 412
  Sarah and William P., twins, 412
  Tabitha, *port.* 413
  T. C., relates Indian Story, 431
  Thomas W., b., 413; enlisted Civil War,
    421; *port.* 421
  Warren C., article by, 155; poem about,
    159-60
  Willard L., b., 372; *port.* 532
  William, Jr., certificate to teach, *facing*
    406; *port.* 406
  William, Sr., biog. 393-400; Contract,
    Chris. Rivers, *facing* 400; Contract,
    Elias Williams, *facing* 402; Land-
    grant, *facing* 398; Letters of Adminis-
    tration, *facing* 396; Permit to settle,
    facing 396; Marriage certificate, *fac-
    ing* 394
  William P., m., 412; *port.* 413; waiter,
    201
  Wilson, b., 415
Bureau, *illus.* 99, 150, 182, 200
Butchering, 277-80
Butter bowl, *illus* 316

Cabin, *illus.* 116, 390
"Camel-back" freight engine, *illus.* 487
Candle box, *illus.* 426
  Moulds, *illus.* 303
  Snuffers, *illus.* 294, 307
  Stick, *illus.* 218, 307, 420
Canes, *illus.* 343
Cap, 427
Cape, *illus.* 427
Carolina to Ohio, move from, 108-13
Carver, Elizabeth, m. and d., 39
Castello, Ellen, biog. 167-69
Cave door, *illus.* 221
Certificate to Teach granted to Wm.
  Bundy, Jr., *facing* 406
Chaddock, Rebecca, m., 39
Chairs, *illus.* 124, 144, 162, 183, 184, 196,
  210, 317, 337
Chest of drawers, *illus.* 99
Chimney breast, *illus.* 223
Clapboard roof, *illus.* 475
Clarke, Frances, 31
  Jeremiah, 31
  Mary, m., 31
Clay Pike, 359-60
Clendenon, Amy, article about, 193; obi-
  tuary, 593; *port.* 193
  Benjamin, saw mill, 197
  Elizabeth B., *port.* 194

INDEX

Clendenon Family, 542
  Hannah, waiter, 201
  Sarah, 208
  Stephen, 197; *port.* 19
Clocks, Stanton, brought
  desc. of, 36-38; ta
  taken to N. C., 37;
  36
Cloth, Pioneer, 462-68
Cobbler's Tools, 486
Coffin, Anna, 71
Cole's Mill, 457-60
Colpitts, Clifford B., d
  600; *port.* 519
  John, 316; *port.* 519
  Mary Bundy, article 1
Comb, *illus.* 426
Broom Corn, *illus.* 25
Compass, *illus.* 274
Conch shell, *illus.* 162
Contract for work, copy
  Between Wm. Bu
  Rivers, *facing* 400
  Between Wm. Bundy
  liams, *facing* 402
Cook, "Bobbie" Peters,
Cookies, Song of, 321-22
Cope, Edith M., m., 333
Coppock, Rachel H., p.
Core Sound Meeting,
  minutes, 53-57
Cradle, *illus.* 402
Cranston, Gov. John, 3
  Mary, 32
Cruet, *illus.* 148, 194
Cups, *illus.* 375
  And Saucers, *illus.* 3.

Davis Family, 544; *ch.*
  Francis, biog., 351-52
  Francis and Mary, ?
  Jane S., b., 326; *port.*
  John, 351; wedding 1
  Mary, biog., 351-52
  Tabitha Stanton, ch.
Dawson Anna, m., 175
  Chalkley, anec. by, !
    article by, 170-71
    port. 170
  Clarence, b., 167
  Ellen Castello, an:
    port. 168
  Family, 546; *chart.* ?
  Henry S., anec. by
    141-43, 418, 455
    port. 167
  Joel, 170; *port.* 178
  Mary P., Bible, 56;
    by, 164-66; *port.*
  Sarah, 170

Clendenon Family, 542; *chart*, 543
  Hannah, waiter, 201
  Sarah, 208
  Stephen, 197; *port.* 194
Clocks, Stanton, brought to America, 35;
    desc. of, 36-38; *illus.* 34, 37, 217;
    taken to N. C., 32, 36; taken to Ohio,
    36
Cloth, Pioneer, 462-68
Cobbler's Tools, 486
Coffin, Anna, 71
Cole's Mill, 457-60
Colpitts, Clifford B., d., 318; obituary,
    600; *port.* 519
  John, 316; *port.* 519
  Mary Bundy, article by, 311; *port.* 519
Comb, *illus.* 426
  Broom Corn, *illus.* 255
Compass, *illus.* 274
Conch shell, *illus.* 162
Contract for work, copy of, 404
  Between Wm. Bundy and Chris.
    Rivers, *facing* 400
  Between Wm. Bundy and Elias Wil-
    liams, *facing* 402
Cook, "Bobbie" Peters, 461
Cookies, Song of, 321-22
Cope, Edith M., m., 335
Coppock, Rachel H., *port.* 188
Core Sound Meeting, abstracts from
    minutes, 53-57
Cradle, *illus.* 402
Cranston, Gov. John, 31
  Mary, 32
Cruet, *illus.* 148, 184
Cups, *illus.* 375
  And Saucers, *illus.* 313

Davis Family, 544; *chart.* 545
  Francis, biog., 351-56; *port.* 352
  Francis and Mary, *port.* 352
  Jane S., b., 326; *port.* 327
  John, 351; wedding certificate, 357
  Mary, biog., 351-56; *port.* 352
  Tabitha Stanton, obituary, 603
Dawson Anna, m., 158
  Chalkley, anec. by, 145, 147-48, 172-73;
    article by, 170-72; coal shaft, 312;
    port. 170
  Clarence, b., 167
  Ellen Castello, article about, 168-69;
    port. 168
  Family, 546; *chart.* 547
  Henry S., anec. by, 154; articles by
    141-45, 418, 433-35; biog. 167, 197;
    port. 167
  Joel, 170; *port.* 158
  Mary P., Bible, 59; biog. 155-58; poem
    .by, 164-66; property of, 149; *port.* 155
  Sarah, 170

Dawson, Stanley F., b., 167
Dew, Joseph, migration, 110-13
Dicky, *illus.* 264
Dictionary, *illus.* 293
Dipper, *illus.* 230
Distaff, *illus.* 260
Door Latch, *illus. facing* 242
Doudna, Anna, anecdote, 139
  Elizabeth, 422
  Family, 422-24, 550; chart. 548-49
  Henry, 422
  Henry, Jr., built barn, 423
  Hosea, Sr., biog. 424; *port.* 423
  Hosea and Mary, *port.* 226
  John, kidnapped, 422
  Joseph W., 116; articles by, 462-68;
    473-75
  Josiah W., 370
  Lillian M., m., 370
  Mary Plummer, 252; article by, 428;
    port. 428
  Rebecca, 430
  Ruth B., 370
  Sarah (Knowis), m., 422
  Tabitha, m., 412; waiter, 201

Edgerton, Anna, 415
  Asenath, *port.* 188
  Richard, left N. C., 457
Engine, Steam, *illus.* 275

Fall butchering, 277-80
Family Charts, introduction to outline,
    535
Fawcett, Esther S., m., 334
Fences, *illus.* 297
Ferry Site, *illus.* 93
Fifth Commandment, 565
Fiftieth anniversary, 377-79
Fireplaces, *illus.* 145, 306
Flax, *illus.* 468, 469
  Breaker, *illus.* 466
  Hackle, *illus.* 467
  Needles, *illus.* 463
  Spinning, *illus.* 471
Flint-lock gun, *illus.* 388
Fly brush, *illus.* 315
Fork, *illus.* 247
Forking the straw, *illus.* 247
Fort Macon, 41; *illus.* 41
Foundation stones, *illus.* 98
Four generations, *port.* 188, 379
Fox skin, 433-35
Frame, Dr. Elizabeth B., 412
  Ira S., m., 415
  Ruanna, breaks wedding custom, 383;
    m., 362
French, Mary, 398
  Sarah, 157
Friends' burying ground, *illus.* 604

Friends' Schools, 451-56
Frontispiece, *port. facing* 3
Fruit preserving, 185

Gardner, Deborah, m., 69
    Dinah, m., 71
    Miriam, 71
    Richard, 69
    Solomon, 71
Garretson, Martha, m., 171
Genealogy Chart, Stanton family, *facing* 536
    Charts, 536-63
    Reverie, 581-82
Gibbons, William, article about, 477-86; *port.* 477
Grain cradle and sickle, *illus.* 245
    Flails, *illus.* 245, 247
Grave stones, *illus.* 166, 360
    Yards, *illus.* 42, 43, 77, 96, 604
Grist, Up to town with a load of, 281-88
Guindon, Albert W., m., 205; *port.* 513
    Bertha R., *port.* 513
    William R., *port.* 513

Hall, Bertha Rebecca, m., 205
    Betty, 252
    Elma and Everett, twins, 292
    Eva, b., 205
    Helen E., m., 205
    Rebecca, 204
    Sarah B., *port.* 512
    Thomas P., 204
    Wilford T., m., 204; *port.* 512
Hames, *illus.* 247
Hammer, *illus.* 419
Hand loom, *illus.* 261
Hanson, Agnes, 158
    Beatrice and Bernice, twins, 292
    Benjamin, 304
    Caleb, 294
    Deborah, m., 179
    Elijah, 208, 289, 304
    Eliza, 208, 289
    Lucinda, relates Indian story, 430
Happer, Margaret T., m., 171
Harbaugh, William, 131
Hat, *illus.* 181, 211
Hinges, *illus.* 223, 246
Hodgin, Agnes Childrey, anec. 430
    Eli, 361
    Elizabeth, 175
    Family, 551; *chart* 552-53
    John E. and Tamer D., 189; *port.* 188
    Mary, m., 175
    Stephen, 175; anec. 178; migration of, 189
    Tamer D. and John E., 189; *port.* 188
    William, article about, 430; b. and d., 432; migration, 108, 189

Hoge, Lydia M., m., 372
Holloway, Harold L., m., 205; *port.* 514
    Helen H., *port.* 514
    Paul W., b., 205; *port.* 514
Homes, *illus.* 76, 79, 140, 147, 152, 174, 176, 195, 196, 202, *facing* 215, 222, 232, 272, 312, 324, 335, 358, 365, 368, 394, 397, 399, 414, 425, 502
Homesite, *illus.* 78, 104
Horndale, Mary, 31
Horse shed, *illus.* 443
House, *illus.* 395, 422
    Eli Stanton's Log, *illus. facing* 215
Hoyle, Benjamin, Minister, 177
    William, 238
Hull, Mary, 32
Hummock field, *illus.* 42

Ice cutter and wagon lock, *illus.* 479
In Appreciation, 9
Indian story, 430-32
Introduction, 7
    To outline family charts, 535
In remembrance, 169
Inventory of Demsey Bundy, 391
    Of personal property of · Benjamin Stanton, *facing* 44
Irish, Ellen K., m. and d., 131

Jars, *illus.* 90, 183, 186, 213
Journey in a Prairie Schooner, 294
Jug, *illus.* 400

Kettle and crane, *illus.* 82
Knitting machine, *illus.* 163
Knives, *illus.* 419
Knowis, Sarah, m., 422

Lamp, *illus.* 451
Lance, *illus.* 126, 129
Land grant to William Bundy, *facing* 398
Lantern, *illus.* 373
Last writing, Henry Stanton, *facing* 146
Lath, hand-split plaster, *illus.* 476
Letter by Aaron Overman, *facing* 404
Letters of administration, William Bundy, *facing* 396
Lever brake and chain, *illus.* 478
Lewis, Lydia, 81
    William, m., 41
Life in the woods, 116
Lighthouse, *illus.* 30
Lock, *illus.* 247
Locomotive of 1922, *illus.* 490
Log house, 215-21; *illus. facing* 215
Logs, *illus.* 224
Lohr, Mrs., m., 172

Macy, Abigail, m. and ch., 39
    David, biog., 71, 75

Macy, Deborah Gardi...
    Dinah, m., 75; w..., 7
    John, biog. 69, 71
    Sarah, d., 69
    Seth, biog., 72
    Thomas, arrival in ..
    69
Making of the book, 4
Maps:—
    Abigail Stanton's H...
    Borden Stanton's M...
    Bundy Farms, Way...
    388
    Core Sound Meetin...
    of, 52
    Farms and mills, Lo...
    Macy Farm, N. C., L
    Mt. Pleasant and v...
    Nantucket Island, &...
    Nantucket Town an...
    Stanton Farms, Ca...
    facing 32
    Warren Township, ...
Marriage certificates:—
    John Bundy, *facing* 4...
    William Bundy, Sr., ..
    John Davis, 357
    Eli Stanton, *facing* 2...
    Henry Stanton, *facin...
    Joseph Stanton, *faci...
    Nathan E. Stanton, ...
Matron, The, poem by ..
    83-90
Maul, Wood Knot, ill...
Medals, *illus.* 374
Medicine mortar, ill...
Meeting House, 439-4...
    illus. 46, 76, 45...
    446, 447, 448
    House Ground, Wes...
Meeting Houses, etc...
    95, 114, 203, 392
Meetings, Friends', 4...
Memories, poem by ...
    164-66
Migration, Carolina ...
Mill, *illus.* 29, 101, 1...
    198, 460
"Mill, Cole's," 457-6...
Mill dam, location of...
Mill-stone, *illus.* 105
Mitchner, Abigail, 81
    Benjamin, m., 41
Mott, Asher, m., 412...
    Sarah (Bundy), m...
Mt. Pleasant boa...
    And vicinity, m...
Mug, *illus.* 186

Nails, *illus.* 24...

Macy, Deborah Gardiner, m., 69
  Dinah, m., 75; will, 73-4
  John, biog. 69, 71
  Sarah, d., 69
  Seth, biog., 72
  Thomas, arrival in America, 67; biog. 69
Making of the book, 491-506
Maps:—
  Abigail Stanton's Home, Location of, 94
  Borden Stanton's Mill, Location of, 100
  Bundy Farms, Wayne Co., N. C., facing 388
  Core Sound Meeting, N. C., Location of, 52
  Farms and mills, Location of, 190
  Macy Farm, N. C., Location of, 80
  Mt. Pleasant and vicinity, facing 80
  Nantucket Island, 66
  Nantucket Town and vicinity, 75
  Stanton Farms, Carteret Co., N. C., facing 32
  Warren Township, facing 144
Marriage certificates:—
  John Bundy, facing 414
  William Bundy, Sr., facing 394
  John Davis, 357
  Eli Stanton, facing 200, 208
  Henry Stanton, facing 142
  Joseph Stanton, facing 176
  Nathan E. Stanton, facing 210
Matron, The, poem by Dr. Benj. Stanton, 83-90
Maul, Wood Knot, illus. 420
Medals, illus. 374
Medicine mortar, illus. 128
Meeting House, 439-40; bench from, 441; illus. 46, 76, 436, 441, 442, 443, 444, 446, 447, 448
  House Ground, Westland, 115
Meeting Houses, site of, illus. 43, 51, 77, 95, 114, 203, 392
Meetings, Friends', 437-38
Memories, poem by Mary P. Dawson, 164-66
Migration, Carolina to Ohio, 108-113
Mill, illus. 29, 101, 102, 103, 104, 105, 106, 198, 460
"Mill, Cole's," 457-60
Mill dam, location of, illus. 102, 198
Mill-stone, illus. 105
Mitchner, Abigail, 81
  Benjamin, m., 41
Mott, Asher, m., 412; port. 412
  Sarah (Bundy), m., 412; port. 412
Mt. Pleasant boarding school, 450
  And vicinity, map facing 80
Mug, illus. 186

Nails, illus. 243, 245, 246

Nantucket, illus. 68; oldest house, 70
Neck handkerchief, illus. 427
Necktie, illus. 163
Needles, flax, illus. 463
Nevin, Sophronia H., m., 131
Newport, R. I., old house, illus. 28; in 1730, illus. 26; stone mill, illus. 29
Niblock, Mary B., anecdote by, 139; articles by, 437-38; 451-56; Indian story by, 432
Norman, Lucy, m., 41
North Carolina, Purchases and sales of land, 48

Obituaries, 584-603
"Old Dobbin," illus. 499
"Our cabin," 116-24
Oven, outside, illus. 310
Overman, Aaron, Letter facing 404
Overman, Sarah, biog., 398, 400
Ox yoke, illus. 236

Palmer, Anna Stanton, ch., 334; port. 522
  Charles W., article by, 339; ch., 334; port. 522
  Charles W. and Anna S., group portrait facing 334
  Eva Stanton, b., 334; port. 522
  Mary Anna, b., 334; port. 522
Patten, Anna Bailey, article by, 361-73; port. 529
  Bertha E., b., 371; port. 529
  Beulah L., b., 371; port. 529
  Clarence R., m. and ch., 371; port. 529
  Family, 554; chart, 555
  Isaac, bought farm and mill, 457
  Oscar M., b., 371; illus. 505; port. 529
  Ruth, 411
  William, migration, 108, 189
  William and Sally, 411, 423
Patterson, Clary, m., 41
  Family, 556; chart, 557
Pegs, illus. 146
Pen and pencil, illus. 175
Pennell, Edna Stanton, b., 534
  Ellen S., appreciation of, 9; article by, 132-34; port. frontis. and 521
  S. Howard, m., 334; port. 521
Permit to settle, issued to William Bundy, facing 396
Picher, Oliver S., m., 131
"Piggin" of silver, 411
Pike, Clay, 359-60
Pioneer cloth, 462-68
  Foods, 308-10
  Fun, 384-88
  Life in Iowa, anecdote, 173
  Samples, illus. facing 242
  Smoke house, 429
  Supper, 304-07

Pitcher, *illus.* 146, 156, 186, 320
Plate, *illus.* 186
Plummer, Elizabeth, m., 383
  Robert, stove, 428
  Robert, Jr., *port.* 177
Pocket book, *illus.* 147
Poem by Demsey Bundy, 409
  About Warren Bundy, 159
Portsmouth, early settler, 27; Friends'
  Burying Ground, *illus.* 604
Postage, 25c., *illus.* 425
Pot books, *illus.* 426
Prairie schooner, journey in, 294
Preserving fruit, 185
Printing house, *illus.* 495
  Press, *illus.* 498
Pump, *illus.* 253
  Making, 253-55
Purchases and sales of land in North
  Carolina, 48-50

Quaker weddings, 382-83
Quilts, *illus.* 214, 249, 252, 317
Quilting, 249-52
  Frame, *illus.* 248

Railroads, 487-90
Rake, *illus.* 247
Reading the proof, *illus.* 497
Receipts, copy of, 404, 408
Records, Section for, 605-37
"Red House," Location of, *illus.* 398
Reed, Hand-loom, *illus.* 262
Reel, *illus.* 256
Rifle, *illus.* 211, 341
Rock, Hollow, *illus.* 403
Roof, Clapboard, *illus.* 475
  Lapshingle, *illus.* 473
Roofs, Shingle, 473-75
Rule, *illus.* 419

Saddle bags, *illus.* 299
Saltcellar, *illus.* 213
Samplers, *illus.* 150, 161, 418, 450
Sap trough, *illus.* 230
Sausage grinder, *illus.* 280
Saw mill, 197, *illus.* location of, 197
Scholars attending Little Brick, *group
  port. facing* 450
School house, Little Brick, *illus.* 449
  Houses, *illus.* 450, 452, 453, 454, 455
  Life, 300-03
Schools, Friends', 451-56
Schooner, *illus.* 33, 510
Scott, Elizabeth, 78
  Joshua, m., 39
Sea captain, 65
Sears family, 559-60; *chart* 558
  Peter, engagement, 139
  Sarah D., poems by, 439-40

Secretary, *illus.* 355
Shacklesford Banks, 41
Shattuck, Sarah, 69
Shaving brush, *illus.* 142
Shaw, Seth, 329
Shawl, *illus.* 214
Sheep-shearing, 418
Sheet from the "Dummy," *illus.* 501
  From the press, *illus.* 500
Shingle roofs, 473, *illus.* 473
Shipyard, Location, *illus.* 40
Shutter, Machinery for, *illus.* 445
  Movable, *illus.* 444, 447
Shuttles, *illus.* 261
Skillet, *illus.* 304
Skin, Fox, 433-35
Slaw cutter, *illus.* 162
Smith, Achsah, article by, 589-92
  Jesse and Anna, 352
  Louise, m., 204, 273
  Lydia Clendenon, *port.* 194
  Mary, biog. 352
  Mary Avice, m. and ch., 207
  Mary C., articles by, 289-93, 308-10,
    457-59; Indian story by, 431; *port.*
    401
  Robert, *port.* 92
  Robert and Maria H., article by, 91-2,
    Thompson, 292
Smoke house, pioneer, 429; *illus.* 429
Snyder, Kate, m., 315
Sock, *illus.* 264
Soap, soft, 187
Spectacles, *illus.* 146, 182
Spinning and weaving, 256-63
  Jenny, *illus.* 263
  Wheels, *illus.* 258, 260, 464, 470, 471,
    472
Spoons, *illus.* 149, 292, 426
Springs, *illus.* 98, 176, 223, 229
Spring house, *illus.* 222
  Lance, *illus.* 129
Stairway, *illus.* 226
  Hannah Clendenon, obituary 593; *port.*
    194
Stanton, Abigail, anec. about, 91-2; bible,
    59, 64; biog., 75-99; clock, 36; poem
    about, 83-90; to Ohio, 101
  Abigail, b., 41
  Abigail and Benjamin, children of, 566-
    70
  Alice, b., 32
  Anna, b., 41
  Anna, 178, 311; m., 179, 290; waiter,
    201
  Anna Clara, biog. 334
  Avis, biog., 16, 27; b., 33; b. and m., 41;
    "Long Stanton," 127
  Benjamin and Abigail, children of, 566-
    70

Stanton, Benjamin, b.;
  b., 31, 33, 41; c
  personal propert;
  Stanton," 127; r
  will, *facing* 42
  Benjamin, 387; obit
  Benjamin, M. D.,
    130-34; poem by,
  B. I., article by, 1.
  Bible, desc., 59-64;
    177
  Borden, anec. con
    101-05
  Dr. Byron, article
    151; biog., 132-54
  Catherine, b., 32
  Clary, biog., 141-4;
  Clary and Henry, c
    74
  Clock brought to A
    8; *illus.* 34, 37, 2
    32, 36; taken to C
  Connection, 139
  Content, b., 31
  Daniel, opp. to slav
  Daniel, 210; obitua
  David, anec., 139;
  Deborah H. B., ar
    03; biog., 289-90
    port. 209, 289
  Edith, m., 134
  Edith Cope, article
  Edith Rebecca, b.,
  Edmund, 141
  Edmund C., 331
  Edna and Ellen m
    dna Macy, appr
    48; articles by,
    port. frontispiec
  Edwin McMaster
    136; Sect. of m
    139
  Ii, 267, 313; b.;
    of barn and ho
    illus. facing 21
    412; marriage c
    208; obituary,
  Eli and Mary, 2
  Elizabeth, b., 39,
    wedding custo
  Ellen, m. and d.,
  Ellen Davis, b. a
  Elwood Dean, b.
  Elwood Dean, J.
  Emma C., biog.
  Esther S., port.
  Eunice, b. and d
  Eva T., biog., 33
  Family, 11-19; c
  Coat of arms, 22

Stanton, Benjamin, bible, 64; biog., 39-45;
  b., 31, 33, 41; clock, 36; inventory
  personal property, *facing* 44; "Long
  Stanton," 127; m., 75; minister, 33;
  will, *facing* 42
Benjamin, 382; obituary, 603
Benjamin, M. D., biog., 125-27; ch.,
  130-34; poem by, 83-90; *port.* 125
B. I., article by, 125-27
Bible, desc., 59-64; *illus.* 58, 60-2, 153,
  177
Borden, anec. concerning, 107; biog.
  101-05
Dr. Byron, articles by, 35-8, 130-31,
  151; biog., 132-34; clock, 32; *port.* 132
Catherine, b., 32
Clary, biog., 141-45; funeral, 154, 175
Clary and Henry, descendants of, 570-
  74
Clock brought to Am., 35; desc. of, 36-
  8; *illus.* 34, 37, 217; taken to N. C.,
  32, 36; taken to Ohio, 32
Connection, 139
Content, b., 31
Daniel, opp. to slavery, 30
Daniel, 210; obituary, 586
David, anec., 139; b., 41; m., 93
Deborah H. B., articles by 256-63, 300-
  03; biog., 289-90; notes by, 295-99;
  port. 209, 289
Edith, m., 134
Edith Cope, article by, 377-79; *port.* 524
Edith Rebecca, b., 210; *port.* 517
Edmund, 141
Edmund C., 331
Edna and Ellen twins, 292
Edna Macy, appreciation of, 9-10, 344-
  48; articles by, 132-34, 191, 199-210;
  port. frontispiece, 334 and 521
Edwin McMasters, biog., 135-38; *port,*
  136; Sect. of war, 81; statues, 134.
  139
Eli, 267, 313; biog., 178, 199; building
  of barn and house, 231-42; log house,
  illus. facing 215; m., 201, 208, 291,
  412; marriage certificate, *facing* 200,
  208; obituary, 594; *port.* 209-511
Eli and Mary, *port.* 201; *port. facing* 199
Elizabeth, b., 39, biog., 361; 178; broke
  wedding custom, 383
Ellen, m. and d., 131
Ellen Davis, b. and m., 334
Elwood Dean, biog., 333; *port.* 523
Elwood Dean, Jr., *port.* 534
Emma C., biog., 206, 291
Esther S., *port.* 523
Eunice, b. and d., 178
Eva T., biog., 330; *port.* 521
Family, 11-18; *chart, facing* 536
Coat of arms, *illus.* and text, 12

Stanton, Lancashire tradition, 19, 20
Longbridge tradition, 20
Miscellaneous English notes, 23
Origin of name, 12
Stauntons of Longbridge, 22
Stauntons of Staunton, 21
Welsh tradition, 18, 19
Farms, Carteret Co., N. C., *map facing*
  32
Francis Wilson, biog., 332; obituary
  597; *port.* 520
Hannah, b., 31, 32
Henry, biog., 31-2, 41; clock, 35-6; min-
  ister, 33
Henry, anec. about, 154; 141-45 har-
  vesting, 92; last writing facing 146;
  "Long Stanton," 127; marriage cer-
  tificate, *facing* 142; visits to, 151-53
Henry and Clary, 141-45; descendants
  of, 570-74
James, 39
Jane Davis, biog., 326-38; *port.* 520,
  523; register of recitations, 341
John, biog., 16, 17, 27, 30-1, 33
John, Jr., b., 31
John Howard, minister, 33
John Lindley, biog., 332; obituary, 598;
  port. 520
Jordan, obituary, 584
Joseph, biog., 32, 41, 175-80; "Long
  Stanton," 127; marriage certificate,
  facing 176; minister, 33; obituary,
  589-92
Joseph and Mary, 175-80
Joseph E., biog., 331; *port.* 521
Katherine Macy, b., 334; *port.* 523
Louise Smith, *port.* 511
Lydia, b., 41; m., 39; "Long Stanton,"
  127
Martha, anec. about, 128; biog., 126
Mary, biog., 16, 30, 31, 32, 175-80;
  obituary, 587-88; persecution, 29
Mary Davis, biog., 331; *port.* 520
Mary P., biog., 199-208; *port.* 511
Mary Patterson, m., 170
Mervin Daniel, b., 210; *port.* 517
Nathan Eli, biog., 208-10; marriage cer-
  tificate *facing* 210; *port.* 517; traveled
  in prairie schooner, 294
Nathan E. and Sarah F., *group port.*;
  wedding company, *facing* 212
Patience, b., 31
Paul, biog., 17
Prudence, b., 30
Rebecca Bundy, 210
Robert, biog., 16-18, 17-30; earliest
  ancestor, 12; not original purchaser
  of clock, 35
Robert, Jr., biog., 16, 27, 31
Ruth Elizabeth, b., 334; *port.* 523

Stanton, Sarah, biog., 16, 30, 33, 39
  Sarah B., biog., 204-05, 291
  Sarah E., m., 210; *port.* 517
  Sidney Fawcett, b., 334; *port.* 523
  Sophronia H., m., 131
  Susanna Morris, b., 335; *port.* 524
  Thomas, biog., 16-18
  William, anec. by, 107; biog., 130-31, 178, 323-38; canes, *illus.* 343; *port.* 130, 179, 520; register of recitations, 340
  William Alonzo, wrote genealogy, 18
  William and Eva S. Palmer, *port.* 333
  William and family, *port.* 336
  William Hanson, b., 210; *port.* 517
  William and Jane Davis, 323-38; *port. facing* 323
  William Henry, articles by, 7-24, 152-53, 167-69, 193, 197, 215-21, 231-42, 249-52, 253-55, 277-80, 281-88, 304-07, 422-24, 429, 460, 461, 477-86, 487-90, 581-82; at work on "The Book," *illus.* 502; biog., 204, 267-74; introduction by, 7-8; "Old Dobbin," Buick Auto, 499; *port. frontis.* and 511; pupil of Deborah Bundy, 291
  William Macy, appr. of, 9; article by, 59-64, 491-506; at work on "The Book," *illus.* 502; biog., 334; poems by, 321-22, 349-50, 380-81; *port. frontis.* and 524
  William Macy, Jr., *port.* 524
Starting under the Meeting House, *illus.* 505
Steer, Laure E., m., 372
Stillwater Valley, *illus.* 10, 324, 329
Stockdale, Sara Lavada, m., 371
Stockings, making colored, 265
Stolen bonnet, 96-99
Stove, Robert Plummer's first, 428
Struck, Alice Clark, article by, 344-48
Stubbs, Isaac, found bear tracks, 299
Sugar bowl, *illus.* 186
Sugar tree by spring, 228-29
  Tub, *illus.* 230

Tar bucket, *illus.* 485
Tail nut, *illus.* 483
Tea-kettle, *illus.* 195
Tea pot, *illus.* 186, 356, 403, 426
Telescope, *illus.* 266
Thomas, Avis, 78, 81
  Jesse, m., 41
Three generations, *port.* 342
Tobacco house, *illus.* 227
Tongs, *illus.* 354
Tools, Cobbler's, *illus.* 486
Tooth puller, *illus.* 129
  Twister, *illus.* 129
Towel, *illus.* 264

Townsend, Joseph and Sarah, Land to Meeting, 115
  Martha, biog., 41, 125
  Mary, m., 41
Trees, *illus.* 51, 97, 185, 228, 229
Trundle bed, *illus.* 216
Turner's Swamp, location of, *illus.* 396
Turning lathe, *illus.* 268, 269, 275

Vase, *illus.* 456
Vernon family, 561; *chart* 562-63
Visits to Henry Stanton, 151-53

Wagon Hub, *illus.* 482
Wagoner, 477
Warren Township, *map facing* 144
Wash bowl, *illus.* 146
Watches, *illus.* 180, 211, 353
Water falls, 564
Weather vane, *illus.* 191
Weaver, Edith M., m. and d., 134
  Rebecca (Stanton), *port.* 127
Webster, Debora H., 99; biog., 207; *port.* 515
  Emma C., biog., 206; *port.* 515
  Harlan S., biog., 206-07; *port.* 516
  Mary Avice S., article by, 294; *port.* 516
  Mary Lydia, biog., 207; *port.* 515
  Raymond Nathan, biog., 207; *port.* 515
  Thomas, biog., 207; *port.* 515
  Willis Vail, appreciation of, 10; article by, 359-60; *home illus.* 502; m., 206; *port.* 515
  Willis William b., 207; *port.* 516
Wedding company:—
  Charles W. and Anna S. Palmer, *group port. facing* 334
  Golden:—Lindley P. and Elizabeth S. Baily, *group port. facing* 378
  Nathan E. and Sara E. Stanton, *facing* 212
  Glove, *illus.* 143
  Guests, *port.* 376
  Reception invitation, *illus.* 338
Weddings, Quaker, 382-83
Wedges, *illus.* 240
Well, *illus.* 424
  Sweep, *illus.* 220
Westland Meeting House, ground, 115; *illus.*, 114
Wheel and shaft, *illus.* 276
  Water, *illus.* 198
  Wool, 472
White, Isaac, m., 32
Williams, Dearman, 151
  John S., 116
  Richard, m., 39
  Sarah, biog., 78; sided with Orthodox Friends, 93
Will of Benjamin Stanton, *facing* 42
  of Demsey Bundy, 390

Will of Dinah Macy, 73-74
Windmill, Wyatt, *illus.* 25
Wind vane indicator, electric, *illus.* 276
Wing Nut, *illus.* 483
Wood popping, 339
Woodward, Eva H., *port.* 512
 Guy, m., 205; *port.* 512

Wool cards, *illus.* 257
Workbox, *illus.* 213, 214
Worth, John, 71
 Judith, m., 71

Years, For Fifty, 380-81

CPSIA information can be obtained
at www.ICGtesting.com
Printed in the USA
BVOW11s1027100717

488951BV00021B/449/P